TRADITIONAL WOODWORKING HANDTOOLS

Graham Blackburn

TRADITIONAL WOODWORKING HANDTOOLS

Written and Illustrated by

GRAHAM BLACKBURN

GRAMERCY BOOKS

NEW YORK

This 2000 edition is published by Gramercy Books™, an imprint of Random House
Value Publishing, Inc., 280 Park Avenue, New York, NY 10017, by arrangement
with The Lyons Press, published in association with Blackburn Books.

Gramercy Books™ and design are trademarks of
Random House Value Publishing, Inc.

Designed by Graham Blackburn

Printed in the United States of America

Random House
New York • Toronto • London • Sydney • Auckland
http://www.randomhouse.com/

Library of Congress Cataloging-in-Publication Data

Blackburn, Graham, 1940-
Traditional woodworking handtools / written and illustrated by Graham Blackburn.
p. cm.
Includes bibiliographical references and index.
ISBN 0-517-16202-4
1. Woodworking tools—Handbooks, manuals, etc. I. Title.

TT186 .B54 2000
684'.082—dc21   00-034742

8 7 6 5 4 3 2

for my father

John Blackburn

WITHDRAWING THE IRON   REPLACING THE IRON
MAKING THE IRON PROJECT FURTHER   MAKING THE LEFT-HAND PORTION OF THE EDGE PROJECT

Four drawings by D. T. Kendrick from WOOD-WORKING TOOLS; HOW TO USE THEM. A MANUAL.
The Industrial School Association. Boston 1884

ACKNOWLEDGEMENTS

Grateful acknowledgement is made to the magazines
Fine Woodworking, *Popular Woodworking*, and *Woodwork*,
which first published in article form much of the material
constituting various chapters of this book.

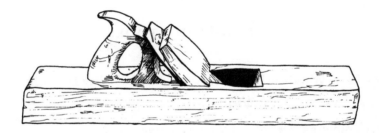

✳

CONTENTS

*

III SAWING TOOLS

*

IV PLANES

*

V EDGE TOOLS

*

VI BORING TOOLS

*

VII MISCELLANEOUS TOOLS

APPENDICES

ILLUSTRATIONS

ILLUSTRATIONS

INTRODUCTION

TRIED & TRUE

THIS BOOK MIGHT WELL BE CALLED 'TRIED AND TRUE' — INDEED MUCH OF THE MATERIAL IN MANY OF THE CHAPTERS FIRST APPEARED UNDER THAT NAME AS A REGULAR COLUMN IN THE PAGES OF 'POPULAR WOODWORKING' — SINCE THERE is probably no epithet more applicable to the tools and devices described in these pages. The expression, meaning something of proven worth and utility, is doubly apt since it originated in woodworking itself. Making a board perfectly flat is still referred to as 'truing', and the trysquare — used for testing or 'trying' the rightness of edges — is still one of the commonest woodworking handtools.

Equally as venerable as the expression but now largely forgotten, even by woodworkers, is a multitude of old handtools, all 'tried and true'. *Traditional Woodworking Handtools* describes many of these tools, the majority of which were in common use from the 18th century to the early

years of the 20th century. This was the period that produced much of what is regarded as 'classic woodwork', and that includes the furniture now known stylistically as Chippendale, Hepplewhite, Sheraton, and Empire (or Federal, depending on which side of the Atlantic you lived), and some of the best interior joinery and woodwork ever seen.

There is a growing interest in these tools, many of which are possessed of an undeniable charm and great intrinsic beauty, and there are several wonderful books (see the Bibliography) which are of great value to collectors and historians attending auctions or rummaging at fleamarkets seeking to classify various items and identify their makers. But *Traditional Woodworking Handtools* does more: it not only lists the tools, it also describes what they did and how they did it. In fact, it is designed to help reintroduce many of these old tools into today's workshop and may be regarded as a user's guide.

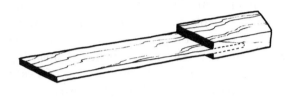

WHY WE NEED THESE TOOLS

THE CONTEMPORARY INTEREST IN CRAFTS parallels the Arts and Crafts movement that flowered around the turn of the century. Both were inspired by a simultaneous dissatisfaction with mass-production and the consequent desire for the more special benefits of individually hand-made items: work that contained both human and esthetic qualities missing from factory-made items. Both movements made small, custom woodworking shops, where quality of work was as important as price, economically viable. But whereas the Arts and Crafts movement was primarily concerned with 'honesty in design' — by which was meant a turning away from the excessive ornamentation that was then common — today's movement has made possible a new examination of past stylistic vocabularies and their inclusion in much stunningly new work.

Nowadays, most small shops are equipped with a standard collection of powertools: tablesaws, bandsaws, jointers, planers, drillpresses, and shapers — but very few handtools. When one considers that much of the best woodwork ever made was accomplished totally without powertools this is somewhat surprising, especially since many people are active in the crafts precisely because they enjoy doing things by hand, and are deeply satisfied and fulfilled by having a one-to-one relationship with their material. Of course, people now generally become woodworkers of their own free will, very often out of a need to indulge some creative and esthetic impulse, whereas yesterday's workers often had less choice in the matter. And yesterday's craftsmen, while perhaps not as artistically motivated as today's, would undoubtedly have availed themselves of every new technological advance possible if it made life easier without sacrificing quality. So I am not suggesting a return to pre-mechanized techniques because I think the old craftsmen knew something that we do not, but rather because I think that a lot was forgotten as a result of the mechanization that began overwhelming small craft shops during the last century.

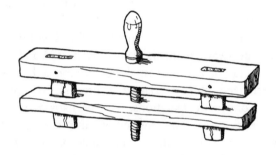

THE INDUSTRIAL REVOLUTION & THE RISE AND FALL OF THE HANDTOOL

UNTIL THE EIGHTEENTH CENTURY MOST things were individually made for individual customers. But with the Industrial Revolution the pattern changed. After centuries of relatively slow advancement, innovations and improvements in manufacturing took place with such rapidity that the whole structure of society was altered. As the revolutionary wheel began to turn, every phase of manufacturing — which up to then had consisted primarily of handwork — was 'improved', which process led eventually to the virtual disappearance of handwork per se.

As manufacturing processes were mechanized, handtools were first improved, then new ones were invented, and finally they were almost completely supplanted by the machine, as engine power inexorably replaced manpower. A brief example of this process may be seen by following the development of plane manufacture.

The story starts with Robert Wooding, the first known professional planemaker, who worked in the first quarter of the 18th century, just before the start of the Industrial Revolution. Before Robert Wooding most woodworkers had made their own planes as the need arose. But towards the end of the 17th century architectural styles changed, requiring the use of a much greater variety of mouldings than previously had been needed. Consequently, instead of being continually forced to stop work to make yet another tool, wood-workers began to turn to specialists who did nothing but make planes. Robert Wooding was the first representative of this distinct and separate trade of planemakers.

Throughout the 18th century as the Revolution built up steam, planemakers like Robert Wooding proliferated, and planemaking became a highly specialized and standardized process. It grew from one-man operations, with perhaps a single apprentice, to concerns employing dozens of workers in small factories. This development was further helped by the growth of the steel industry in Sheffield, which, long a center of the cutlery trade, was now bursting at the seams with new developments in iron smelting and steelmaking, including businesses that specialized in making joiners' edge tools — such as plane irons. By the middle of the 19th century, planes that are still eagerly sought after today were being made by firms such as Spiers of Ayr, Alexander Mathieson and Sons of Glasgow, and Slater of London. These planes were extremely well made, with dovetailed metal bodies and rosewood and ebony infills, and were designed for the very best class of work. They are unquestionably the highest expression of the planemaker's art.

Ironically, they appeared at the very moment when the entire process of woodworking was being changed by the introduction of new labor-saving and cost-efficient machinery. The very technology that had made such tools possible was now rendering them irrelevant by causing the disappearance of the small shops that employed the craftsmen for whom these tools were developed.

Of course, this did not happen all at once. Old traditions die hard, and in some areas change is slower to occur than in others, but in general by the turn of the century it was true to say that the woodworking plane had reached its peak only to become obsolete. From that moment on it was increasingly replaced by cheaper, mass-produced tools called on to perform ever less-exacting work. The long tradition of handcraftsmanship was moribund, and most furniture and millwork was now mass-produced. To make matters worse, as the handtools faded away, so did the skills of using them.

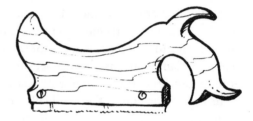

AN IMPOVERISHED WORKSHOP

IT IS A CURIOUS AND SAD FACT THAT although most machines are developed not to cheapen quality but to lessen cost, this is precisely what usually happens. The most strik-ing example of this can be found in the buildings we live in. Look at the typical woodwork of a contemporary house — the window frames, the doors, the staircases, all of which are now built quickly and efficiently with powertools and factory-made components — and compare the skimpy proportions, poor finish, and lack of sophistication with the woodwork of a house built before the turn of the century, rich with ornate mouldings, gorgeous architraves, and magnificent staircases. It is true that there is more to the equation than the quality of the woodwork — we now enjoy the benefits of insulation, central heating, electricity, and indoor plumbing — but is it not regrettable that attention to detail should have been lost in the rush towards efficiency and progress?

This process has left contemporary furniture-making with an oddly impoverished workshop. What used to be a hand process, performed with skill, has become largely a factory process in which design has been made increasingly subservient to the exigencies of the machine, and handtools and techniques have been increasingly discarded. But with the resurgence of small custom shops the level of individual craftsmanship is on the rise again, and the machines that now dominate the workshop are being called upon for ever finer and more creative work. In some respects they are more than equal to the task. They can, for example, saw, plane, and joint far faster and with far greater accuracy than any hand could ever do. And in an age when apprentices who might be expected to perform all the grunt work of stock preparation for no pay are none too common, we would be sorely pressed to make a living doing everything ourselves by hand. In fact, machines have become indispensable.

But it is a mistake to rely on powertools alone for such a reliance forces us into designing only with the capabilities of the machine in mind. In a surprising number of cases, especially in a custom shop where one-of-a-kinds are the rule and large runs the exception, it is frequently easier to use a purpose-made handtool than a machine or a powertool requiring lengthy setup time and the use of auxiliary jigs.

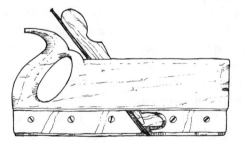

THE NEED TO REINVENT THE WHEEL

THE REPLACEMENT OF THE MOULDING plane by the electric router is a case in point. Mouldings that can be made with moulding planes are legion, but only a few are duplicated by modern routers and shapers. For example, while there are only a few profiles and even fewer sizes of these profiles available for router bits and shaper cutters, the range of available moulding planes is much greater. There are common beads, reeds, coves, ogees, and astragals in an almost never-ending range of sizes, plus dozens of varieties of these basic shapes, such as reverse ogees, greek ogees, and roman ogees, as well as infinite combinations such as astragal-and-cove, quirk-ogee-and-bead, quirk-ogee-and-astragal, or greek-ovolo-and-bead, and so on and so on. Moreover, not only is there a far greater variety of shapes and sizes available to the user of moulding planes than there is to the router or shaper user, but also, in a small shop where production is limited to a few feet at a time of any particular moulding, the ability of the machine to produce hundreds of feet of a particular moulding in short order is largely irrelevant and more than outweighed by the comparative ease and speed with which the right moulding plane can be picked up and used instantly, rather than having to set up a machine with all its attendant jigs, fences, and safety devices. Furthermore, a moulding cut by a moulding plane is one crisp cut polished by the sole of the plane's wooden body — ready in fact for the finish — unlike a moulding made by the rotary cutter of a machine. And lastly, there is the by no means inconsiderable matter of cost. A moulding plane costs on average between ten and fifteen dollars — and will last several lifetimes (indeed, it probably already has). A router bit or a shaper cutter can cost fifty or sixty dollars (and much more for panel-raising bits and the like) and has a very limited lifetime, for too many sharpenings and the diameter is necessarily reduced, and consequently the profile is changed.

Another aspect of particular relevance to the designer-craftsman is the ease with which unique and distinctive mouldings can be formed by the use of those moulding planes known as hollows and rounds. These planes, as the name implies, cut simple convex and concave shapes, but they exist in such a large number of widths and curves that almost any conceivable shape can be easily built up by their use in various combinations, aided sometimes by various finishing planes such as side snipes and snipe bills. Invest in a few hollows and rounds and you will be able to design and fabricate endless profiles, whereas if you are dependent on shapers and routers it will cost a considerable amount to have just one new profile custom made.

All this is akin to reinventing the wheel, but mouldings are only one aspect of the potential wealth of old handtools. For almost every operation now performed by the tablesaw, shaper, or jointer, for example, there exists a specialized handtool. It is often far easier to reach for and use a simple handtool than it is to stop everything and set up machinery and prepare jigs. Where is the sense in spending an entire morning making jigs and setups for an operation that takes a minute and a half when there is a handtool that will do the job quietly, safely, and efficiently in five minutes?

There are also handtools for which as yet no machine has been designed, and there is, of course, an entire armory of commoner handtools which, when used with knowledge and skill, will still outperform the most powerful machine. No amount of speed attainable on the jointer or thickness planer is worth while if it results in tearout on wood with an awkward grain pattern, especially when there is a handplane with the pitch and mouth to handle such a condition.

Unfortunately, the few handtools that have survived complete obsolescence and are still being manufactured are very often only poor shadows of their predecessors. Compare, for example, a contemporary handsaw, with its cheap blade, pressed teeth, and uncomfortable plastic handle, to a tool of eighty or ninety years ago — a tool replete with brass screws in an elegant and comfortable beech handle, and a blade made of the finest cast steel originally sold in a variety of teeth-per-inch and a set for every conceivable job.

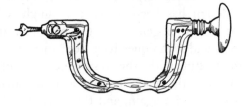

OLD TOOLS: A USEFUL LEGACY

CONTEMPORARY FURNITUREMAKERS SHOULD not be limited by what is fastest and cheapest, but only by what tools and techniques are available. By turning to the past we can augment the admittedly impressive array of contemporary machinery at our disposal with a wealth of traditional handtools and techniques.

In the pages that follow, the tools that created the marvels that now sell as priceless antiques are described in detail and their purpose and methods of operation explained. It may be noted that a slight amount of overlap occurs in the first few chapters of the section on planes. This is partly a result of each chapter originally having been a stand-alone article, and partly because similar subjects are given different emphases within the context of different chapters. In any event, the material presented here is important enough to bear the occasional repetition. Since *Traditional Woodworking Handtools* is intended as a manual, the chapters may be read in any order as you have occasion to experiment with older tools.

It is my sincere hope that historians will gain a deeper understanding of how society's fabric was constructed; collectors a greater appreciation of the often beautiful objects of their passion; and, most importantly, woodworkers a valuable addition to their technical vocabulary.

I
HOLDING TOOLS

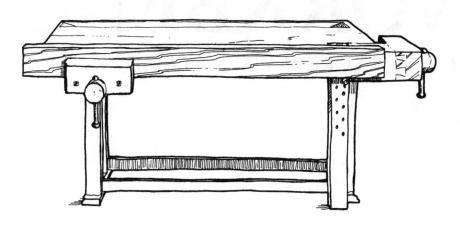

1

THE CLASSIC WORKBENCH

WOODEN-SCREW VISES & SLIDING DEADMEN

IT WAS WHILE MOVING MY SHOP THAT I WAS FORCED INTO A CONSIDERATION OF ALL THE EXTRA STUFF THAT SEEMS TO ACCUMULATE BETWEEN MOVES. SINCE IT IS HARD FOR ME TO WORK IN A DISORGANIZED ENVIRONMENT MY SHOP IS GENERALLY QUITE neat and I think I know what is what and where everything is, but it is truly astonishing how much extra creeps in and becomes forgotten until something as radical as a move forces it out into the open.

THE DISAPPEARING BENCH

IT IS EASY TO UNDERSTAND HOW AN EXTRA screwdriver or two picked up at a yard sale and thrown into a drawer can become quickly forgotten, and how one soon loses track of numerous other small items acquired here and there, but a bench is another matter. Even small workbenches are substantial objects and difficult to overlook, yet I had become oblivious to the fact that my shop now housed an extra, 8½ ft.-long, antique cabinetmaker's bench! It sounds impossible, especially when you consider that my old shop was not much bigger than a two-car garage, but somehow the bench had disappeared from view, and I was quite taken by surprise when I began packing and uncovered this large behemoth lurking in the shadows.

'Uncovered' is, of course, the operative word here. The extra bench had been acquired several years earlier as a restoration project and eventual incorporation into my regular workspace. The usual press of day-to-day business had delayed the proposed restoration, and in the meantime the bench had been used first as an extra work surface, and then as an extra storage surface, finally to disappear completely under a welter of boxes containing painting supplies, carving samples, special hardware, scales, glue containers, cans of linseed oil and tung oil, lacquer thinner, boxes of roofing nails, a big shop fan, and my emergency electric heater. I had erected a temporary shelf above the bench for jars of assorted nuts, bolts, washers, and screws, and had rapidly filled the space below with boxes of rags and other finishing supplies. One end of the bench had become completely obscured with automotive equipment that I was forced to keep in the shop, and the other end had been pressed into service as a convenient place to rest a collection of wooden sash-clamps that had unexpectedly come my way. The result of all this was that the bench had literally vanished from sight.

I have always loved tools for their own sake, but I have never admitted to being a tool collector. I try to abide by the self-imposed rule that if I have not used something in the last two years it is time to get rid of it; I need the space to work in. Furthermore, I am very happy with my regular bench, a large European model of classic design, which I periodically resurface and refinish. The fact that I had completely forgotten about the very existence of the antique bench originally slated for restoration seemed adequate proof of the fact that it was not really needed and should be disposed of, according to rule. This decided, I went about the awful business of packing everything else into boxes, trying very hard to be conscientious about labeling, and forgot about the bench for the moment, sure that when the time came I would have no trouble finding a home for such a desirable item.

The days passed, and gradually the old shop grew emptier since I was not moving far and could take things bit by bit. Slowly, the antique bench was revealed in greater relief against the denuded walls until finally it was the only thing left in the otherwise vacant space. It stood there in all its magnificence, its ancient patina glowing in the deserted shop, looking larger than ever, and I could not avoid examining it more closely than I had before. As its presence grew more powerful, it became more difficult to do anything about disposing of it. This was no ordinary bench, no mere convenient extra work surface for the occasional helper or student, this was a king among benches, and I remembered how excited I had been when I first saw it.

It had been a completely serendipitous find. I had been helping a friend move out of an old house, and the bench, which had been there when he had first moved in, now had to go as part of the general clearing out for the new owner. To my friend it had been no more than a cumbersome object to be dealt with, but I had seen it not only as something to do with woodworking — which always arouses my interest — but also as something obviously very old and of great potential use in my own shop. At that moment there had been no time to do more than quickly move it, and its subsequent fate, after a few more moves on my part, has been explained above. Now I looked at it more carefully and my resolve began to waver.

It was, as already mentioned, 8½ ft. long. Apart from the extra labor involved in the resurfacing of such a large bench — necessary from time to time as changing moisture conditions move the surface out of absolute flatness — a large bench is much to be preferred over a smaller one, unless you are forever dedicated to the fabrication of tiny jewelry boxes. It not only provides good working space and support for planing long and wide boards, but is also invaluable for assembly, especially of things with legs that must all be referenced off the same flat surface.

VISES: TAIL, END, FACE, & LEG

CABINETMAKER'S BENCHES HAVE EVOLVED over the last two hundred years into a fairly standard form distinguished by being equipped with a pair of vises: one at the right-hand end (as

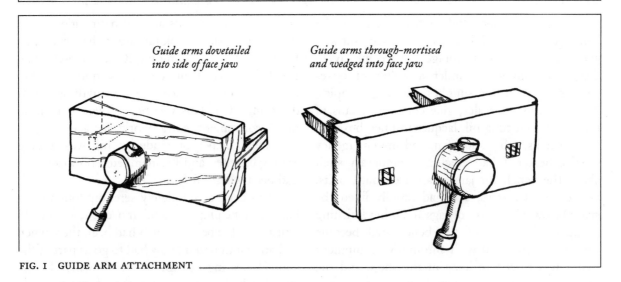

Guide arms dovetailed into side of face jaw

Guide arms through-mortised and wedged into face jaw

FIG. I GUIDE ARM ATTACHMENT

you stand in front of the bench), and one on the front of the bench, towards the left-hand end. The former is known as a tail vise or end vise, and the latter as a face vise or, if it extends all the way from the top of the bench to the floor, as a leg vise. This bench was fitted with a well-made, massive tail vise, nicely dovetailed and operated by a large wooden screw, and a full-length leg vise (also operated by a large wooden screw) complete with a bored adjustment bar at its foot.

Most of the time when wooden-screw vises are found today, they are in such a sad state of repair that it can be difficult to believe that they ever functioned very efficiently. But when adjusted properly and kept in good condition these screws make possible vises that have great holding power combined with a surprising niceness of grip, capable of holding equally firmly a large, heavy board or a thin piece of paper. Unfortunately, such old vises have often been terribly abused, and it is sometimes difficult for them to grasp even a two-by-four with any reliability. There are, however, really only two parts that need attention to keep these wooden-screw vises working efficiently: the guide arms and the screw garter.

Regardless of the condition of the bench top and the mating surface of the vise, which can be improved if necessary later, the first thing to see to when you come into possession of a bench

equipped with one or more of these vises is the proper operation of the guide arms. They must be rigidly fixed in the wooden face of the vise itself. Two common methods of attachment are shown in FIG. I, and any repairs are straightforward. Furthermore, they must run smoothly and truly in whatever form of guide block has been provided for them. This is usually something very simple, fixed to the underside of the bench top or to the supporting frame. Common faults may include: a guide block loose in its fixing; excessively worn slots or cutouts that permit too much play for the guides; or misalignment of block and guides, making a wider and sloppy adjustment necessary if the vise is to be fully opened and completely closed. It may be necessary to replace the guide block if it is too worn or broken, or it may simply be a question of firmly resecuring it to the bench. The guides, once rigidly fixed to the face of the vise, should slide through the block with as little slop as possible; their fit should be so tight that waxing them is necessary before they will slide through easily (assuming, of course, that they are properly aligned).

The second part that may need attention is the garter. The garter keeps the screw attached to the face of the vise, while at the same time allowing it to turn. The garter may be simply made out of wood (see FIG. 2), or it may consist of a two-part

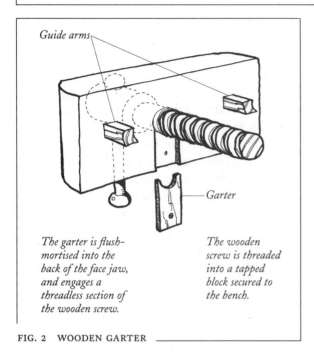

The garter is flush-mortised into the back of the face jaw, and engages a threadless section of the wooden screw.

The wooden screw is threaded into a tapped block secured to the bench.

FIG. 2 WOODEN GARTER

cast-iron piece (see FIG. 3). Once located, it is usually quite obvious how it is, or ought to be, attached, and all that is necessary is to see that it, like the guide arms, is securely in place and will allow the screw to turn with the minimum of play, possibly with the help of a little lubrication: grease in the case of a metal garter, and wax in the case of a wooden garter.

The screws themselves, unless they have deformed severely, are usually perfectly adequate for their task even if they have lost a few threads. If they appear beyond repair, and the rest of the bench warrants it, turn to chapter 38, which describes the tools for making the wooden threads that were used on a variety of objects, including the large wooden ones common on cabinet-maker's benches.

The above holds true for all bench vises: tail, face, and leg. Leg vises, however, because of their extra size, are usually provided with an additional adjustment at their foot. There are various ways in which the foot of the leg vise may be held securely so that the face of the vise remains parallel to the face of the bench no matter how widely the vise is opened, including some

ingenious patented devices consisting of scissor-like adjustments, but the commonest method is a simple bar or beam, fixed to the face of the vise in the same way as the guide arms. The beam runs through a slot usually formed in the leg of the bench, and is bored with a series of holes so that a pin may be inserted at the appropriate point maintaining the vise's parallelism with the bench (see FIG. 4).

Once the vise opens and closes properly, its top surface must be made perfectly flush with the top of the bench. This is part and parcel of properly dressing the bench top. Depending on the condition of the bench and the degree of flattening and refinishing necessary, this may be accomplished with the judicious use of a pair of winding sticks (as described in chapter 17) in conjunction with a power hand-planer, a jointer plane, a smooth plane, or nothing more than a scraper. I would like to correct the often-held erroneous belief that refinishing a bench top as old as the one under discussion — which apart from much needed truing was grievously covered with old paint, globs of glue, and other embedded

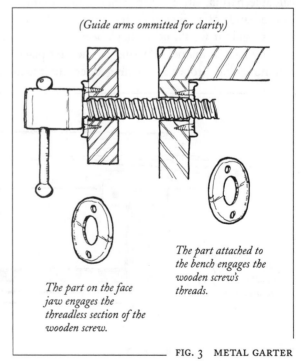

(Guide arms ommitted for clarity)

The part on the face jaw engages the threadless section of the wooden screw.

The part attached to the bench engages the wooden screw's threads.

FIG. 3 METAL GARTER

The bored bar attached to the bottom of the leg vise runs through the bench leg and is held in position by a removable peg.

FIG. 4   LEG VISE ADJUSTMENT

sanding the surface clean and applying a coat of polyurethane, as is so often done by misguided, over-zealous antique shops and other 'restorers'. Sandpaper should never touch a bench top for fear of loose grains of abrasive damaging finely sharpened cutting edges, and polyurethane is a hideously inappropriate finish.

The inside surfaces of the vises, as well as those parts of the bench against which the vise closes, should all be maintained in a smooth and closely matching condition. A badly abused vise may have its inside face built up with additional wood to restore its correct planar relationship to the bench. It also helps to glue thin pieces of card to these surfaces. The card, which is easily replaced when it deteriorates, not only protects the jaws of the vise but can also prevent the denting or damaging of soft pieces clamped in the vise. For real protection of a freshly finished workpiece it helps to glue pieces of baize, felt, or even carpet to the inside of the jaws.

The antique bench in my shop needed a little of all the attention described above, but basically its massive tail vise and handsome, full-length leg vise were still as effective as on the day they were made. But there was more. Benches have not always had vises, and many of the holding devices that were used before vises became common may still be incorporated to good effect on modern

bits of debris — constitutes wanton destruction of valuable patina, since if the bench had remained in the hands of a diligent craftsman from the day it was made it would never have been allowed to develop such a shameful 'patina' in the first place. But note that proper refinishing does not mean

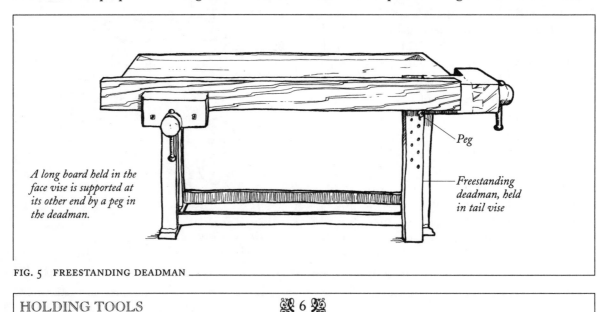

A long board held in the face vise is supported at its other end by a peg in the deadman.

Peg

Freestanding deadman, held in tail vise

FIG. 5   FREESTANDING DEADMAN

benches. This bench had its share of these, too, of which the most impressive was a sliding deadman.

THE DEADMAN & OTHER ATTRIBUTES

A DEADMAN IS AN UPRIGHT PIECE, freestanding or held in the tail vise, provided with a peg that can be positioned in any one of numerous holes bored in its face so as to support the end of a long board held in the face vise, as in FIG. 5. A more sophisticated version is a deadman made integral with the front of the bench, and not needing to be supported in the tail vise. Sometimes, such an integral deadman can be moved closer to, or farther from, the face vise in order to support boards of varying length at the most convenient place. This bench had such a superior deadman (FIG. 6), whose top and bottom ends were grooved to run over matching projections under the front of the bench top and on top of the bottom rail.

The bench top was also provided with a series of mortises for the insertion of a bench dog to be used in conjunction with the spring-loaded cast-iron bench stop set in the top of the tail vise — which had a mate mortised into the bench top itself at the other end. It is true that modern aluminum replacements might be preferable to cast-iron ones as potentially less tool-damaging, but the originals had such a handsome 19th century quality that it was hard to contemplate replacing them, even though they themselves were obvious later replacements for wooden bench stops, whose slots had been partially filled but whose locking-screw holes were still visible beneath the bench. There were even several holes bored in the top for the accommodation of an iron holdfast — a simple, angled piece of iron with a small flattened face at one end, which by being wedged into a convenient hole will hold a workpiece securely to the bench (see FIG. 7).

All these accommodations had been made in a very professional manner; the vise screws and garters, while hand-made, were not the least bit

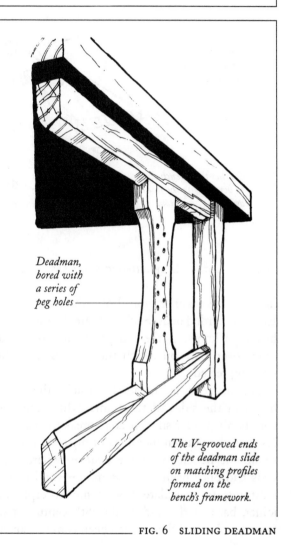

Deadman, bored with a series of peg holes ——

The V-grooved ends of the deadman slide on matching profiles formed on the bench's framework.

—— FIG. 6 SLIDING DEADMAN

amateurish, and the dovetailing of the various members of the tail vise, and the finishing details of the leg vise, together with the regular, neat way the dog mortises had been made, were every bit as good as those in a factory-made bench. It was still obvious for a couple of reasons, however, that this was a hand-made bench, and this lent an even greater charm to the piece. First, although the back piece of the top was thinner than the two massive pieces forming the main surface, there was no tool tray. And second, the undercarriage appeared to have been built from parts that originally must have formed part of an early bed-frame, since they were bored with a series of

The holdfast is wedged into a hole bored in the bench top.

Mortises for a bench dog are bored along the front edge of the bench top.

Bench stop

The bench stop is held at the required height by a spring fitted to its shank.

FIG. 7 HOLDFAST & BENCH-DOG MORTISES

holes in the manner typical of 18th century New England corded beds. Such beds are distinguished by a rope, known as the bedcord, which forms the interwoven base on which the mattress and the bedding rested.

The bedcord is threaded through the holes bored in the sides of the frame, which are also commonly given a small bead to break their edges, just like the bottom members of my bench. I had found the bench in Connecticut — where rope beds had once been very common — and it was tempting to speculate that some enterprising joiner, back at the end of the 18th century, had traded a new bed that he had been commissioned to make for the older rope bed it was replacing, and then used the parts in the construction of his new workbench.

By this point in my assessment of the bench I realized I was too attached to its quality, its workmanship, and its romance to be able to get rid of it. Somehow I would have to find room in my new shop, and I secretly promised myself that this time I would see it put back into service, and not allow it to become once again a mere glorified shelf or storage facility. I would have to bend my rule about usability a little, but then what are rules for if not to be broken occasionally?

2

CLAMPS CRAMPS & PIN VISES

GETTING A GRIP ON THINGS

A COMMON WOODWORKING ADAGE STATES: YOU CAN NEVER HAVE TOO MANY CLAMPS. THE TRUTH OF THIS IS PROBABLY THE RESULT OF A CLAMP GENERALLY BEING PERCEIVED AS A LESS GLAMOROUS AND EXCITING TOOL TO BUY THAN A NEW PLANE, powertool, or machine. Its memorability on the other hand is doubtless the result of discovering its truth right at the moment when one is in the middle of a clamping-up job and realizes there are indeed not enough clamps in the shop to do the job properly. And yet, in any shop that has been in existence any longer than for a very short time, the number of pipe clamps and bar clamps visible is certain to be awe-inspiring to a novice, who simply cannot imagine what all those long things are needed for.

There is not much that can be done completely freehand in woodworking. Even if we dispense with guides and jigs, it is almost impossible to do anything with any degree of accuracy unless what we are working on is firmly secured in place. Even a very sharp plane taking a very thin shaving will push a surprisingly large board across the bench unless it is prevented from moving. Only when a fairly large piece is nearing completion is it sometimes possible to rely on the piece's own integral weight and mass to provide sufficient stability to resist movement while being sawed, sanded, planed, or cut. To deal with this problem the standard cabinetmaker's bench has gradually developed into a very efficient holding tool, equipped with all manner of devices for securing the work in progress (see chapter 1).

This is only half the problem, however, for there are numerous other occasions when work needs to be securely held — and indeed more, when it needs to be very tightly held, and even compressed — for which the workbench is of little or no help. For these instances an entire range of freestanding holding devices has been developed, including clamps (or cramps, as they are known in Britain) of an astonishing variety, and many other contraptions ranging from items big enough to grasp entire doors or wall-sized panels to tools small enough to hold securely the tiniest pin. There are even ways to hold things with surprising security that are not strictly tools, but which may more properly be called jigs or simply methods of work.

Many of the tools and some of the methods are very old and yet, for all their antiquity and possible unfamiliarity to the modern woodworker, work as well today as they ever did.

WOODEN CLAMPS & HANDSCREWS

THE ORIGINS OF BOTH THESE CLASSES OF holding tools are extremely distant, but it is likely that the basic clamp — from which sash clamps, bar clamps, and the now ubiquitous pipe clamp

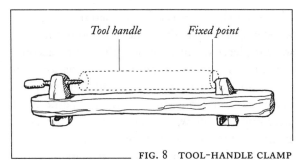

FIG. 8 TOOL-HANDLE CLAMP

are all descended — came first, and was developed from a very simple device, used in the making of handles, known as the tool-handle clamp (FIG. 8). The earliest-known examples of tool-handle clamps are found in those parts of America originally settled by the Dutch, and it is probably for this reason that 'clamp' is the preferred spelling in America, the word deriving from the Dutch: *klamp*. In Britain, on the other hand, where there was little Dutch influence (and where tool-handle clamps are almost unknown), the spelling has remained 'cramp', reflecting its descent from the much older German words: *krampe* and *chrampf*.

A tool-handle clamp — designed to hold a piece of wood needing to be worked in the round

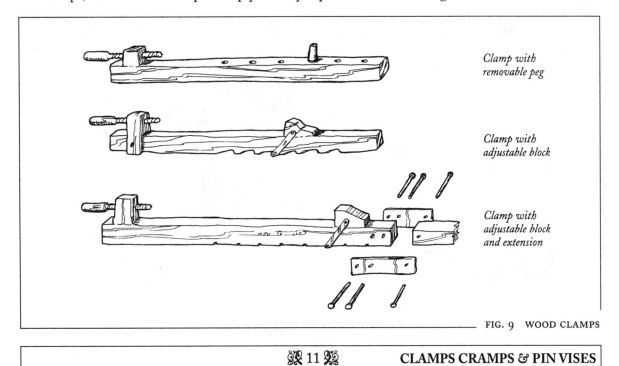

Clamp with removable peg

Clamp with adjustable block

Clamp with adjustable block and extension

FIG. 9 WOOD CLAMPS

with a drawknife — is easily turned into a regular wooden clamp by making the fixed point movable so that pieces of differing length may be accommodated. There are innumerable variations on this simple theme representing different ways to make the foot adjustable, different methods of attaching the screw, and even different ways of extending the stock or bar (see FIG. 9).

The handscrew (FIG. 10) is considerably more sophisticated and can cause trouble for someone unfamiliar with its operation. The tool consists of two wooden screws turned by hand (hence the name) which are inserted from opposite sides into a pair of wooden arms. One screw passes through a plain hole near the center of one arm and on through a tapped hole near the center of the other arm. The second screw is tapped through this arm but turns freely in a blind hole in the first arm. Both screws assist in tightening the grip of the arms, but care must be taken to turn them in unison or the arms will be forced out of parallel and soon bind.

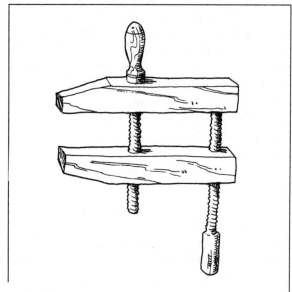

FIG. 10   HANDSCREW

METAL BAR CLAMPS & ADJUSTABLE HANDSCREWS

IF YOU ARE EQUIPPED WITH A SCREW BOX (see chapter 38), wooden bar clamps and, indeed, wooden handscrews possess the advantage of being easily made in the shop as needed, often out of scrap material, but factory-made metal versions are nowadays far commoner. Like their wooden counterparts, metal bar clamps (FIG. 11) have been made in an astonishing variety of designs and given an equally large number of classifications. Most of these — for example, carpenter's clamps, builder's clamps, cabinetmaker's clamps, joiner's

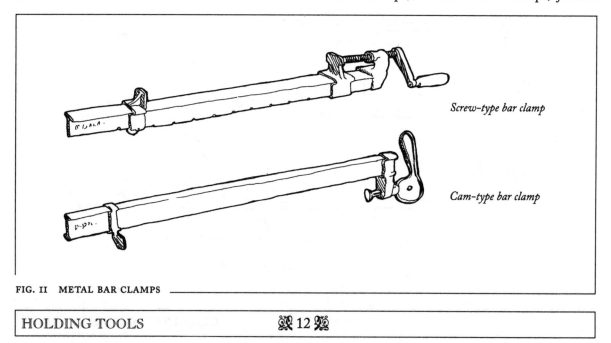

Screw-type bar clamp

Cam-type bar clamp

FIG. 11   METAL BAR CLAMPS

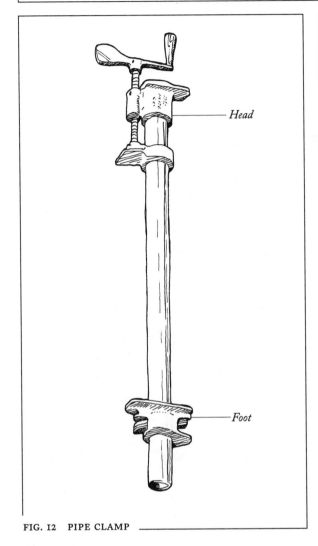

FIG. 12   PIPE CLAMP

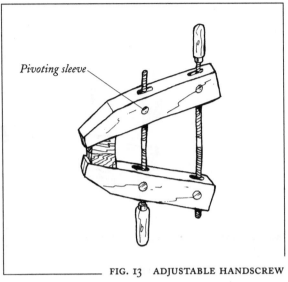

Pivoting sleeve

FIG. 13   ADJUSTABLE HANDSCREW

clamps, pianomaker's clamps, sash clamps, and finishing clamps — merely reflect differences in size, length, and sturdiness. The function and operation of all remain essentially the same. The biggest difference comes with the newest variety, the pipe clamp (FIG. 12), which like many other contemporary innovations is markedly inferior to its predecessors. The pipe clamp's chief advantage is its relative cheapness. For the price of a head and foot bought individually, and any length of pipe that is convenient, you can quickly make a clamp without having to incur the greater cost of a steel bar clamp. But much is lost in rigidity and stability, to remedy which deficiencies you must

spend more on accessories, thereby losing much of the savings.

There are, of course, various hybrids that partially address the problem of cheapness versus quality. Such are the removable metal assemblies designed to be used on a user-supplied wooden beam. The metal screws and clamping feet are undoubtedly longer-lasting and often easier to use than their wooden forebears, but even a stout piece of oak will not be as strong as a similarly sized steel bar. This type of clamp is nevertheless to be preferred to the basic pipe clamp.

The term 'adjustable handscrew' refers almost exclusively to those handscrews with metal screws running through pivoting sleeves in their arms. The design was patented by Jorgensen™ and they are often called simply 'Jorgensens' (FIG. 13). The advantage of the pivoting sleeves is that there is no longer any need to keep the arms perfectly parallel. This not only makes their operation easier, it also makes possible clamping together items that have no parallel clamping surfaces. An additional advantage not always appreciated by those who have never used the wooden handscrew is that it is easier to clean glue from the threads, which themselves are far more durable than the wooden kind which are prone to chipping and even breakage if over-tightened.

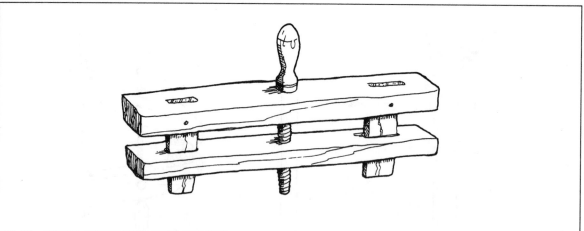

FIG. 14   SINGLE-SCREW VISE, 19TH CENTURY

SPECIALIZED CLAMPS

EVER SINCE WOODEN THREADS BECAME feasible there have been other types of clamping devices than the two commonest just described. FIG. 14 shows a 19th century form using a single screw and two leaves (fixed to the upper arm and riding through slots in the lower arm designed to keep the arms parallel), which is related to the commoner double-screwed veneer vise, shown in FIG. 15 below.

Another single-screw clamp, known simply as a wood clamp (FIG. 16), became the progenitor of the now universal C-clamp (FIG. 17), known in Britain — perhaps a little more accurately — as a G-cramp. C-clamps, which, like bar clamps, may

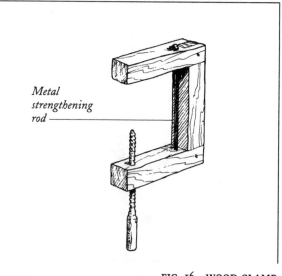

Metal strengthening rod

FIG. 16   WOOD CLAMP

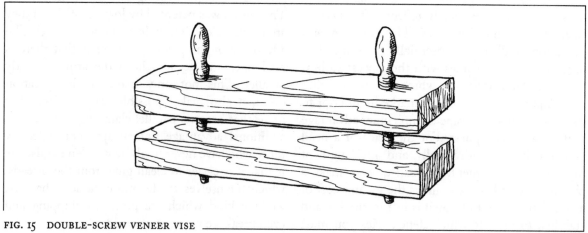

FIG. 15   DOUBLE-SCREW VENEER VISE

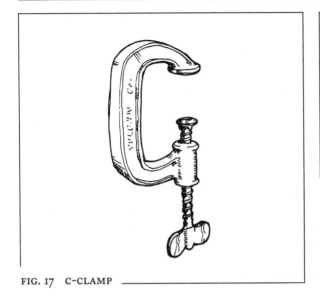

FIG. 17 C-CLAMP

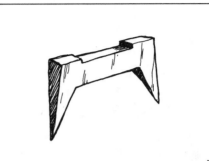

FIG. 19 JOINER'S DOG

not always be operated by screws but sometimes are cam-operated, are made in a huge range of sizes, from tiny 1 in. models to giant versions used in industries other than woodworking.

NON-SCREW DEVICES

TWO EXTREMELY SIMPLE DEVICES DESERVE to be mentioned since they are now largely forgotten. The first one, the drift pin (FIG. 18), is admittedly not needed now so much as formerly,

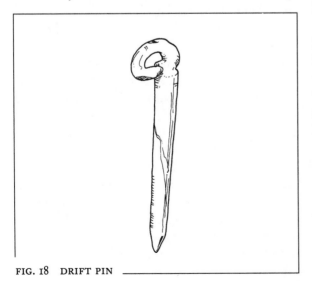

FIG. 18 DRIFT PIN

since its chief use was for holding together heavy wooden framework designed to be secured, when finished, with trenails (wooden pins). The second one is the joiner's dog or joint cramp (FIG. 19). This little device, 2 in. to 4 in. long, is handy for driving into the ends of boards to keep them together while glue sets. The wedge shape of the points pulls the boards closer the more they are driven in. The joiner's dog, it should be noted, is very closely related to all sorts of other non-canine dogs, such as cant dogs, hewing dogs, ring dogs, and strake dogs, all of which are much larger and used simply for holding large pieces (such as whole logs or parts of wheels) together without necessarily drawing them tighter.

SPECIALIZED DEVICES, LARGE & SMALL

BEFORE EXAMINING THE TECHNIQUES involved in using some of the commoner clamps, there are some more unusual types to record. Saw vises, both the wooden kind designed to be held in a bench vise as well as the metal adjustable kind, are also kinds of clamp and are well known. Hand vises and pin vises, such as those shown in FIG. 20, may be found in such variety that they are often the subjects of large collections.

It is interesting to note that in America the word for the tool is spelled with an 's', reflecting its derivation from *vis*, the French word for screw, which is the operative part of most vises, whereas the word used to describe a pernicious habit or

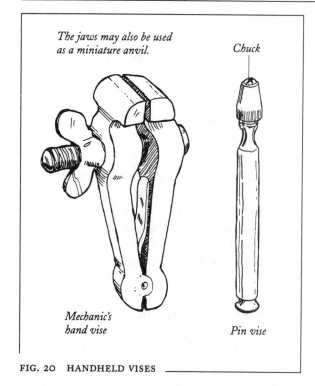

The jaws may also be used as a miniature anvil.

Chuck

Mechanic's hand vise

Pin vise

FIG. 20   HANDHELD VISES

moral depravity is spelled 'vice'. In Britain, on the other hand, tool catalogues [sic] make frequent reference to 'vices' in an uncharacteristic abandonment of a useful spelling differentiation.

The principle of the clave (FIG. 21) — basically a receptacle in which the object to be held is

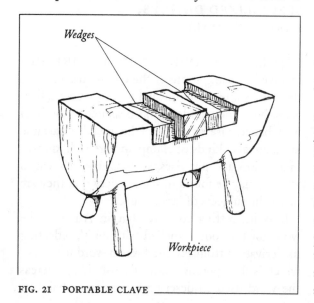

Wedges

Workpiece

FIG. 21   PORTABLE CLAVE

secured in place by the use of wedges — deserves to be remembered since it may be adapted for an object of almost any size. Indeed, even the floor may be used as a form of clave.

Instrumentmaking has also developed a number of specialized clamps that are often useful in a general shop. Of these, violin clamps are perhaps the best known and the simplest. They consist of nothing more than a threaded rod with round blocks at each end, one block being fixed and the other being adjustable.

Perhaps the largest holding devices are those used as veneer presses, which are often capable of holding entire 4 ft. by 8 ft. sheets of material, but there is no reason why much smaller and more convenient versions might not be made for the home shop. Equally useful are benches or tables set up to contain a series of pipe or bar clamps recessed in their top surface so that large panels, doors, frames, or even carcases can be clamped up for gluing or assembly.

CLAMPING TECHNIQUES

THE PRIME RULE WHEN USING ANY KIND OF clamp is to ensure that the clamp, and especially its jaws, do not mar the work. Plastic pads are available that may be slipped over the jaws of pipe-clamp fittings, but blocks of soft wood should be kept on hand when using otherwise unprotected metal (and even wooden) shoes and jaws, and inserted between these and the work.

The second major rule is to avoid over-zealous and unequal clamping. Ideally, surfaces to be joined should mate perfectly without being forced into position by the thoughtless use of clamps, for seldom is severe pressure advisable for securing a good gluebond. If the surfaces mate well, excessive clamping merely squeezes out the glue and 'starves' the joint. If the joint is poorly prepared and extreme pressure is required to bring the mating surfaces together, both misalignment and starved joints are likely. Misalignment can also occur if the joint is well prepared but the clamps are poorly positioned. Always test for squareness and winding when clamping up framework, and adjust the clamps as shown in FIG. 22 if necessary. Remember that clamps may be quite heavy, and their weight alone can have an effect on the piece being clamped; what looks square in clamps may appear differently when the clamps are removed.

For extra length, bar clamps may often be bolted together with their feet removed — both ends of the resulting unified clamp now being adjustable. And pipe clamps may have their feet hooked over one another if a longer length of pipe is not available. When using very long pipe, a support (in the form of a small block or saddle) in the middle of its length is usually necessary, but take care that the support does not act like a fulcrum and press the work out of shape.

Wooden handscrews are quickly adjusted as follows: Firstly, making sure that the jaws are parallel, grasp a handle in each hand and revolve one around the other. In this way the jaws remain parallel whether they are being opened or closed. When the opening is close to what is required, position the handscrew on the work and tighten the jaws by turning the inner screw first, followed by a turn of the outer screw, in the directions indicated in FIG. 23. This last action, which has the effect of levering over the jaw onto the wood, should only need to be very slight. If too much turning is needed the jaws should be made more nearly parallel and closer onto the work first. In any event, maintaining as much parallelism as possible at all times is of paramount importance.

Jorgensen™ handscrews relieve you of this burden, but be aware that unevenly adjusted jaws will have the same misaligning effect as unevenly applied bar clamps (remembering of course that this effect may sometimes be needed and used to advantage).

Keep all wooden jaws, on whatever clamps, planed smooth and clean. A light coat of wax will help prevent glue adhesion from glue squeezeout, but it will also increase the likelihood of unparallel jaws slipping off the work when

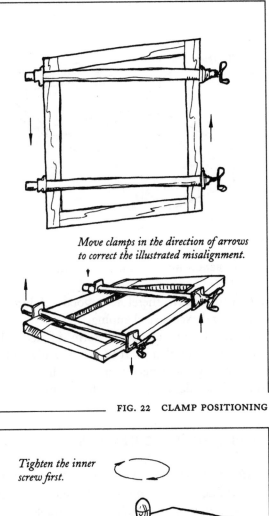

Move clamps in the direction of arrows to correct the illustrated misalignment.

FIG. 22   CLAMP POSITIONING

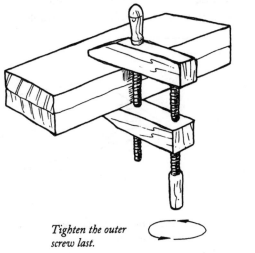

Tighten the inner screw first.

Tighten the outer screw last.

FIG. 23   TIGHTENING WOODEN HANDSCREW

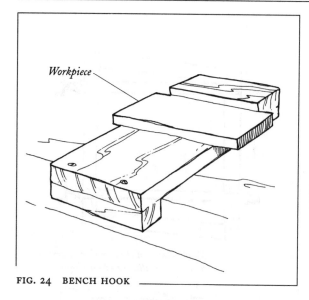

Workpiece

FIG. 24   BENCH HOOK

tightened, and is therefore a good inhibitor to careless and excessive clamping.

Lastly, do provide some form of accessible storage for your clamps. If they constantly end up in an inconvenient heap you may well doubt the truth of the adage concerning too many clamps.

SIMPLE HOLDING DEVICES

APART FROM THE VARIOUS DEVICES USED for holding things common to most modern benches — such as catch pins, movable bench dogs, holdfasts, deadmen, and a variety of attached vises — there are items that while separate nevertheless function with the bench as an indispensable partner. Of these the simplest and perhaps oldest (Moxon pictures it in use in 1678,* and its use certainly predates this) is the bench hook or side rest (FIG. 24), used for providing a support for work being sawed on the bench.

There is a whole class of holding devices in the form of purpose-shaped jaws designed to match what needs to be held, and which in turn are designed to be held either in a bench vise or in another clamp (perhaps also held in a bench vise).

Sticking boards (FIG. 25) may also be purpose-made and are the traditional method of securing work that is too small to be held any other way. The board may be built up or rabbeted, and it may be held on the bench by a holdfast, between dogs, or in the vise by means of a keel attached to its underside. It may even be made adjustable with the addition of a sliding fence.

Bridge clamping is another useful technique for awkwardly shaped pieces that cannot be otherwise held. The method consists of clamping a stout bridge-piece on the work and on an equally thick auxiliary piece (see FIG. 26).

Clamping picture frames is a branch of woodworking that has developed virtually its own

* Joseph Moxon. *Mechanical Exercises: or the Doctrine of Handy-Works.* London 1678

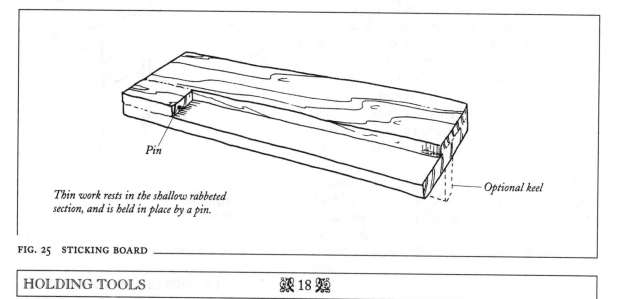

Thin work rests in the shallow rabbeted section, and is held in place by a pin.

Pin

Optional keel

FIG. 25   STICKING BOARD

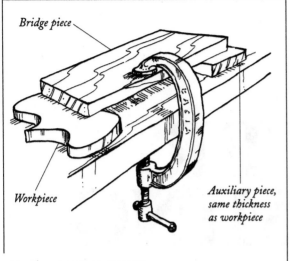

Bridge piece

Workpiece

Auxiliary piece,
same thickness
as workpiece

FIG. 26 BRIDGE CLAMPING

toolkit, but every woodworker should be familiar with the various proprietary corner clamps available, as well as factory-made and user-made belt, strap, or rope clamps that work with ratchets or simple tourniquets.

Finally, remember that wedges, especially when used in opposing pairs, may be used (as in the clave) to hold many things, from tiny pieces secured on the bench, to large objects like doors, held in situ — or anywhere else that may be convenient. Offcuts from tapered legs and pieces of shimming shingles are useful items to save from the scrap bin and keep hung up somewhere out of the way for just this purpose. Ideally, the wedges should be made from a softer species than the workpiece to avoid denting.

3

MITER TRIMMING

DEVICES TO ENSURE ACCURACY

MANY OF TODAY'S WOODWORKERS IF REQUIRED TO MAKE SOME FORM OF MITER WITHOUT THE AID OF THE TRUSTY TABLESAW WOULD NO DOUBT BE UP TO THE JOB OF DOING IT BY HAND. AFTER ALL, MUCH OF THE PREPARATORY WORK necessary even when working in a shop equipped with a tablesaw still has to be done by hand. We usually have to measure with a tape or a rule, and we typically have to use trysquares and bevels to mark where the cuts must be made. It is a short step to acually making the cut by hand rather than bringing the work to the machine. And the majority of toolkits still contain at least some form of elementary miter box, even though most carpenters would nowadays not dream of going to work without a powered portable miter-saw, often called a chopsaw.

What happens after the cut has been made, however, is another story. All is probably well, or at least well enough, if the miter is relatively small and has been made in a regularly rectangular piece, and if the operator has used a sufficiently sharp and finely toothed saw, paying careful attention to the 'line'. If a miter box has been used — especially a metal miter box with saw guides and clamps for the stock — the cut is probably quite accurate. But should the miter concerned require anything more involved, such as the use of larger or irregularly shaped stock, then the job is liable to be regarded with a certain amount of apprehension. If anything goes the slightest bit askew and recourse is had to some form of trimming, then the chances are good that the job will have to be started over or accepted as less than perfect. Taking a block plane — or any other kind of plane — to the surface of a miter joint is an extremely risky proposition for any but the most skilled: those possessed of a sharp eye, a firm hand, and a very keen plane.

Cutting an awkward or irregular miter is the kind of operation that causes many beginners to despair of ever being able to produce neat work with tight joints; it can also cause experienced workers to wonder at the consummate skill of the old-timers who worked without benefit of such modern-day marvels as the electric tablesaw and the radial-arm saw.

The truth is, of course, that although not having the powertools we enjoy today and being consequently more used to working with hand-tools alone and as a result more skilled in their manipulation, the old-timers had what we would consider a few tricks up their sleeves. While many of the tools that were common in pre-powertool days are still with us — and are sometimes even used by us — many of their adjuncts — the jigs, gauges, guides, and assorted implements that accompanied them — have become so forgotten that most people have no idea there ever were such things.

MITER SHOOTING-BOARD

THE SIMPLEST OF THE VARIOUS APPLIANCES devised for ensuring accuracy when trimming miters is known as the miter shooting-board (FIG. 27). This operates on the same principle as a regular shooting-board, holding the work so that a plane may be presented to the face to be trimmed at the correct angle. Whereas a regular shooting-board is fitted with a stop, against which the work is held, mounted at right angles to the path the plane takes, the miter shooting-board's stop is mounted at 45°, and is usually mounted in the middle of the shooting-board, rather than at one end, so that it may be used from either direction.

Miter shooting-boards are invariably user-made since their construction is so simple. All that is needed are three pieces of fairly dense, straight-grained material such as maple, quarter-sawn to minimize warping and wear longer (side grain wears better than face grain). The bottom piece may be anything from 18 in. to 30 in. long by roughly 1 ft. wide. On top of this, just as long but only half as wide, is fixed the second piece. This forms a wide rabbet in which the plane rides on its side. On the very top, and in the middle of the length, the short third piece is fixed. The work is held against this top piece so that the face of the miter to be trimmed overhangs the wide rabbet very slightly.

When making a miter shooting-board, two tips are worth bearing in mind: Firstly, provide a dust groove by chamfering the bottom of the second piece. Without this there is the risk that dust buildup may force the sole of the plane away from the fence that this piece forms, and you will no longer be trimming the miter at exactly 45°. Secondly, take the time to mortise the top piece — the stop for the work — into the top of the second piece rather than relying on screws or nails alone. This obviates the danger of the fasteners being pushed in the direction of the planing — with concomitantly unfortunate results to the accuracy of the trimmed face.

Providing the stop is cut and affixed carefully so that the angle formed between the work and the plane is exact, and providing the bottom piece is flat and lies in a perfectly parallel plane to the top of the second piece (on which the work rests), this is a foolproof device. Of course, a plane whose

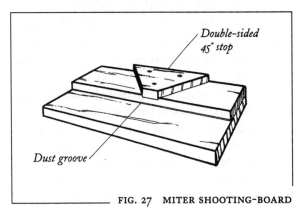

Double-sided 45° stop

Dust groove

FIG. 27　MITER SHOOTING-BOARD

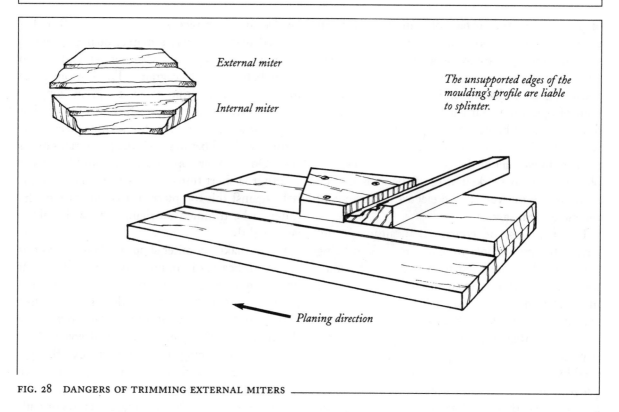

External miter

Internal miter

The unsupported edges of the moulding's profile are liable to splinter.

Planing direction

FIG. 28   DANGERS OF TRIMMING EXTERNAL MITERS

sides are at perfect right angles to its sole is also required, but most of today's low-angle block planes are usually quite exact. Before the advent of the metal block plane — a comparatively recent invention, first appearing towards the end of the last century — a miter plane (see chapter 18) would have been used with the miter shooting-board. Metal or wooden, these planes had low-angle blades and straight, parallel sides which made them easy to hold and work in the sideways position required by the shooting-board.

The miter shooting-board is ideal for trimming internal miters on relatively small stock, such as applied mouldings. However, be aware that unless the plane iron is very sharp and set very fine, unsupported corners of external moulded miters are liable to be splintered off (see FIG. 28).

By fixing stops cut at different angles, miters other than those at 45° can be trimmed. It is sometimes found practical to make a series of interchangeable stops to fit in the same mortise if you have much work to do at certain angles.

An additional level of sophistication can be achieved with the use of appropriately cut wedges on which the work is rested. Used in conjunction with the differently angled stops just mentioned, these wedges permit the exact trimming of compound miters such as may be encountered in splayed work. The determining of the shape and size of the wedges and stops is made clear in FIG. 29. A little trickier is the provision of some kind of support for the work. Once it is resting on the miter shooting-board at the correct angle, it is usually best to secure it with the use of a bench holdfast. But with a little ingenuity other clamps can be arranged to do the job as well.

The only limit to the size of a miter shooting-board is the width of your largest low-angle plane's iron. When faced with the necessity of trimming miters that are larger than can be accommodated by the miter shooting-board, recourse may be had to two other miter-trimming devices: the donkey's ear shooting-board and the miter shooting-block.

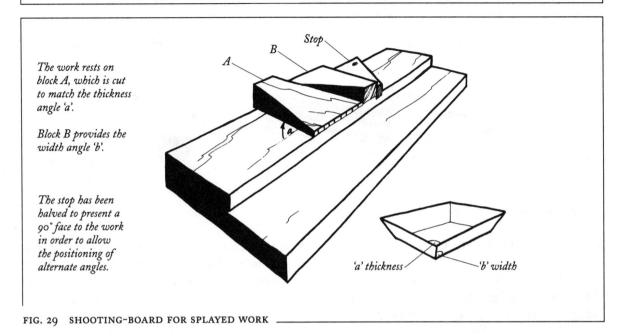

The work rests on block A, which is cut to match the thickness angle 'a'.

Block B provides the width angle 'b'.

The stop has been halved to present a 90° face to the work in order to allow the positioning of alternate angles.

'a' thickness   'b' width

FIG. 29   SHOOTING-BOARD FOR SPLAYED WORK

DONKEY'S EAR SHOOTING-BOARD

THE DEVICE KNOWN AS A DONKEY'S EAR shooting-board (FIG. 30) is used for trimming tall, narrow miters, such as those needed for fitting tall baseboards or moulded skirtings. It is actually the same beast as a regular shooting-board, with the difference that the bed on which the workpiece rests is made at 45° to the plane bed, thereby forming the miter angle, and its 90° stop is centered in the board's length (as in the miter shooting-board shown in FIG. 27) instead of being fixed at one end.

The work to be trimmed is frequently quite long. This forces the shooting-board to be positioned close to the edge of the bench so that long pieces of wood can hang unobstructedly over the side of the bench. The commonest way of accommodating this need and still being able to hold the shooting-board securely when using it is to fit the shooting-board with a keel-like member which can be held in the bench vise. The same could be done for the miter shooting-board, but this is generally unnecessary since the work is usually much smaller and the shooting-board can be held sufficiently securely simply by using it against a bench dog or bench stop.

When trimming a tall miter it is generally best to work in from the top of the work. This will require holding the work against the appropriate side of the center stop. In this way any tendency to split off the end of the miter is restricted to the bottom of the miter, where it will matter less.

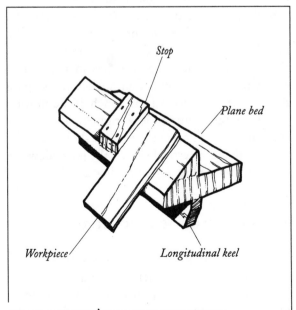

Stop

Plane bed

Workpiece

Longitudinal keel

FIG. 30   DONKEY'S EAR SHOOTING-BOARD

MITER TRIMMING

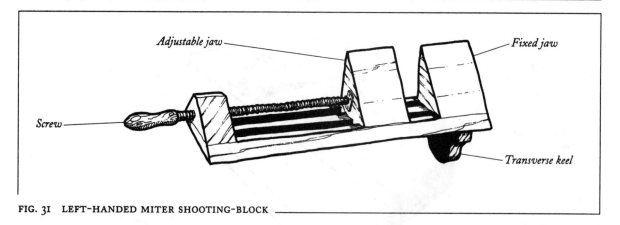

Adjustable jaw

Fixed jaw

Screw

Transverse keel

FIG. 31 LEFT-HANDED MITER SHOOTING-BLOCK

MITER SHOOTING-BLOCK

FOR LARGE MITERS OF ANY SIZE OR SHAPE the miter shooting-block (FIG. 31) is almost indispensable. This device is invariably fitted with a keel (bottom piece) that may be clamped in the bench vise, sometimes so that the block is used parallel to the front of the bench and sometimes so that it is used across the bench. Cabinetmaker's benches fitted with side vises and tail vises of course permit the use of the miter shooting-block in a variety of directions, according to whichever way is most convenient for the work concerned.

The miter shooting-block consists of two jaws, one of which is fixed and the other of which may be moved by a long screw so that the work can be clamped securely between them. The plane used for trimming, which may be a smooth plane or a block plane, but most efficiently will be a large miter plane (see chapter 18), rests on the wooden jaws, and is moved over them in any direction so that the miter being trimmed may be approached from the best angle. This is usually into the miter if the work is moulded and some sides cannot be supported by the jaws of the miter shooting-block. To protect the jaws themselves from being planed away it is usual to glue thin sheets of card or cardboard over them. Replacing such protective carding when worn, torn, or cut is much easier than retruing inadvertently planed jaws.

Many of these miter shooting-blocks are found with jaws that have been abused and therefore require careful trimming to be brought into truth. Furthermore, since they are frequently quite large, jaws are often made up of several pieces, which may have shrunk or warped at different rates. But do not despair, for all that is really necessary is that both jaws be perfectly flat and lie in the same plane. Since the work is held between the jaws it may be fixed at any angle without necessarily having to lie on the frame of the block. It is, of course, preferable if the work can be supported in this way, and this will require that the faces of the jaws lie at exactly 45° to the frame. Frequently, however, the work itself is of such a shape or size that it cannot be held against the frame.

Both left-handed miter shooting-blocks and right-handed miter shooting-blocks may be found, but most work can be accomplished on either variety. The difference lies in the end at which the moving jaw is found when the sloping sides of the jaws face off the bench: if the moving jaw is to the right, it is a right-handed miter shooting-block, and vice-versa. It should also be realized that the vertical side of the jaws allow the device to be used as a regular shooting-board.

ADJUSTABLE SHOOTING-BOARD

ALTHOUGH A REGULAR SHOOTING-BOARD cannot be used as a miter-trimming device, any shooting-board that is provided with some form of adjustable stop, the angle of which may be

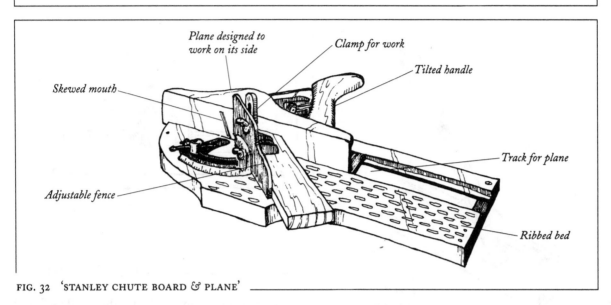

Plane designed to work on its side

Clamp for work

Tilted handle

Skewed mouth

Track for plane

Adjustable fence

Ribbed bed

FIG. 32 'STANLEY CHUTE BOARD & PLANE'

changed from 90° to the direction of the plane to any other angle, automatically becomes a form of miter shooting-board, since a miter is, by definition, the joining of two pieces of wood at any angle other than 90°. A regular wooden shooting-board is not easily fitted with such an adjustable stop; it is far easier to provide a different stop, angled as desired, than to attempt to adjust the primary right-angled stop. However, around the turn of the century, those remarkable inventors of plane technology improvements Justus A. Traut and E. A. Schade (without whom the Stanley Rule and Level Company would have had a far smaller inventory of tools) developed precisely such a device, complete with a special plane for cutting end grain, designed to be used on its side. Accordingly, in 1905 the 'Stanley Chute Board and Plane' (FIG. 32) was put on sale, and remained in the catalog until 1943.

Although the Stanley Tool Company is to be credited with having resuscitated English names for various planes which it marketed over the years — names such as 'fore plane' and 'jointer plane', which by the time Stanley™ used them had long since become archaic and obsolete in England — it curiously chose to avoid the use of the English term 'shooting-board' (which was in general use everywhere in America) in favor of the

French-derived term 'chute board'. Despite the strange nomenclature the device was a great success with patternmakers and cabinetmakers, as well as with printers and electrotypers, all of whom were required to work with exceptional accuracy. In 1909 the price was ten dollars for a new board and plane; that today the price, even for a 1940-vintage model, is in the neighborhood of a thousand dollars is a testament not only to the enthusiasm of tool collectors but also to the continuing worth of such an item to serious woodworkers.

Other manufacturers offered adjustable metal shooting-boards, but none is so common as the Stanley™ model; all are worth having, however, and will be found to make accuracy easily attainable when trimming a miter of any angle.

MITER TEMPLATE

ANOTHER MITERING DEVICE, MUCH SMALLER and usually made of wood as and when needed, but which has also been manufactured in metal by various companies over the years, is the miter template (FIG. 33). Often referred to as a 'templet' (especially in Britain, where 'miter' is also spelled 'mitre'), this is used for guiding a chisel when

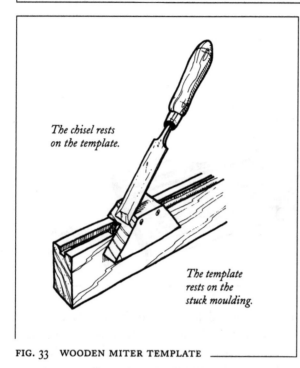

The chisel rests on the template.

The template rests on the stuck moulding.

FIG. 33   WOODEN MITER TEMPLATE

trimming stuck mouldings on mortised-and-tenoned framing. In section this is an L-shaped device with both sides of the long arm making an angle of 45° from a centerline. When pressed against the side of the framing, a chisel held on the template's long arm will trim any moulding to a perfect miter more nicely than any scribed joint and without the unavoidably fragile thin edge that a scribed joint creates.

While metal templates may be more exact than wooden ones, they are also more easily bent out of truth and may even break when dropped. Furthermore, a wooden template is less likely to damage the edge of a chisel and the work it is held against than would sudden and untoward contact with a piece of iron. Templates are easily made, and a selection of them fitted to various widths of

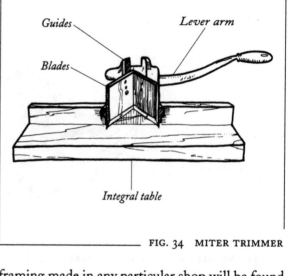

Guides   *Lever arm*

Blades

Integral table

FIG. 34   MITER TRIMMER

framing made in any particular shop will be found to be very useful.

MITER TRIMMER

ANOTHER DEVICE THAT ORIGINATED IN THE 19th century, but which is still made and sold today, is the miter trimmer (FIG. 34), sometimes called a miter machine. This tool actually sits on the border between miter-making tools and miter-trimming tools, but is properly used to finish an already roughed-out miter. Developed primarily for use with small mouldings and picture frames, some of these trimmers are large enough to cut through fairly substantial pieces of wood. Workpieces to be trimmed are secured at the desired angle on the tool's integral table. A powerful lever then lowers the blade or blades, set in guides, into the work. When used often, the trimmer is frequently fitted into a much longer table, in the same manner as a radial-arm saw.

II
SETTING-OUT TOOLS

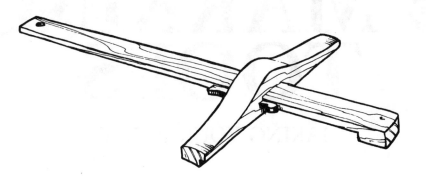

4

MEASURING & MARKING TOOLS

MAKING YOUR POINT

'MEASURE TWICE AND CUT ONCE' IS AN OLD PIECE OF ADVICE JUST AS VALID TODAY AS IT EVER WAS. AN EQUALLY USEFUL TIP IS TO MEASURE TWICE BEFORE MARKING. FURTHERMORE, MARKING CAREFULLY AND APPROPRIATELY IS ALSO important, for no matter how carefully you saw or chisel, if the job has not been set out properly, good results will be a matter of luck.

All too often we pay scant attention to the actual procedures whereby we measure and mark, and are consequently frustrated by poorly fitting work. Disappointing results are not always simply the fault of a blunt edge on the chisel, or uneven and dull teeth on the saw, or even the lack of skill in manipulating the particular tool that may have been used, but frequently merely the result of inappropriate measuring and marking techniques. Any old pencil, picked up at random and used in combination with the nearest measuring tape, is not necessarily good enough.

DEGREES OF EXACTITUDE

FOR MUCH CARPENTRY, SUCH AS HOUSE framing and general woodworking with two-by-fours and similar stuff, measuring to the nearest ⅛ in. is usually sufficient. When a greater degree of niceness is needed it is common to hear carpenters express measurements as so and so many inches and a 'fat' or 'thin' eighth. Sometimes, other more colorful expressions are used, such as 'five-eighths and a hair', or so many eighths 'full' or 'bare'. To mark such measurements on construction-grade lumber, a normally sharpened pencil is fine. But for finer work, such as finish carpentry and trimwork, cabinetmaking, and especially furnituremaking, more care is needed. This chapter examines the tools and devices used for measuring and marking different kinds of work, and how they may be best used for the degree of exactitude required by the particular job.

PENCIL & CHALK

THE CARPENTER'S PENCIL IS OVAL, WITH an extra-thick lead, barely exact enough even for rough carpentry — unless it is constantly sharpened to a flat point. It is practically useless for most woodwork. Its oval shape (see FIG. 35), while presenting a good surface for messages from the lumberyards or tool companies that often give such pencils away as advertising vehicles, makes keeping it behind your ear difficult. It sometimes comes in handy for making large, easily legible marks on concrete or foundation work, but the soft lead quickly wears down to a point often as thick as ¼ in. Far more useful is a regular pencil of medium hardness, sharpened either to a conical point or a chisel-like point (see FIG. 36). Pencils labeled 'H' will keep their point longer but leave a fainter line. Pencils labeled with 'B' leave nice black marks but wear very quickly. The ideal is a pencil marked 'HB', indicating a medium hardness and a fairly visible degree of blackness.

The chief disadvantages of using a pencil to mark layout lines and points on wood are that the mark often leaves an impression and the graphite is not as easily removed as a mark made with chalk. The use of ballpoint pens, felt-tipped pens, and other ink markers is similarly frequently undesirable. Felt markers in particular are inadvisable since the ink is especially liable to bleed far beyond the point you intend to mark.

Chalk has thus long been a favorite medium for marking wood since most traces of it are quickly rubbed away, and any particles that may remain are easily hidden when finish is applied. Nowadays, the encased chalk line is a common tool, especially useful for marking a long and straight line between two points on material such as plywood, gypsum board, and other pieces of wood too long to be easily marked by the use of a pencil and straightedge. The case is filled with powdered chalk, often colored, and the line is usually provided with a hook or loop that may be attached to a nail at one end of the line to be marked. This allows the operator to extend the line much farther than he or she could reach unaided. The line is withdrawn from the case and stretched tautly between two points marking the ends of the line to be described, and then 'snapped' smartly so that a line of chalk is shaken off the line onto the work (see FIG. 37). To produce a perfectly straight line, care must be taken to lift the string or cord perpendicularly, and not at an

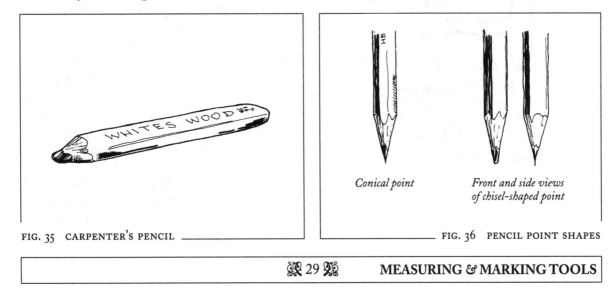

FIG. 35 CARPENTER'S PENCIL

Conical point

Front and side views of chisel-shaped point

FIG. 36 PENCIL POINT SHAPES

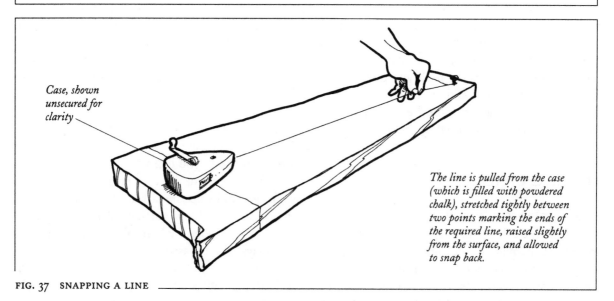

Case, shown unsecured for clarity

The line is pulled from the case (which is filled with powdered chalk), stretched tightly between two points marking the ends of the required line, raised slightly from the surface, and allowed to snap back.

FIG. 37   SNAPPING A LINE

angle to the work. The tighter the line is stretched the less it will have to be lifted above the surface of the work, and consequently the easier it will be to ensure that it is not pulled away from the perpendicular.

Before the introduction of such encased lines, wooden reels (FIG. 38) were common. The line was wound by hand around the reel when not in use. This method required the use of a solid lump of chalk, against which the line was rubbed to 'chalk it up'. More primitive methods included the use of any non-elastic line kept wrapped around a convenient stick and rubbed with charcoal, redding (red ocher, once commonly used for marking sheep), or even brick dust.

It is interesting to note that Japanese woodworkers developed a method halfway between the chalk line and reel and the modern encased chalk line, consisting of a line wound through an inked reel.

KNIVES & AWLS

WHEN ABSOLUTE PRECISION IS NEEDED neither chalk nor graphite will do. In these cases the best method of leaving a mark is to use some form of incision. Most commonly this means scratching a line or making a mark with a sharp point or knife edge. Depending on the sharpness of the instrument, this method makes possible accuracy up to $1/64$ in. There are a large number of awls, all basically no more than sharp metal points with wooden handles, intended primarily for making small holes, including belt awls, bradawls (so common that they are invariably spelled as one word), carpet awls, magazine awls (which contain different sizes of points within their handles), marking awls, peg awls, scratch awls, stabbing

FIG. 38   WOODEN REEL, LINE, & CHALK

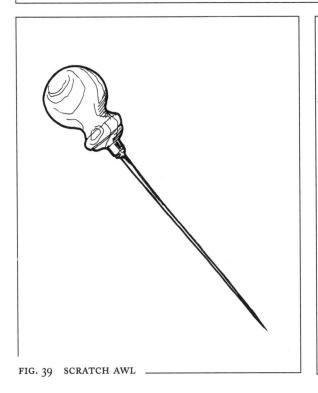

FIG. 39   SCRATCH AWL

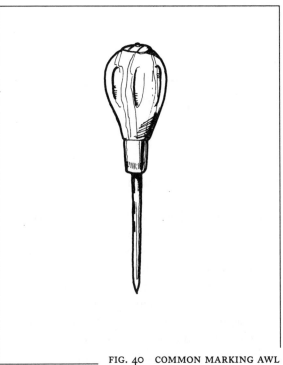

FIG. 40   COMMON MARKING AWL

awls, and upholsterer's awls. Of all these, long-bladed scratch awls (FIG. 39) are the best for general woodwork since the length of their blade enables them to be used in otherwise inaccessible places, such as when scribing around dovetails to lay out the matching pins. But far commoner is the marking awl (FIG. 40), a much shorter tool often provided with a small metal cap at the end of the handle. The cap allows the tool to be hit with a hammer without damaging the handle. Unfortunately, not only is the blade often too short, but it is also considerably stouter than that of a scratch awl and is rarely sold with anything more than the mildest of sharp points. This is because it is intended to be driven into the wood — a procedure which might break off a thinner point.

Knives intended for marking are made in a variety of designs. A design once so common that it was virtually the standard bench knife is the Sloyd knife (FIG. 41). This is useful for marking only if it is kept sharp, and if its tip is kept pointed.

Combination marking awls and marking blades (FIG. 42) also exist, but since they are double-ended and have no handle they can be dangerous to use.

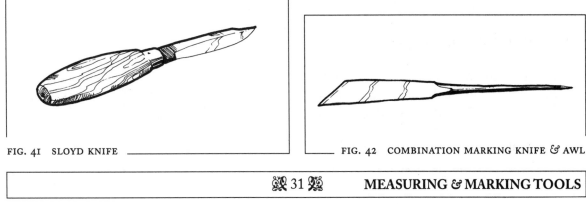

FIG. 41   SLOYD KNIFE

FIG. 42   COMBINATION MARKING KNIFE & AWL

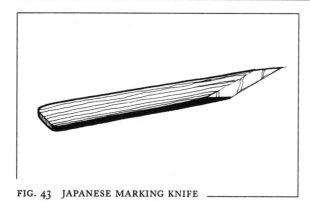

FIG. 43 JAPANESE MARKING KNIFE

A traditional Japanese tool that is extremely useful is the marking knife (FIG. 43). Usually sold unhandled, it should be provided with both a handle and a sheath before use since it is capable of taking a very sharp edge. Because it is made of laminated steel, it should be sharpened with the same degree of care as a high-quality chisel. Its characteristic, diagonally formed single-bevel blade is especially useful for marking in combination with straightedges and trysquares, since the flat side of the blade allows it to be drawn along the guiding tool with utmost accuracy.

Whatever tool you use, it is often helpful to run the point of an extremely sharp pencil along the scribed line. This makes the line more visible and avoids the danger of strong grain deflecting an unguided thin pencil point.

Although there are a number of other tools that mark, most of them do so as a function of some other purpose, such as the various marking and mortise gauges (see chapter 7) that may be used to scribe lines, and instruments such as compasses and trammel points that can be used in woodworking to mark lines.

STRAIGHTEDGES, RULES, & TAPES

REGARDLESS OF WHICH INSTRUMENT YOU may have chosen to mark the wood, you will need some form of measuring or guiding device. This means not only some form of calibrated or graduated rule or tape, but also some form of edge — straight or curved — against which to guide the marking instrument.

The unit of measurement is unimportant. Although inches and feet are common in America and the metric system is the norm in most other parts of the world, any standard will work if used consistently. Of course, it helps if your tools are made in the same units as those of the the measurement system you use — so that a ¼ in. groove may be conveniently cut with a ¼ in. chisel — but relative proportion is more important than actual measurement where good design is concerned. Nevertheless, using straightedges, trysquares, bevels, and other guiding and layout tools that are graduated in some form is invariably a real advantage.

A simple length of straight wood may serve as a convenient straightedge for testing and marking. It may be made in almost any size convenient for the job at hand, but bear in mind that a good straightedge should be straight two ways: along the flat and along the edge. FIG. 44 illustrates a good shape for a straightedge and also a method for proving its accuracy. You should also remember that under different conditions some woods remain more dimensionally stable than

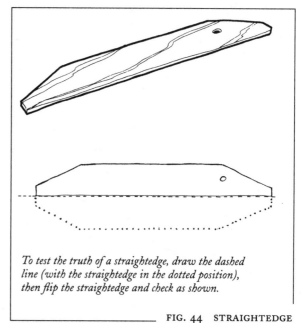

To test the truth of a straightedge, draw the dashed line (with the straightedge in the dotted position), then flip the straightedge and check as shown.

FIG. 44 STRAIGHTEDGE

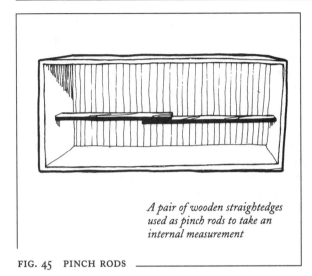

*A pair of wooden straightedges
used as pinch rods to take an
internal measurement*

FIG. 45   PINCH RODS

others. If you intend keeping a user-made
straightedge for any length of time it pays to make
it out of a relatively straight-grained and close-
grained wood such as mahogany or maple.

For extreme accuracy, indeed, for accuracy
greater than it is possible to take advantage of
with a material so essentially alive and constantly
changing as wood, a machinist's straightedge is
the best possible tool to use. Despite its apparent
simplicity (it is invariably ungraduated), the
machinist's straightedge is an expensive precision
instrument. It should be handled with care, laid
down flat, protected from extremes of temperature, and kept in a case when not in use. If you do
all this, you will have at your disposal a sure way
of gauging perfect joints.

One wooden straightedge graduated in inches
may be used to measure distances, but two plain
straightedges may also be useful for measuring
distances not otherwise conveniently measurable.
Such a pair of straightedges are known as pinch
rods, and can be used to take off inside measurements as shown in FIG. 45.

A pair of short wooden straightedges may also
be used to measure flatness, twisting, or winding
in a board, or of a surface such as your bench top,
by being used as winding sticks (see chapter 17).

Graduated metal rules are extremely common
in a wide variety of lengths from as short as 1 ft. to

as long as 6 ft. While not truly straight, longer
ones may be fitted with right-angled crossbars,
enabling them to be used as giant T-squares or
trysquares. This is useful when measuring and
marking sheet material such as plywood, composition board, or gypsym wallboard.

For many years woodworkers used folding rules
(FIG. 46). Many older woodworkers still maintain
that these have advantages as yet unsurpassed by
the now more common metal tape measure. Made
in a variety of lengths from as short as 6 in. to as
long as 4 ft., sometimes once-, or twice-, or even
three-, but most commonly four-folding, the
folding rule may be conveniently carried in an
apron or back pocket. An interesting example of
the marriage of the traditional with the contemporary is the introduction of two-fold one-meter
rules in a recently metricized Britain.

Whatever the variety, the folding rule is usually
a good deal more sophisticated than its cousin the
tape measure. Pretty much all that can be done
with a tape measure is to measure a given length,
and this is usually limited by the length of the
tape. The usual loose-pin arrangement at the
hook, supposedly allowing exact measurements to
be taken with the hook inside or outside, is not
terribly exact, and unless you get into the habit of
always using the tape measure one way only,
annoying discrepancies are liable to appear. The
folding rule, however, is exact, and can not only
measure off a scribed line or a given distance, but,

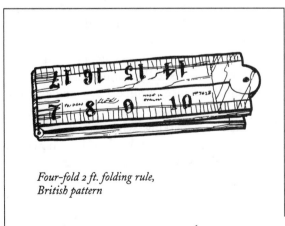

*Four-fold 2 ft. folding rule,
British pattern*

FIG. 46   FOLDING RULE

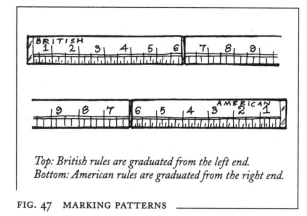

Top: British rules are graduated from the left end.
Bottom: American rules are graduated from the right end.

FIG. 47 MARKING PATTERNS

by virtue of the various scales marked on it, can also be used for directly measuring actual distances on a scale drawing. It is also useful for measuring or laying out angles, since it can be used as a protractor with the aid of a simple table giving the angles corresponding to the various openings of the unfolded arms.

Relatively cheaper and more simply marked rules were used for general work, but more expensive varieties made of ivory (even more stable than the very dense and stable boxwood usually used), with better-constructed joints and brass edgings, and fitted with little spirit levels and even calipers, were also offered by many manufacturers. The better rules were also marked with graduations in eighths, tenths, twelfths, and sixteenths of an inch, as well as various architect's scales and protractor markings around the knuckle joint. In short, these tools were made to last longer and do much more than today's virtually disposable tape measure.

The rule also has the advantage of being rigid, and will not unexpectedly rewind itself. It can be held with confidence at almost any angle to the work. To accommodate other personal preferences, different marking schemes are used. For example, for the near-sighted, rules known as 'blind man's rules' with extra-large numbers were available. And depending on whether you were left-handed or right-handed you had the choice of 'British marking' or 'American marking'. Rules with British marking are graduated from left to

right, like the words on a page of English. American-marked rules are graduated from right to left (see FIG. 47). I grew up using the British system, which seems more logical than having the numbers run backwards, but the American system has the advantage that when the rule is held in the left hand the right hand is free to use the marking instrument without obscuring any of the numbers.

Skilled users become adept at flicking folding rules open and shut, but the beginner is often frustrated by a tool that can always seem to be folded the wrong way. Furthermore, while it is true that the folding rule does not clip on your belt like a tape measure, neither does it unexpectedly fall off; it usually finds a secure home in your back pocket, shirt pocket, or apron. In practice I use both now: the tape for hooking over the ends of boards to be marked off and crosscut, as well as for measuring longish distances to be filled, such as window or door openings where there is no wood yet to be measured and where I can get the tape to stand rather rigid; and the rule for precise layout and marking. The rule also comes in handy as a marking gauge preparatory to ripping boards (one's hand forms the stock and the rule forms the stem, with a pencil or awl held at the far end of the rule) and as a depth gauge for checking mortises too narrow to admit the hook at the end of a tape.

Four-fold 1 ft. rules were frequently given away as promotional and advertising pieces. Together with the small 6 in. versions, often fitted with sliding calipers (made left- and right-handed), these are also extremely handy to carry about.

The other main type of wooden rule useful in the shop is the zig-zag rule (FIG. 48). 'Zig-zag' was the Stanley Rule and Level Company's patented name for this design, but it has now become a generic term for a folding rule that opens in a zig-zag fashion. The chief advantage of these rules is their rigidity and length. It is hard to get a metal tape to stay straight when extended much more than 6 ft., especially when held horizontally, but zig-zag rules can be found that unfold up to 12 ft.,

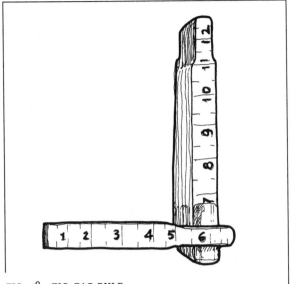

FIG. 48   ZIG-ZAG RULE

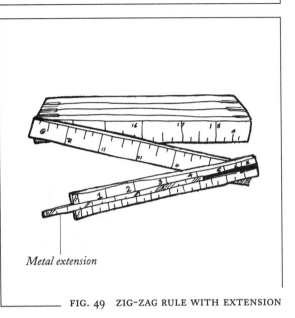

Metal extension

FIG. 49   ZIG-ZAG RULE WITH EXTENSION

and which will remain rigid when completely extended. A further feature of some zig-zag rules is a sliding extension (see FIG. 49) which allows inside measurements to be read directly without having to calculate, rather inaccurately, the width of the tape measure's case. Two drawbacks to this kind of rule are the time it takes to refold the rule compared to the virtually instant retractability of a spring-loaded tape measure, and the vulnerability to being broken precisely because you have not had the patience to refold it in the first place.

The ancestor of today's metal tape measure was, as the name implies, originally made of cloth. The tape was wound up by hand into a leather case. It was itself a descendant of the chains used by surveyors for measuring distances (whence the actual distance known as a 'chain'). Like today's metal tapes, its end was prone to wear and eventually tore off. But while when this happens to a modern tape measure the tape disappears with a sudden and alarming whirring into the case, and must either be replaced or thrown away, the cloth tape could simply be neatly trimmed and, provided you always remembered to add the missing inch or so, continue to be used.

For long distances, such as 50 ft. or more, a tape is still a useful tool. Despite the fact that cloth tapes may stretch, they can be easier to use than metal ones, which tend to remain intractable when you are trying to measure something not quite flat. For the shorter lengths that you are likely to need to measure in the shop, however, wooden rules have distinct advantages.

MARKING TECHNIQUES

MENTION WAS MADE AT THE BEGINNING of this chapter of the necessity for a fine instrument if exact measurements are needed. It is also important to use such instruments skillfully and with an appropriate guiding device. For instance, when taking off measurements from a graduated rule, accuracy will be increased if the rule is held so that the graduation is in direct contact with the work. Since most rules are inscribed only on their top surface, this means tilting the rule so that the actual indentation touches the work. If the instrument is sharp enough it will ride in the indentation and your measurement will be precise.

Although metal tapes are usually provided with a hook at the end, so fixed that it moves by as much as its own thickness, allowing accurate

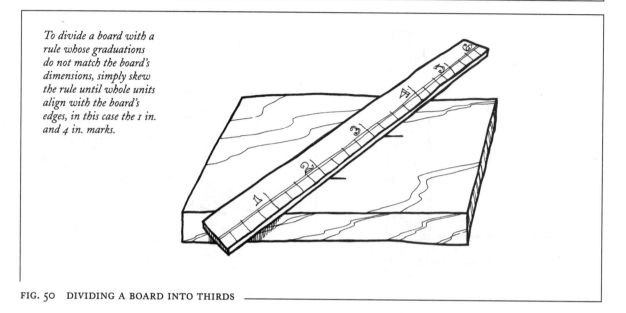

To divide a board with a rule whose graduations do not match the board's dimensions, simply skew the rule until whole units align with the board's edges, in this case the 1 in. and 4 in. marks.

FIG. 50   DIVIDING A BOARD INTO THIRDS

measurements to be taken with the hook over the end of the work or inside it, much greater accuracy will be assured if you get into the habit of measuring from within the tape. This means starting from some other point than the very end — the 2 in. mark, for example — and subtracting this amount from the final figure. The same procedure is advisable when using wooden rules, especially those that may have become worn and irregular at the end.

It is very common to find that you need to divide a piece into equal parts for which there are no convenient units on your rule. The solution is to skew the rule or tape until the required number of divisions on the rule can be fitted across the piece. This is clearly illustrated in FIG. 50.

5

THE SQUARE

NORMAL PERFECTION

EVEN WITH PRECISELY SET-UP FENCES AND ACCURATELY ALIGNED BLADES ON TODAY'S TABLESAWS, BANDSAWS, AND RADIAL-ARM SAWS — ALL OF WHICH CAN BE RELIED ON FOR CONSISTENTLY PERFECT RIGHT-ANGLED CUTS — WE STILL NEED the simple trysquare.

In the past the trysquare provided the main guidance for the majority of handsawing operations. Using it we made the marks that showed us where to saw. How accurately the cut was made depended not only on the saw and our skill in using it, but also to a great extent on where and how accurately the trysquare had been used. With powertools, on the other hand, often all that is necessary to make a perfect cut is simply to mark a single point indicating the required length, and leave the rest up to the predetermined accuracy of the tool in question. Nevertheless, the trysquare is still far from redundant. Not only does it remain one of our most important layout tools, but it is often the very tool used to check the accuracy of the powertools that would appear to have rendered its primary use superfluous in the first place.

A LONG HISTORY

THE SQUARE, AS YOU MIGHT EXPECT OF such a basic tool, is one of the oldest known to us. Its form being largely dictated by its function, it has remained basically unchanged for hundreds of years. Indeed, many 19th century shop-made wooden squares are virtually identical to the Roman squares described by Pliny and Vitruvius over two thousand years ago. Our word 'normal',

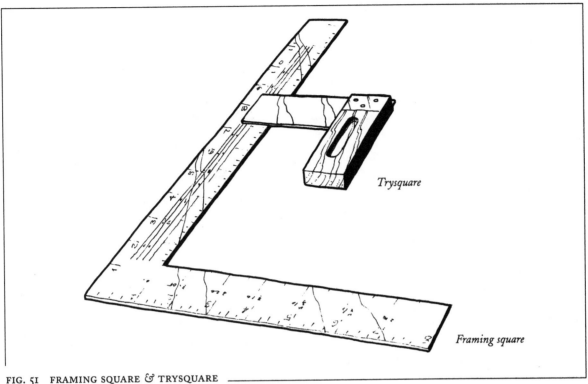

FIG. 51 FRAMING SQUARE & TRYSQUARE

which long ago meant something that was a right angle, then came to mean something that was the rule or the pattern, and which is now used to mean simply something that is customary or usual, comes directly from the Latin: *norma*, which was the Romans' word for a carpenter's or mason's square. The carpenter's square in more senses than one is a very normal tool.

THE WOODEN TRYSQUARE

MENTION 'SQUARE' TO A WOODWORKER AND two main types spring to mind: the all-metal framing square used by carpenters, and the much smaller, wooden-handled trysquare used in the shop (see FIG. 51). But there are other types: the machinist's square, miter square, combination square, adjustable square, sliding square, and sash square — not to mention the humble set square and T-square used mainly by draughtsmen but which are also useful in the shop.

The tool now called a trysquare is the grandfather of them all, but it is only in the last hundred years or so that it has had a metal blade. For centuries the common form was that of two wooden arms, one thicker than the other, fastened together to form a right angle (see FIG. 52). A curious feature often noticed by the first-time user is the way in which the two arms are joined,

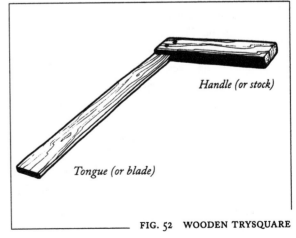

FIG. 52 WOODEN TRYSQUARE

THE SQUARE

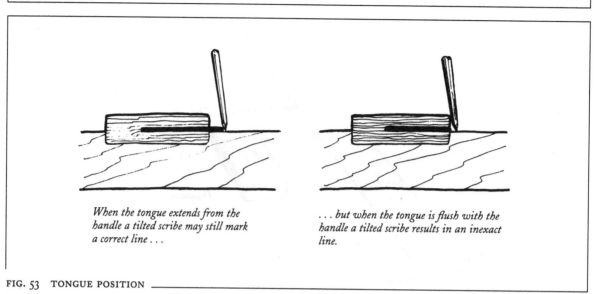

When the tongue extends from the handle a tilted scribe may still mark a correct line . . .

. . . but when the tongue is flush with the handle a tilted scribe results in an inexact line.

FIG. 53   TONGUE POSITION

whereby the thinner arm (often called the tongue or blade) is not let completely into the fatter arm (often called the handle or ſtock). Joseph Moxon, who, in 1678, wrote the firſt book in English on joinery, explained it thus:

> . . . the reason why the Tongue hath not its whole breadth let into the end of the Handle is, because they [the users] may with less care ſtrike a line by the side of a thin than a thick piece: For if inſtead of holding the Hand upright when they ſtrike a Line, they should hold it never so little inwards, the shank of a Pricker falling againſt the top edge of the Handle, would throw the Point of a Pricker farther out than a thin Piece would . . .
>
> Another Reason is, That if with often ſtriking the Pricker againſt the Tongue it becomes ragged, or uneven, they can with less trouble Plane it again when the Stuff is all the way of an equal ſtrength, than they can, if Cross-grain'd Shoulders be added to any part of it.*

The truth of the firſt reason is shown in FIG. 53. The second reason remains true even though it is not advisable to plane a damaged contemporary metal blade; filing is more appropriate, but ſtill

* Joseph Moxon. *Mechanick Exercises: or the Doctrine of Handy-Works.* London 1678

easier if the entire length of the edge remains proud of the handle.

Wooden versions, similar to the common shop-made square (FIG. 54) that was once the only kind available, may ſtill be usefully made, especially when a larger tool is needed. It is true that framing squares are typically made with 18 in. and 24 in. blades, and that extra-large joiner's squares with brass-faced rosewood handles and 18 in. tongues may sometimes be found at fleamarkets, but the former are not as easy to use as wooden versions, and the latter can be both expensive and damaged.

The advantage of a large wooden square over a framing square is that, having a handle thicker than its blade, it is easier to hold square to the work if you want the blade to reſt flat on the surface. A framing square may be held square to the work with security only if the tool is tilted so that the part used as the handle is allowed to bear againſt the back of the far edge of the workpiece. This is often inconvenient, since it raises from the work precisely that edge of the tongue from whose graduations you are likely to want to take measurements. If made from aluminum, the framing square is liable to damage — and an out-of-square square is no square at all — and if made from ſteel, it is liable to be heavy and awkward to

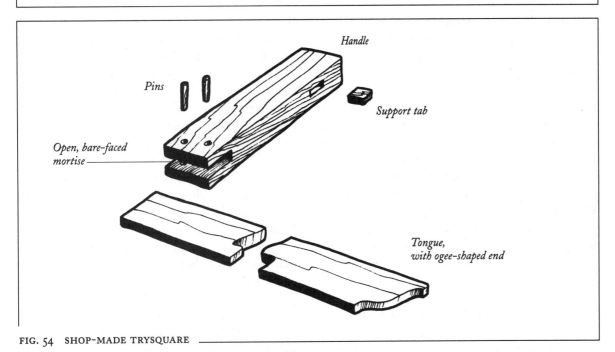

FIG. 54   SHOP-MADE TRYSQUARE

keep precisely tilted. The wooden square, if made precisely (and kept tuned, as Moxon suggests, by being planed to perfect accuracy), is a better tool to use for squaring across wide boards. Note that larger wooden trysquares are commonly fitted with a small support tab mortised into the inside of the handle, at the opposite end from the tongue and in the same plane, to rest upon the work and so prevent the handle from tilting.

Shop-made trysquares are best made from well-seasoned, stable, straight-grained wood such as mahogany. Care should be taken to shoot both sides of handle and tongue perfectly straight and

parallel so that both sides of the tool may be used with accuracy, and so that the square may also be used to check the squareness of internal and external angles. Let the tongue into the handle with an open, bare-faced mortise, and fix the two together with glue and wooden pins. Older, wooden trysquares often have the end of the tongue finished in the shape of an elegant ogee.

While making a wooden trysquare you may want to make another old tool that was well known to generations of woodworkers but is now virtually unseen: a wooden miter-square (FIG. 55). Although originally made in two pieces like the

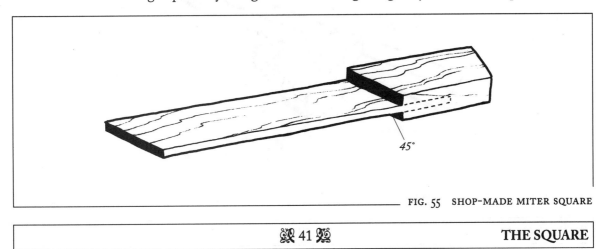

FIG. 55   SHOP-MADE MITER SQUARE

trysquare, its tongue being mortised into its handle and then glued and pinned, if you have a tablesaw it is just as easily made from a single piece. Start with an 18 in. length of 1 in. by 3 in. seasoned material, and set the tablesaw's blade to cut to a depth of slightly less than ⅜ in. Hold the workpiece against the miter gauge — set to precisely 45° — and make a pass, cutting the wood about 4 in. from one end. Continue to pass the wood over the blade, each time moving the workpiece so that the cut is made closer to the far end. When the first side of the tongue is thus formed, reverse the 45° angle of the miter gauge, turn the workpiece over, and reduce the second side of the tongue to match the first.

TRYSQUARES WITH METAL BLADES

THE ADJUSTABLE COMBINATION-TRYSQUARE (FIG. 56), whose handle slides up and down the blade (allowing it to be used as a depth gauge or a marking gauge) and which may be used either as a trysquare or a miter square, and which often contains a built-in spirit level together with a removable pin for striking (marking) a line, is a masterpiece of many-tools-in-one, equaled only by the famous general-purpose layout tool once made by Stanley™ known as the 'Stanley "Odd Jobs" Tool No. 1'. But it lacks the comfortable familiarity of a dedicated trysquare such as the standard joiner's-trysquare. Even a cheap contemporary model with a mahogany-colored handle and a plain, unmarked steel blade is a nicer tool to use. Best of all is an old model with a rosewood or ebony handle, its inside edge faced with brass, and its steel blade smooth to the touch.

These beauties, one of the nicest classes of tools to grace any bench, were made in a wide range of sizes. Their blades vary from 3 in. long to as much as 30 in., although giants this extreme are now very rare. The commonest and most generally useful sizes have blades measuring from 6 in. to 10 in. long. Top-of-the-line models were made with built-in levels, graduations, and blades embellished with ornate photo-etched designs similar to those seen on old saw blades. All but the cheapest were sold faced with brass wear strips. The distinguishing feature of all these tools is the brass plate or plates set in the handle, through which the iron rivets that secure the blade are driven. When cleaned and restored to use, the gleam of the brass in the rich rosewood or ebony handle creates an effect of old-world luxury, of a bygone era of exemplary handwork far removed from the plastic-handled powertools

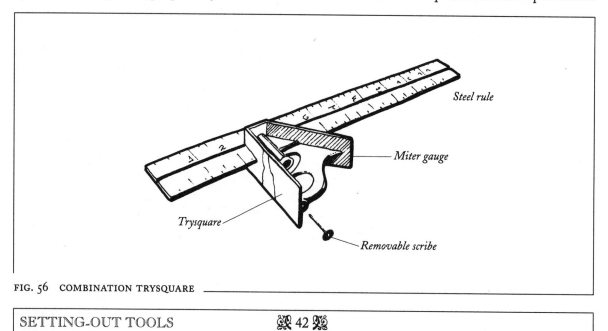

Steel rule

Miter gauge

Trysquare

Removable scribe

FIG. 56   COMBINATION TRYSQUARE

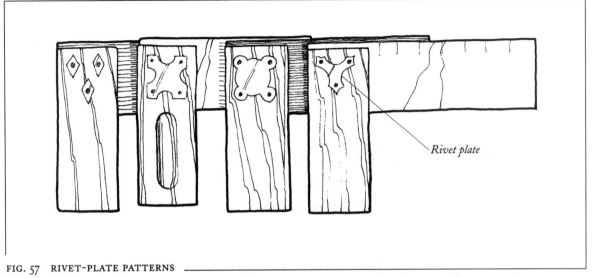

FIG. 57   RIVET-PLATE PATTERNS

now the norm. That this appeal is still strong is shown by the premium tools sold by several enterprising present-day companies, albeit at prices far exceeding the cost of the older tools.

A USEFUL INLAY TECHNIQUE

THE PLATES THEMSELVES, WHICH WERE made in a great variety of patterns from simple diamonds to stars and fanciful multi-armed designs (see FIG. 57), have been responsible for the start of many a tool collection, but they also embody a little-known routing technique of interest and possible use to woodworkers interested in routing designs with acute internal angles. These tools were mass-produced; indeed, it was the cheapness of their mass-production which enabled them to supplant the older user-made all-wooden trysquare as the standard tool. Nevertheless, one aspect of their manufacture remained handwork for the longest time: the routing of the mortises for the brass rivet plates.

This was done with a setup similar to a bow drill (see chapter 36), used in conjunction with a breast plate of the type that used to be worn by craftsmen who had much heavy boring to perform and who needed to bear down on the end of the

brace with their chests (see FIG. 58). The two-edged cutter, called a parcer or parcee, was turned with the help of the bow, its cord being given a turn around the parcer's bobbin. The depth of cut was a function of the length of the parcer's cutting tips. The outline of the shape cut depended entirely on the shape cut in the template. The

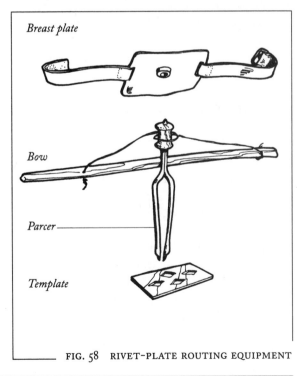

FIG. 58   RIVET-PLATE ROUTING EQUIPMENT

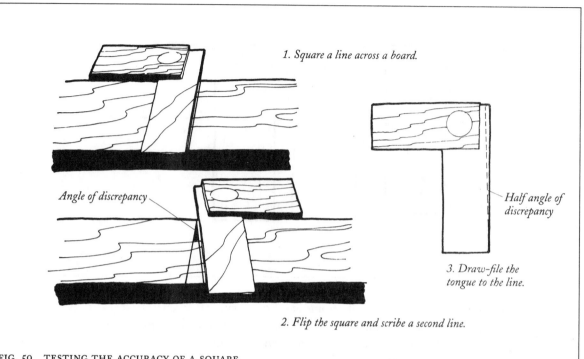

1. Square a line across a board.

Angle of discrepancy

Half angle of discrepancy

3. Draw-file the tongue to the line.

2. Flip the square and scribe a second line.

FIG. 59   TESTING THE ACCURACY OF A SQUARE

parcer was kept cutting within the confines of a hardened ſteel template by being pressed againſt the breaſt plate, which in the 19th century was usually spelled 'breſt plate', perhaps juſt as bevel was commonly spelled 'bevil', and mortise-and-tenon was referred to as 'mortess and tenaunt'.

GUARANTEEING ACCURACY

THE WAY TO TEST THE ACCURACY OF A trysquare is well known: ſtrike a line, flip the trysquare and ſtrike a second line. If both lines coincide the blade is set accurately at 90°. Few trysquares are perfeĉt, even when new, and old models are particularly liable to have been dropped or suffered subtle deformation as the result of fifty years or more of drying out. But before you rush off to buy an all-metal (and expensive) machiniſt's trysquare for those all-important referencing operations when setting up bandsaw tables and jointer fences, consider how easy it is to true a trysquare.

All that needs to be done is to perform the accuracy teſt, leaving an observable pair of converging lines on the wood used for the teſt. Now scribe a line on the edge of the trysquare's blade at exaĉtly half the angle of the marked discrepancy, as shown in FIG. 59. Use machiniſt's blue and a hardened ſteel point so that the result is clearly visible on the blade. Then draw-file down to this line using a flat mill-file. Smooth the filed edges very lightly and your square should now produce parallel or coincident lines when flipped, indicating a perfeĉt 90°.

VARIETIES

SEVERAL MODERN MANUFACTURERS OF trysquares, including Disſton™ and Stanley™, have made tools which, while patterned on the older rosewood-handled models, are all metal. Although these are not as nice to the touch or the eye, they do have the advantage, so long as they are maintained in good condition, that like the all-metal machinist's squares (typically those manufactured by the L. S. Starret Company) they can be used with a little more precision when measuring or checking internal angles, since the metal handles are unlikely to become rounded over at the edges like their wooden-handled counterparts. They are also more commonly graduated, although personally I have never found the graduations on a trysquare to be of much help except for rough use. An exception to this is the use of the trysquare as a gauge: Holding a scriber or a pencil against the required graduation while pressing the inside of the tool's handle against the edge of a board allows you to make a long gauging mark by pulling the tool along the workpiece.

This is similar to the trick of using your hand (while holding a pencil) as a rough gauge, but can give you a greater range.

Machinist's squares, it should be noted, are more than simple metal versions of joiner's or carpenter's trysquares. They are made to higher tolerances and can be used to check surfaces and angles to a degree of precision not practical when working with wood, which no matter how finely machined remains by virtue of its composition a material not susceptible to the same level of accuracy as metal. Since most woodworkers own metal tools such as metal-bodied planes or powertools, a machinist's square is nevertheless a useful thing to have around the shop.

6

BEVELS

ANYTHING BUT SQUARE

THE BEVEL, AN APPARENTLY STRAIGHTFORWARD TOOL, FAMILIAR EVEN TO THE NOVICE WOODWORKER, SUFFERS FROM AN AILMENT UNUSUAL FOR SOMETHING SO COMMON: A SURFEIT OF OFTEN ERRONEOUS NOMENCLATURE. A GLANCE AT THE indexes of a random selection of books on woodworking will confirm this; the tool may be listed under square, bevel square, T-bevel, sliding bevel, or various other inventive combinations.

The word 'bevel' refers to any angle that is not square (90°). Strictly speaking, it also excludes angles of 45°. Since there are 'squares', known as 'miter squares', designed to aid in the measuring and marking of 45° angles this would seem implicitly to exclude bevels from this area of geometry. But since a bevel can be, and indeed often very usefully is, used to take off 45° angles, we should not be too pedantic on this point.

The tool used to measure and mark any angle other than one of 90° is therefore properly known to masons and woodworkers as a bevel. To call it a bevel square without intending an oxymoron is to define something that cannot exist. Of course, it could be argued that the use of the word 'square' in this context is really a contraction of the term 'trysquare', but then by extension a tool used to test angles other than those of 90° should be known properly as a 'try bevel', and this is one variation that, perversely, does not seem to exist.

Most of the other names by which this innocent tool may be known are simply descriptive of the various levels of sophistication in its design that have been achieved over the years. At first glance one might be tempted to think, to paraphrase Gertrude Stein, that 'a bevel is a bevel is a bevel',

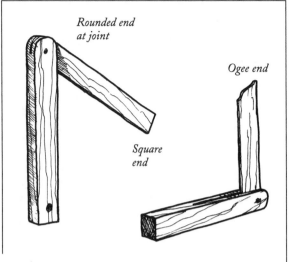

FIG. 60   PRIMITIVE USER-MADE BEVELS

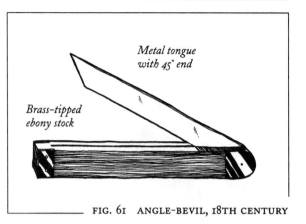

FIG. 61   ANGLE-BEVEL, 18TH CENTURY

and yet, to paraphrase Thomas Jefferson, 'not all bevels are created equal'.

Although the bevel was known to and used by the ancient Romans, it first made its appearance in the form familiar to us today at the end of the 18th century, at which time it was known as a 'bevil'. It was also commonly called an 'angle-bevil' — thereby proving that tautology is not confined to 20th century advertising. The first manufactured tools were modeled directly on the common wooden user-made tool: a straight stock, slotted at one end to receive a thinner arm, or tongue, which, being stiffly secured in the slot, could be set at various angles to the stock.

While many primitive examples are finished with square ends on both stock and tongue, the end where both join is usually rounded (see FIG. 60). The outer end of the tongue, when made of wood, was often finished with an ogee-like profile, similar to many wooden trysquares. Metal tongues are most commonly found with the outer end of the tongue finished at 45° (see FIG. 61), though larger angles from 60° to 75° also exist. The reason for this is twofold: first, it aids significantly in folding the tongue back into the stock if the end of the tongue is cut back at less than 90° (just as beveling the edge of a door aids in its closing tightly against the jamb); and second, the angle produced by the tongue and the stock just before the tongue enters the stock provides a useful and ready-made auxiliary angle for such purposes as laying out dovetails (FIG. 62).

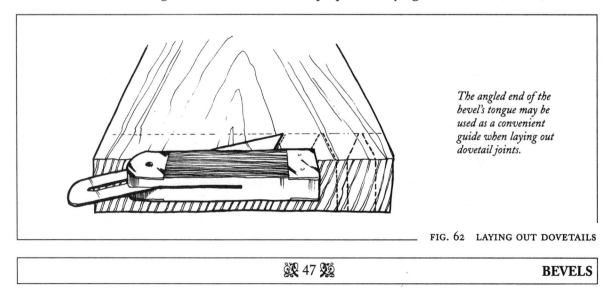

The angled end of the bevel's tongue may be used as a convenient guide when laying out dovetail joints.

FIG. 62   LAYING OUT DOVETAILS

BEVELS

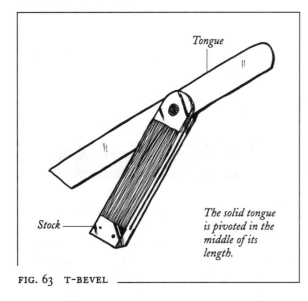

FIG. 63   T-BEVEL

The solid tongue is pivoted in the middle of its length.

middle of its length within the ſtock, but with one great difference: a slot is cut in the tongue, reaching from the pivot point back to that end of the tongue which was the pivot point in the earlier angle bevels. This is the form that has remained basic down to today's mass-produced models. It combines the usefulness of creating, like the T-bevel, both complementary angles at once, with the convenience of the angle bevel's end pivot point — frequently required by the tightness of the work, where a protruding end of tongue would get in the way or actually prevent the bevel from being held againſt the work at all.

SOME REFINEMENTS

WITHIN THESE THREE BASIC TYPES THERE are yet further differences to be noted, differences so important that over the years many patents have been taken out by their inventors. Moſt have to do with the method of securing the tongue within the ſtock, but others have affected different aspects of the bevel's conſtruction, such as the design of the tongue itself, making for greater versatility in an already surprisingly agile tool.

The firſt major improvement over the simple 'angle-bevil' was the invention of the 'T-bevil' (FIG. 63). A T-bevel's tongue is fixed to its ſtock in the middle of its length rather than at one end. By this simple expedient the use of the tool is doubled, for now any angle set at one end of the tool automatically produces its complementary angle at the other end.

It was but a short ſtep from the T-bevel to the next development, the sliding bevel (FIG. 64). The sliding bevel is arranged in the same manner as the T-bevel, its tongue being pivoted in the

Early examples had the tongue fixed in the ſtock by a simple metal rivet or a tightly fitting wooden pin. The disadvantage of this method of fixing was that with continued use the tongue would inevitably become so loose within its ſtock that the required angle could not be securely maintained. The cure for this defect was to use a screw, or a nut and bolt, which could be tightened so as to hold the tongue securely at any desired angle. Of these two methods, that of the nut and bolt soon predominated, the nut soon becoming a wingnut which could be loosened or tightened by the fingers alone without recourse to an additional tool such as a wrench or a pair of pliers.

While this expedient produced a tool of great reliability and convenience (so much so that moſt contemporary tools are ſtill made this way), it suffered from one annoying drawback: the wingnut all too often protrudes on the wrong side of the

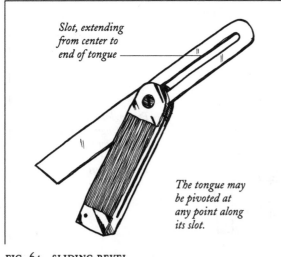

Slot, extending from center to end of tongue

The tongue may be pivoted at any point along its slot.

FIG. 64   SLIDING BEVEL

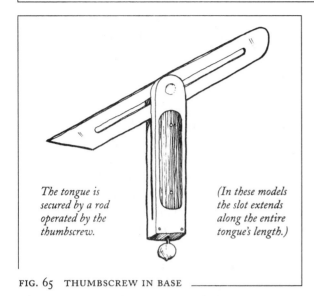

The tongue is secured by a rod operated by the thumbscrew.

(In these models the slot extends along the entire tongue's length.)

FIG. 65   THUMBSCREW IN BASE

stock, making it impossible to lay the bevel flat on the work. The user is then forced to set the tongue in the opposite direction and take the angle again. When involved with any casework where alternate angles are constantly required to be taken, this is not only an inconvenience but also an opportunity for error to creep in. You could, of course, equip yourself with two bevels, but even so there would still be a certain amount of inconvenience occasioned by the necessity of constantly having to put down one tool and pick up another. The first patented solution to this

problem was recorded on June 14, 1870, by one Isaiah J. Robinson of St. Johnsbury, Vermont. It consisted of a mechanism for securing the tongue at any desired angle controlled by a thumbscrew located in the base of the stock, conveniently out of the way regardless of which way around the bevel might be used (see FIG. 65).

The end of the 19th century in America was a period of unprecedented invention, especially in the area of tool development, and in the ensuing years many more patents were taken out for methods of securing the tongue in such a way as not to interfere with the tool's use. Aside from the wingnut-in-base type, soon developed by major manufacturers such as Sargent™, Stanley™, and Disston™, a second major type appeared that consisted of various tongue-locking devices all located at the pivot point of stock and tongue. These were recessed so as to be below the general level of the stock when laid on its side (see FIG. 66). Diamond-shaped locking nuts, lever nuts, and regular wingnuts were all used and all patented, but one form, which was really a far simpler solution to the problem than all this clever Yankee ingenuity, was one that had been prevalent in Britain since much earlier in the century — the countersunk pivot screw (FIG. 67).

The advantage of the British method is one that is often cited by its opponents as being its major

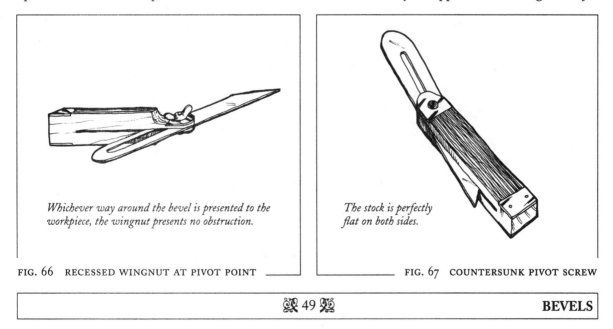

Whichever way around the bevel is presented to the workpiece, the wingnut presents no obstruction.

FIG. 66   RECESSED WINGNUT AT PIVOT POINT

The stock is perfectly flat on both sides.

FIG. 67   COUNTERSUNK PIVOT SCREW

disadvantage, which is that a screwdriver is required to set the tongue. American woodworkers apparently valued the ability to alter the setting with one hand — the wingnut or lever nut often being positioned so that all the user had to do was to move slightly the thumb of the hand holding the tool to release the tongue and then resecure it. The British seemed to think that there was less likelihood of inadvertently changing the angle if doing so required that the tool be put down and readjusted with a screwdriver. The same principle was applied to British gauges (see chapter 7), many of which are set by means of recessed screws. The comparison is not strictly fair, since the American tools were primarily intended for carpenters and workmen employed on work demanding more speed than exactness, while the British tools so made were invariably those representing the top of the line in their class, and were intended for the less rushed and more exacting work performed by cabinetmakers and high-class joiners.

All three types of sliding bevel (those with a surface-mounted wingnut, those with a recessed wingnut or lever nut, and those with an in-base securing device) continue to be made today, but strangely, it is a representative of the least-useful type (the surface-mounted securing nut) that is

now the most expensive bevel, often costing more than fifty dollars in mailorder catalogs. On the other hand, the most useful type (that with a tongue secured from the base of the stock) is now the most cheaply made, the handsomely shaped brass wingnut seen on older models having been replaced by a piece of bent rod.

Since 1897 many bevels manufactured by the Stanley Tool Company in all its various incarnations have been made with elongated recesses formed in the sides of the wooden stock. This feature supposedly provides a better grip, but the advantage is minimal, and in any event is not duplicated on metal bevels.

Aside from variations in size and design intended for specific uses and trades, there are other features that commend older bevels over contemporary versions. One is, of course, the use of finer materials such as rosewood or ebony for the stock, and silver-plated tongues. Additional enticements included brass-plated sections on the stock, built-in levels, and graduated tongues, together with all manner of engraving on both tongues and metal stocks (see FIG. 68).

OPERATING TECHNIQUES

BEFORE LOOKING AT SPECIALIST BEVELS let us first examine the basic uses of the average, all-purpose sliding bevel. Its primary use is, of course, for marking and testing angles that are not right angles — this job being accomplished by the trysquare. Whereas the trysquare's blade or tongue is permanently fixed, that of the bevel must be fixed by the user. Whichever method of securing the tongue is used the process is the same: First set the bevel to the required angle and then tighten the tongue — but only enough to prevent it from slipping. You will usually discover, when you compare the bevel with the angle to which it has been set, that during tightening the tongue has moved a little. Make the final adjustment by lightly tapping the bevel on the bench and then screwing it up tightly, but do not

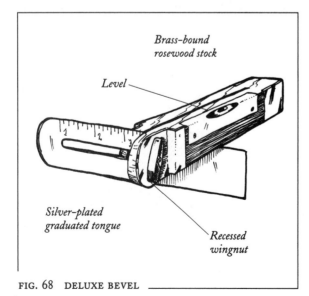

Brass-bound rosewood stock

Level

Silver-plated graduated tongue

Recessed wingnut

FIG. 68 DELUXE BEVEL

overdo it, for remarkably little pressure is needed to secure the tongue firmly.

When using a sliding bevel, a little forethought is necessary to determine whether the tongue should be slid out to the end of the slot before being set, or whether it may be left pivoted at its center. If the work will allow the bevel to be used from either direction it is frequently more useful to leave the tongue pivoted at its center, as this method will provide you with both the acute angle and the complementary obtuse one. This is not always possible, however, and the tongue will have to be slid out to the end of the slot. In so doing, take care that the sides of the tongue align perfectly tangentially with the end of the stock. There is usually a certain amount of free play from side to side of the tongue on the pivot, and you will not get a true reading if the end of the tongue is misaligned with the end of the stock. This is another case in which older bevels are frequently superior to modern ones. The curved end of older tongues is usually a perfect semi-circle, which perfectly matches the shaped end of the stock. New models, on the other hand, are often not machined as nicely, and the end of the tongue is rounded in such a way that shoulders or corners are formed which interfere with a perfect alignment. The tongue also fits better on the pivot in older models, and is therefore less likely to sink below the level of the slot in the stock.

It should be obvious that in order to take true readings from either side of the tongue, the tongue must be made with perfectly parallel sides. Care should be taken to ensure that the edges do not become dented or bent.

A related aspect of good bevel care and use has to do with the condition of the stock. This should be formed with perfectly square sides, for otherwise the tongue will not lie flat on the surface to be marked or measured. Indeed, you may often get into trouble by marking an erroneous line as a result of not having pressed the stock firmly enough against the work.

Sometimes, however, there are situations in which it is necessary to take off an angle with the bevel, but where either the end of the work is too narrow to provide sufficient support for the stock or there is an obstruction in the way. The best way around this problem is to use a spacer block to provide a bearing surface for the stock, as shown in FIG. 69.

Since most bevels now have an angled end on the tongue, should you find it necessary to disassemble the tool, be sure to reassemble the tongue the right way round, or the end of the tongue will not fit into the slot in the stock.

If you have a bevel with a side adjustment, particularly on a non-recessed model, you may need to take the bevel apart. Sometimes the end of the wingnut or lever interferes with the work in such a way that the bevel cannot be held quite flat against the work. You could file off the end of the obstructing nut, but there is an easier and less radical solution: completely unscrew the nut and gently tap out the bolt. On many modern bevels it will be seen that this bolt fits into a hexagonal hole in the stock (to prevent the bolt from turning when the nut is secured). By repositioning the bolt one place to the left or right you will usually find that next time, when the securing nut is

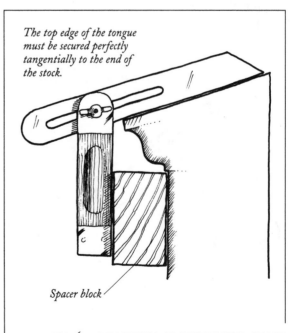

The top edge of the tongue must be secured perfectly tangentially to the end of the stock.

Spacer block

FIG. 69   MEASURING AN OBSTRUCTED ANGLE

tightened down, it ends up in a position that no longer interferes with the work. Not all older bevels have their pivot screw made this way; some are actually screwed into the stock, and wanton attempts to beat out the screw will merely break off the somewhat vulnerable end of the stock.

SETTING THE ANGLE

THERE ARE SEVERAL WAYS TO ACHIEVE THE correct angle adjustment with the bevel. The first is to take off the angle directly from the work, the only precaution necessary being that both stock and tongue be held tightly to the work. The second way is to take off the angle from drawings or plans. Since the stock is thicker than the tongue, use straight strips of wood at least half the thickness of the stock to place along the lines on the drawing with which the tongue is to be aligned, as shown in FIG. 70. This effectively raises their height so that the bevel does not have to be tilted to come into contact with both sides forming the required angle. A third method is by using a protractor. Here, care must be taken that the edge of the tongue intersects exactly with the center of the protractor. A method useful for carpenters

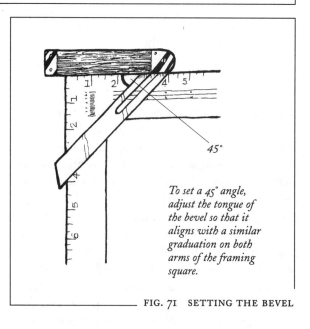

To set a 45° angle, adjust the tongue of the bevel so that it aligns with a similar graduation on both arms of the framing square.

FIG. 71 SETTING THE BEVEL

equipped with a framing square consists in laying the stock of the bevel along one side of the square and adjusting the tongue so that its edge coincides with the desired graduation on the other arm of the framing square. Studying FIG. 71 will clarify the method. An easy way to achieve an angle of 45° is by arranging the bevel so that the outside point of intersection of stock and tongue lies at the same graduation on one arm of the square as does the outside edge of the other end of the bevel's tongue. The tongue thus positioned forms the hypoteneuse of an equilateral triangle — which contains 45° angles.

Equipped with sine and cosine tables, or a pocket calculator designed to render these values, the bevel and the framing square can be arranged to produce any desired acute angle (and by sliding the tongue back past the pivot point, the complementary obtuse angle as well). The method is as follows: let the side shown in FIG. 72 marked 'a' be the sine, and the side marked 'b' be the cosine; then divide the value of the cosine (obtained from table or calculator) by the value of the sine of the required angle; multiply the ratio thus obtained by any assigned value of side 'b', and the product will be the corresponding length of side 'a'; arrange the bevel on the square so as to

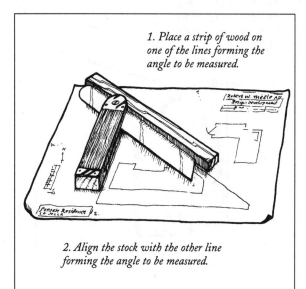

1. Place a strip of wood on one of the lines forming the angle to be measured.

2. Align the stock with the other line forming the angle to be measured.

FIG. 70 TAKING MEASUREMENTS FROM DRAWINGS

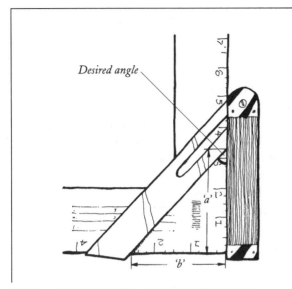

FIG. 72   SETTING BEVEL TRIGONOMETRICALLY

represent these two lengths, and the angle formed by the junction of stock and tongue will be the angle originally required.

SOME HYBRIDS

THERE ARE ONE OR TWO SPECIALTY BEVELS that deserve mention, and of these the boatbuilder's bevel (FIG. 73) is the most venerable. This tool is distinguished by having two tongues, one long and one short, each pivoted at the opposite end of the same stock and having their meeting ends angled complementarily. The stock is further distinguished by frequently being graduated, in distinction to ordinary bevels, which, if graduated at all, bear the graduations on the tongue. Such an arrangement is of considerable help when measuring the compound angles encountered in the curving lines of planks and frames found in ships and boats.

Another bevel that has two tongues (or two stocks, depending on how it is used) is the combination bevel (FIG. 74). Both tongue and stock are slotted, which allows the bevel to adapt to adjustments that could not be obtained with a common bevel. A necessary sophistication of this bevel is that the back of the securing screw's head is let in flush with the back of the stock so that the tool may lie flat on the work.

A bevel that might not be recognized as such is the bricklayer's bevel. Used for marking bricks to be cut into various shapes, the inside face of the stock, when made of wood, is plated with brass, the better to withstand the hard usage occasioned by the rough bricks. Otherwise it looks identical to a common angle bevel. All-metal versions with slotted stocks and slotted tongues are used by

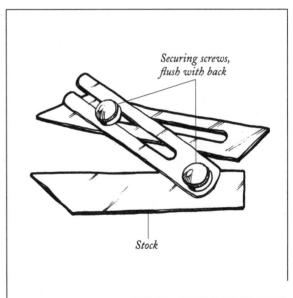

FIG. 74   COMBINATION BEVEL

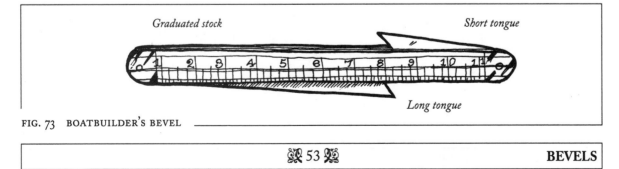

FIG. 73   BOATBUILDER'S BEVEL

masons. In Britain this specialty bevel is also known as a shift stock.

One last observation: as with so many venerable tools developed by tradition and highly individualistic tradesmen, there is little standardization. You might not think that in a tool so eminently simple and straightforward there was much cause for concern over standardization, but a lack of this very quality has caused great confusion over the years. It is manifested in the question of size. There is a considerable range in available sizes, and indeed, it is a definite advantage to have several bevels in your toolkit. While the bevel with the longest tongue will most easily give you the most exact reading, there will be many situations where only a much smaller bevel may be used. They can be found in sizes measuring from 6 in. to 16 in. long, but beware of the fact that there is little agreement as to which part is taken as the measurement. Some measure the tongue, others measure the stock, and yet others compute the length of the bevel by measuring the combined length of tongue and stock when the tongue is folded back into the stock.

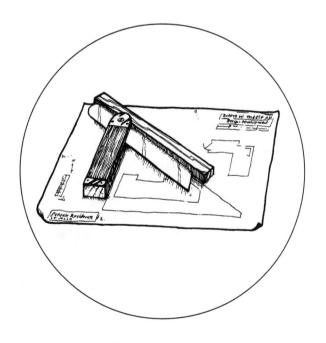

7

GAUGES

STOCK & STEM

'**G**AUGE', MEANING EXTENT, DIMENSION, CAPACITY, OR MEASUREMENT, IS A MYSTERIOUS WORD. IT IS FIRST NOTICED IN OLD NORTHERN FRENCH, WHERE IT IS THOUGHT TO HAVE HAD SOMETHING TO DO WITH A MEDIEVAL WINE container used as a standard for quantity. In American English it is sometimes spelled 'gage' but since this is also the term describing one sailing vessel's position relative to another's and the wind, keeping the older spelling when referring to the various tools and instruments used in woodworking is a useful distinction.

According to the basic definition of 'gauge' there are many tools used in woodworking that ought to qualify for inclusion under this head, but convention and usage — ultimate arbiters of what is finally considered 'correct' — have decreed that 'gauge' be reserved for those measuring and marking tools which conform to the stock-and-stem construction. Although 'gauge' means simply to measure, the woodworking gauge usually does something more: it marks. It may do this lightly or in a more permanent fashion. Accordingly, the stock, or head as it is also called, which acts as a fence or guiding block, moves along a rod-shaped part, known as the stem or the beam, which contains some form of marking or cutting device, such as a pin, pencil, or small knife (see FIG. 75).

Simple though this description and definition may seem, woodworking gauges exist in a surprising number of types and varieties, some of which are so complicated as to defy interpretation by the uninitiated. While every woodworker is surely familiar with the basic marking gauge — it is, indeed, one of those items invariably included in

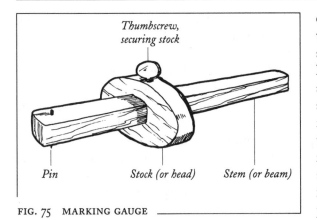

Thumbscrew, securing stock

Pin *Stock (or head)* *Stem (or beam)*

FIG. 75 MARKING GAUGE

even the smallest kit of woodworking tools — how many are on working terms with, amongst many others, the panel gauge, the slitting gauge, or the butt-and-mortise gauge?

Leaving aside the other numerous woodworking tools that might qualify as gauges in the broadest sense — many of them actually being called gauges, including, for example: auger-bit gauge, button gauge, caliper gauge, chisel gauge, clapboard gauge, cylindrical gauge, depth gauge, limit gauge, plane gauge, stairbuilder's gauge, and thickness gauge — true stock-and-stem gauges may be divided into three main groups: marking gauges; cutting gauges; and panel and slitting gauges.

Apart from various panel gauges, which tend to be larger, these three groups all look so similar that the casual observer might not at once be able to discriminate between them. However, a closer examination of what 'gauging' is all about will make apparent niceties of difference much appreciated by the careful worker.

GAUGING BASICS

THE SIMPLEST GAUGE IS THE HAND ITSELF. By holding a pencil between thumb and forefinger, and running the hand down the edge of a board with the little finger hooked over the edge, a surprisingly straight and accurate line can be drawn up to as much as 5 in. or 6 in. from the edge. By using a graduated rule with the hand that holds it as a fence pressed against the edge of a workpiece, an even straighter and more precise line can be drawn with the aid of a pencil held against the end of the rule (see FIG. 76). Substitute a wooden stock for the hand that holds the rule, make this adjustable and securable by means of a thumbscrew, and fix the pencil in the end of the rule or stem with a screw, and you will have made a simple, pencil marking-gauge. The common, factory-made marking gauge, fitted with a steel point instead of a pencil, is essentially the same tool. Even a metal tape measure can be used as a marking gauge: the hook at the end of the tape, usually hooked over the end of a workpiece, is often made with a hole or notch in it that will securely locate a pencil point. Use a pencil with the tape measure similarly to the rule and pencil; the locking device found on many tapes further increases the accuracy of any line drawn this way.

The simplest and most basic marking gauge constitutes a quantum leap forward from either of these techniques in terms of ease and exactness. For one thing, the required measurement may be locked into place and stored, as it were, freeing your hands from the necessity of maintaining their grip for as long as you need to keep the gauge at the desired measurement.

The other main advantage of using a purpose-built gauge lies in the control that may be exercised over the scribed line. It does not take much

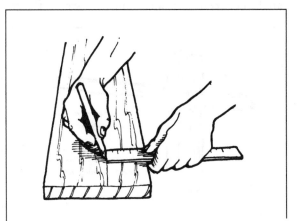

FIG. 76 RULE & PENCIL GAUGE

GAUGES

Hold the stock close to the workpiece.

Tilt the gauge in the direction it is being moved.

Gauged line

Keep the leading edge of the stem against the workpiece.

FIG. 77   USING THE MARKING GAUGE

practice to be able to manipulate the gauge so that the drawn or scribed line is always perfectly parallel to the edge of the work and always inscribed with the same pressure, leaving a mark of regular depth or definition.

Two main techniques are practically all that is required for successful use of virtually any gauge — marking, cutting, panel, or slitting. These are the necessity of keeping the stock or head pressed closely to the work (and note that I said 'closely' and not 'tightly', for the object is to avoid any space forming between the stock and the work and not to attempt to bury the stock in the work. Excessive pressure does not increase accuracy but merely wears the face of the stock unnecessarily and can also damage the edge of the work); and developing the knack of maintaining a constant angle between the gauge and the work. Exactly

what this angle is will vary according to whether you are marking or cutting, and also according to the material you are working with — experience will be your guide here — but the degree of success will depend on the level of consistency you are able to maintain. Of less importance are the questions of whether the tool should be pushed or pulled and of which hand should be used to hold the tool. Individual circumstances will dictate different methods; you may need to see part of the work, the job may be too big to reach from any one angle, or there may simply be too many obstructions to afford a clear pull through in any one direction. FIG. 77 illustrates one way of holding the marking gauge.

THE DEVELOPMENT OF FACTORY-MADE GAUGES

THE TIME WAS WHEN IT WAS COMMON practice for most woodworkers to make their own gauges. But as a man's business thrived and he began to take pride in his tools beyond what his own toolmaking ability could provide, and increasingly as the 19th century saw the appearance of specialized toolmakers, more elaborate and sophisticated forms than the simple homemade gauge became common. A few home-made gauges still survive, especially those made for specific purposes in some of the more specialized woodworking trades such as coopering, wheelwrighting, and waggonmaking (see FIG. 78). Apart from a lack of factory finish, and the frequent use of woods other than the beech most commonly used by full-time toolmakers, these

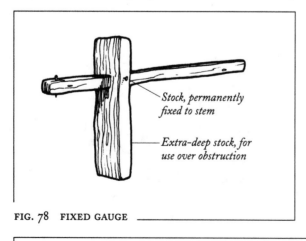

Stock, permanently fixed to stem

Extra-deep stock, for use over obstruction

FIG. 78   FIXED GAUGE

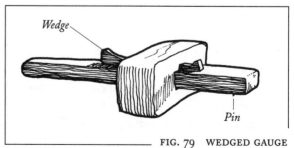

Wedge

Pin

FIG. 79   WEDGED GAUGE

user-made tools are usually characterized by the simple wedge that secures the stock at the desired position on the stem (see FIG. 79).

One of the first improvements that factory-made gauges had to offer was a better method of fixing the stock. This consisted of using a thumb-screw instead of the wedge. You are less likely to move the stock from its desired position when securing it with a thumbscrew than when attempting to fix it with a wedge. Practically all the cheapest lines of marking gauges featured this arrangement, and, indeed, today it is virtually the only method employed by contemporary tool-makers such as Stanley™ and Marples™. There were, however, other forms that used neither the wedge nor the screw, such as the threaded stem (FIG. 80), and the type made with a stem cut in the shape of an interrupted cam (FIG. 81). This type has a matching mortise in the stock, which may be loosened and tightened as desired simply by twisting the stem.

A superior method of securing the stock, surpassing both thumbscrew and cam method, was achieved with the development of gauges that featured a screw sunk into the stock so that its head was flush with the surface of the head (see FIG. 82). The chief advantage of this method is that it is virtually impossible to alter the setting inadvertently. There is also no obstruction in the event it is necessary to turn the gauge in the hand during use.

Another factory-made improvement was the inclusion of a wear plate in that part of the stock which bears against the work (see FIG. 83). Often taking the form of a simple inlaid brass strip, this piece was sometimes very elegantly shaped, and sometimes, indeed, covered the whole face of the stock. The value of providing a more durable face to the stock becomes apparent when another improvement that gradually became popular is taken into account. This is the practice of marking the stem in inches and fractions of an inch, starting at the point of the actual marking pin. With the addition of stem graduation the gauge can be set to any desired measurement without

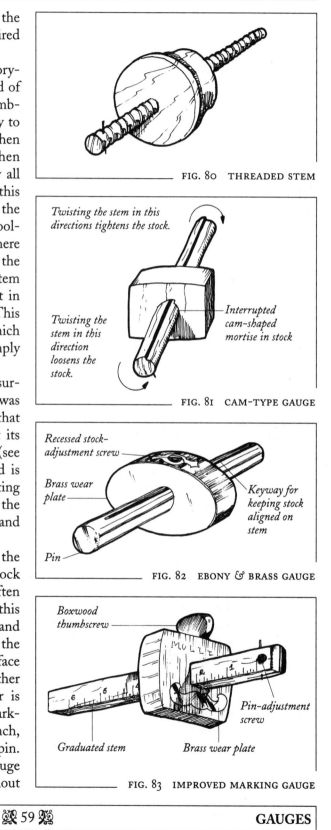

FIG. 80   THREADED STEM

Twisting the stem in this directions tightens the stock.

Twisting the stem in this direction loosens the stock.

Interrupted cam-shaped mortise in stock

FIG. 81   CAM-TYPE GAUGE

Recessed stock-adjustment screw

Brass wear plate

Keyway for keeping stock aligned on stem

Pin

FIG. 82   EBONY & BRASS GAUGE

Boxwood thumbscrew

Pin-adjustment screw

Graduated stem

Brass wear plate

FIG. 83   IMPROVED MARKING GAUGE

having to juggle a rule, the stem, and the stock in two hands while trying at the same time to secure the locking screw or wedge. Another advantage of a hard-faced stock is the avoidance of a worn face, which can make alignment with stem graduations increasingly difficult.

Hand-in-hand with graduated stems goes the need to keep the marking pin precisely located. The pins eventually wear down and become otherwise blunt and then need to be resharpened or replaced. Better-quality gauges make provision for this by having the pin secured with its own screw, which can be loosened for easy removal of the pin and precise alignment.

FINE TUNING

ALTHOUGH THE MARKING GAUGE APPEARS to be a relatively simple instrument there are several things that can be done to enhance and ensure its efficiency and accuracy. The first has to do with the actual marking point.

Contemporary gauges are invariably supplied with pins that are far too long, or at least which protrude far too much from the stem. The idea is not to inscribe a line in the work that is ¼ in. deep, but merely a surface scratch. Consequently, the pin does not need to protrude more than ⅛ in. at the most. If you use a gauge with a pin that sticks out much farther than this you run the risk of having the gauge tilt while in use and losing the parallelism that is the gauge's whole purpose. Of course, cheaper gauges that have square stems require their pins to protrude a little more than gauges with round or oval stems, in order to allow the stem to be rotated slightly when being pushed or pulled along the work. If you attempt to use the gauge with the pin vertical to the work there is a danger that the gauge will stick — and then jump free, with unfortunate results to the straightness of the line being marked. The gauge must be tilted a little in use so that the pin is not vertical.

The reason a gauge with a square stem should be cheaper is not that it is easier to make a square

mortise in the stock — it is not — but that a round stem requires some form of keying to keep it aligned within its stock. Should the stock be free to revolve around the stem, it would be impossible to keep wear-bearing plates and graduation marks in a consistent relationship to the stock. It is, however, much nicer to use a gauge with a round or oval stem, and for that matter, a gauge with an oval stock is much easier to use than one with a square stock. In any event, reduce the amount of point protrusion by repositioning the pin, or by filing it if it cannot be easily repositioned.

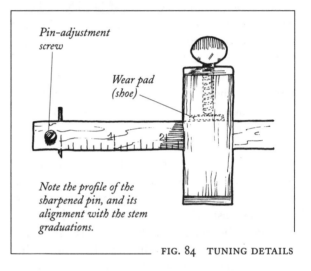

Pin-adjustment screw

Wear pad (shoe)

Note the profile of the sharpened pin, and its alignment with the stem graduations.

FIG. 84　TUNING DETAILS

To ensure absolute accuracy when using a gauge with a graduated stem, file or sharpen the point not only so that the tip is exactly at 'ground zero', but also so that the inside edge of the pin is flat, and any beveling is effected on the outside of the pin — the side farthest away from the stock, as shown in FIG. 84.

That the stock should not rock on the stem is also important; mere torquing down on the retaining screw will not necessarily ensure this. If the mortise in the stock is too worn the gauge may have to be discarded in favor of a unit that fits more tightly — but check first that the shoe or pad that should be provided inside the stock of a better-quality gauge to prevent the screw from eating into the stem is not missing. A new one can

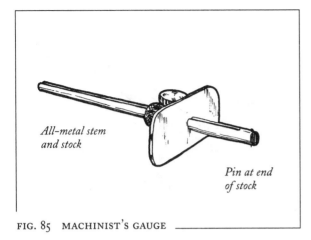

FIG. 85 MACHINIST'S GAUGE

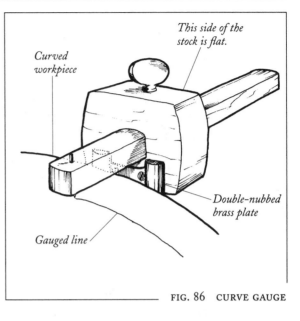

This side of the stock is flat.

Curved workpiece

Double-nubbed brass plate

Gauged line

FIG. 86 CURVE GAUGE

usually be easily provided with a piece of scrap brass or a blind washer.

VARIETIES & ADAPTATIONS

EVEN THE HUMBLEST BEECHWOOD GAUGE devoid of wear plate and adjustable pin will provide accurate service, but keep an eye open for the aristocrats: ebony masterpieces with stocks faced entirely with brass; gauges with flush-mounted stock-securing screws; oval-stocked models and models with solid-brass stocks; and gauges made entirely of metal. These last examples, often intended as machinists' metalworking gauges, are extremely useful since the pin is often placed much nearer the end of the stem than it is in wooden models (see FIG. 85), thereby enabling the gauge to be used close up in a rabbet or corner.

An especially useful find is a marking gauge that has a head designed to be reversible: one side is flat (for regular straight work), and the other face is fitted with a double-nubbed brass plate enabling the gauge to be drawn along curved work (see FIG. 86).

THE MORTISE GAUGE

A MUCH COLLECTED VARIETY OF MARKING gauge, because of the many ingenious and often pleasing varieties made over the years, is the mortise gauge. A mortise gauge scribes two parallel lines, rather than one. It is used typically to lay out the sides of a mortise to be cut in a workpiece. A simple marking gauge will do the job just as well, but will, of course, need to be reset to scribe the second line. However, if there are many mortises to be laid out, all of similar size, or if one particular size of mortise is most commonly used in your work, two marking gauges, each permanently set to one side or the other of the mortise, are more convenient. Similarly, a marking gauge with two pins set in the stem, at the requisite distance apart, will save even more time. Many user-made mortise gauges are precisely of this sort. They possess the great virtue of being instantly ready and always correct.

A mortise gauge whose second pin is adjustable is a refinement useful only if you commonly need to lay out mortises of different sizes. If this is the case then the choice of adjustment systems available to you is staggering. The simplest is a user-made type common in shops at the turn of the 19th century, consisting of two stems, each with its own pin, tightly fitted in a common stock but positioned at right angles to each other. There are no wedges, screws, threads, or fancy brass parts,

GAUGES

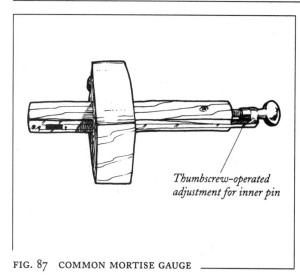

FIG. 87   COMMON MORTISE GAUGE

Thumbscrew-operated adjustment for inner pin

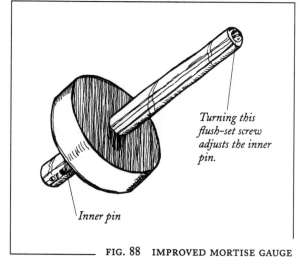

Turning this flush-set screw adjusts the inner pin.

Inner pin

FIG. 88   IMPROVED MORTISE GAUGE

just three pieces of wood and two small nails. The stems are simply pushed in or out to the needed measurement and stay there as a result of the tightness of the fit. At the other end of the scale are rosewood, ebony, and brass marvels fitted with hidden threaded rods and flush-mounted adjusting screws, polished, lacquered, graduated, and gleaming. They are a tool fancier's delight, and they work just as well as their humbler cousins. In between are innumerable varieties with double arms, sliding inserts, double-ended pins, screws, and wedges too cunning to detail.

In common with most other gauges, the shorter the pin the better, but in the case of mortise gauges it is also important that both pins be of the same height. Better-quality mortise gauges make provision for pin adjustment and replacement, but cheaper ones work just as well when you take care to file the pins properly, remembering to file the bevel on the inside edges.

The most common form of mortise gauge is that whose inner pin's adjustment mechanism is operated by a thumbscrew located at the end of the stem (see FIG. 87). But unless the adjustment is kept scrupulously in order this type of gauge can be prone to sudden and unaccountable inaccuracies. By far the best kind is that whose inner pin is adjusted by means of a screw set in the end of the stem (see FIG. 88). Not only does this

arrangement prevent inadvertent readjustment but it also provides for a tighter and more secure movement of the pin.

An equally secure adjustment is also possible with another type of mortise gauge, but at the price of a certain cumbersomeness and an extra motion. This is the two-bar mortise gauge that has each pin set in its own bar, both bars being contained within the same stock. It is rather cumbersome to use, since only one line at a time can be scribed and the gauge must be turned over and used a second time in order to achieve the marking of two lines. There is also the commensurate difficulty of having two stems to adjust and secure instead of only the one. However, very handsome models of this type were occasionally made in ebony and brass, and perhaps the sheer pleasure of handling such an attractive tool offsets any inconvenience in using it.

The butt-and-mortise gauge mentioned earlier is a do-it-all tool once sold by Stanley™, designed to allow the user to set three different depths at once in order to speed up the layout of mortises for butt hinges (see FIG. 89). The modern three-edged butt template that is simply banged onto the door jamb, leaving an inscribed outline, is an eminently simpler tool, but it lacks the undeniable charm and mystery of the wood and brass masterpiece that preceded it.

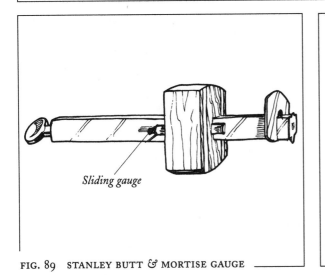

Sliding gauge

FIG. 89   STANLEY BUTT & MORTISE GAUGE

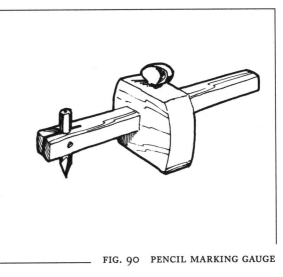

FIG. 90   PENCIL MARKING GAUGE

THE PENCIL MARKING GAUGE

YOU DO NOT ALWAYS WANT TO LEAVE A line after having marked something. Contemporary woodworking sometimes suffers from the reverse snobbism of pointing out scribe lines left on work as evidence of the work having been hand-made. Dovetailed pieces are the most common examples of this. But to leave a scribe line that was made to guide the work and not to form part of the design is simply sloppy workmanship. I am not advocating a return to the 19th century ideal of constructing pieces so that no joinery per se is in evidence; I believe joints themselves can be used decoratively to good effect and should not necessarily be consigned to the position of invisible servants in the service of the overall form. But scribe lines and other scratches are hard to justify

esthetically. Consequently, it is sometimes very useful to mark with a pencil rather than a pin. To make or adapt a regular marking gauge to hold a pencil as shown in FIG. 90 is a worthwhile and fairly simple project. Whether you are lucky enough to buy one or whether you make one for yourself, keep the point sharp, for a line thicker than a saw kerf is too thick for accuracy.

CUTTING GAUGES

BY REPLACING THE PIN OR PENCIL WITH A knife a whole new class of gauge is created, one that is capable not only of marking and layout but also of scoring or cutting the work. A cutting gauge (FIG. 91) is typically somewhat larger than a marking gauge. It is used where the marks

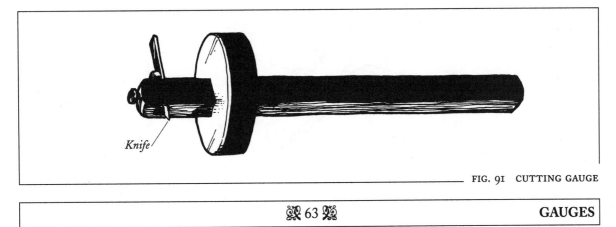

Knife

FIG. 91   CUTTING GAUGE

GAUGES

required for layout coincide with future cuts to be made by chisel or saw. It can therefore be an ideal marking tool. When laying out dovetails, for example, the groove left by the knife edge forms a fail-safe starting location for the chisel that will clean out the final joint. When marking rabbets, grooves, or dados to be planed, the cutting gauge will sever the fibers cleanly, especially across the grain, allowing a clean edge to be worked. Like the pin on a marking gauge, however, it is important that the knife edge be properly sharpened. It should have a single bevel, the inside of the knife being perfectly flat. This makes possible accurate gauging as measured from the inside of the stock, and takes advantage of the bevel to keep the stock close to the edge of the workpiece, since when the bevel is on the inside there is a tendency for the cutting edge, especially when it encounters pronounced grain, to be forced closer to the edge, in turn forcing the stock away from the edge of the workpiece and so producing an inaccurate line. But note that when using the cutting gauge for laying out dovetails, as mentioned above, the knife should be reversed so that the beveled side enters the work on the waste side of the line.

In addition to reversing the knife the shape of the actual cutting edge may be formed so that the gauge may be pushed or pulled (and worked in either direction when the blade is reversed). As with the pin on a marking gauge, set the knife so that the smallest amount of blade that is practical

protrudes through the stem; this will increase accuracy and give you greater control.

Just as with other classes of gauges, cutting gauges exist in a wide variety of qualities. Look for those whose blades are easily adjusted and removable for sharpening.

PANEL & SLITTING GAUGES

THE LAST GROUP UNDER DISCUSSION IS defined mainly by the larger size of its members. These tools tend to be around 18 in. in length, although longer examples are not rare. Panel gauges (FIG. 92) typically have flattened and lengthened stocks, usually with a small rabbet formed in the bottom inside edge so that the stock may ride more securely against the work. This is useful and, indeed, even necessary since the work is commonly a thin panel which may well be rather wavy and present an edge against which the holding of a regularly shaped stock would be a difficult accomplishment.

In the contemporary workshop the panel gauge can function usefully as an extra-large marking gauge, for there are frequently occasions when you need to mark a line farther from the edge than the common marking gauge can accommodate. Panel gauges are especially useful when working with sheet material such as plywood and composition board.

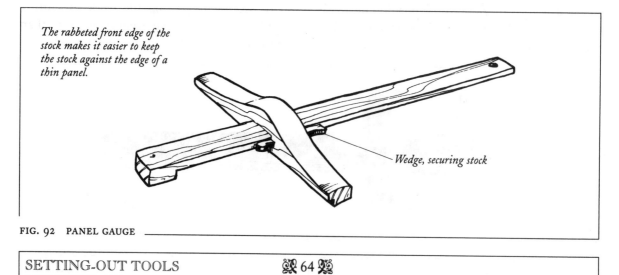

The rabbeted front edge of the stock makes it easier to keep the stock against the edge of a thin panel.

Wedge, securing stock

FIG. 92 PANEL GAUGE

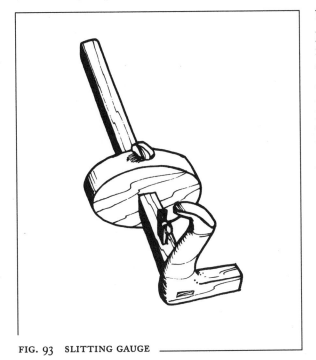

FIG. 93   SLITTING GAUGE

blade. To facilitate forward movement while pressure is being applied, better models are often fitted with a small wheel or roller directly under the handle. Whether the roller bears on the work or the bench will depend on how wide the work-piece is, but if the waste is to be reused it is good practice to place a thin piece of scrap under the roller. The amount of pressure is critical: too much and the cut will be too deep and the tool will bog down, all progress being halted or rendered totally inaccurate; too little and the cut will be too shallow.

Slitting gauges are useful for cutting out thin boards such as drawer bottoms and veneer, and may also be used to cut thin strips such as the stringing used in inlay and banding work. If the stock is first reduced to the proper thickness, and the stock or head of the slitting gauge adjusted to the width of one piece of stringing, repeated cuts can be made working from the same edge of the stock to produce as much length as is needed. They may also be used for slicing off battens or lathing strips, as well as to separate beading when it is being made into doweling.

As with many other classes of tools, it is not until you incorporate many of these gauges into your arsenal that you begin realize quite how indispensable they are. Keep a sharp eye out for unusual models; they are not always what they might appear at first glance.

Slitting gauges (FIG. 93), the big cousins of the cutting gauge, have stems as long as panel gauges but smaller, beefier stocks. The end of the stem housing the blade is usually fitted with a handle similar to the tote (handle) of a jack plane. This is not merely a convenience for a large and otherwise unwieldy gauge-type tool, but an important design feature for a cutting edge that requires a substantial amount of pressure applied over the

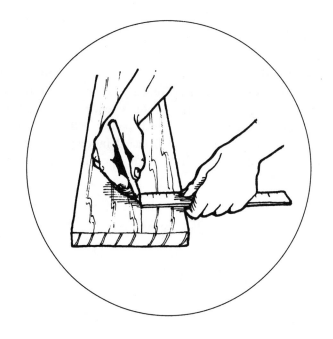

III
SAWING TOOLS

8

HANDSAWS

A QUIETER APPROACH TO LUMBER CONVERSION

MY CIRCULAR SAW HAS SEEN MANY HOURS OF USE. APART FROM BEING DEAFENED BY ITS WHINE AND SHOWERED BY THE SAWDUST IT THROWS UP, I HAVE TO ADMIT THAT I HAVE DEPENDED ON IT GREATLY AND AM GRATEFUL FOR ITS EXISTENCE. But several times it has come very close to inflicting serious injury, admittedly through my own fault. Most especially I shall never forget the time when I had been sawing a lot of particularly resinous pine and had failed to notice that the blade guard had become jammed by an accumulation of sawdust. I put the saw down at the end of a cut only to watch it race across the floor before the blade finished spinning. I was devastated by what it did to the new floorboards I was installing, but horrified at the thought of what it might have done to my feet if it had run the other way.

Over the years I have become more cautious, and I now don goggles, mask, and sometimes earplugs before pulling the trigger. I also try to restrict its use to times when friends and neighbors are least likely to be driven crazy by its noise, although I do not like to use it when I am completely alone just in case I need someone to drive me to the hospital. I have similar concerns when using the tablesaw. This is not to denigrate this extremely useful invention — tablesaws can be capable of great accuracy and can do a great deal of work with minimum effort — but I do not have any of these problems when I use my handsaws.

Handsaws are also capable of great accuracy, and can do a lot of work with far less effort than might be thought possible, but you have to know how. This should not be seen as an obstacle, since it is equally inadvisable to switch on a tablesaw or pull the trigger of a circular saw without some instruction. The argument that the use of handsaws requires a special skill should not preclude their use any more than does the need to recognize certain precautions and to learn certain techniques when using their powered cousins. While it may be unreasonable to expect handsaws to replace powered saws at this stage of the game, there are still many occasions, quite apart from a power outage or a machine breakdown, when you might be glad of an alternative. For example, crosscutting long, heavy boards is much more easily done with a crosscut handsaw and a couple of sawhorses than by trying to manipulate them across the top of a narrow tablesaw. Avoiding kickback and binding while ripping warped or twisted boards on a tablesaw can also be a dangerous operation, but there is no such danger when using ripsaws. At the other extreme, very small pieces are more safely and easily cut on a bench with a handsaw than by trying to feed them through the tablesaw with fingers only a slip away from the blade. Yes, it is true that by taking advantage of the vast array of support systems developed for the tablesaw, such as additional tables, jigs, featherboards, holding devices, and even power-assisted feeders, the tablesaw can be used safely, but this seems like an awful lot of extra work to get back to the simplicity already available with a handsaw. Moreover, apart from being quieter, making less mess, and posing fewer threats to life and limb, handsaws consume no electricity; they offer instead a modicum of exercise and the opportunity to proceed with your work on a more thoughtful level.

One of the more surprising aspects of handsaw use is the cheapness with which a quality saw can be found. I am not talking about new saws, the vast majority of which are worse than useless, although the better mailorder companies do offer decent saws for upwards of fifty dollars, but about the many second-hand saws that can be found at fleamarkets and in junk stores for anything between three and fifteen dollars. Many of these are inferior and damaged beyond repair, but under the rust and paint spatters there are aristocrats to be found that with a little refitting will reward you with a lifetime of use.

THE HANDSAW FAMILY

STRICTLY SPEAKING, ANY SAW OPERATED BY the power of the hand (and arm) alone may be called a handsaw. This definition includes an astonishing range of tools, from tiny gent's dovetail saws and jeweler's saws to giant, two-man felling saws of the type used in the American Northwest a century ago to cut down trees as tall as 200 ft. In this and the following chapters the term is restricted to the narrower but more usual sense used in woodworking: those wide-bladed, single-handled saws used to convert boards and lumber into workable sections for the job in hand. These are: the crosscut saw, the ripsaw, and their smaller relative, the panel saw, all shown in FIG. 94. Nowadays it is hard to buy a new handsaw that is anything else, but still turning up in second-hand shops, in fleamarkets, and at auction are many other types of wide-bladed handsaws,

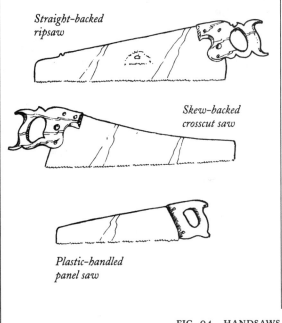

Straight-backed ripsaw

Skew-backed crosscut saw

Plastic-handled panel saw

FIG. 94 HANDSAWS

such as ship saws, gauge saws, pruning saws, joiner's saws, and plumber's saws. All these are true handsaws by virtue of the fact that they average 2 ft. in length and have a wide blade with a single handle. It is also important to realize that the term 'handsaw' does not mean simply any saw used by hand rather than by power; there are many other types of saw used by hand that are not referred to as handsaws, of which coping saws, fretsaws, keyhole saws, and compass saws are just four examples.

It is possible to cut a board in any direction relative to the grain, but if the direction of the cut is more *with* the grain than across it this is called 'ripping', and if the direction of the cut is more *across* the grain than along it this is called 'crosscutting' (see FIG. 95). Where you draw the line may be open to discussion, but more often than not, when converting boards into sections for any given project, you will discover that in fact most cuts are distinctly either rip cuts or cross cuts. Because of this, handsaws are made with two forms of teeth: those designed for ripping and those designed for crosscutting. This is the origin of and reason for crosscut handsaws and ripsaw handsaws.

While it is possible to cut teeth of either design into any handsaw blade, there are other differences between crosscut saws and ripsaws. These differences have to do with blade width, weight, the way the blade is ground, the shape of the handle, and overall length. All these factors make the saw in question particularly well suited for either ripping or crosscutting, and it is literally 'going against the grain' to try to rip with a crosscut saw or crosscut with a ripsaw. It can be done, but it will be unnecessarily laborious, and is often the reason why the uninitiated thinks handsawing is such hard work: the wrong tool is being used for the job.

THE PANEL SAW: A COMPROMISE

AS EARLY AS THE EIGHTEENTH CENTURY smaller saws called panel saws were being made. Shorter than regular crosscut saws and with finer teeth, they were designed for use where a smoother cut was required and where the piece being sawed was of relatively small dimension. Panel saws occupied a place between full-sized crosscut saws and the smaller tenon saws, or backsaws (as they became known in America) used more for cutting joints than for converting lumber to size. By the end of the 19th century, machinery had taken over much of the conversion process and the panel saw had become more popular as a general-purpose handsaw, useful for crosscutting and ripping small pieces. The woodworker was often advised that if only a single handsaw could

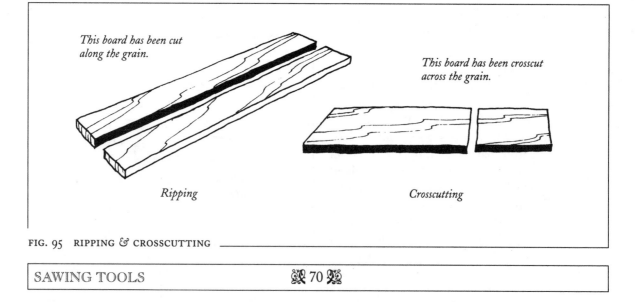

This board has been cut along the grain.

This board has been crosscut across the grain.

Ripping

Crosscutting

FIG. 95 RIPPING & CROSSCUTTING

be afforded, the panel saw was the most useful. It would not rip as quickly as a ripsaw nor crosscut as well as a crosscut saw nor yet be as handy as a tenon saw for small work, but would, in a pinch, do the work of all three.

The panel saw, usually provided with teeth cut like those of a crosscut saw, remains useful for small work and especially for sawing large tenons, since the strengthening strip fixed along the back of the saws usually employed in cutting tenons limits the depth of cut to however deep the blade may be, usually little more than 4 in. or 5 in. The panel saw is an especially useful saw to have handy for the odd cut, and can often accomplish its job before a tablesaw can be properly set up. Even though some shops keep panel saws cut with both rip teeth and crosscut teeth, for serious ripping or crosscutting it is still best to use the saw designed for the purpose.

THE CROSSCUT SAW

CROSSCUT SAWS VARY FROM TWENTY-TWO inches to 26 in. in length. The number of teeth per inch may also vary, six being the most common. More teeth produce a finer and smoother kerf but take longer to cut down the line. Saws with fewer teeth cut more rapidly but leave more rag. The shape of the blade may also vary. Most saws were originally made with straight backs, but a concave profile, known as a skew-back, became popular since, in conjunction with a taper-ground blade (a blade made thickest at the teeth and becoming thinner towards the toe and the back), this design produces less drag and enables the saw to move more easily through the wood.

Of great importance is the quality of the steel used for the blade. It should be light for ease of use but at the same time strong enough to resist buckling. A good-quality blade may be bent so that the toe of the blade will almost touch the handle and still spring back perfectly straight. Performing this test, however, on a saw is a little like shaking a lightbulb to see if it rattles in order

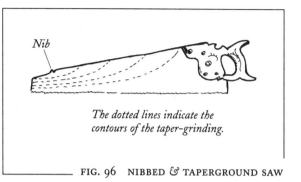

Nib

The dotted lines indicate the contours of the taper-grinding.

FIG. 96   NIBBED & TAPERGROUND SAW

to determine whether it is broken. If the blade is inferior, the test will seal the matter, whereas a more cautious approach might have made a little more use possible.

Old saws frequently have a small nib on their back at the toe end (see FIG. 96). Thought to be a vestige of the original curved shape of the first wide-blade handsaws made by the Dutch towards the end of the 17th century (when the new process of rolling steel strip in water-driven mills made saws with wide blades possible for the first time), this nib is useful for sighting along the blade when sawing — not for cutting nails, as many old-timers maintain. Do not worry if it has broken off.

Although, when the new wide blades were first introduced, Dutch and other European saws continued to be made with the older-style pistol-grip, English saws were treated differently. In Sheffield, sawmakers developed a completely new method, essentially the same as we use today, whereby the handle, instead of being bored to receive a tang formed in the blade, is slotted and fitted over the end of the blade, handle and blade then being riveted or screwed together (see FIG. 97).

Present-day handsaw handles, especially the cheaper models made of plastic, often bear only a vague resemblance to the beautiful and extremely comfortable shapes first designed this way. Even if, in the name of economy or contemporary design sensibility, you disregard the elegant curves and cutouts intended to lighten the handle, the intricate carving designed to provide a more secure grip, and the way in which the bottom part

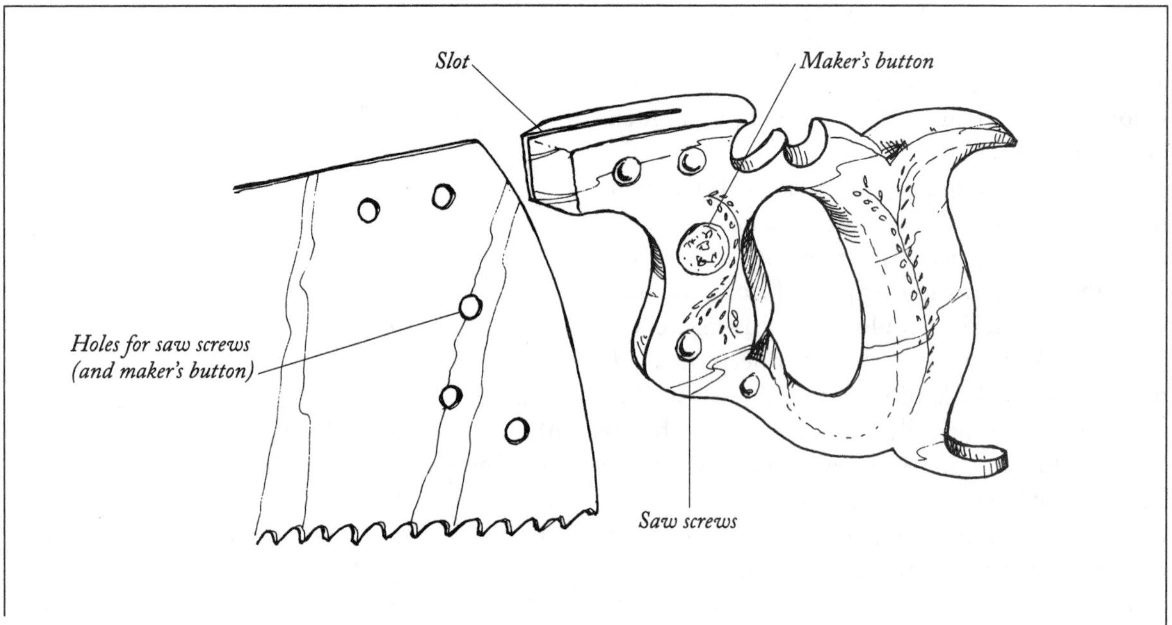

Slot

Maker's button

Holes for saw screws (and maker's button)

Saw screws

FIG. 97   SAW-HANDLE ATTACHMENT

of the grip was frequently carved to give the appearance of the handle having been folded into place while in an almost fluid state, it is hard to deny the superior comfort afforded by an old handle. These handles were designed for hours of blister-free use. But when considering a second-hand saw, do not reject it simply because a handsomely shaped handle is damaged. Missing tips and ears can be easily repaired. And as a last resort, the entire handle can be replaced, using the original as a pattern. Remember, better saws were usually provided with better handles made of choice applewood or mahogany and fitted with extra screws to hold the blade. A handle with five screws, including the inscribed maker's-button screw, indicates the top of the line.

Keep an eye out for ripsaws fitted with handles designed for overhand ripping (see FIG. 98). It used to be common practice to rip boards not on the sawhorse, but secured to the bench. This has the advantage of eliminating the bent-back posture now commonly associated with hand ripping. Overhand ripping is less tiring, since the back is straight and both hands are used (see FIG. 99). Many handles were factory-made to

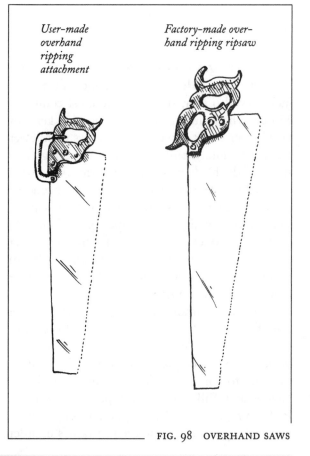

User-made overhand ripping attachment

Factory-made overhand ripping ripsaw

FIG. 98   OVERHAND SAWS

Since the board is clamped to the bench, the operator remains upright.

FIG. 99   OVERHAND RIPPING

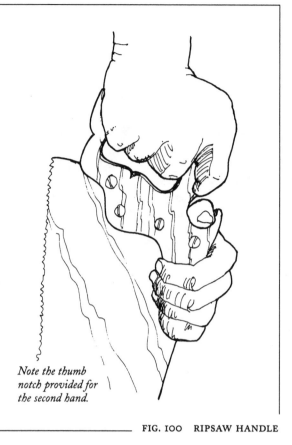

Note the thumb notch provided for the second hand.

FIG. 100   RIPSAW HANDLE

accommodate the second hand or adapted by the user for this purpose.

Lastly, and most importantly, is the condition of the teeth. For the saw to work at its best — that is, to cut straight without having to be forcibly held to the line, and to cut easily without undue effort (if the saw is held in the kerf and allowed to drop of its own weight it should continue to cut) — the teeth must be not only keen, but also sharpened to the correct angle, cut at the right rake, jointed and crowned evenly, and set according to the material being sawed. If all this sounds too specialized and complicated, take heart: a competent saw-sharpening service should be able to do all this for you very reasonably, certainly more cheaply than the price of a new circular-saw blade. At the same time, no self-respecting hand-saw user should ever be content to let someone else sharpen his or her saws. The various procedures are described in detail in chapter 9. Once you know how, and have readjusted your saws, maintenance is very easy and takes no longer than sharpening a plane iron or a carving chisel.

THE RIPSAW

APART FROM A RADICALLY DIFFERENT FORM of tooth and a tendency to be larger and heavier, much of what has just been said about the cross-cut saw holds true for the ripsaw. Most ripsaw blades, at least when new and before numerous sharpenings have worn them down, are typically wider from tooth to back. Furthermore, since ripsaws are often used overhand, the handles are sometimes differently formed, as in FIG. 98. Other models may have provision for a two-handed grip, or a special notch for one's thumb as shown in FIG. 100. Overall lengths from 28 in. to 30 in. are common, and the number of teeth per inch is around four.

9

SAWFITTING & SAWING

SHARP TEETH BITE BEST

A T FIRST GLANCE ONE HANDSAW MAY LOOK VERY MUCH LIKE ANOTHER, BUT TRYING TO RIP WITH A CROSSCUT HANDSAW OR VICE-VERSA CAN BE A FRUSTRATING EXPERIENCE. EQUALLY AS IMPORTANT AS USING THE RIGHT HANDSAW FOR THE JOB in hand is using one that is in good condition. This is not necessarily something that can be taken for granted simply by buying a new saw. There are many things affecting a saw's fitness for work, including the shape, set, number, and size of its teeth, as well as the quality of the actual materials from which the sawblade and the saw handle are made. Few of these factors are readily apparent to the inexperienced. But knowing what a saw is designed to do is halfway to being able to use it well.

In addition, there is the skill necessary to use the tool properly and effectively. A beginner can have as much trouble with a well-conditioned saw as with one in poor shape and blame it all on the tool, not realizing that the right tool can make all the difference in the world.

THE DIFFERENCE BETWEEN SAWS

THE PREVIOUS ABUNDANCE OF HANDSAW types was such that merely classifying them as crosscut or rip is not very helpful. Nevertheless, knowing whether a saw is designed to crosscut or rip is a good place to start, since in practice almost every time you put saw to wood you are inevitably doing one thing or the other. FIG. 101 illustrates the difference between saw teeth designed to crosscut and saw teeth designed to rip. Notice not

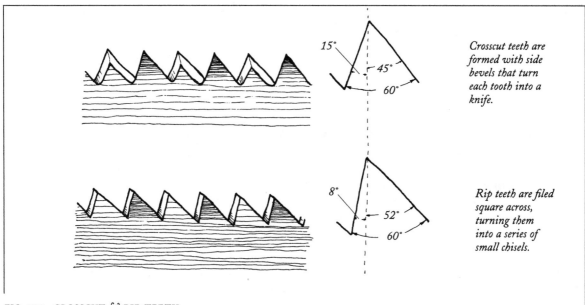

Crosscut teeth are formed with side bevels that turn each tooth into a knife.

Rip teeth are filed square across, turning them into a series of small chisels.

FIG. 101   CROSSCUT & RIP TEETH

only the different angles of the teeth's profiles but also the fact that crosscut teeth are beveled to cut like a series of knives, while rip teeth cut only at their tips, like a series of tiny chisels. Guessing at a glance whether a saw is designed to crosscut or rip by looking at the size of the teeth alone can be deceptive; both sorts are made with different numbers of teeth to the inch — a feature usually described as the point size. Calculating the point size is done by counting the number of teeth in a lineal inch, as shown in FIG. 102. Ripsaws in general have fewer points than crosscut saws (the reason for different point sizes is discussed later), but a 7 pt. ripsaw can have teeth the same size as a 7 pt. crosscut saw, so judging the type by the teeth size alone is not reliable (see FIG. 103).

ONE INCH

├─── 8 ───┤

To determine the point size of a saw, count the number of tooth tips contained in a lineal inch, starting from the tip of any given tooth. When determining the point size of an older ripsaw, count teeth in the middle of the blade, since end teeth were sometimes cut smaller in order to make it easier to start the cut.

FIG. 102   DETERMINING POINT SIZE

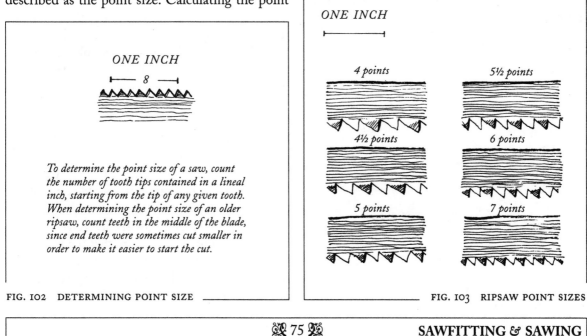

ONE INCH

4 points   5½ points

4½ points   6 points

5 points   7 points

FIG. 103   RIPSAW POINT SIZES

Although the cut of the teeth is the most important distinction between saws, the rest of a saw's design can also vary, not only from cross-cut to rip but also within each type. Overall length is the most obvious difference. Examples may range from as short as 10 in. to as long as 3 ft. The width of the blade at the heel (the handle end) and the toe (the small end) may also vary considerably, both separately and in various combinations.

The shape of the blade is another important distinction, and is governed by the intended use and the way in which the blade is made, as well as by a variety of novelty 'improvements', such as those designed to render the saw additionally useful as a measuring device or by making its depth of cut self-regulating.

A final distinction concerns the handle: its shape, position, and manner of fixing all affect the way the saw can and should be used.

TEETH

A NEWLY BOUGHT SAW SHOULD AT THE VERY least have evenly formed teeth. With use (or abuse) and frequent sharpenings the regularity of the teeth may be lost, possibly ending up as bad as those illustrated in FIG. 104. A saw with teeth like this should be recut by a professional, but

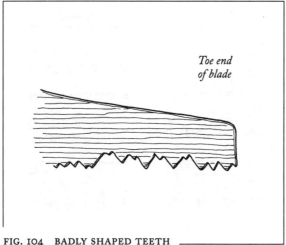

*Toe end
of blade*

FIG. 104   BADLY SHAPED TEETH

moderate unevenness can be corrected by the user in the course of regular sharpening.

Evenly formed teeth are, however, no guarantee of correct shape or adequate sharpness. Knowing what to do requires a little study, but the actual sharpening is easier than sawing itself, and there is generally no excuse for not sharpening your own saws. It is certainly cheaper than sending them out, and you are guaranteed a quicker and, with a little practice, equally good job.

JOINTING

ASSUMING A SAW'S TEETH ARE ALL FAIRLY uniform in size and shape, the first step in any sharpening is to joint the saw. Using a factory-made handsaw jointer (FIG. 105) or a simple user-made device (FIG. 106), run a mill file lightly along the top of the teeth until a small land is formed on the top of every tooth. You may have to squint to see the light reflected from the flat part you have filed, but it is important to produce such a land on all the teeth. Of course, the more uneven the teeth are, the greater will be the disparity between the sizes of lands on individual teeth. If it is too great it will be better not to make all the teeth the same height the first time, but joint only the highest, then shape and sharpen them, and then joint the teeth a second time. Be careful when jointing to keep the file perpendicular to the blade. Not letting it tip from side to side is the advantage of using a handsaw jointer.

SHAPING

THE NEXT STEP SHOULD NOT BE NECESSARY with a new saw or even with an old saw that has been properly sharpened, but only if the profile of the teeth has become grossly irregular. Shaping the teeth is done to make sure that the fronts and backs of the teeth are at the correct angles, and that the gullets are all of equal depth. The process is simple and requires no more than filing at right

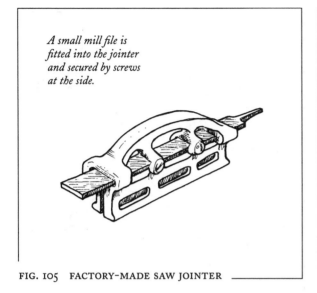

A small mill file is fitted into the jointer and secured by screws at the side.

FIG. 105   FACTORY-MADE SAW JOINTER

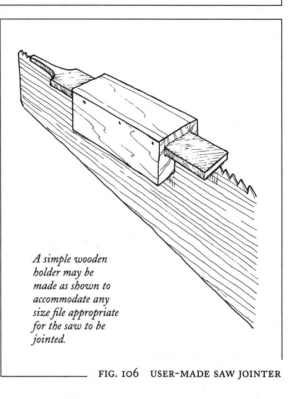

A simple wooden holder may be made as shown to accommodate any size file appropriate for the saw to be jointed.

FIG. 106   USER-MADE SAW JOINTER

angles to the blade. Start work by holding a small triangular file well down in the first gullet so that the requisite angles of the fronts and backs of the teeth are formed properly. If the teeth are of unequal size, press more against the largest, filing until you reach the center of the land created by jointing. Continue along until all teeth are of equal size and all finish in a point.

Note that it is not necessary at this stage to worry about any bevel that crosscut teeth may require; be sure only to file at right angles. The triangular file most useful for this operation is one sometimes known as a 'slim taper' and which has the cross-section of an equilateral triangle whose sides form angles of 60°. Since the angle formed by the front and back of the saw's teeth is also 60°, whether measured at the tip or in the gullet, using a 60° file will guarantee this angle. But it is up to you to control the angle that the front (and the back) of the tooth makes with the perpendicular. This angle is known as the angle of rake. The angles indicated in FIG. 101 are all-purpose angles for ripsaws and crosscut saws, but experienced sawyers will prefer slightly different angles according to the kind of wood being sawed and the angle at which they work. The effect of changing the rake is similar to the effect that different rakes, often known as positive and negative,

have on bandsaw teeth. Many woodworkers are familiar with specifying rake when ordering bandsaw blades; you can achieve the same thing when shaping handsaw teeth.

SETTING

SETTING IS THE PROCESS OF BENDING NO more than half the height of a tooth to one side and then bending the next tooth similarly to the opposite side. When all teeth are set the kerf made by the saw will be wider than the thickness of the sawblade by as much as they have been bent. This provides positive clearance for the blade and prevents binding. If the set is too little or the wood too wet the friction caused by sawing can cause the wood to swell and bind the saw. Consequently, how much set is appropriate is a function of the wood being sawed. Crosscutting dry hardwood requires less set than ripping unseasoned softwood. The well-equipped shop will contain several crosscut saws and several ripsaws

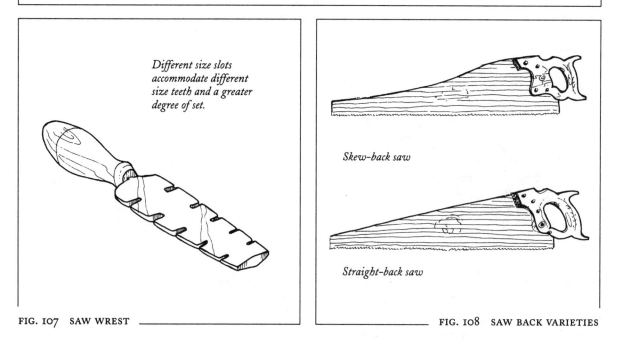

Different size slots accommodate different size teeth and a greater degree of set.

FIG. 107   SAW WREST

Skew–back saw

Straight-back saw

FIG. 108   SAW BACK VARIETIES

with different sets for this reason. Although the process of setting used to be accomplished with a simple tool called a saw wrest (FIG. 107), patented saw sets are now more common and somewhat easier to use since many contain anvils that may be adjusted according to the point size of the saw being set, thereby providing a preset — albeit only average — amount of set. The perfectionist will prefer the saw wrest, since any amount and degree of set can be achieved at will.

As with shaping, setting should not be necessary every time the saw is sharpened. Experience will be your best guide as you become more sensitive to small changes in set and how they affect the sawing of different kinds of wood. You should be aware that a taper-ground saw, by virtue of the fact that its blade becomes progressively thinner from teeth to back, requires very little set.

How do you tell a taper-ground saw from one that is not? If it is a new saw it will undoubtedly have been advertised as such. Many older, better-quality saws — made when pride of manufacture resulted in ornate inscriptions, often still discernible if you clean the blade well enough — will bear a message to the effect. Among really old saws, those with skew backs are the more likely to be taper-ground than are straight-backs (see FIG. 108), but simply measuring the thickness of the blade at the gullet and at its back is the easiest way to tell taper-ground from flat-ground.

4½ pt., 5½ pt., 6 pt.	7 in. slim taper
7 pt., 8 pt.	6 in. slim taper
9 pt., 10 pt.	5 in. or 6 in. slim taper
11 pt., 12 pt., 13 pt., 14 pt., 15 pt.	4½ in. slim taper
16 pt. and over	5 in. superfine metal saw
for jointing:	8 in. or 10 in. mill bastard
	(or smaller to fit factory-made jointer)

TABLE I   FILE SIZES FOR SHARPENING & JOINTING

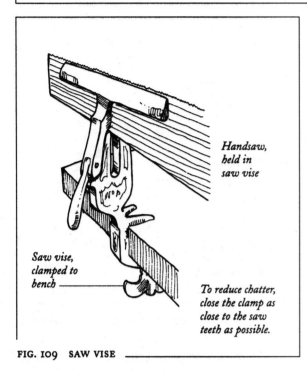

Handsaw, held in saw vise

Saw vise, clamped to bench

To reduce chatter, close the clamp as close to the saw teeth as possible.

FIG. 109 SAW VISE

SHARPENING

WHETHER SHARPENING RIPSAW TEETH OR crosscut teeth you will need some form of saw vise or saw clamp (FIG. 109) to hold the saw firmly just below the level of the gullets, otherwise the saw will chatter and scream when you try to file it, and the file will quickly become dulled. The only other requirement is the correct size file, as indicated in TABLE I.

Both kinds of saw should be given a light pass with a file, as when jointing, sufficient to produce the tiniest land. Make sure that you are working in a good light so that you can see this tiny shiny area, then proceed as follows.

CROSSCUT FILING

FIX THE SAW IN THE VISE AND STAND AT position one, as shown in FIG. 110. Starting at the toe of the blade, pick out the first tooth that is set towards you. Place the file in the gullet to the *left* of this tooth, holding the file level with the floor

and angled to the saw as indicated. Make sure that the file sets down well into the gullet. Check constantly that the file remains horizontal, and notice that the angle at which the file should be held to the saw corresponds to the angle of the bevels cut on the edges of the teeth. If this is not easy to see, try looking at the teeth nearest the handle. These teeth are generally used less and retain their factory grind longer. Try letting the file find its own bearing against these bevels to get the feel of where the correct angle should be. File gently until you have worn away half the land formed on the tips of the teeth. This should not take more than a stroke or two.

Now lift the file out of the first gullet, skip the next gullet (to the left of the next tooth, set to the right), and place it in the third gullet (to the left of the next tooth set towards you). File as before, and then repeat the process all the way down the blade.

On reaching the heel of the blade, reposition the saw in the vise, and yourself and the file, as shown in FIG. 111. Now place the file in the gullet to the *right* of the first tooth set towards you. This should be the first gullet you skipped when filing from position one. This will be obvious if the saw has been previously used or is somewhat old, since the filed gullets will now all be shiny and this gullet will be noticeably darker. When you have filed away the remaining half of the land on the top of every tooth the saw will be sharp.

RIPSAW FILING

THE METHOD OF FILING RIPSAWS IS exactly the same as that for crosscut saws, with the single difference that the file must be worked straight across the saw, at right angles to the blade. Look in FIG. 101 again to see why ripsaw teeth must have no side bevel. However, do not be tempted into thinking that simply because there are no alternating side bevels to be filed it will be quicker to start at one end and file every tooth until you reach the other end. While it is true that

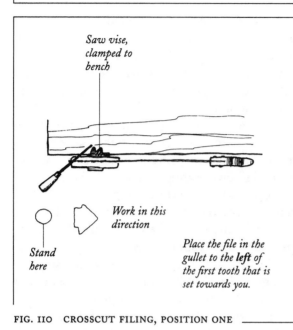

FIG. 110   CROSSCUT FILING, POSITION ONE

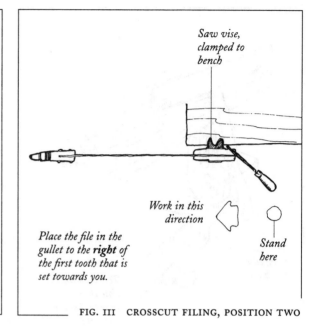

FIG. 111   CROSSCUT FILING, POSITION TWO

there are no alternating bevels and you should file straight across, in practice this is hard to do perfectly, and a ripsaw that has been filed this way is likely to lead (favor one side over the other, making sawing to a straight line difficult). By working in the same way as when filing crosscut saws, and filing first all those teeth that lean towards you, then reversing the saw and your position and filing the remaining teeth, any slight inaccuracy in filing is equalized and the saw will run straight with little guidance.

BLADE & HANDLE

PROVIDING ALL TEETH ARE AT THE SAME height (check this by sighting along the tips — a slight crown along this line is preferred by some woodworkers), the angle of rake is consistent and appropriate to the work in hand, the bevels exact, and the set sufficient, the saw is now ready to be used. But before starting to saw, check the condition of the blade and the handle. The blade should be securely fastened to its handle, since any effort transferred through a wobbly handle is wasted. It is a simple matter to retighten the saw

screws with a screwdriver from which a small section of the middle of the blade has been filed away (see FIG. 112). Equally importantly, the blade should be straight and free of rust, kinks, bends, and any warping. These last defects can be cured by judicious hammering of the blade. The blade must be placed perfectly flat on a firm surface — an anvil is ideal — and the hammer struck on those areas that are concavely distorted. The effect of the hammering, which should be done with a slightly round-faced hammer, is to stretch the metal, thus making concavities convex. This only happens if the blade is held on a perfectly flat surface, otherwise the effect is merely to dent the

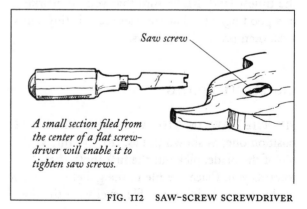

FIG. 112   SAW-SCREW SCREWDRIVER

blade further. A little experimenting on an old blade will soon show you how to remove all manner of dents, kinks, and warping. Scratches can be filed or steel-wooled away.

THE WAY TO SAW

APART FROM USING A CROSSCUT SAW FOR crosscutting and a ripsaw for ripsawing there are various other choices that can influence the efficiency of your handsawing. Although it used to be common practice to recut and use broken saws, the attribute of good balance is vital to a saw's ease of use. Balance is affected by a saw's overall length, the shape and weight of its blade, and the design and positioning of its handle. Naturally, a larger saw will make heavy work easier, and there is little point in wielding a 26 in. heavyweight where an 18 in. panel saw would suffice, but you should try to use a saw that feels most comfortable for you.

Some people prefer the lighter weight of streamlined skew-backs; some prefer the greater rigidity of straight-backs (also made in lighter versions). But probably most critical is choosing a saw with the appropriate number of points for the job. The choice is simple: fewer points result in faster cutting, more points produce finer work and a smoother cut. To rip eight-quarter hardwood, a 5 pt., straight-back ripsaw is very efficient; using such a saw to crosscut six inches of ½ in.-thick pine would be like using a pickaxe to remove a tiny splinter from your thumb.

Once you have chosen the right saw, select the appropriate mode of operation. For ripping heavy timber the kneeling position is best: one knee on the work, and the blade held at 60° to the surface of the wood (see FIG. 113). For lighter ripping it is often more comfortable to stand upright, secure the work higher than when supported on saw-horses, and use the overhand method. Some saws may be found that have handles designed to be held this way (see FIG. 98, chapter 8), but even those that do not can still be used like this.

Whether crosscutting or ripping do not force or press the saw; properly sharpened it will cut very well on its own. All you have to do is guide it. If it seems difficult to keep to a straight line, you may be pushing too hard and forcing the teeth to follow the path of least resistance up soft grain before they have a chance to cut their way along the line. If the set of the teeth is biased towards one side or the other, the saw will lead — the cut will tend to curve towards the side with the greater set. Either reset the teeth or try running a file lightly down the side of the teeth whose set is greatest.

Avoid all kinds of jigs and tips purporting to help you hold the saw exactly perpendicular, since you will never develop a reliable eye if you become addicted to such crutches. Position yourself directly over the line to be cut, and try to keep sight of both sides of the blade.

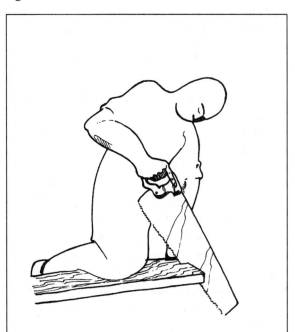

After the kerf is begun, this should be your position at the end of the upstroke, with your eye positioned directly over the back of the blade.

FIG. 113 RIPSAWING POSITION

Some wood is cantankerous. No matter how carefully you saw, it will twist and flex, and the kerf cut by the saw will close up behind the saw, binding the blade tighter than a vise. Use softwood wedges — better than screwdrivers, which can bruise the wood — to keep the kerf open. Saw slowly and gently. It should be an easy process if you are doing it correctly.

Next to planing, sawing should be one of the great pleasures of woodworking, allowing you to discover the true nature of your material, safely and with an abundance of tactile and aromatic delights totally impossible with a 5 HP motor screaming and showering dust everywhere.

STARTING THE KERF

AFTER MEASURING AND LAYING OUT THE workpiece you will be faced with the most difficult part of the operation: starting the cut. The beginner often makes several stabs at the cutline, and in so doing erases it as the teeth bounce up and down on the edge of the wood, often cutting stray fingers instead of the wood. The trick is to position your thumb close to the cut with the thumbnail pointing at the line, rest the edge of the sawblade against your thumbnail somewhere in the middle of the blade's length, and pull the saw gently towards you (see FIG. 114). Some people prefer to rest the side of the sawblade against the back of the thumb's knuckle when making these first strokes. If you do nothing but pull the blade towards you there is no danger of any injury in either case. Now lift the teeth away from the wood, reposition the blade, and repeat the pulling action. Although the teeth are designed to cut on the push-stroke, when pulled they will nevertheless score the wood sufficiently to start a kerf. After two or three pulling strokes, the kerf thus formed will usually be deep enough — ⅛ in. is all that is needed — to keep the blade on course when it is pushed. Your thumb will no longer be needed as a guide and you should move it out of harm's way.

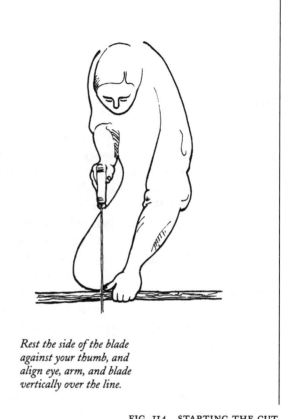

Rest the side of the blade against your thumb, and align eye, arm, and blade vertically over the line.

FIG. 114 STARTING THE CUT

A properly sharpened saw does not need to be pressed into the work. All you have to do now is exert just enough force to move the blade forwards; the teeth will do the cutting. The first few strokes should be especially light, and it will help to make them short until you become more practised. If you sense any danger of the teeth leaving the kerf, stop, and then take a few more pull-strokes to deepen the kerf before proceeding.

DEEPENING THE CUT

ONCE THE KERF IS FAIRLY BEGUN THERE ARE two points to remember throughout the rest of the cut: do not press on the blade, and use the entire length of the saw. Long strokes are more efficient and require less energy than many short strokes. This is the reason the saw is provided with a long blade in the first place. If you attempt to force the blade, the teeth will simply dig in more deeply than necessary, and the work will be that much harder. You will not saw through the wood any faster, and the saw will be more difficult to guide. You may increase your speed as your stroke becomes surer, but in the beginning it is usually a case of 'more haste, less speed'. What you are trying to do is not difficult but there are several things to bear in mind, apart from guiding the saw, which is explained below. It is like playing the piano: practise slowly at first until you can perform every aspect of the operation correctly, and then gradually increase your speed. Soon you will be able to saw quickly and faultlessly.

ANGLE OF SAWING

THE TEETH ON A PROPERLY CUT HANDSAW will have been carefully designed to work most efficiently on a particular material and for a particular cut when used at a specific angle to the wood, but all you need to concentrate on now is the angle at which to hold the blade to the wood. At the start of the cut, keep the angle low, around 20°. After a good start has been made, raise the angle closer to 45° (see FIG. 115). In practice it will

be found that varying the 45° angle, sometimes higher and sometimes lower, will help things along, and in certain circumstances it will also be found possible — perhaps even preferable — to saw at radically different angles, as, for example, when ripsawing in the overhand manner or when sawing large tenons.

KEEPING TO THE LINE

THE ABILITY TO FOLLOW THE LINE AND SAW where you intended is often regarded as the acme of handsawing skill, but if everything else has been properly attended to it is really very easy. There are two aspects to a properly aligned cut: horizontal and vertical. Only the latter requires any real practice.

Correct positioning is everything here. If you stand — or as is more usual, place one knee on the workpiece — so that your eye is immediately above the blade and your body centered over the cut, you will have little difficulty in noticing whether the blade is perpendicular to the wood. If you have any doubt, place a trysquare on the wood with its blade at right angles next to the sawblade. As you make the initial pull-strokes to start the kerf, sight down the back of the blade with your

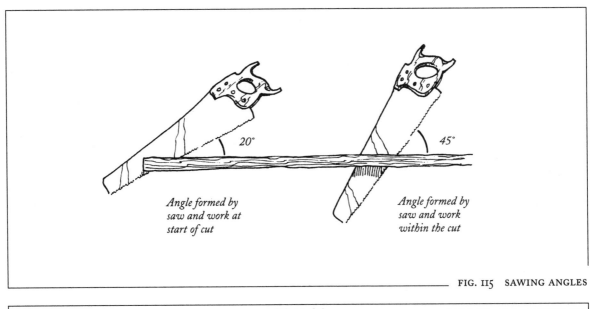

Angle formed by saw and work at start of cut

Angle formed by saw and work within the cut

FIG. 115 SAWING ANGLES

eye directly above the line to be cut, trying to keep the blade so positioned that neither one side nor the other is tilted more in one direction than another. This simple expedient alone will do much to guarantee success. So often a thoughtless operator will try to saw a perpendicular cut while positioned far to one side of the cut.

At the same time as you are paying attention to the verticality of the cut, you must also control the longitudinal direction. Once again, if you position yourself directly in line it will be easier to keep the saw on track. Where possible, and assuming you are right-handed, saw to the right of the line. Furthermore, try to position the workpiece so that the waste is to the right. Consistency will improve your relationship to the kerf, and if any error is to be made it will be better to make it on the waste side of the cut.

Just as when paying attention to verticality, sight down the back of the blade. Older saws frequently have a small nib, often thought to be the vestige of a much older and more ornamental sawblade design, cut in the back of the blade near its toe (the end farthest from the handle); this nib can be used in the manner of a gun sight to help keep things aligned: try to keep it in line with the back of the blade. Additionally, if you hold the saw so that your first finger, rather than being wrapped around the handle with its friends, points forward, you will discover this also helps to saw in a straight line.

A certain amount of guidance may be necessary no matter how carefully you have started the cut. The grain structure and density of the wood being sawed may exert an influence on the blade, and you should pay constant attention to the line, stopping frequently if necessary to blow away any sawdust that may build up and obscure the mark. When saws seem determined to wander, pulling always to one side or the other, it is usually a result of bad set. If the teeth on one side are set farther out than the teeth on the other side the kerf will tend to curve in this direction no matter how hard you struggle to keep to a straight line. The proper cure is to reset the teeth evenly, but a quick improvement may be made by running a file down the side that is set too far out. This is not as good as a complete reset since it can have the effect of altering and blunting many of the angles that form the cutting edges of the teeth, but it can help in an emergency if you do not have your saw wrest or saw set with you.

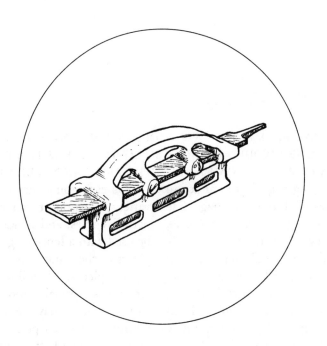

10

FRAMED SAWS

LIFE BEFORE THE BANDSAW

O F ALL THE MACHINES AND POWERTOOLS IN THE CONTEMPORARY SHOP, LARGE OR SMALL, THE ONE I WOULD BE MOST SORRY TO LOSE IS THE BANDSAW. TABLESAWS, JOINTERS, AND PLANERS CAN MAKE LIFE EASIER AND SPEED UP MANY PROCESSES, even imparting a satisfying degree of accuracy to many jobs, but if pressed I could manage fine without them. To lose my bandsaw, however, would be a very heavy blow. It is a relatively mild-mannered machine, generally quieter than most stationary powertools, and although like all powertools it still needs to be treated with respect, it is not so fiercely or so noisily threatening. Even very large bandsaws (except perhaps certain resaw models equipped with extra-wide blades) hum along relatively quietly, making just a gentle tick-tick-tick where the weld joining the blade into a single loop passes through the blade guides, and unthreateningly invite the workpiece to be fed into the blade and twisted and turned at will.

This easy-going machine is capable of a great variety of work: It can rip, crosscut, resaw, cut perfect circles, and make repeated pieces. It can be used with a fence or guide to produce multiple pieces of the same dimension, turn out matching tapered pieces, and follow the most intricate patterns; it is especially good for following freehand curves. There may be other, more specialized machines that can perform each of these operations somewhat better, but in most circumstances the bandsaw is a perfectly adequate substitute, and in a small shop where time or money does not permit a complete array of machinery, the bandsaw is regarded by many as the best all-purpose machine to own.

LIFE BEFORE THE BANDSAW

BUT WHAT IF YOUR RESOURCES DO NOT stretch even to a bandsaw, let alone to a whole array of stationary machines? The answer lies in how people managed for generations before the bandsaw was invented. A quick look around museums and antique shops should make it obvious that woodworking did not begin with the advent of the bandsaw, and that very fine and complicated work was somehow wrought without this, or any other, powertool. How was it done? With handsaws, of course, but not always and only with the kind of saw that now springs to mind when the word 'handsaw' is used. The saws that for most of history formed part of the woodworker's toolkit, from Greek and Roman times, down through the Middle Ages, right up to the beginning of the Industrial Revolution, were members of the framed saw family.

Apart from the common coping saw and its slightly more specialized cousin, the fretsaw, today's handsaws belong to the unframed family of saws. Although the very earliest saws — those dating from prehistory and consisting of pieces of serrated bone and stone — were technically without frames, unframed saws, such as the common crosscut handsaws and ripsaws still available in hardware stores, have been with us only since the end of the 17th century. Before that time most saws belonged to the framed family.

FRAMED VERSUS UNFRAMED

AN UNFRAMED SAW CONSISTS OF A FLAT blade usually held by a single handle fixed at one end. Some large unframed saws, such as two-man crosscut saws (FIG. 116), are made with a handle at both ends. What distinguishes an unframed saw is the lack of any framing holding the blade straight and taut; whatever rigidity the blade possesses depends solely on the strength of the metal itself. It was not until the 17th century, when certain improvements in steelmaking were made, that a blade could be made strong enough to be used without any supporting frame.

Although the unframed saw has virtually supplanted the earlier framed models in America, in other parts of the world, notably the Far East and Europe, framed saws have remained popular and continue to be used by both a small number of discerning traditionalists as well as woodworkers too poor to afford anything else. It is a large family and not all its members may be useful today, but there are some that can still play a useful role, especially for the woodworker without a bandsaw.

THE FRAMED FAMILY

FRAMED SAWS MAY BE DIVIDED INTO TWO main groups: those known as frame saws and those known as bow saws. Frame saws were designed primarily for ripping, that is, cutting with the grain, such as when converting logs into timbers, balks, and boards, or when resawing or ripping smaller boards into the desired width or thickness. It is this use that inspired the development of the first bandsaws.

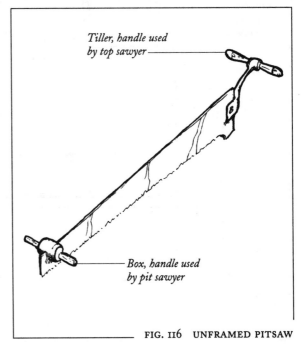

Tiller, handle used by top sawyer

Box, handle used by pit sawyer

FIG. 116   UNFRAMED PITSAW

FRAMED SAWS

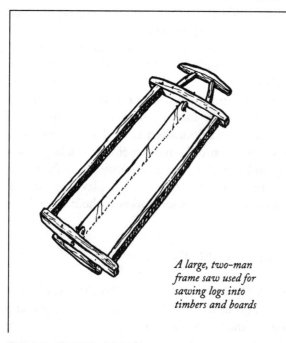

A large, two-man frame saw used for sawing logs into timbers and boards

FIG. 117 FRAMED PITSAW

The frame saw (FIG. 117) was designed with a blade held between two stretchers of a frame, the end pieces of which provided the attachment points for the blade. These stretchers were made far enough apart so that they would clear the sides of the wood being ripped, different size frame saws being used for different classes of work, such as giant pitsaws, smaller felloe saws (for cutting out felloes, sections of wooden wheels), and even smaller veneer saws.

The bow saw was designed to hold a blade that was generally narrower than that of a frame saw. The blades of British and American types are held between the ends of bow-like arms separated at their mid-point by a rigid crosspiece. The other ends of the arms are connected by an adjustable cord or bar. As this cord or bar is tightened, the crosspiece acts as a fulcrum, and the ends holding the blade are stretched apart, tensioning the blade. European types are made somewhat differently

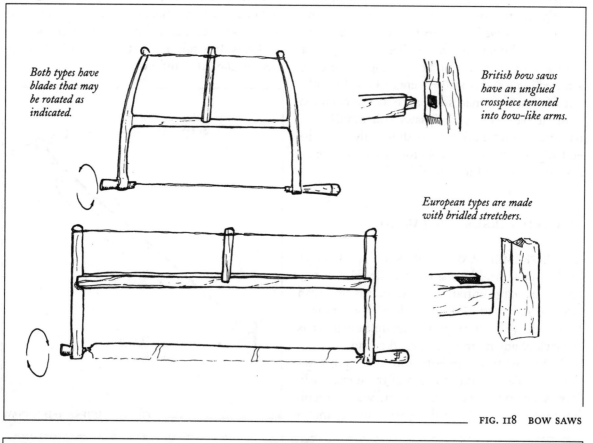

Both types have blades that may be rotated as indicated.

British bow saws have an unglued crosspiece tenoned into bow-like arms.

European types are made with bridled stretchers.

FIG. 118 BOW SAWS

but the principle and effect are the same (see FIG. 118). Apart from the turning saw, whose blade is wider and intended mainly for ripping, the blades of most bow saws are formed for crosscutting.

The blades of frame saws are fixed and cannot rotate in their frame. Being intended for ripping, their wideness helps the blade cut straight, despite any tendency the grain of the wood being cut might have to twist the blade out of its path. The blades of bow saws are much narrower, since it is easier to control the direction of cut when cutting across the grain, and also to allow the bow saw to cut tightly curved shapes. Additionally, the blades are often capable of being turned in the bow so that the direction of cut may be at any angle to the plane of the frame and not necessarily in a straight line with it. This is useful when crosscutting extremely wide boards, since the bow may be turned to clear the end of the board.

This, indeed, is the principle behind one of the smallest members of the bow saw subsection of the framed saw family: the fretsaw, whose blade, like that of its more common cousin, the coping saw, may be turned at any angle relative to the plane of its frame. This, plus the fact that its frame is especially deep, makes it ideal for twisting and turning when cutting detailed patterns in the center of a board. A jeweler's saw by comparison has a fixed blade and is therefore a true frame saw. All three are shown in FIG. 119.

USING A FRAMED SAW

FEW PEOPLE ARE LIKELY TO USE A PITSAW anymore, although there are still parts of Asia where its use continues. Felloe saws became obsolete together with wooden waggons and wainwrights. But the smaller members of the family still have their adherents, despite the fact that using a framed saw is not as intuitive as using many other tools. At first grasp they can seem awkward and unwieldy and, when considered as a possible alternative for a bandsaw's effortless

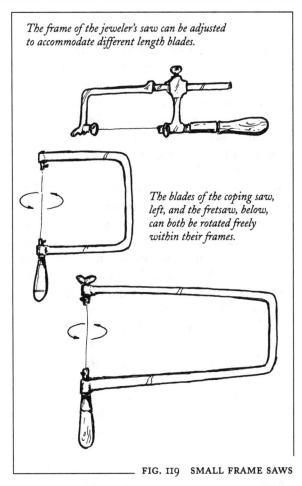

The frame of the jeweler's saw can be adjusted to accommodate different length blades.

The blades of the coping saw, left, and the fretsaw, below, can both be rotated freely within their frames.

FIG. 119   SMALL FRAME SAWS

operation, bow saws can present an appalling prospect of the kind of hard work that used to make woodwork an often unenviable trade, rather than the pleasant hobby it is for many people today.

The larger saws were in several ways easier to use. Their wide blades guaranteed a straight cut, and their sheer weight helped the teeth bite into the wood. Neither of these advantages obtain with the smaller bow saws. They may not be heavy and tiring, but it can be hard to get the blade to start a cut and even harder to follow a line. A certain amount of technique is necessary.

Firstly, the blade needs to be properly sharpened, just like any other sawblade, sufficiently tensioned, and perfectly aligned with itself and the frame. Secondly, the saw should be grasped in both hands, the work being secured on the bench or saw horse. This provides greater power and better control over the direction of the cut.

How much tension is necessary depends on the width and length of the blade, the overall size of the saw, and the size of its component members. Too much tension can damage both blade and saw. Some saws are made with the cross member tenoned into the bowed arms. The tenon is typically shouldered and, assuming a blade of the length originally designed for the saw is fitted, the shoulders of the stretcher's tenons are designed to bear evenly against the arms when the tensioning cord or bar is tight enough. After much use, or a little abuse, this relationship may no longer remain ideal, however, and it will prove necessary either to fashion a longer stretcher, with fresh, clean shoulders, or to fit a shorter blade. This can often be made from the old blade simply by hack-sawing off a little bit and boring a new hole for the pin that commonly secures the end of the blade in the arm, or in the turning handle that is sometimes fitted through the arm.

Other types are made with a stretcher that fits over the arms with an open housed joint. This permits more rocking of the arms in the stretcher, and care must be taken to center the stretcher properly before tightening the adjustment.

The aim is to secure the blade tightly enough so that it will not buckle on the cutting push-stroke, an effect that varies depending on the hardness of the wood being sawed.

Unless there is a good reason to the contrary, the blade should be straight and untwisted from end to end, and fitted in the same plane as the arms. If the bow saw in question is not a turning saw there is no other choice: the blade is secured directly to the arms, or to pieces that will fit in the arms only in one way. Other saws allow the blade to be twisted in relation to the frame. One variety of turning saw designed for cutting dovetails actually makes use of a twisted blade that allows one end of the blade to be entered into the work at one angle and then, as the bottom of the dovetail is approached, the other end of the twisted

blade is used so that, without changing the angle of the saw too much, the blade now cuts somewhat perpendicularly to its first action, thus cutting the bottom of the joint. But for general cutting it is most efficient to keep the blade straight and aligned with the saw.

Some bow saws and turning saws have one arm longer than the other. The longer arm extends below the blade and is intended to be held. The bucksaw (FIG. 120) is an example of this. These saws are best held (by the right-handed) with the right hand on the extension, immediately below the blade, the left hand being brought across one's chest to grasp the bow above the blade. If the saw has no such extension, the right hand is still the hand that grasps the arm closest to the blade, and the left hand is positioned above this. Keep the saw aligned with your right shoulder and use the frame's height and length to ensure that the cut remains perpendicular to the work and proceeds directly in front of you, much as you would sight along the top of a handsaw's blade.

Start the kerf by drawing the blade backwards a few times until enough of a groove is made to guide the saw, and then saw lightly, without excessive downwards pressure, keeping the blade at

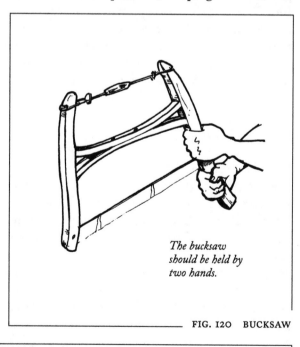

The bucksaw should be held by two hands.

FIG. 120 BUCKSAW

approximately 45° to the work. If the saw wanders from the line, increase the angle to about 10° from vertical until the correct relationship is again achieved. This is the method for general crosscutting. When ripping with a frame saw, an overhand method is often used, the saw being held more vertically, but still with two hands.

ARE THESE SAWS REALLY FORGOTTEN?

BOW SAWS ARE ONCE AGAIN BEING SOLD BY many woodworking-tool suppliers. Turning saws are still common in Europe. Practically everyone has a coping saw, often referred to erroneously as a jigsaw. And even bona fide fretsaws are not unknown, even if the craze for fretwork has lessened. Not often regarded as such, and not strictly a woodworking tool despite being found in almost every woodworker's toolkit, the metal-cutting hacksaw is also a form of framed saw. But two other forms of framed saws are also occasionally met with: a metal-framed bow saw used for horticultural work, consisting of a large-toothed blade held in a metal bow, and the bucksaw, so called because it was commonly used in conjunction with the sawbuck, usually a user-made X-shaped sawhorse designed to hold logs being sawed into firewood. Every barn and antique store used to have a few bucksaws on hand, mostly in familiar red-painted wooden frames. Although designed for crosscutting, bucksaw blades are quite wide and coarse-cut. Despite the current prevalence of chainsaws, there is still much to be said for the bucksaw, especially if you only need to cut the occasional piece of firewood. It does not need to have its spark plug changed, it starts every time, and best of all it is neither smelly nor noisy.

11

BACKED SAWS

STRENGTHENED, SUPPORTED, & REINFORCED BLADES

To WORK WELL A SAWBLADE NEEDS TO BE STRONG. THE STRENGTH REQUIRED HOWEVER IS NOT NECESSARILY MEASURED AGAINST THE MATERIAL IT IS DESIGNED TO CUT. IT IS TRUE THAT BRUTE FORCE OF A SUPERIOR ORDER WILL USUALLY prevail in an otherwise equal contest — the larger of two giants will generally be able to knock the smaller one down — but strength in a sawblade can be obtained in various ways, the chief of which is a result of the cunning invention of teeth.

A relatively small saw, made with a surprisingly thin blade of metal, can fell a tree many times its size and weight simply by taking advantage of the principle of the cutting edge applied, in the case of the saw, to a large number of small teeth. We take this for granted (unless suddenly asked to fell such a tree with a blunt saw) but the ability of a relatively tiny tool to achieve such huge results would doubtless seem miraculous to most people unfamiliar with the secret strengths of a saw.

There are, however, other aspects of the saw's ability that even those who are familiar with saws might not be aware of, which stem from satisfying opposing needs in the saw's design.

Cutting edges and teeth alone are not sufficient to constitute a useful saw. Despite such 'scientific' advantage, a certain amount of strength relative to the material being worked remains necessary. But progressively providing a saw with more and more strength simply by making it bigger — and so heavier and stronger — increasingly detracts from the efficiency of the mechanism by which the cutting edge performs its apparent miracle.

Without becoming too complicated, suffice it to say that the principle of cutting depends partly on the relationship of an ideally fine edge slicing into the material with a wedging action. If you have ever looked at micro-photographs of supposedly sharp edges formed on plane irons or chisel blades you will no doubt be familiar with the fact that there is no such thing as a perfectly sharp edge finishing smoothly into nothingness. The granular composition of metal limits the formation of any edge to a series of irregular blunt serrations. The wedging action is what really constitutes the 'sharpness' of any given edge. When we judge a sharp blade to cut well we are really commenting on the fact that the wedging action which pushes apart and then severs the fibers of the wood being cut feels relatively easy compared to the resistance encountered by the particular density of the wood.

This is where the opposing needs come into the picture. On the one hand, the wedging will be easier as the blade is made thinner and sharpened to a narrower edge; but on the other hand, the sharper and narrower the blade is made the less able it will be to push its way through the wood.

Thinness can be maintained, however, if the strength required to enable the blade to push through the wood is provided by some other means than merely thickening the blade. Hence the development of a surprisingly extensive range of strengthened, supported, and variously reinforced sawblades.

STRENGTHENING THE BLADE

THE COMMONEST WAY, AND FOR A LONG time the only way, to support a thin sawblade was by means of a framed saw (see chapter 10). The blades in framed saws are all provided with the requisite strength by being held tautly tensioned in variously designed frames. We use several of these saws today: websaws, turning saws, and even the lowly bucksaw, still sold at most hardware stores for gardening and yardwork.

The other way of providing a thin blade with sufficient strength to prevent its buckling is to 'back' it, by fixing some strengthening material to its back. There are several examples of prehistoric and Roman saws that appear to have been backed (see FIG. 121), but the principle seems not to have been generally adopted until quite recently in the history of woodworking tools. Only in the 18th century do illustrations begin to appear showing various backed saws.

Interestingly, it was about this time that improvements in steelmaking made possible the fabrication of sawblades from rolled steel wide enough and strong enough to form backless and frameless handsaws of the type still common today, known as ripsaws and crosscut saws. Previous saws, made of bronze or iron, all required strengthening. Even the apparent exception to the necessity for somehow strengthening a thin blade represented by Japanese saws, which avoid much of the danger of buckling by being made with teeth designed to cut on the pull-stroke rather than the push-stroke, is a result of their being made with high-grade steel, a material much stronger than what was generally available for most of woodworking's recorded history.

The reason for this late development may have to do with the fact that a backed saw has a necessarily limited depth of cut. For most purposes it is much more useful — indeed, absolutely necessary — to be able to saw right through the material,

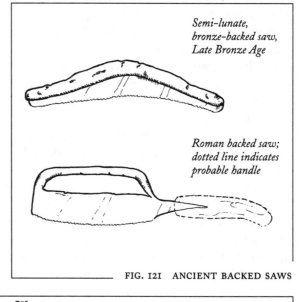

Semi-lunate, bronze-backed saw, Late Bronze Age

Roman backed saw; dotted line indicates probable handle

FIG. 121 ANCIENT BACKED SAWS

from one side to the other. Framed saws, because they have the blade mounted at right angles to the frame, can — provided the frame is large enough — easily saw down the longest and largest balk of timber. It is hardly practical to make a backed saw with a blade much wider than 8 in., and a depth of cut limited at most to 8 in. imposes serious limitations on much woodworking. This was especially true so long as most woodworking was relatively massive and crude. Only when joinery became finer, and parts became smaller and more exactly made, was there even a need for smaller saws.

To make finer cuts possible, a smaller blade with finer teeth is needed. Finer teeth and thinner blades demand strengthening, and so the backed saw was born.

THE TENON SAW OR BACKSAW

OF ALL BACKED SAWS THE TENON SAW IS the best known and the commonest, still useful even in today's tablesaw- and bandsaw-equipped workshop. Although generally referred to in America as the backsaw, it was first known as a tenon saw, and since there are several other backed saws substantially different in design and use that could also be meant by the same name, the confusion caused by the change of name is regrettable. Its chief use is, in fact, for cutting tenons, both across and with the grain. For this job, which requires as neat a cut as possible with as little rag and as much smoothness of surface as can be achieved, a relatively fine-toothed saw is needed.

In some areas it is still known as a 'tennant saw', reflecting a very old spelling that is believed to derive from the nature of the joint now known as a mortise-and-tenon. Old carpenters sometimes explain that the tenon part of this joint is the 'tenant' of the mortise, occupying the cavity — as does a tenant a house. Since both spellings derive ultimately from the Latin word: *tenere*, meaning 'to hold', both senses are meaningful and correct.

To be useful for more than general, shallow crosscutting performed with the use of the bench hook (FIG. 122), the backsaw requires relatively fine teeth, usually cut between twelve and fourteen to the inch. The commonest form of the saw consists of a parallel blade about 12 in. to 24 in. long, cut with crosscut-type teeth. Since tenon-making requires kerfs both across the grain (best made with crosscut teeth) and along the grain, some people like to keep a backsaw filed with square teeth in the manner of a ripsaw.

Another difference between backsaws and other handsaws concerns the set of the teeth. Since handsaws, both crosscut and rip, are generally used for coarser work than finished joinery, their operation can be made easier by providing them with a fairly generous set (the amount by which adjacent teeth are bent to alternate sides), creating a wider kerf less likely to bind the saw, especially when working in wood whose moisture content in conjunction with the heat built up by the friction of the working blade can cause the wood to swell. Backsaws, both because the kerfs involved are typically smaller and shorter, and because the wood being sawed is likely to be better seasoned and drier, can be conveniently used with less set,

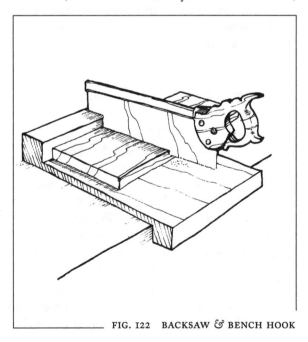

FIG. 122   BACKSAW & BENCH HOOK

which will also result in a smoother cut. If a new backsaw makes too wide or too coarse a kerf, run a file held flat against the side of the teeth down the length of the saw, doing this on both sides evenly.

Older backsaws, especially top-quality models, were frequently backed with strips of brass. Some models can still be found brass-backed, but the usual variety is now steel-backed. The back is simply pressed on, being crimped at both ends, and is not hard to remove should the blade ever require de-kinking by judicious hammering on the convex side of the kink, bump, or buckle. In addition to brass backs, older saws were often made with blades narrower at the toe than the heel (the end nearest the handle). While these saws also tend to be narrower overall and consequently capable of relatively shallow cuts, they are better balanced and easier to use, especially when you consider that the bulk of the work is most easily done with the toe end of the blade, since using this part gives greater control in the attempt to saw 'to the line'. The slightest deviation in the longitudinal angle of approach is inevitably magnified the farther away from the handle the blade is used.

THE DOUBLE-EDGED VARIETY

WHEN CUTTING TENONS, BY HAND OR ON any machine, one of the most important points to watch is that the cut is not allowed to extend past the shoulder line. Besides weakening the joint, the fault usually remains visible and advertises sloppy workmanship. Depth stops can be clamped to saw tables to limit the cut, but when using a backsaw you must try to hold the saw as level as possible and keep an eye on both ends of the kerf if you are to avoid cutting below the line. There is, however, a way to guarantee the perfect shoulder cut which is the logical development of one of a backsaw's most annoying limitations. Most backsaw users sooner or later make the mistake of trying to make a cut deeper than possible and discover that the saw is riding backwards and forwards on the backing strip with the teeth no longer cutting into the wood. A little thought will suggest that by clamping an additional strip to the side of the blade as in FIG. 123 (two clamps are sometimes better than one) you can provide a useful depth stop at precisely the right spot — assuming you are trying to make a cut for which the blade is indeed wide enough.

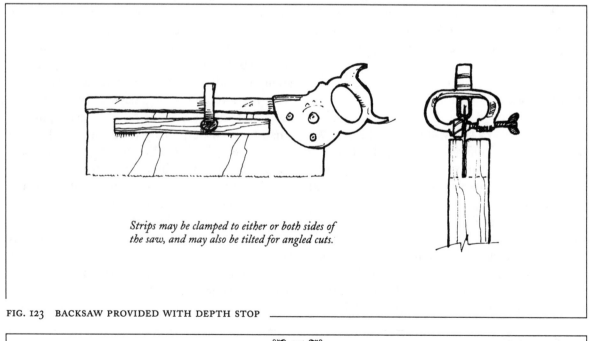

Strips may be clamped to either or both sides of the saw, and may also be tilted for angled cuts.

FIG. 123 BACKSAW PROVIDED WITH DEPTH STOP

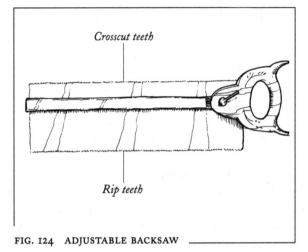

FIG. 124   ADJUSTABLE BACKSAW

Crosscut teeth

Rip teeth

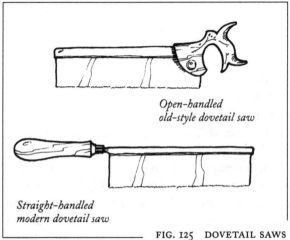

FIG. 125   DOVETAIL SAWS

Open-handled old-style dovetail saw

Straight-handled modern dovetail saw

At least one manufacturer thought of this and produced a backsaw with an adjustable back; one that, moreover, could be tilted out of parallel with the cutting edge, guaranteeing a perfectly angled cut such as is occasionally required for canted, tilted, or splayed work. Since the back may move up or down the width of the blade it made eminent sense to cut teeth on both sides of the blade's width, thereby providing crosscut and rip capabilities to the same saw, combined with a fail-proof depth stop. The only disadvantage to this type of saw (FIG. 124), still to be found from time to time at auction and with old-tool dealers, is that the handle is not quite as perfectly comfortable as one designed to be held always in the same way.

FINER WORK

THERE ARE SEVERAL SMALLER BACKED-SAWS distinguished by different names and differently shaped handles that may be called backsaws. These include the gent's saw, the dovetail saw, and the dowel saw.

A modern dovetail saw looks just like a smaller backsaw with a proportionately narrower blade but with a straight handle similar to the original handles found on antique Roman and Egyptian saws. Older dovetail saws from the 19th century were invariably furnished with the dolphin or pistol-grip type of handle common on contemporary handsaws (see FIG. 125). Since the saw is considerably smaller, these pistol-grip handles are, however, open, rather than formed into a completely closed oval. There is a slight advantage to the pistol-grip type in that it allows you to keep your eye on the line being sawed and feel whether the saw is being held in the correct plane by the position of the handle. A round, straight handle offers no such clue.

The variety known as a gent's saw (a contraction of the term 'gentleman's saw') originated in the 19th century as one of a number of tools made somewhat smaller than the regular tradesman's size and intended primarily for use by gentlemen hobbyists. Gent's saws were invariably made with straight handles like modern dovetail saws. They were the forerunners of today's do-it-yourselfer's tools, but can be very useful as general-purpose small backsaws, especially since they usually have crosscut teeth in distinction to a true dovetail saw which should have ripsaw-type teeth. The true dovetail saw has square teeth, frequently as many as twenty-two to the inch, since cutting out dovetails and pins typically involves sawing with the grain and requires as smooth and exact a cut as possible.

The third type, known as a dowel saw (FIG. 126), may be identical to either of the previous types except for a cranked neck formed by a bent tang

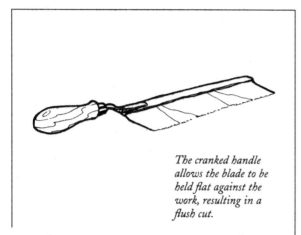

The cranked handle allows the blade to be held flat against the work, resulting in a flush cut.

FIG. 126   DOWEL SAW

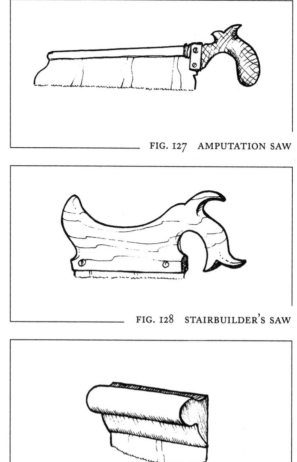

FIG. 127   AMPUTATION SAW

FIG. 128   STAIRBUILDER'S SAW

FIG. 129   VENEER SAW

to which its handle is attached. The crank allows the side of the blade to be held flat on the face of the work — ideal for sawing off protruding dowels or other proud parts.

OTHER BACKED SAWS

ADDITIONAL VARIETIES OF REINFORCED blades and backed saws include the rather gory amputation-saw (FIG. 127), once used by doctors and veterinary surgeons, and prized for its top-quality steel and the usually cross-hatched handle which provides a superior grip; the stairbuilder's saw (FIG. 128), which is essentially a narrow blade, sometimes made adjustable to different widths, designed so that the backing — which constitutes the majority of the tool's bulk — functions as a depth stop, allowing evenly formed kerfs to be sawed when making shallow grooves such as are required for housing the treads and risers of stairs

to each other; small veneer saws (FIG. 129); and even comb saws, which have two narrow blades side-by-side, one slightly shallower than the other to act as a guide by running in the previously cut kerf.

IV
PLANES

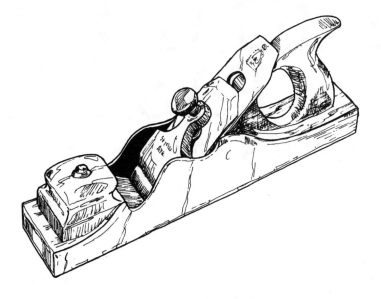

12

A PLANE FROM THE PAST

CLUES TO A WOODEN PLANE'S AGE

IT WAS THE THIRD ANTIQUE SHOP I HAD VISITED THAT AFTERNOON. SO FAR THE PICKINGS HAD NOT BEEN GOOD: A COUPLE OF UNDISTINGUISHED SMOOTH PLANES WITH BROKEN-OUT CHEEKS AND ONE OR TWO MOULDING PLANES MISSING THEIR wedges and irons. I was losing interest rapidly. I was beginning to think that perhaps antique shops were becoming less fertile hunting grounds for old tools than they had been in the past. And then it happened.

From a distance it was the curve of the tote that grabbed my attention. The plane itself seemed common enough, somewhere between 18 in. and 2 ft. in length, and in the usual dirty, grey cond-ition, paint-spattered, stained, and replete with a rusty iron. But the tote was altogether different from the handle seen on most bench planes. As I came nearer I could see that not only did the top part curl back much farther than usual but also that the entire tote was peculiarly proportioned.

Something odd like this usually means that you are looking at a repair or perhaps even a home-made tool. I went over and took a closer look, not really expecting to find anything more than another sad example of an abused plane rescued from total oblivion in some damp basement, and now destined for retirement as a piece of antique atmosphere in someone's weekend country house.

The tote had been repaired, the tail having been broken off and somewhat crudely nailed back on, but it was original, and it was apparent that it had been made by a professional. The proportions were different from the standard 19th century tote: squatter, with a more circular hole, longer overall, including the elongated curl at the top that had originally caught my attention (see FIG. 130), but the plane nevertheless had an air of that sure professionalism that diſtinguishes the factory-made article from a product of a hand less practised. The curves were smoothly cut and flowed nicely from one to the other, and the shaped edges of the hole were evenly rounded. My intereſt was aroused; what was this?

I picked it up and immediately noticed it felt heavier than is usual for a plane of this length. Moſt of the time this is because the tool is made of a heavier wood than the usual beech. Rosewood is fairly common, especially in a tool a craftsman might make for himself that was made to be better than the ordinary, and this would account for the unusual tote. But rosewood does not turn grey, and as I looked more closely I recognized the familiar speckled grain of beech. Beech that is heavier can indicate age or a possible British anceſtry. Now I began to get excited. Was it possible that I had found a truly old plane?

NOT JUST ANOTHER OLD PLANE

THE PROPORTION OF NINETEENTH AND early 20th century planes to 18th century examples is overwhelmingly in favor of the former, but it is ſtill possible to ſtumble across isolated examples of early rabbets, dados, and moulding planes. But 18th century bench planes (smoothers, jointers, and trying planes) are extremely rare, probably because they saw much more use than the relatively infrequently used moulding planes. So it is never wise to rush to the conclusion that an odd-looking bench plane is that old; it is more likely some form of recent hybrid. But if it should prove to be genuinely old the excitement and thrill are that much greater.

It was time for a more careful examination. The firſt thing to look for when attempting to date a plane is a maker's mark. Will it be that of the firſt-known British planemaker, Wooding, or perhaps his equally legendary American counterpart, Nicholson? More often than not, when anything

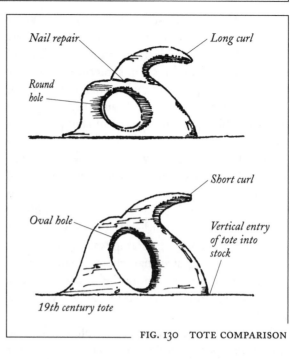

FIG. 130 TOTE COMPARISON

at all is visible, the ſtamped imprint on the plane's toe (the front end of the ſtock) turns out to be nothing more exciting than that of one of the common 19th century giants of planemaking firms: Auburn, Ohio, Greenfield, or the like. But, as is all too often the case, I could make out nothing on this plane. The toe had been so badly hammered and dented that any mark that may have once exiſted was now completely obscured. Nevertheless, it was ſtill possible that this was an early — if unidentifiable — tool. I checked the heel of the ſtock juſt in case something had been ſtamped on the back. I have never seen a regular maker's mark ſtamped on this end, but you never know. An early maker might have left his mark here before the practice of imprinting ſtamps on the toe became ſtandard. Besides, in the absence of a maker's mark, there is often much to be learned from any owner's marks that may exiſt, and owners are liable to ſtamp their names all over a tool, wherever there is space. Even if the owner is unknown and his hiſtory cannot be traced, the ſtamp may ſtill help date the tool since typefaces and imprint borders of particular eras are shared by both maker's ſtamps and owner's ſtamps. But

A PLANE FROM THE PAST

there was no owner's stamp to be seen anywhere on the toe, heel, sides, or top of the plane. There was nothing to be learned from this line of enquiry, but I had forgotten something: irons are frequently stamped with maker's names and logos. Finally I hit pay dirt: a beautifully clear and unmistakably 18th century type of stamp adorned the iron.

The stamp possessed what is known as a zig-zag border, the name 'James Cam' being enclosed in a recessed oblong with an indented edge. This is a typically early form of stamp; by the middle of the 19th century unbordered stamps were more common. Moreover, the stamp was upside-down. This further suggested that whoever had stamped the iron had done so before the practice became standardized and formalized in the way we know it today.

The name 'James Cam' rang a bell, but I could not remember whether Mr Cam had been a planemaker or a blademaker, let alone when he had been working. Then I noticed that the top of the iron was not formed in the usual straight-edged way with trimmed-off corners, but ended in a flat curve (see FIG. 131). This shape is almost exclusively pre-19th century. Of course, irons can be replaced as they are worn down by sharpening, and are therefore not a foolproof way of either dating or identifying a plane, but in this case, taken together with the unusual shape of the tote, the likelihood of the iron being original was strong. And there was still stronger proof in evidence.

Firstly, when I turned the plane over to look at the sole I noticed that there were a couple of cracks extending from the corners of the mouth (see FIG. 132). It was clear that these cracks had been formed by the stock shrinking in width until the iron had become caught tightly in the mouth. Further shrinking against the unyielding iron had caused cracks to develop at the weakest part of the stock, namely the narrow wall at either side of the mouth. Such shrinking takes quite a while to occur since plane bodies were commonly made from very well seasoned stock because the maker's

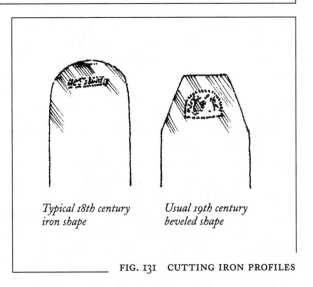

Typical 18th century iron shape *Usual 19th century beveled shape*

FIG. 131 CUTTING IRON PROFILES

reputation depended largely on the material he used and how careful he was in its preparation. Of course, any wooden tool will shrink appreciably when brought from the damp and rainy British Isles to the relatively drier climate that obtains in much of the United States. If the plane was not

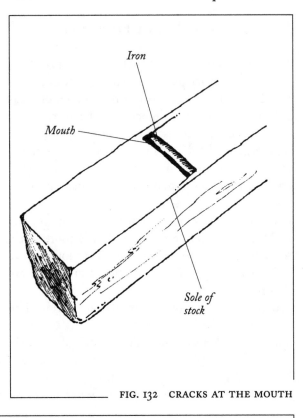

Iron

Mouth

Sole of stock

FIG. 132 CRACKS AT THE MOUTH

early American it was very likely an early example from Britain.

Secondly, and more excitingly, when I turned the plane upside-down the wedge fell out and I saw that the iron was uncut. An uncut iron is one that has not had a slot cut out of its center for the bolt that holds a capiron to the cutting iron. Before capirons became common at the end of the 18th century, all irons were naturally uncut. In itself an uncut iron does not conclusively establish an early date of manufacture, since the improvement was not adopted everywhere at the same time. Cheaper grades of tools continued to be supplied with the old-fashioned single irons well into the 19th century. Indeed, certain classes of planes, specifically those made with blades set at very low or very high cutting-angles, such as block planes and miter planes, have to this day never been provided with capirons. However, since it was apparent that the abutments cut in this plane's throat had been made to contain a single iron and its wedge, without the added space that

would have been necessary for a capiron, it was obvious that this was not a replacement iron. It is unlikely that anyone who cared enough about a particular plane to furnish it with a new iron when the old one wore out would not have taken the opportunity to upgrade to a more efficient double iron. The iron was almost certainly original, and since it was an early type on three counts (its rounded shape, the form of the upside-down stamp, and the fact that it was uncut), this lent a great deal of weight to the idea that the plane was truly old.

TAKING THE PLUNGE

AT THIS POINT I KNEW I HAD A TWENTY two inch trying plane made of old and possibly British beech fitted with a very old iron. It was time to buy it and take it home for closer examination. The asking price of twenty-two dollars was fair, even for an early 20th century tool, if not for a collector, then certainly for any woodworker who knows how to restore it to good working order. A lot of the iron remained and it did not appear to be terribly rusted, and the stock was in very good shape with no damaging checks or cracks except the minor ones at the mouth. The wedge and tote were complete and, most importantly for potential use, there was no splitting of the cheeks or abutments caused by inexperienced attempts to remove or insert the iron and its wedge. Such splitting (FIG. 133) so weakens the abutments' ability to hold the wedge and iron securely that the plane becomes useless as a working tool. As a possible 18th century example of the planemaker's art it might be worth much more, especially at an auction or sale attended by knowledgeable tool enthusiasts. Depending on its condition and provenance it might bring anything from one to five hundred dollars.

I paid the asking price without the customary dickering and was promptly rewarded for my open-handedness by being given a small discount. I almost felt guilty at making off with such a find until I remembered that there had been much

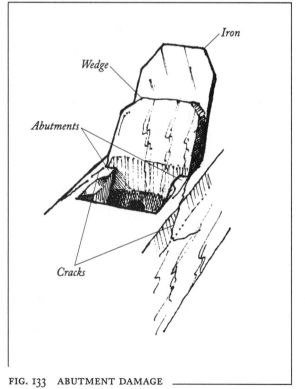

FIG. 133   ABUTMENT DAMAGE

Labels in figure: *Iron*, *Wedge*, *Abutments*, *Cracks*

that was obscenely overpriced in the store. Most things come out even in the end.

A CLOSER LOOK

ONE WAY TO LEARN AS MUCH AS POSSIBLE about a tool is to disassemble it completely. The wedge, as previously noted, was no problem: it fell out whenever the plane was turned upside-down. The iron, however, was firmly caught in the shrunken throat, and its removal required the careful assistance of a pair of pliers. The tote, originally mortised into the stock as is normal, had loosened at some time in the past and had been rather inexpertly secured with a screw inserted through its base. The stock, having subsequently shrunk, had not only cracked around the iron but had also started to crack around the front of the tote, pushing the tote out a little so that it no longer sat as deeply as originally intended, nor as straight. This could be easily rectified by slightly enlarging the mortise, but the situation in the throat was a little more difficult. There would be a difficult decision to be made between enlarging the throat and possibly weakening the cheeks of the stock or filing the sides of the iron until it was reduced in width sufficiently to fit properly, thereby tampering with the shape of something that ought by virtue of its venerability to be left alone. Meanwhile, I was now able to consider the plane's constituent parts in greater detail.

The stock had no strike button and, as was to be expected, the top of the stock just in front of the throat was somewhat crushed from having been struck here repeatedly. This is the normal method of loosening the wedge and is the reason why best-quality planes are provided with a strike button, a round section of hardwood inserted end grain up, at this point (see FIG. 134). This plane had not been the top of the line. Nevertheless, all other details of its construction were nicely attended to. The arris at the junction of the top and the sides had been finished with a typically broad 18th century chamfer, which had been run

down the sides for 1 in. and finished with a neat gouge-cut. Very early planes often have chamfers that finish in neat lamb's tails. This model showed signs of incipient standardization.

The very top edges of the abutments had been slightly chamfered — a nice detail usually omitted in factory-made planes — and the wedge was made with wider chamfers than usual, finishing in a little curve. Otherwise everything was unremarkable. The sole was in very good shape. There was none of the gouging or chipping that is common in old wooden planes that have fallen into inexperienced hands during the last fifty years of their life. The stock was a good ⅛ in. smaller in front than at the heel end, indicating that it had been repeatedly jointed over the years as it wore unevenly, but the mouth was not excessively wide.

I turned my attention now to the name stamp on the iron, and after a little research discovered that my original guess had been close to the mark. James Cam had been a well-known plane-iron maker, active in Sheffield, England, between 1781 and 1838. Furthermore, one of the planemakers in whose planes James Cam's irons have been found, a certain John Day, who is known to have been apprenticed to Thomas Phillipson of Cheapside in London in 1756, is also noted as the maker of several planes found in the United States. It was not possible to tell whether this plane was in fact

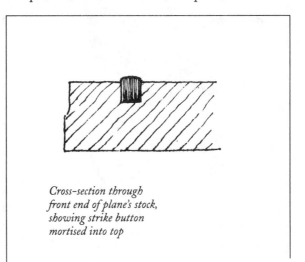

Cross-section through front end of plane's stock, showing strike button mortised into top

FIG. 134   STRIKE BUTTON

made by the Englishman John Day, but its appearance in an upstate New York antique shop would be consistent with its having been made for the American market, since many English makers exported tools to the East Coast in the early 19th century. Indeed, after James Cam's death his business was acquired in 1838 by the firm of Marsh and Shepherd, which firm sold many tools, including plane irons with the James Cam imprint, through agents both in New York and in Philadelphia. By this late date, however, the stamp used on the irons had changed to a more modern pattern than that on the plane before me, and the irons were moreover square-edged and double.

The evidence was now all before me and the verdict was in. The iron was an early example of James Cam's work and obviously original with the plane, since it was uncut and fitted the abutments. The plane could thus be securely dated from at least the first quarter of the 19th century, and was very probably even older, since James Cam was known to have been active since 1788.

It is reasonable to assume that this trying plane was originally bought and owned by an American woodworker, who no doubt, before it became too worn down, set it aside when planes with double irons became available. In the years that followed it must have been lucky enough to have remained out of the hands of inexpert abusers, tucked away somewhere relatively dry until the present day.

One last note of interest: the prices quoted in various contemporary catalogs for planes of this length with single irons averaged close to a dollar in 1830. Considering how much a tradesman using this tool would have earned per hour then, and comparing this with what any similarly skilled woodworker might be expected to earn per hour today, our plane had maintained its relative value remarkably nicely.

13

BENCH PLANES

THE FIRST FAMILY OF HANDTOOLS

PLANES, ESPECIALLY BENCH PLANES, ARE ARGUABLY THE TOOLS THAT DEFINE FINE WOODWORKING. YOU CAN MAKE A LOT OF THINGS OUT OF WOOD, AND YOU CAN WORK WITH WOOD IN MANY WAYS, BUT IF WHAT YOU DO IS RELATED TO FURNITURE or joinery it is a practical certainty that planing will be an indispensable part of your life. The fact that for many people planing is now undertaken primarily by powered handplanes, or for those better equipped, by stationary machines known as planers, does not alter the fact that the operation of planing remains as central to fine woodworking as it ever was. Without planing it would just not be woodworking as we know it.

But in common with many other aspects of contemporary life that, after having remained relatively constant for centuries, are now changed dramatically, planing also has altered radically. Nevertheless, the operation is essentially the same as it has ever been: the production of a flat and smooth surface from the rough and irregular material of raw wood.

Where speed, economy of time and labor, and overall consistency are concerned, the machine is supreme. There are few handplanes to be found in the great furniture factories of America these days, and indeed even many small shops have abandoned such tools in favor of thickness planers and jointers that work quickly and efficiently. But as those at the top of the craft know, there is still no substitute for the quality of the surface produced by a properly tuned plane in the hands of a skilled user. If you are concerned about revealing as much of the wood's inherent beauty as possible, then abrading and machining the surface of wood into technical flatness is no match for the effects possible by cutting fibers and cells so cleanly that you can literally see into the wood.

Furthermore, when it comes to difficult grain and boards with features such as knots that machine users call defects, a well-tuned plane can out-perform the average jointer or planer. The fear of tearout is well known to every machine operator, and inordinate amounts of time and energy are commonly expended in adjusting knife depth, speed of rotation, feed rate, and depth of cut in an effort to avoid the price we must all too often pay for mechanical speed.

Unfortunately, competent planing is no longer as common as it once was, and few people have ever seen a properly tuned tool being used with skill. Disbelief of the claims made above is common. And even if all the pre–machine age woodwork of the past is offered as evidence of what can be done with such tools the response is often: 'Perhaps, but who has the time for that today?'

The fact is that it does not take as much time as you might think to acquire the skill and put it to use, and in any case time is not necessarily the most important element in the pursuit of woodworking. If you have to produce a given number of items in a given period of time in order to pay the rent and stay afloat then admittedly time counts. But if quality is important, and if love of the material and enjoyment of the process are also important, there may be other ways to reach your goal. The bench plane can be your secret weapon if you know how to use it. But it is important to realize that what is commonly sold as a bench plane today is in many cases only a poor imitation of the bench plane as it once was. Nevertheless, adjustments can be made, and even a new tool can be made to perform surprisingly well in knowledgeable hands.

MEMBERS OF THE FAMILY

BENCH PLANES ARE THOSE PLANES USED AT the bench to prepare and finish the surface of boards. The most important members of this family are the smooth plane, the jack plane, and the jointer plane. Of course, every plane is used to work the surface of a board, but what is meant here is not cutting grooves, making joints, or forming special shapes, but the straightforward preparation of stock into tried and true material. Usually the first operation that is performed on any piece of wood, once it has been sawed to a workable length and width, is to produce at least one flat or true surface. Without this all subsequent operations are difficult if not impossible. Before the days of power jointers and planers this first step in almost every project was accomplished with the jack plane (FIG. 135).

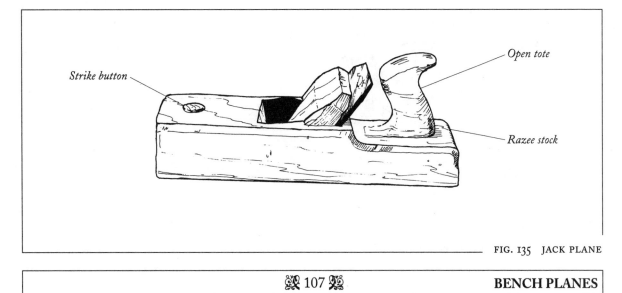

Strike button

Open tote

Razee stock

FIG. 135   JACK PLANE

	UNITED STATES		GREAT BRITAIN	
	19TH CENTURY	20TH CENTURY	19TH CENTURY	20TH CENTURY
16 in.	Jack	Fore	Jack	Fore
18 in.	Fore	Fore	-	-
20 in.	Fore	-	Trying	Jointing
22 in.	Jointer	Jointer	Trying	Jointing
24 in.	Jointer	-	Long	Jointing
26 in.	Jointer	-	Long	Jointing
28 in.	Jointer	-	Jointer	Trying
30 in.	Jointer	-	Jointer	Trying

TABLE 2   BRITISH & AMERICAN BENCH PLANE NOMENCLATURE

Nineteenth century ingenuity, which produced an unprecedented plethora of specialized planes, developed a close cousin of the jack plane, known as the scrub plane. The scrub plane, made of metal and fitted with a narrow blade set in a wide mouth, was designed to be used as a kind of preliminary jack plane to remove gross unevenness before getting to work with the jack plane (see chapter 15). The scrub plane is efficient, but unless you are working with logs or extremely rough-sawn material it can be overkill, since the curved profile of its hungry blade removes very large quantities of material at each pass.

After a board has been cleaned up and made basically flat, it is then possible to pay attention to considerations such as width, thickness, and relative parallelism. If the required thickness is less than can be conveniently achieved by sawing, then the jack plane is used again, but when it is time to achieve trueness over length, whether of edge or surface, as well as to produce a greater degree of flatness and smoothness, then the mid-range bench planes are called for (see FIG. 136).

Mid-range bench planes include: jointers, or jointing planes; fore planes; try planes or trying planes; and the less-common panel plane. There is

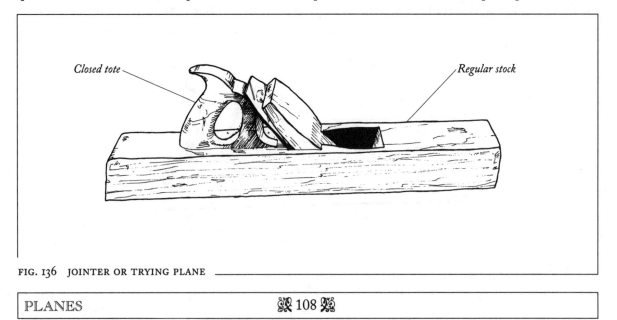

Closed tote   *Regular stock*

FIG. 136   JOINTER OR TRYING PLANE

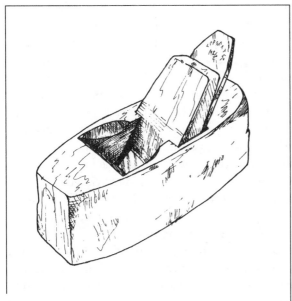

FIG. 137 SMOOTH PLANE

Finally there are smooth or smoothing planes (FIG. 137). These planes are well named since their purpose is simply to finish a presumably already flat surface to the utmost level of smoothness and perfection.

WHAT MAKES THESE PLANES WORK?

WHEN THOMAS CHIPPENDALE WORKED IN St. Martin's Lane, producing many of the masterpieces that became the standard of 18th century excellence by which we still measure the greatest examples of our craft, planing was not one of his daily tasks. Undoubtedly, had he had the machines he would have used them — up to a point. Chippendale was a designer and a businessman first and foremost, and as soon as he could he employed apprentices and journeymen to perform much of the so-called grunt work. Such workers spent the majority of their time planing.

considerable confusion concerning all mid-range planes, especially regarding their length, since naming conventions have varied over the years and from Britain to America. TABLE 2 gives the approximate sizes implied by the various names at various times in the two countries, but they can all be considered as belonging to the second major group of bench planes.

These workers may have constituted cheap labor, but it was still important to keep costs to a minimum. Business was business even in the 18th century. Consequently, the tools they used were the most efficient available. Made throughout of

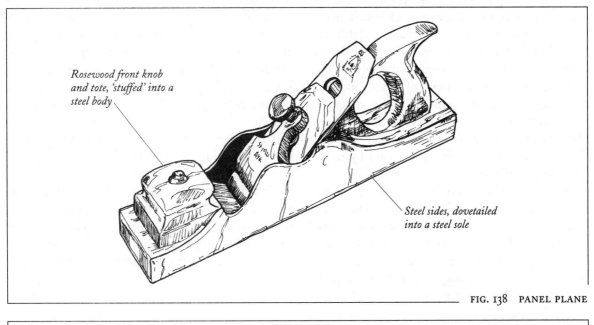

Rosewood front knob and tote, 'stuffed' into a steel body

Steel sides, dovetailed into a steel sole

FIG. 138 PANEL PLANE

BENCH PLANES

wood, except for the irons, their form had remained relatively unchanged for hundreds of years. The angle of the iron, the shape of the stock, and the design of the throat and wedge, though apparently very straightforward, are, in fact, masterpieces of sophisticated tool design honed to perfection by long centuries of practical experience. To use one of these tools correctly adjusted and properly sharpened is to understand at once that the production of an 18th century masterpiece with what are now often regarded as 'primitive' handtools is not totally the miracle that it might seem.

THE LAST HUZZAH

IN THE MID—NINETEENTH CENTURY, JUST as the advances of the Industrial Revolution were starting to make themselves felt in the toolmaking industry, and just as toolmaking was approaching an all-time high of excellence, technology was sowing the seeds for the obsolescence of the best handtools ever made. Right at the point when many tools were being made to standards never before attained, the introduction of power was ousting them from the workplace. This is most clearly seen with bench planes. As mentioned earlier, the design and fabrication of bench planes had remained essentially unchanged (although their manufacture had passed from the individual user-maker to small firms engaged solely in toolmaking) for many hundreds of years. Suddenly these designs were reinterpreted using dovetailed metal bodies filled in with exotic hardwoods and fitted with irons, capirons, and screw wedges. These tools, made largely in Scotland by only a few firms, continue to represent the absolute pinnacle of the planemaker's art. Two particular firms, Spiers of Ayr and Norris of London, whose 'stuffed' planes (as they are sometimes known) were among the best, chose to call certain models measuring between 13½ in. and 17½ in. 'panel planes' (FIG. 138). Similar in size to some jacks, they are, however, so superior in their ability to produce a finished surface that they may be used as a combination smooth plane and jointer plane. The term is now used for any superior-quality stuffed plane of approximately this size regardless of maker.

Designed originally for the most demanding craftsmen, stuffed bench planes were never copied in America, where firms were more concerned with economies of mass-production and the conveniences that could be attained by designing simpler, iron-bodied tools. Many varieties of these were produced, of which the Stanley™ model is perhaps the predominant example, and which remains the type common today. They require less skill to maintain and use than either wooden planes or the Scottish type, albeit at the expense of a diminished capacity for truly top-quality work.

Regular commercial production of the dovetailed and stuffed-body type of plane ceased shortly after World War Two, but such has been the demand from collectors and discriminating users that several specialty firms are once again making copies, along with new designs embodying the best features of the archaic types. Although the hunt for such a plane is well worth while, simply finding one of these tools, old or new, will not necessarily guarantee you a new world of planing pleasure. What follows will help put you on the right path. The remainder of this chapter is concerned with how to appraise a tool's condition and, if necessary and possible, how to improve it. Chapters 14 through 17 focus on actual planing techniques and particular members of the family.

It is important to bear in mind that in reality these two things usually proceed hand-in-hand. Only the practised user can competently assess a tool's worth and condition, and only with an at least moderately well-tuned tool can anyone begin to appreciate the niceties of its use. Thus the path to a successful planing technique depends on a sort of back and forth approach: Tune the plane as well as you can and then use it for a while, appreciating the improvements and becoming aware of further deficiencies. Then refine the tuning again and experience the improved performance, repeating this process infinitely to rhykenological* Nirvana.

THE IMPORTANCE OF FLATNESS

THERE ARE A NUMBER OF VARIABLES THAT must be recognized if any bench plane is to perform well enough to make its use worth while. These vary from plane type to plane type as well as according to the work being attempted and the material involved. One thing that is common to all types, however, is the necessity for flatness of the stock's sole. This is true for a wooden plane or a metallic plane, an old plane or a new plane, since you will never be able to plane anything flatter than the degree of flatness represented by your plane's sole.

Judging flatness is almost as hard as achieving it. You need a reliable reference. True flatness is very hard to come by in the average shop, and ends up being relative at best. For practical purposes acquiring a 3 ft.- or 4 ft.-long machinist's straightedge is the best that can be done. These

* rhykenological: from the Greek word for plane: *rhykane*

are precision tools, and can cost as much or more than a good-quality plane. There is little need to buy one that is graduated — a regular rule or tape is good enough for measuring distance in the shop — but to do good work accurately and with the greatest ease, you need something approaching the flatness measurable by a machinist's straightedge. Although they may look for all the world like no more than a simple length of steel, they are precision instruments and must be treated with a great deal of care. Always make sure that they are laid down flat over their entire length, and are not pivoted on some other object. Protect the beveled edge as you would the edge of a cutting tool, and never pick them up by one end. Realize also that they are sensitive to extremes of heat.

To judge the flatness of a plane's sole, hold a machinist's straightedge against the sole of the plane, as in FIG. 139, and see if any light is visible between straightedge and sole. Make sure the iron is retracted into the mouth so it does not interfere with the straightedge, but is nonetheless wedged in place, so that any deformation caused by wedging is taken into account. Unlike Japanese planes, whose soles are required to be in the same plane only in vital areas (other parts being slightly hollowed), there should be no light visible anywhere, regardless of how you swivel the straightedge.

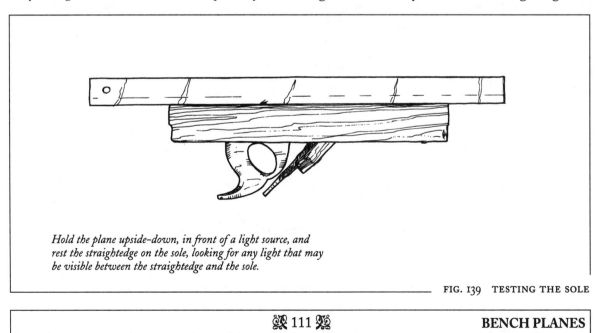

Hold the plane upside-down, in front of a light source, and rest the straightedge on the sole, looking for any light that may be visible between the straightedge and the sole.

FIG. 139   TESTING THE SOLE

The degree of flatness measurable this way is perfect for fine woodworking. If you have a plane that passes muster, and use it to plane two edges to the same standard, using the straightedge to test them, edge joints will almost hold themselves together by suction alone.

If your plane does not measure up — and it is extremely unlikely that it will unless it comes from a master's toolkit — there are various remedies at your disposal. Metal-bodied planes can either be surface-ground at machine shops, or laboriously hand-lapped at home. Wooden-bodied planes can be hand-dressed and planed flat using other planes. But before embarking on any of these solutions, bear the following points in mind:

A machine shop will charge upwards of forty dollars and must be made aware of the fact that the plane should be ground with iron and wedge (or lever cap, in the case of a Stanley™-type plane) in place, but retracted, of course. The shop also needs to know that you are concerned that the sides be held carefully so that they do not become scratched or marked, and that it is not just a question of flattening the sole but that perfect perpendicularity to the sides of the body must be maintained. Remember that grinding the sole necessarily enlarges the mouth. Wooden-bodied planes can be remouthed, but if a metal-bodied plane's mouth becomes too large this invariably

spells the end of the plane's usefulness for fine work, no matter how flat the sole. Obviously you will only want to submit an intrinsically good-quality plane to such a process, making sure that the machinist is skilled and sensitive to the needs of the job. It is hardly going to be worth while doing this with a second-rate tool from your local hardware store.

Right off the bat this would appear to put top-quality planing beyond the reach of the average woodworker, but there are other options. Before dismissing the stuffed Scottish aristocrats and panel planes costing two to three hundred dollars as too expensive, consider how much is typically spent for routers, chopsaws, and ½ in. drills, not to mention small jointers, planers, and tablesaws. If you are still unconvinced, you might adopt a cheaper alternative of acquiring a regular wooden-bodied bench plane. Fifty or more years after general production ceased there is still a wealth of easily salvageable planes of this type to be found. With patience and a straightedge, these can be given very flat soles.

The same requirements hold true for wood as for metal. The sole must be kept perpendicular to the sides. With many wooden planes, especially the longer sizes, this is made difficult, though not impossible, by the fact that shrinkage over the years may have caused a slight bulging around the

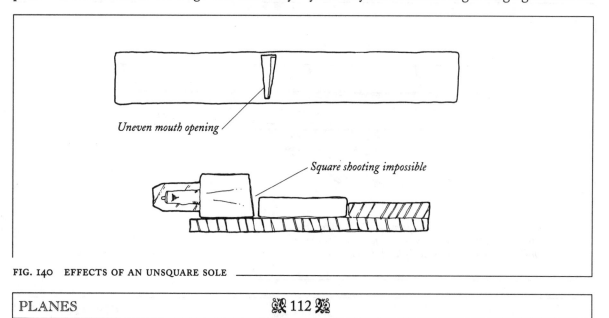

Uneven mouth opening

Square shooting impossible

FIG. 140   EFFECTS OF AN UNSQUARE SOLE

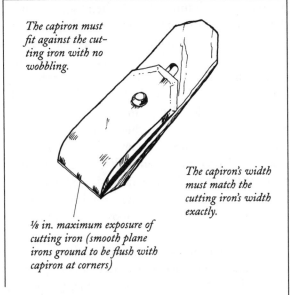

The capiron must fit against the cutting iron with no wobbling.

The capiron's width must match the cutting iron's width exactly.

⅛ in. maximum exposure of cutting iron (smooth plane irons ground to be flush with capiron at corners)

FIG. 141   CAPIRON ADJUSTMENT

throat area where the iron has prevented the ſtock from becoming as narrow as at each end. Planing this bulge flat may result in dangerously weakened cheeks, but perpendicularity is necessary for two reasons:

Firſtly, anything less will produce a mouth that is wider at one side than the other. This will mean that the iron will have to be wedged in place somewhat askew if it is to projeċt equally across its width. Alternatively, the iron will have to be reground out-of-square. Neither of these solutions is desirable, since the work necessary to accommodate them defeats the prime purpose of having an easily adjuſtable tool. Secondly, using the plane on a shooting-board becomes impossible without the use of wedges to compensate for the exaċt degree of non-perpendicularity in the plane's sides. Both conditions are illuſtrated in FIG. 140.

UNDERSTANDING THE MOUTH

NO MATTER HOW WELL SHARPENED THE cutting iron may be, unless its capiron is properly fitted and the two together bear the correċt relationship to the plane's mouth, good results will be hard to come by. The capiron muſt fit perfeċtly againſt the back of the cutting iron and be set extremely close to its cutting edge (see FIG. 141). Even for a plane designed to take relatively coarse shavings, such as those produced by the jack plane, this diſtance should not be more than ⅛ in.

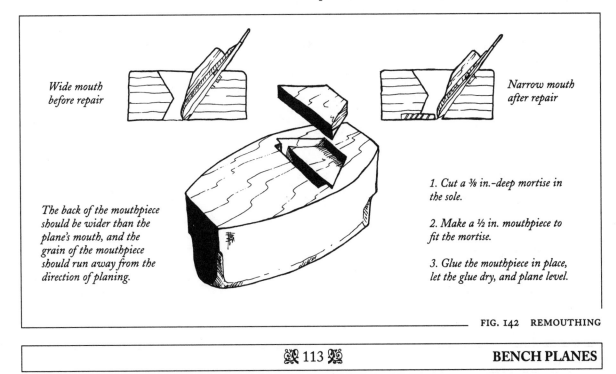

Wide mouth before repair

Narrow mouth after repair

1. Cut a ⅜ in.-deep mortise in the sole.

2. Make a ½ in. mouthpiece to fit the mortise.

3. Glue the mouthpiece in place, let the glue dry, and plane level.

The back of the mouthpiece should be wider than the plane's mouth, and the grain of the mouthpiece should run away from the direction of planing.

FIG. 142   REMOUTHING

BENCH PLANES

For finish work, where only the finest shavings are taken, a gap less than 1/32 in. is none too small.

A properly sharpened and fitted cutting iron and capiron is not enough, however. The size of the mouth is all-important. While it may be obvious that the mouth must be large enough for the substantial shavings that are taken by the jack plane, what is perhaps not so obvious is that for the finest of all possible shavings the mouth must be so small that it may seem for all practical purposes to be closed up.

Close examination of the mouths of stuffed planes, when they are fitted with properly sharpened irons, will show how small mouths should be. The range of frog adjustment (the frog is the assembly to which the irons are affixed) which is usually possible in Stanley™-type planes will also demonstrate how small a mouth may be made for the finest work.

Remouthing, which is the term for the process of providing a used wooden plane with a small mouth, is shown in FIG. 142 (and described more fully in chapter 16). Since wooden planes wear down with use and should therefore be periodically rejointed (have their soles planed flat), remouthing becomes a normal part of maintenance. If a metal plane has too large a mouth it may be possible to build up the bed (the part against which the iron rests) so that the iron is positioned further forward, but this can be difficult with Stanley™-type metal planes since their bed is the frog to which the capiron is held by a screw. Stuffed planes' beds are, of course, made of wood, and present no difficulty. In any event, a small mouth is an absolute necessity if the plane is to be able to take thin shavings without tearout and deal successfully with opposite, cross, curly, or rowed grain.

One last consideration is the condition of the cheeks and the consequent wedge-holding ability of the plane. No matter what its type, the plane's body must be able to hold the wedge securely. Broken abutments or cracked cheeks make this impossible, as do faulty capscrews and wobbly irons. The iron should not wobble. If it does, check the fit of the wedge, and see whether the bed needs adjustment, reflattening, or perhaps nothing more than a careful cleaning.

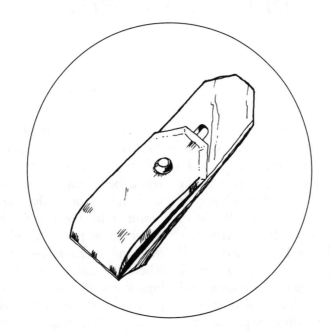

14

SUCCESSFUL PLANE RACING

ODDS-ON FAVORITES

WHEN IT COMES TO RACING HANDPLANES, PUT YOUR MONEY ON THE OLD ONES, ESPECIALLY IF THEY ARE WELL FETTLED AND IN THE HANDS OF A SKILLED CRAFTSMAN. ALL OTHER THINGS BEING EQUAL, CONTEMPORARY BENCH PLANES of the Stanley™ type will be no match at all for similarly sized wooden or stuffed planes of respectable vintage. The older ones will win in the straightaway, producing clean, chatterless shavings, and they will win hands down in all the specialized categories, such as Thinnest Shaving, Smoothest Cut against the Grain, and Best Performance over Gnarly Rowed and Interlocked Surfaces; they will even produce the Longest Shavings on End Grain.

The sport of plane racing, once a vital part of every cabinet and woodworking shop, has all but died out. In the days before powered machinery for planing, thicknessing, jointing, and other basic surfacing operations became commonplace there

was a lot of time-consuming and tedious hand-work. It was absolutely essential for the economic health of the shop that this be done as well and as efficiently as possible, and this meant that both tools and mechanics be of top quality. One way to relieve the tedium and simultaneously encourage high standards was for the apprentices, who were given most of the grunt work, to engage in racing tourneys. Even wagering was not unknown. The excitement was always particularly intense when a job came in that involved a particularly trouble-some species. Wood with a high mineral content, such as zebrano (also known as zebrawood), that required steeper cutting angles to preserve the plane's cutting edge for the maximum time, wood with interlocked, rowed or twisted grain, such as is common on many mahoganies, and wood that was highly figured, with areas of different resiliency and density, such as bird's-eye maple and even hemlock, all raised the stakes.

It may not be practical or even desirable to revive this obsolete sport, but since it can be very rewarding to use tools of 'competition caliber', it makes a lot of sense to develop the skills that were common among the competitors. If you consider keeping even a single plane in your shop worth while, then you owe yourself the experience of using it with all the skill, grace, flair, and efficiency that it is capable of.

FIRST REQUIREMENTS

A PLANE'S PERFORMANCE DEPENDS AS MUCH on the condition of the plane as it does on the operator's skill. The two things go inextricably hand-in-hand, for inasmuch as you cannot hone your operating skills on a deficient tool, neither can you fully understand what is required to fettle a tool if you have no experiential way of appreciating what is required of it. As your skills improve, so you become increasingly sensitive to possible improvements in the tool's condition; and as the tool's condition improves, so it becomes possible for you to discover increased levels of proficiency regarding its use.

But you must start somewhere, and to do so requires taking a certain amount on faith since results may not seem to warrant the effort at first. Persevere, and as your fettling skills improve so will your technique, and vice-versa. Soon the time will come when you may even begin to regret the passing of the old plane-racing days, for you too will be eager to compete.

At the beginning remember that it is false economy to start with an inferior tool since you will need all the help you can get. There is little point in burdening yourself with an additional disadvantage. When experienced, you will be able to make even a cheap tool perform so that it will amaze those not in the know. But at the same time be respectful and try not to wreak too much havoc on the unsuspecting tool with over-zealous grinding, filing, and sharpening. The golden rule is: 'Little by little and bit by bit'.

FLATNESS ABOVE ALL THINGS

FLATNESS IS THE 'SINE QUA NON' OF THE planing world. Regardless of any other ingredient in the equation it is impossible to plane anything flatter than the plane itself. If the sole of the plane is not perfectly flat then no amount of skill or sharpening will produce a perfectly flat surface on the work. By 'perfectly flat' in woodworking is meant flatness to within a few thousandths of an inch. Given the non-contiguous nature of matter at microscopic levels and beyond, absolute flatness may turn out to be a mere philosophical concept. Even flatness as defined in machining and toolmaking is not truly perfect, although its tolerances are far greater than those required for woodworking. In any case, we are ultimately limited by the material we are working with. Wood, being cellular in composition, can only ever present an average surface flatness to the world. This fact is readily apparent when we consider the differences between the various types of wood. Open-grained, large-celled species, such as oak, can never be made more than averagely flat across their surface when compared to denser, more evenly structured species such as boxwood, whose apparent flatness is much more continuous.

The flattest thing in the typical shop is the top surface of the tablesaw or some other stationary powertool. But examine this surface with a machinist's straightedge and you may discover that even this is not truly flat. Hold the machinist's straightedge against the sole of your plane (as in FIG. 139, chapter 13), and you are likely to be amazed at the number of places light shines between straightedge and sole. This then is your first job: to perfect the flatness of your plane's sole with a machinist's straightedge.

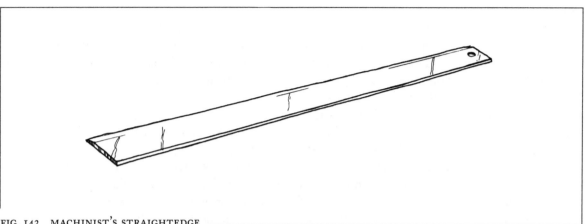

FIG. 143 MACHINIST'S STRAIGHTEDGE

MACHINIST'S STRAIGHTEDGES

A SMALL DIGRESSION ON THE SUBJECT OF straightedges is useful here. They are relatively expensive — even a 3 ft.-long, ungraduated, single-edged machinist's straightedge (FIG. 143) costs around fifty dollars — but as a basic and essential standard for everything you do in the shop there is no useful alternative. Not only do they provide a guide to the condition of your planes (and items such as tablesaws and jointer tables), which depend on the supposed accuracy of their flatness for their proper use, but they are also invaluable when checking the accuracy of your work. There is little in woodworking that demands greater accuracy than that measurable by a machinist's straightedge. Using this tool as your basic reference when checking trueness of joints, surfaces, cuts, and layouts will ensure the very best work of which you may be capable.

Since they are expensive precision instruments they require respectful handling. New ones are usually sold with cautionary notices regarding proper storage, such as always to lay them down on a flat surface, not to allow them to bang up against other items, and not to subject them to extremes of temperature. It is worth protecting your investment as well as your ability to benefit from their accuracy by providing them with their own home somewhere safe in your toolchest or at the bench.

FIRST SHAVINGS

HAVING DONE THE BEST YOU CAN FOR THE moment regarding the flatness of your plane's sole, and having sharpened the iron as well as you can, stand at the bench and try a few passes.

The first thing that is liable to cause difficulty is securing the work. The Japanese manage well by pulling the plane towards them, with just a knee or a toe holding the work, the work simply butting up against a single stop. In the West we are accustomed to pushing planes away from us on a waist-high bench, and securing the work with all manner of vises, clamps, and holdfasts. Even so, no matter how firmly the work may be secured, if the surface of the bench is not flat we may still run into trouble.

Another new idea for many woodworkers is that the bench itself is a tool and must also be trued. Since it is usually made of wood, it is subject to wear and tear and all the ambient moisture-content changes that play fast and loose with wood's dimensional stability. Dressing the bench top is easy — once you are equipped with properly tuned planes and a reasonable degree of skill in using them — but this is easier said than done in the beginning. In the meantime, however, if your bench top is hollowed, and you cannot get a board that you intend planing to lie flat, use shavings, or even thin wedges, to keep the bottom of the board reasonably flat (see FIG. 144).

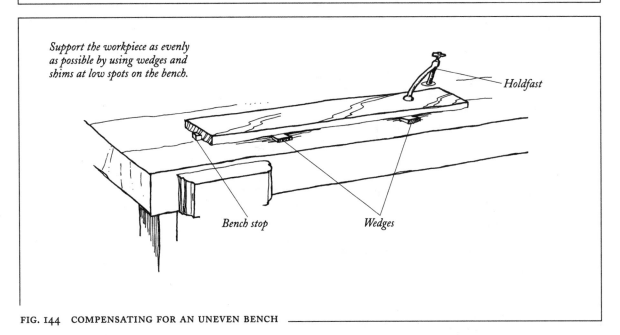

Support the workpiece as evenly as possible by using wedges and shims at low spots on the bench.

Holdfast

Bench stop

Wedges

FIG. 144   COMPENSATING FOR AN UNEVEN BENCH

Edge planing, of course, usually takes place with the board being held in the vise, perhaps with the assistance of a deadman (see chapter 1), but here too, successful planing can often depend on how accurately the vise operates. Ideally, the vise should be adjusted so that the top surface of the outside jaw — and inside jaw too if this is separate from the bench top itself — is exactly in the same plane as the bench top, and that the vise, when closed, will securely grip a single sheet of paper. Furthermore, any board held in the vise should remain perfectly vertical, and not have its bottom edge pulled in towards the center of the bench, as so often happens if the vise's front jaw is not properly adjusted.

Apart from these basics, which are direct characteristics of the bench, there are numerous other aids more or less attached to a bench, such as stops, dogs, and holdfasts, all of which need to be perfectly adjusted and in proper working order if their use is to produce anything other than frustration and poor results.

But to return to the actual planing. Different planes are designed to do different jobs: a jack plane is intended to remove fairly thick shavings from material that is not terribly flat or smooth to

start with; a jointer's job is concerned with an evenly thicknessed shaving taken from the edge of a board, often a very long board; a smooth plane is designed to remove the merest whisper of a shaving. Each of these needs is reflected in the different cutting-iron angles, differently sized mouths, differently adjusted capirons, and differently ground profiles of the various planes' cutting-irons' edges (see FIG. 145). Nevertheless, every plane should be able to bite cleanly, cut without tearing, and produce shavings all day long without choking. If any of the above should not be the case, the plane needs work. If all of the above is true, however, and you still cannot get the board flat, true, or smooth, the fault is with you.

THE THREE ORDERS OF PLANING

TO ACHIEVE A FLAT SURFACE — USUALLY the first requirement in stock preparation — a board may be roughly bandsawed, or ripped to shape and size on the tablesaw. Thereafter, in a mechanized shop, it is usually run through the jointer and maybe the planer. Lacking these appliances, however, life can still go on. If the

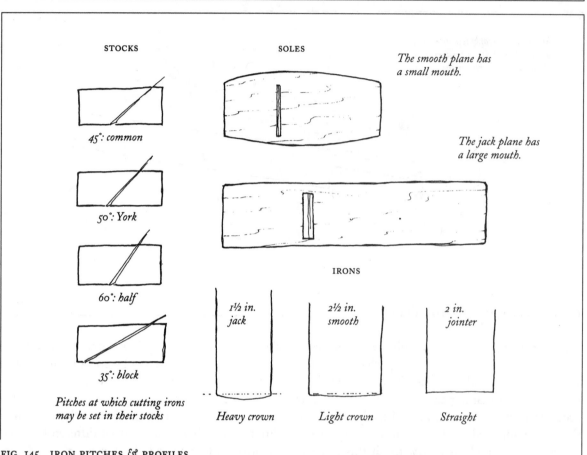

STOCKS

45°: common

50°: York

60°: half

35°: block

*Pitches at which cutting irons
may be set in their stocks*

SOLES

*The smooth plane has
a small mouth.*

*The jack plane has
a large mouth.*

IRONS

*1½ in.
jack*

*2½ in.
smooth*

*2 in.
jointer*

Heavy crown

Light crown

Straight

FIG. 145 IRON PITCHES & PROFILES

board is totally rough, a scrub plane is useful to remove the saw marks and gross unevenness. Thereafter, a jack plane is used to bring the surface into flatness. A board that is not flat may be cupped, bowed, warped, propellored, crowned, twisted, or any combination of these deformities. All these may be easily observed and measured with the use of winding sticks (see chapter 17).

Mark the high spots or other areas that need to be reduced in order to create a flat surface, and use the jack plane in any direction you feel like. If only one corner is high, plane across the grain or even diagonally until the area has been corrected. Then plane with the grain. When removing high spots do not worry about tearing the surface of the wood. Theoretically your plane should be so well sharpened and adjusted that this will not happen, but until you are able to do this remember all you

are really concerned with is removing the extra material.

This kind of planing is hard on the plane and is also the hardest work. For this reason, a wooden jack plane is superior to a metal one. Being lighter, it is less tiring to use, and being wooden, it is easier to keep its sole flat by periodically planing it with another known flat-soled plane. Since the jack plane needs to take fairly large shavings, frequent jointing and consequent enlarging of the mouth is not a problem. Keep the cutting edge of the iron sharpened somewhat convex, so that its center is about ⅛ in. proud across a 2 in. width, and set the capiron to be at least ¹⁄₁₆ in. above the cutting edge (FIG. 146). Lastly, make sure the ends of the wedge finish smoothly, and that there are no obstructions to the smooth passage of the shavings up through the throat.

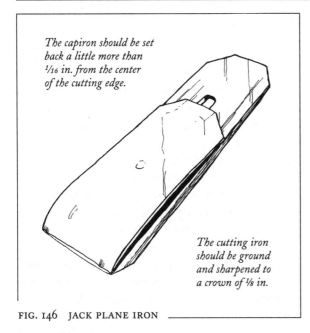

The capiron should be set back a little more than 1/16 in. from the center of the cutting edge.

The cutting iron should be ground and sharpened to a crown of 1/8 in.

FIG. 146   JACK PLANE IRON

JOINTING

HAVING ESTABLISHED SURFACE TRUTH, THE next operation is to achieve a straight and square edge. This is what a power jointer is used for, but there can be problems associated with the powertool that its handtool counterpart, the long jointer plane, makes light of.

The jointer plane is a bench plane longer than 18 in. fitted with a perfectly square iron; no crown to the cutting edge is necessary since the plane is rarely asked to cut any width greater than that of its blade. Like the power jointer's need for an absolutely flat bed, the jointer plane demands a flat sole over its entire length. This is easy to achieve with a wooden jointer: the plane is simply planed flat using another perfectly flat plane. A metal plane's sole is not only a bigger proposition to resurface but also, because of the inherent weakness in the sole's design and extra stresses caused by the frog mechanism precisely at the weakest part of the body, more likely to warp out of perfect flatness along its length. Once the jointer plane is in good shape, however, the iron and capiron may be so finely set as to make light and easy work of grain irregularities that would result

in tearout on a power jointer. Furthermore, the finished cut will be one smooth surface, not a series of parallel knife lines.

There is no question that it takes some practice to hold a 22 in. jointer squarely on the edge of a 6 ft.-long board — holding it slightly askew as in FIG. 147 will help a lot — but once this skill is developed you will never want to sacrifice the niceness of control that you are able to exercise with this tool for the faster but riskier efficiencies of the powertool.

Developing the skill needed is made easier if you use the machinist's straightedge as a constant guide to check lengthwise straightness, and an exact trysquare to monitor squareness. Shorter lengths may be made square more easily by being shot: laying them down flat on a shooting-board and using the plane on its side. This, of course, demands perfectly square sides to the plane. Once again, this is an easier thing to accomplish with a wooden stock than with a metal plane.

SMOOTHNESS

BRINGING THE SMOOTH PLANE INTO PLAY IS usually the last planing operation. The smooth plane's job is to produce a finished surface. The

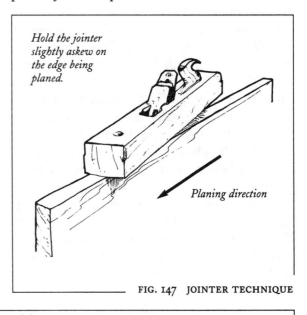

Hold the jointer slightly askew on the edge being planed.

Planing direction

FIG. 147   JOINTER TECHNIQUE

SUCCESSFUL PLANE RACING

board should already have been made flat and true, and possibly cut for jointing and maybe even partly or wholly assembled. There are very few occasions when sanding need be the finishing operation; a surface finished with a smooth plane will usually result in a better job. For this to be true your smooth plane must be in top shape, its sole perfectly flat and square to its sides, the mouth small, the capiron set so closely to the cutting edge that at the corners no iron is visible at all (this supposes a crown of no more than ¹⁄₁₆ in. across a 2 in.-wide blade), and the whole assembly tightly secured in the plane body with no rocking against the bed.

One of the great advantages of a wooden smooth plane is the ease with which the sole may be kept perfectly true. Armed with a machinist's straightedge and — this is the Catch-22, at least at the beginning of your career — another well-tuned and sharpened plane, preferably a jointer, since jointer irons should be ground straight across with no crown like that on the smooth plane's iron, it is a quick and simple job to touch up the smooth plane's sole until perfection is reached. This is often more easily accomplished in reverse: the jointer being held upside-down in a vise, and the smooth plane — its blade retracted but not removed, since removal would alter the stresses and possibly the shape of the stock — being moved across the upturned jointer's sole. In addition, after this has been done a number of times and the mouth has become consequently too wide, a wooden plane is easily remouthed (see FIG. 142, chapter 13). Such a plane needs only a wipe or two of paraffin wax from a candle kept handy by the bench to glide smoothly over the surface to be planed, actually creating a certain amount of suction as it works, making it difficult to lift off.

If you make sure the corners of the sole are slightly rounded and that the corners of the iron do not cut into the surface, a shaving may be taken that is no more than one or two cells thick in the center and that disappears completely at the edges. Plane across the grain to start, working

your way along the length of the board, and then plane in the normal fashion.

Any difficulty at this stage may usually be traced to inadequate sharpening, but a less frequent cause may have to do with choking. If the plane's throat chokes up with shavings it is because the shavings are not being broken efficiently by the capiron or because they are running into an obstruction in the throat.

Capirons were introduced towards the end of the 18th century when it was discovered that by presenting the newly cut shaving with a steeper exit angle it could be broken and thus prevented from causing possible tearout. For the capiron to be effective it must be positioned as closely as possible to the cutting edge in order to break the shaving at the earliest opportunity. At the same time, the position of the capiron controls the maximum possible thickness of the shaving, so while a very close setting is needed with smooth planes, a somewhat greater setting is better for jointers and jacks.

If the front edge of the capiron is not perfectly smooth — indeed, polished — it can impede the shaving's smooth passage even while it is being broken. Similarly, if anything else gets in the way of the exiting shaving, such as a less than perfectly tapered or chamfered wedge, the shaving may catch and immediately concertina into a throat-choking blockage.

SHARPENING

SHARPENING IS EXTREMELY IMPORTANT. Regardless of which method is preferred — and there are many equally good — bear in mind that how it is done, and the results aimed for, will vary from job to job, from plane to plane, and from one situation to another. For this reason you will find that as you gain experience it will be a great advantage to keep several planes, each set up slightly differently. But any smooth plane, when properly fettled, should be able to remove a continuous shaving from end grain if the end grain is first slightly dampened. The truest test of a racing plane, however, may be the old trick of placing two planes side-by-side at the end of a board and then slowly tilting the board to see which one will slide away first, taking a perfect, lace-thin shaving as it goes.

15

SCRUB JACK & JOINTER

STOCK PREPARATION BY HAND

I HAD GONE TO BUY SOME CHERRY FROM A HARDWOOD DEALER ON THE WEST COAST, WHERE ADMITTEDLY IT IS NOT AS COMMON AS IN THE EASTERN UNITED STATES, AND WAS SURPRISED TO FIND IT SURFACED ON BOTH FACES. I HAD WANTED EIGHT-QUARTER stock (2 in. thick), expecting that after milling and dressing I would end up with boards ¾ in. thick, just right for the project in hand. When I asked the lumberyard operator why the boards were already surfaced, and as a result already reduced to ¾ in., I was told that his customers preferred it that way, the better to see the grain pattern. I gave him a cock-eyed look and went elsewhere. For one thing, despite having been surfaced, the boards were still as warped, bowed, and propellored as you would expect any reasonably seasoned rough-sawn stock to be: admittedly not much, but still far from perfectly flat. After basic stock preparation to get the material to the point where parts could be measured and sawed out, I would

be lucky to end up with ½ in.-thick boards. For another thing, none of these boards was wider than 4 in., and most showed considerable white sapwood; what did he expect the prospective purchaser to admire?

The experience demonstrated two things: an increasing unwillingness to prepare one's own stock, and a misplaced zeal on the part of the dealer to provide the customer with what was perceived as the desired end-product.

At the other end of the scale, I have known people who take a great deal of pleasure in felling their own lumber, using a chainsaw milling-attachment to convert it to boards, stickering it themselves, and then leaving it to season for a number of years. Not all of us have this much time to spend, nor even the opportunity or access to standing lumber.

THE BEST WAY TO BUY LUMBER

BETWEEN THESE TWO EXTREMES LIES A route quicker than the latter and guaranteed to yield better results than the former. It involves buying lumber in dimensions as large as you can afford and as are available, and reducing it and preparing it yourself.

It might seem a bit excessive to have fifty or a hundred feet of twelve-quarter (3 in. thick) oak, in random widths and lengths, delivered to make a small bookcase, all the parts of which will measure exactly ¾ in. thick, but if you intend making anything else, such as pieces with parts consisting of varying dimensions, especially tables with 2 in.-square legs or cabinets that have five-quarter (1¼ in. thick) rails and stiles, it is the only way to go. You will have the ability to determine whether parts are flat-sawn or quarter-sawn. This means it will be your choice how the face of the part is oriented to the center of the tree from which it is cut. This determines the grain pattern and often affects its stability. You will also have relieved yourself of the tiresome necessity of lamination or making do with pieces smaller than ideal. In the long run, you will end up with less waste.

"This is all very well for someone with a large shop, equipped with industrial-strength jointers, planers, and surface thicknessers," I hear you saying, "but the prospect of reducing an 8 ft. length of lumber measuring 3 in. or 4 in. thick by 10 in. wide to something I can cut dovetails in defies the imagination. And this does not even address the problem of making the reduced piece perfectly flat and square."

My reply to this is that it is just not true. A properly conditioned handsaw (see chapter 9) will cut anything to length very easily. And while a bandsaw is an undeniable asset when resawing (ripping, or sawing wood lengthwise with the grain, into thinner slices or boards), a traditional ripsaw, with five or six teeth to the inch, set appropriately for the type of wood at hand, is remarkably efficient. In any case, a 14 in. bandsaw is not an expensive piece of machinery and is quite common in many small shops, as any tour past the open garages of a residential neighborhood on a Saturday morning will demonstrate. The amount of extra effort involved in getting out a 4 ft. board, 1 in. thick, from a large balk by hand is not tremendous. It is not even very time-consuming. Machines were invented to save time and labor for those faced with the same task all day long. It would not make any sense to attempt to produce ten thousand feet of material by hand, but when dealing with one piece of furniture or one project at a time, not having any heavy machinery is hardly an obstacle.

"But this still leaves the question of producing a board, no matter how large or small, that is flat and square," you continue to object. "Isn't this a formidably difficult and pointlessly laborious task to attempt by hand in this day and age of jointers and planers?" Again, the answer is a resounding 'No!' Not only is it not impossibly difficult, but there are also frequently advantages, especially for the small shop on a budget unable to afford premium lumber. It can also be a more rewarding experience, closer to that which attracts many people to woodworking in the first place. Not everyone wants to be a production shop making the same piece every day; many simply like to make things out of wood, one at a time, and enjoy the feel, smell, and texture of the material as they work. Noisy, dust-producing, and potentially dangerous machinery is not part of this dream. Planing a board by hand is. The tool investment is less, you can still hear the birds sing while you work, and masks, goggles, and an expensive array of safety devices are all unnecessary. It is also far better for your fitness, your utility bill, and the environment. I may be making a virtue out of what for some is a necessity, but remember that for centuries, long before any machine appeared, countless beautiful pieces were produced by hand.

WHAT YOU NEED

APART FROM THE SAWS MENTIONED ABOVE all that you need to prepare flat, tried and true pieces are a pair of winding sticks, a scrub plane, a jack plane, and a jointer plane. If you decide to continue the process by hand to finished perfection, and avoid the use of abrasives, which bludgeon the surface to smoothness and destroy its clarity and luminescence, you will also need a panel plane and a smooth plane. Also useful for basic stock preparation, and even more so when you start joining boards and cutting joints, is a quality straightedge. For rough work, anything that is reasonably straight will serve, such as a wooden yardstick or a 4 ft.-long metal rule. But for the degree of perfection needed to produce impeccable joinery in wood — by nature an often irregular and variable material — a machinist's straightedge (FIG. 143, chapter 14) is invaluable.

The first two items on the list may be unknown to many woodworkers, but they are far from unobtainable. Winding sticks (see chapter 17) are simply a pair of parallel sticks, invariably user-made, that are used to check overall flatness and determine whether a board is 'in winding'. This is another way of describing a board that twists like a propeller, one part lying in a different plane from another. Note that winding has nothing to do with smoothness or localized flatness.

A scrub plane is simply a wide-mouthed and relatively short (10 in.) plane with an iron that has a very pronounced crown to its cutting edge. Many people are familiar with the metal version sold by the Stanley Tool Company from 1896 to 1962 (FIG. 148), but wooden versions have been used for hundreds of years, most simply being adaptations of ordinary jack planes. Similarly, many contemporary metal jack planes can also be turned into workable scrub planes, as described below.

PLANING FOR FLATNESS

FACED WITH A PIECE OF WOOD THICKER than will be ultimately needed, and given that it is also wide and long enough, the first job is to make one surface completely flat. When this has been done the board may be thicknessed and brought to the correct width, using this flat surface as a reference for all the other dimensions.

If the board is already dressed (made smooth, but not necessarily flat), the jack plane is the first tool to use. But if the board comes straight from the saw, and is still furry and irregularly surfaced, then you need to use the scrub plane. As a precautionary measure to protect your plane from unwanted nicks and scratches, both to its cutting edge as well as its sole, use a stiff brush — a wire-haired, file-cleaning brush is ideal — to clean any grit, loose particles of dirt, wood, or other debris from the surface.

Having chosen which side you wish to prepare first, place the board with this surface uppermost on the bench so that it is held firmly in place and does not rock. Do this with the use of wedges (as shown in FIG. 144, chapter 14) rather than by forcing the board flat, since a board bent flat will spring back to its bowed shape when released.

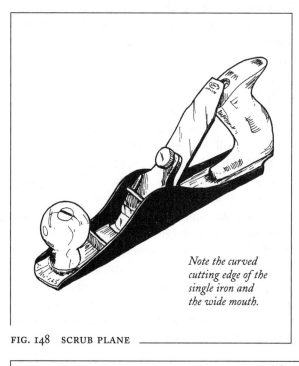

Note the curved cutting edge of the single iron and the wide mouth.

FIG. 148 SCRUB PLANE

The idea is to create a flat surface on the board that is naturally flat and not in tension.

A metal scrub plane is relatively narrow. It has a single, thick iron with a pronounced crown to its cutting edge. If you set the iron so the entire cutting edge projects through the plane's sole, you will cut a deep, curved groove in a flat piece of wood. Adjust the set according to the roughness of the surface, deeper as the surface is rougher and more irregular.

In lieu of an actual metal scrub plane you may use a medium length (10 in. to 18 in. long) jack plane, wooden or metallic. Sharpen the iron to a somewhat more pronounced curve than shown for the jack plane's iron in FIG. 145, chapter 14, and set the mouth as wide as possible. With a metal plane this can usually be accomplished by moving the frog (the assembly that holds the cutting iron and capiron to the plane's body) backwards. Most metal-bodied planes' frogs are attached by two screws; superior models also have a longitudinal adjustment screw. A wooden plane's mouth may be made wider by jointing the plane's sole. If you obtain a second-hand wooden jack plane it will usually be necessary to do this anyway in order to make the sole flat and true. Lastly, set the capiron

back from the cutting edge a good ⅛ in. so that thick shavings can be taken. Do not try to use an unaltered jack plane as a scrub plane since the mouth will continually clog up with all the loose fibrous material and the cutting edge will quickly dull. Once you discover how efficiently a scrub plane works you will be tempted to attack whole logs; it is almost as satisfying as using a broad axe or an adze to make a usable timber out of a log.

The scrub plane is used to remove the roughness and leave the board ready for the jack plane. This process is sometimes referred to as 'hogging'. It is not terribly important to take note of grain direction or even knots at this stage; you are not interested in producing a surface that is perfectly smooth. As soon as most of the saw marks are gone and you can see the grain, it is time to switch to a regular jack plane.

The next step is to make this now relatively smooth surface flat. Place the winding sticks at right angles across the board, one at the far end, and the other successively closer to you along the length of the board. Sight from the stick closest to you to the stick placed at the far end of the board as shown in FIG. 149. In the unlikely event the board is perfectly flat — not in winding — the top

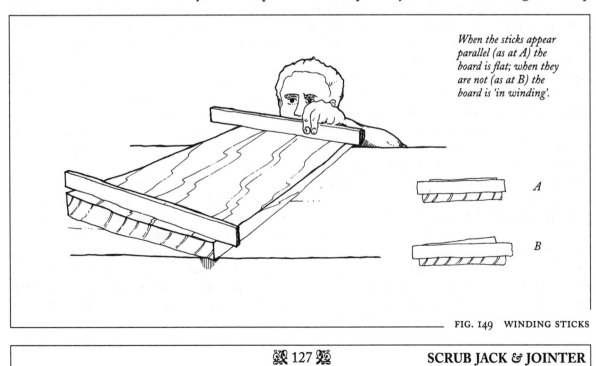

When the sticks appear parallel (as at A) the board is flat; when they are not (as at B) the board is 'in winding'.

A

B

FIG. 149   WINDING STICKS

edges of both sticks will be perfectly parallel. But if one stick's edge is higher than the other's, you will now know where to plane in order to achieve flatness.

At the same time as you use the jack plane to produce flatness along the entire length of the board, you should also be concerned with two other things: removing the curved marks of the scrub plane and not curving the board. The latter requires special attention, for there is a tendency to round over the ends of the board unless you concentrate on how you plane. At the beginning of each stroke be sure to press more on the toe of the plane, and at the end of each stroke be sure to press more on the heel. In fact, plane as if you were attempting to produce a hollow board.

The biggest surprise to most beginners is that the use of the jack plane does not consist simply in planing from one end of the board to the other, in a straight and lengthwise fashion. By all means begin in such a way, but where use of the winding sticks indicates that one corner or other area of the board needs to be reduced more than another, it is often more efficient to plane diagonally in localized areas. Furthermore, in order to remove the longitudinal marks of the scrub plane in the most efficient manner, alternate a complete lengthwise planing of the entire board with a complete diagonal planing, and then with a complete transverse planing. Transverse planing is especially effective in reducing high spots, both side-to-side and end-to-end. It will also make obvious which areas need more attention, since when you plane across the board any hollow areas that are left will still show the marks of the lengthwise passes, and when planing lengthwise transverse planing marks will be similarly visible.

These methods work well only if the plane is properly adjusted. This implies that the iron is well sharpened, properly shaped, well seated, and correctly adjusted for depth, and that the capiron is set so that at the edges of the iron's cutting edge there is zero clearance. If the crown is sufficient, the distance between the capiron and the cutting edge at the center should be about 1/16 in. to 1/8 in.

Proper adjustment also implies that the plane's sole is flat and smooth. Both wooden and metal planes will work more easily if their soles are waxed slightly. A candle stub is useful for this. Lastly, the gap between the front of the cutting edge and the front of the opening in the sole of the plane (the mouth) should not be excessive. This distance is critical when attempting to produce ultimate smoothness with a smooth plane, since the smaller it is made the finer are the shavings that may be taken and the more quickly they will be broken, thus preventing tearout, even on a minute scale.

With practice your need for the winding sticks will diminish to the point that one or two sightings will be sufficient to produce the required results. Holding the bottom edge of the jack plane itself across the board is another quick way to check the progress being made. An alternative method is periodically to turn the board over onto the side being planed and see if it rocks; any fulcrum point obviously needs to be reduced. A final check for hollows and rises can be made by holding the straightedge against the board in various directions: lengthwise, across the board, and diagonally.

By the time you have produced a flat surface, the board should also be quite smooth. A few passes with a more finely set panel plane (or any close-mouthed plane from 16 in. to 22 in. long with a medium-crowned cutting edge, known variously by different manufacturers as a fore plane, a short try plane, or even a long smooth plane) can remove areas of roughness or tearout. If your jack plane has been properly sharpened, even though it be set to take fairly thick and coarse shavings, it should have been possible to plane in virtually any direction, regardless of grain, and still produce a smooth surface. Nevertheless, by virtue of the more pronounced crown typical of a jack plane's iron, planing strokes will still be visible as shallow depressions in the surface of the wood. These should not be enough to affect the next operation, that of marking the board for thickness.

PLANING FOR THICKNESS

ONE ADVANTAGE OF SURFACING A BOARD BY hand over using a jointer to produce the first reference surface is that there is no limit to the width of the board that may be so planed. The next operation is to achieve the required thickness. Thicknessing by hand may also be accomplished with no regard for any limitations imposed by jointer or thicknesser or planer. Moreover, it is almost as easy to produce a tapered board as it is a parallel board; the only difference lies in the marking out.

A marking gauge is used to scribe a line around the edges. Since these are usually still unplaned and therefore in a fairly rough state, marking will cause no permanent disfigurement. Hold the face of the gauge closely to the finished surface of the board. A sharp pencil run in the groove left by the gauge will make the line easier to see.

Secure the board face side down and proceed as before. This time there should be no need for any wedges, since a flat board will not rock, and your bench top should also be perfectly flat if it has been periodically dressed (using the winding stick technique if necessary). Use the scrub plane if necessary. Change to the jack plane as soon as the surface is clean enough to permit continuous shavings to be taken with the jack, and this time pay attention to reducing the board to the level of the gauged line around all edges.

When close to this line, throw the winding sticks on to check your progress, even though it should be easy enough to see whether you have approached the line at all points to the same degree. If you have, the board will be fairly flat since this surface has been referenced off a known flat surface.

A useful trick is to set the marking gauge a hair thicker than needed. This will allow you to see when you have reached the desired level more easily than by having to bend down and peer at the edges continually, since when the plane reaches the mark a thin sliver of wood that was the upper edge of the marked line will appear. At this point you should proceed a little more slowly until the sliver has been produced on both sides, indicating that you have reached the required thickness at both edges.

The remarks made earlier about planing across, and even against, the grain apply even more to smooth planing. If you have flattened and thicknessed the board in the manner just described and have, despite your best efforts at sharpening and tuning your plane, been unable to avoid some tearout, this may be corrected with the smooth plane. The smooth plane, even more so than its larger and cruder relatives, should be capable of working in any direction without raising or tearing the grain. If it cannot, the fault lies with a mouth that has become too wide, a cutting edge that is insufficiently sharp, or, more probably, a combination of too much iron protruding through the sole and the capiron not being set closely enough to the cutting edge.

In any event, use a panel plane or a smooth plane to bring the thicknessed board to perfect thickness, working alternately along the board and then, when the entire surface has been planed, across the board, finishing with the merest shavings taken in a lengthwise fashion.

Basic planing techniques are applicable: a slightly skewed approach is easier than planing straight ahead, and in the final stages little downwards pressure should be necessary. In fact, one measure of an adequately sharpened plane is that you should be able to place the plane at one end of the board, tilt the board, and watch the plane slide down the board unaided, removing a perfect shaving, feathered to nothing at its edges, as it does so.

PLANING TO WIDTH

IT IS CONCEIVABLE THAT YOU WILL HAVE reached this point with as yet no straight edges, especially if your board was resawed from waned or flat-sawn material straight from the bole. If the edges vary more than ½ in. from straight it will be

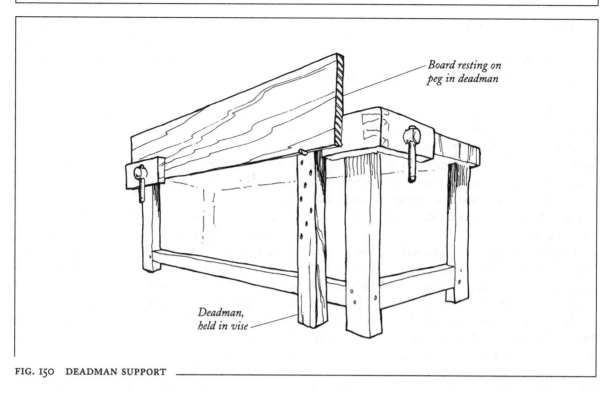

*Board resting on
peg in deadman*

*Deadman,
held in vise*

FIG. 150   DEADMAN SUPPORT

quickest to mark a line and rip to it. It is more likely, however, that at least one edge will be fairly straight, even if it is nowhere near square. In this event the next step is the same should you now wish either simply to true this edge or to remove an area from the center of the thicknessed board.

Secure the board with the edge to be straightened and squared uppermost in the face vise of your bench. If it is long, the near end may have to be supported by a deadman or pegs inserted in the leg of the bench as in FIG. 150. Having marked a line with a pencil and straightedge, or even a chalk line if the board is very long, and having squinted along this line to check that it is indeed straight, proceed to reduce the board to the mark. If there is ¼ in. or more material to lose, start with the jack plane; if less, use a jointer plane. In both cases use the longest plane you own, since the greater the length the easier it will be to establish a straight cut. A long plane will bridge hollows and cut only high spots until the entire edge lies in the same plane. A short plane will ride up and down

the curves cutting all equally as it goes, as shown in FIG. 151.

Aside from planing to the line, which needs only to be marked on the face side, since the attempt to mark a perfectly placed line on the other side is difficult and prone to error, your chief concern is to plane the edge squarely. (In the event you are aiming for a beveled edge, it is still easier and safer to plane a square edge to the height of the upper edge of the bevel first, and then mark the lower edge and plane to it, with or without special guides such as auxiliary shoes or fences attached to the plane or the work.) Your chief assistance in this search for perfect squareness should be a small trysquare, whose truth you have tested or trust. Use it frequently at various places along the length of the board. You will quickly see where the angle changes. Mark the high spots, and on the next stroke move the plane so the center of the cutting edge passes over the marked areas. Since a properly shaped jointer plane's iron has only a slight crown to it, rather than the exaggerated curve of the jack plane or the scrub

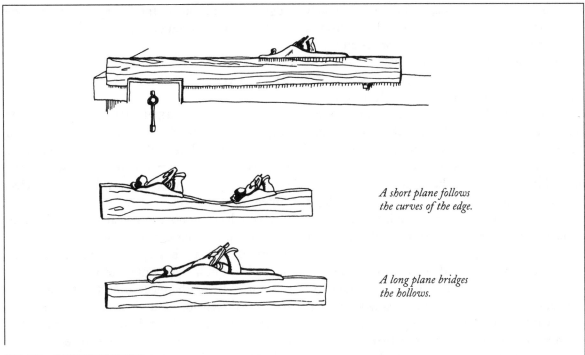

*A short plane follows
the curves of the edge.*

*A long plane bridges
the hollows.*

FIG. 151   LENGTH PLANING

plane, nothing will be removed at either edge of the typical 2 in. to 2½ in.-wide iron. As a result, the effect illustrated in FIG. 152 is easily obtained, and a simple manipulation of the plane from side to side as required is all that is necessary to remove any unwanted out-of-squareness.

Though the edge you are planing will typically be quite narrow — narrower than the jointer plane — it is still a good idea to plane with as much skew as is possible while still keeping the entire length of the plane resting on the edge. Additionally, and in contrast to the way in which other planes are used, two fingers of the left hand held beneath the plane so that they form a fence resting against the side of the board will also prove useful. But if you do this, do not attempt to maintain a grip on the knob at the front of the plane. On metal-bodied planes this knob is so prominent that it demands to be held, but it is really only there as a result of the tool manufacturer's desire for a consistent design across his entire range of planes, even on the very smallest planes, most notably the diminutive Stanley™ 1 and 2,

whose knobs are far too tiny to be grasped by any but small children. Most British and American wooden planes have no such knob, and even stuffed planes (top-quality, metal-soled planes with wood infill, such as those made at the beginning of the 20th century by firms such as Norris™, Spiers™, and Mathieson™) have no such attention-demanding protrusion. So-called

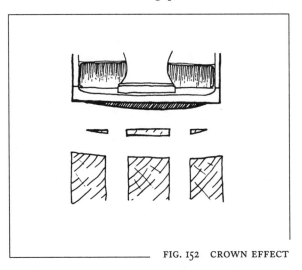

FIG. 152   CROWN EFFECT

horn planes do, of course, feature an extremely large 'horn' at the front, but these derive from a different tradition. They are far more common in Europe than in Britain or America.

While continuing to check and adjust for squareness as you approach the line, use the machinist's straightedge to check for straightness to a degree not observable by looking at the line. Place the straightedge lengthwise on the planed edge and see if it rocks or can be rotated around any point. Furthermore, bend down so that your eyes are level with the edge and look for any light that may show beneath the straightedge. This is made easier if there is a white wall or a light behind the bench.

The second edge should be produced in a manner similar to the first. If it is to be parallel you may mark the line on both sides, using a marking gauge with a long stem — or a panel gauge if the width is too great — the face of either tool's head held closely to the first edge of the board. If this edge is indeed square, the lines you mark will be exactly opposite each other.

RELAXING

JUST AS WHEN REDUCING STOCK FROM large balks by machine, it is a good idea, no matter how well seasoned you may think your material is, to prepare the stock in two stages. Otherwise you may be surprised by unexpected dimensional changes.

If you have removed a relatively small piece from material much larger, the side that was innermost may not be as perfectly in balance with the ambient moisture-content of your shop as the outer side. Bring the piece almost to the required finished dimension and then set it aside for a while — a week at least, longer if you are in the middle of an extreme season — to relax before reducing it to the final, required measurement.

16

THE SMOOTH PLANE

EVALUATING A FORGOTTEN ICON

IN NINETEEN SEVENTY-FIVE RAPHAEL SALAMAN STATED, IN A BOOK THAT REMAINS A STANDARD REFERENCE WORK FOR ALL WOODWORKING-TOOL ENTHUSIASTS, BE THEY COLLECTORS OR USERS, THAT THE SMOOTH PLANE WAS STILL TO BE FOUND IN MOST woodworking shops.* He went on to remark that it was often so worn on the sole that its original thickness was considerably reduced. Today, not only is the first part of this statement somewhat less than an absolute truth, but the second part is liable to make many people wonder: thin planes — what could he have meant!? What Salaman was talking about, of course, were wooden smooth planes; nowadays, if smooth planes exist at all in a woodworking shop, they are likely to be the metal type of plane, most commonly represented by the Stanley™ model.

* R. A. Salaman. *Dictionary of Tools used in the woodworking and allied trades, c. 1700–1970*. London 1975

A FORGOTTEN ICON

FROM TIME TO TIME ARTICLES APPEAR IN woodworking magazines on how to make these metal smooth planes more efficient. Instructions may be given on improving the adjustments of the moving parts, refining the casting, or flattening the sole, but the sad truth of the matter is that the technique of using these tools is becoming less and less a part of the typical woodworker's basic knowledge about his or her craft. A tablesaw and a belt sander are often more frequently found than a smooth plane. A wooden smooth plane (FIG. 153)

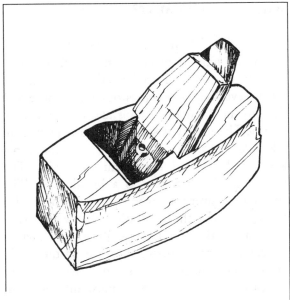

FIG. 153 SMOOTH PLANE

is now more the icon of antique-tool collecting than it is the icon of contemporary woodworking.

Tablesaws, while potentially more dangerous and noisier than their handtool counterparts, are admittedly useful and can save a lot of labor. For those for whom the product is more important than the procedure — a preference equally as reasonable for practising woodworking as liking the smell of wood, or taking pleasure from the tools, or any other of the numerous reasons that turn people into woodworkers — the tablesaw probably deserves to be the icon of contemporary woodworking. But the sander, in whatever form — belt, oscillating, reciprocating, or stationary — is a less defensible invention.

It is true that one of the most fundamental joys of woodworking derives from the impulse to make wood smooth, and that using some form of abrasive to achieve this has been common since at least Roman times. It would be hard to deny the practice completely, for there are situations where it is the only expedient, and sometimes occasions where its unique effects are impossible to duplicate by any other means, but as the pre-eminent way to smooth wood it leaves a lot to be desired. A surface that has been sanded by no matter how

fine a grit remains an abraded surface. This is fine for many materials such as metal, and can result in an impeccable smoothness and shine, but because of its cellular structure wood can never be rendered as smooth by abrasion as it can by being cleanly cut by a knife edge. The effect is easily seen after using a relatively coarse-grit abrasive: the ends of the fibers are torn, frayed, and bent; individual particles of abrasive have left scratches in the surface; and sanding residue composed of both loosened abrasive and wood dust fills the pores and surface of the wood. If the process is repeated using ever-finer grits, as is common practice, it is true that the scratches become smaller, but the other effects remain the same. A wood surface smoothed no matter how finely with abrasive can never have the shine or clarity of a well-planed or scraped surface. The effect of being able to see into the wood, and the crisp clarity of the grain figure, is lost.

The sander, however, is very fast. It achieves its second-rate effects far more easily than a plane in the hands of an unpractised beginner, although there is much to be learned; tell-tale gouges and rounded edges are common signs of inexperience with the belt sander. But you do not have to learn how to sharpen it; you just need to know how to change the belt. A handplane by comparison can seem an arcane and inefficient relic of the 'good old days' before powertools were invented.

Nevertheless, if you want the incomparable look and feel of a surface that has been cleanly cut, a surface that is at once smooth, flat, and alive, you must learn how to use a plane and a scraper. Both have edges designed to cut rather than bludgeon or tear the surface. There is a limit, depending on the composition of the cutting edge's material, beyond which you cannot get any sharper, and under a very powerful microscope even the most keenly sharpened edge will be seen to be more saw-like than knife-like, but taken in conjunction with the burnishing action of the plane's sole, especially a wooden plane's sole, this cutting edge is capable of producing a far superior smoothness than can any abrasive.

THE SMOOTH PLANE

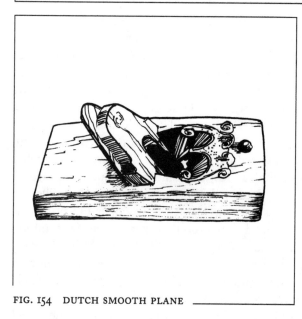

FIG. 154 DUTCH SMOOTH PLANE

A FAR FROM RARE TOOL

ALTHOUGH IT MAY NO LONGER BE AS common as Salaman reported, the wooden smooth plane is far from rare. Plenty of planes may still be found at fleamarkets, in antique stores, and in the inventories of old-tool dealers throughout the country. America shares many of its woodworking tools in common with Britain, and across the Atlantic wooden smooth planes may be found that are virtually identical to their American cousins, along with many more from slightly different European heritages, such as those of France, Holland (FIG. 154), and Germany. Tools from these and other European countries may look a little strange to the American eye — their proportions may be slightly different, handle shapes may vary, and they may be ornamented and finished as the result of a different sensibility — but they will still be instantly recognizable as smooth planes. Farther afield are Oriental planes, of which the wooden Japanese plane (FIG. 155) is perhaps unique in representing a class of tool, virtually obsolete in America, that is actually becoming more popular to the point where, unlike its Western counterpart, it can be regularly found for sale in mailorder tool catalogs.

WHICH ONE IS BEST?

ALTHOUGH ITS GENERAL SHAPE AND USUAL size is enough to make a smooth plane easily recognizable as such, a bewildering variety of types nevertheless becomes observable once you start to hunt out these tools and examine them closely. The variety is such that you may want to ask: "Are they all intended to do the same job, and how do I know which is best?" The answer to the first part is a broad: 'Yes'. The ability to answer the second part will come with experience and the realization that which type of plane works best for any given individual is largely a matter of personal choice. In the world of wooden smooth planes, apart from certain hopeless cases noted below, almost any plane can be made to perform like a champion once the working principles are understood.

There are so many planes still in existence that you need not bother with any tool that is incomplete. In the majority of cases 'complete' means a tool consisting of a stock or body, a wedge, and an iron usually consisting of two parts: a cutting iron and a capiron, held together by a bolt (see FIG. 156). In American-made irons the short bolt holding the cutting iron to the capiron is screwed

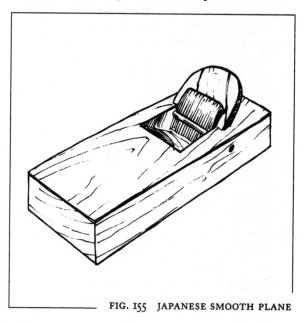

FIG. 155 JAPANESE SMOOTH PLANE

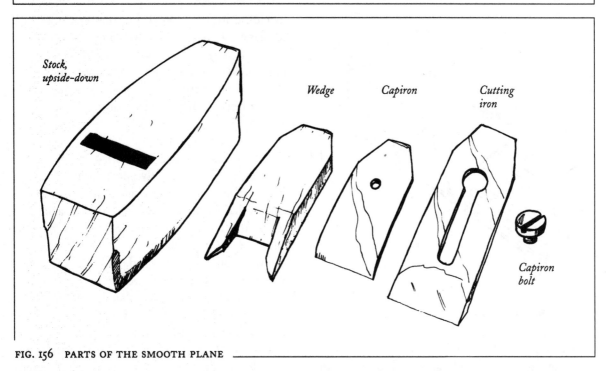

Stock, upside-down

Wedge *Capiron* *Cutting iron*

Capiron bolt

FIG. 156 PARTS OF THE SMOOTH PLANE

directly into a threaded hole in the capiron; in British-made irons there is often a small brass boss fixed to the top face of the capiron (see FIG. 166), and the short bolt is threaded through the capiron into this boss. In its simplest form that is all there is: stock, wedge, and iron.

Planes dating from earlier than the beginning of the 19th century, as well as cheaper models produced well after this date, sometimes into the 20th century, have single irons. Since these single irons were not designed to be used with a capiron, they may be identified as such by the fact that they are 'uncut', that is, there is no slot through which the capiron bolt may be inserted. Old-tool dealers sometimes offer for sale irons, or packets of irons, manufactured expressly for wooden planes, and identify them as 'cut' or 'uncut'.

Armed with this knowledge you ought not to be fooled by a plane loosely fitted with a single, cut iron; you will know at once that the capiron is missing. At the same time, you should be aware that a plane designed for use with a single iron will necessarily have a narrower slot cut in the sides of its throat than a plane designed to

accommodate a double iron. If you find a plane with a wedge and a single, cut iron that appear to fit well, you should entertain the possibility that the original iron was either used up or lost and has been replaced. A cut iron will function equally as well as an uncut iron — although the reverse is not true — and the substitution of cut for uncut is perfectly reasonable and acceptable.

Apart from certain specialized designs, some of which, like the modern block plane, still exist, a double iron is usually to be preferred, since the capiron adds superior chip-breaking capability to the plane's mouth. This translates into the ability to plane without tearout in any direction, with or against the grain. Additionally, a capiron lends support to the very end of the cutting edge. Therefore, choose a double-iron smooth plane over a single-iron model.

Having assured yourself that all parts are present and the plane is complete you need to check the throat (see FIG. 157). This is the hole in the center of the plane where the iron is inserted. There is much damage that can be repaired in a smooth plane to make it good as new: you can

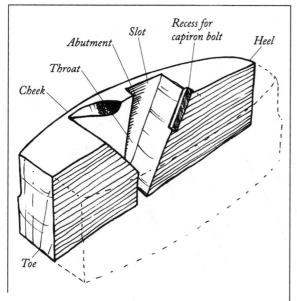

FIG. 157   PARTS OF THE STOCK

unyielding iron — something that can happen if the plane has been left untouched for years and allowed to dry out, as well as happening much more quickly if the plane is suddenly brought into a drier environment — the thin cheeks may crack. It is extremely difficult to restore them to the degree of integrity necessary to hold the wedge and iron assembly in use.

Other cracks and checks may appear more alarming, and occasionally you may find a plane with a crack so big that it is obvious the wedge will not hold, but in general, small cracks and checks affect only the appearance and not the performance of the plane.

As with any piece of wood, its essential soundness should be considered before taking it home, but wormholes, other insect damage, and even rot are not necessarily terminal. A smooth plane is an object sufficiently small that complete and safe elimination of any insect pest is very easy: simply place the stock in a sealed plastic bag, thereby keeping out any moisture, and leave it in the freezer for a couple of days.

replace irons, make new wedges, close the mouth by inlaying extra wood, and add buttons and handles; but there are two things that are almost impossible to repair: broken abutments and cracked cheeks (FIG. 158). Either of these conditions is generally cause for immediate and total rejection of a plane. Both determine the fitness of the body to hold the wedge and iron accurately and securely. If this is not possible you will never be able to plane with any nicety or efficiency.

The abutments are the protrusions at the side of the throat immediately in front of the iron. They are formed by the slot into which the iron is inserted, and are what the wedge is forced against when the iron is secured. If they are broken or partially missing the wedge's holding ability is compromised.

Cracked cheeks generally result from the wedge having split the sides. This happens because the wedge is a stout and unyielding piece of wood and the cheeks are the thinnest part of the stock's sides. If the wedge is banged in too forcefully, especially by an uninformed user hitting the top of the wedge to set it in place instead of by using the correct method of tapping the front end of the stock, or if the stock has simply shrunk around an

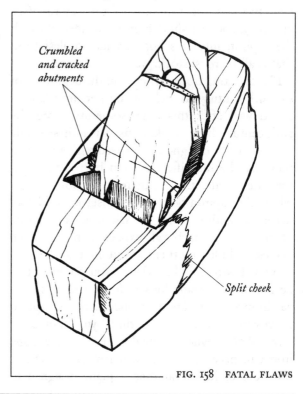

FIG. 158   FATAL FLAWS

Small areas of punky wood or incipient rot can be prevented from spreading by normal care, such as keeping the plane in a reasonably dry and well-ventilated area like a toolbox, rather than in the dank and moldy basement where you may have found the tool. If they do not appear to compromise the throat or consume too large a proportion of the sole, these defects can be ignored.

Once the condition of the stock has been stabilized by finding it a home suitable for any other woodworking tool, it will require very little care. Apart from shooting the sole from time to time to ensure absolute flatness (the very procedure which results in the reduction of the tool's thickness mentioned by Salaman), normal use will generally transfer sufficient oil from the hands to keep the wood in good condition. If in doubt, rub the stock occasionally with linseed oil. An extremely dry stock — one that appears grey and dusty — may even be immersed in linseed oil for a while, but should need this treatment only once if subsequently used normally.

BASIC CONDITIONING

STARTING FROM THE PREMISE THAT MOST wooden smooth planes you are likely to find will be old, second-hand, and often abused or neglected, you will almost certainly find one or more of the following procedures necessary. Do not let this dismay you; using the smooth plane efficiently requires a certain amount of skill, attainable only after a certain amount of practice — even using a sander requires a little practice — and being familiar with the way the tool is constructed will make it less likely that you will try to use it the wrong way, and you will be able to produce good results more quickly.

REMOUTHING

MOST WOODEN SMOOTH PLANES ARE MADE from beech, which is a fairly close-grained and hard-wearing wood. Nevertheless, constant use will eventually wear the sole down. Beech is also a fairly stable species, but despite the fact that well-made planes were cut from the raw material in such a way as to optimize its stability and hard-wearing characteristics, changes in ambient moisture will affect the plane body, just like any other piece of wood, with the result that the sole of the plane will require flattening from time to time. Unlike the soles of Japanese planes, which are designed to bear on the work only at certain points, the sole of a Western smooth plane must be perfectly flat over its entire area. This is guaranteed by occasional shooting of the sole as the need arises.

These two facts, wear and the subsequent need for shooting, eventually result in the plane's stock becoming thinner from top to bottom than when originally made. This in itself is of no great importance, the overall loss in the weight that is sometimes helpful when planing certain materials is insignificant, but thinning has a serious effect on the plane's mouth (the aperture in the sole through which the cutting edge of the iron projects). Because the cutting iron, and the capiron if so fitted, is held in an angled, wedge-shaped slot, the mouth becomes wider as the stock becomes thinner. This is not good.

When new, the width of the mouth is just sufficient to accommodate the width of the iron plus a little sideways movement enabling the cutting edge to be angled slightly as the need dictates. The measurement of the mouth from front to back largely determines how fine a shaving can be taken and how well the plane can be used against the grain. Yes!, for all those who have been told that one should always plane with the grain, note that a properly set-up smooth plane should be able to plane equally well in any direction; it is the adjustment of the capiron and cutting iron in combination with a properly proportioned mouth that makes this possible.

The larger the mouth, the thicker is the shaving that can be taken, simply because this allows a fatter shaving to pass up into the throat of the plane.

A thick shaving taken against the grain with a wide mouth can lead to tearout.

FIG. 159   TEAROUT

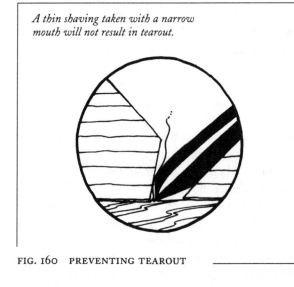

A thin shaving taken with a narrow mouth will not result in tearout.

FIG. 160   PREVENTING TEAROUT

But if such a fat shaving is taken against the grain, there is a tendency for the cut to run ever more deeply into the wood as it follows the sloping grain (FIG. 159). By making the mouth extremely narrow, only a thin shaving can be taken, which upon entering the throat is forced backwards by the combined relationship of the curved front edge of the capiron and the narrowness of the mouth, and is consequently broken, thereby eliminating the possibility of tearout (see FIG. 160).

Some planes are needed for general stock-reduction and surfacing, and their mouths may be such that there is as much as ⅛ in. gap in front of the cutting edge. But for a smooth plane meant to be used for final surfacing, the narrowest possible mouth is preferred. If the gap has become too great it may be narrowed by inlaying a small piece of wood as shown in FIG. 161, using either a small

The mouth has become wider as the sole has worn.

A small mouth piece (shown after gluing but before being planed flush) narrows the mouth.

FIG. 161   COMPENSATING FOR WEAR

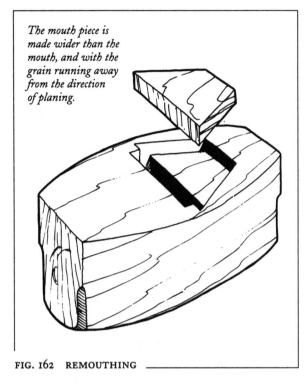

The mouth piece is made wider than the mouth, and with the grain running away from the direction of planing.

FIG. 162 REMOUTHING

router, a Dremel™-type tool, or a mallet and chisel. Take care to orient the grain of the inlay, known as the mouth piece, so that it runs away from the direction of planing, and inlay the piece so that its corners have some bearing and will resist any backwards pressure (see FIG. 162). Make the mouth piece first, and then scribe around its outline on the plane's sole, cutting away the waste area to form a tight fit. It need not be any thicker than ¼ in., but it should be inlaid so that when glued — never nail or screw it in place — its surface will be a little proud of the plane's sole. This way the entire sole can be shot level after the glue has dried.

It is possible to remouth planes with fanciful inlays in odd shapes, even human profiles, as well as using color-contrasting wood, but try to find something of similar hardness to the beech, or whatever your particular plane's stock is made of, so that the whole sole will wear evenly. Make sure the mouth piece is long enough; the rear edge can always be trimmed to make the mouth wider, but it cannot be made narrower.

SHOOTING THE SOLE

IN ORDER TO MAINTAIN AN ABSOLUTELY flat sole the bottom of the plane is itself planed as needed. You can do this by running the plane over a power jointer, but this method is generally only safe for longer wooden planes. To shoot a smooth plane it is easier to push it across a longer wooden plane, such as a jointer plane or a jack plane, held upside-down in the bench vise. This, of course, implies that you have such additional planes and that they too have perfectly flat soles.

In the beginning this can result in a Catch-22 situation: how can you achieve flatness without something flat to start with? The answer is bit by bit. Treat the sole of the plane just as you would any other piece of wood requiring to be made absolutely flat, but do not sand it because you do not want to allow any abrasive particles anywhere near the cutting edge or to become embedded in the sole where they may scratch the very surface the plane will be trying to smooth.

After a while you may be able to true up the sole simply by holding it upside-down in the bench vise and taking a few passes with another well-adjusted smooth plane. Eventually the shooting will become less radical as both you and your planes become more sensitive to what is truly flat.

Whenever shooting the sole is necessary be sure to do so with the iron and wedge in place, albeit retracted into the throat, so that any deformation caused by the pressure of a secured wedge and iron assembly is accounted for. If you take the assembly out and then shoot the stock you run the risk of creating a flat sole that might deform out of flatness when the iron assembly is reinserted.

Equally as important as perfect flatness is the perpendicularity of the sole to the vertical axis of the plane. Measure this by holding a trysquare against the side of the stock and the sole as shown in FIG. 163. Although the typical coffin-shape of smooth planes makes them less useful than longer planes such as jacks and jointers for shooting edges (a method of planing perfectly square edges on boards accomplished by running the plane on

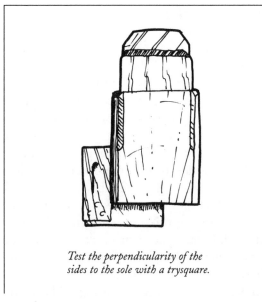

*Test the perpendicularity of the
sides to the sole with a trysquare.*

FIG. 163   TESTING FOR SQUARENESS

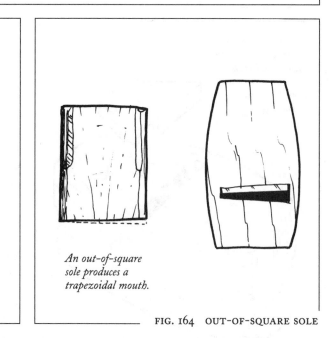

*An out-of-square
sole produces a
trapezoidal mouth.*

FIG. 164   OUT-OF-SQUARE SOLE

its side against the edge of a workpiece held in a shooting-board), if their sole is not absolutely perpendicular to their vertical axis the shape of the mouth will not be a perfect rectangle, and the front and back edges will not be parallel, with the result that the cutting edge of the iron will not project evenly from side to side (see FIG. 164). Although some slight sideways tilting of the cutting iron should be possible (in case it should be necessary to compensate for less-than-perfectly squarely sharpened edges, or to make possible other specialized planing operations that may require differently thicknessed shavings), there will be rarely enough adjustment to compensate for a trapezoidal mouth.

After shooting the sole, gently round the perimeter edges and rub some candle wax onto the sole. This last will make the plane slide more easily and provide a certain measure of protection against further moisture-content change.

THROAT WIDTH

AS MENTIONED EARLIER, THE IRON SHOULD fit in the mouth with just a little room to spare at either side for slight sideways adjustment. Over the years some planes may have shrunk in width to the extent that the iron may have become a very tight fit in the throat. This not only makes any sideways adjustment impossible but can also make depth adjustment difficult and iron removal hard. It can even cause damage to the cheeks of the stock if allowed to continue, for an iron blade will eventually split a shrinking wooden stock. The obvious cure may be to widen the slot by filing or chiseling the inside of the throat, but resist this temptation. It is better to file or grind the iron assembly to a narrower width and preserve the integrity of the stock's strength in this vulnerable area.

A PERFECT BED TO LIE ON

NO MATTER HOW WELL SHARPENED THE cutting edge and how well fitted and adjusted the capiron may be, if these cannot be held securely by the wedge in the throat all will be in vain, and chattering, choking, and frustration will attend every effort to produce that perfect surface. The wedge should fit its slot well, and the cutting iron should seat flat on the bed of the throat without rocking. Both conditions can be compromised by resinous buildups. Keep both the wedge and the iron clean. The wedge, being wooden, is subject to wear and, like the sole, may occasionally need to be planed smooth again. Do this with care, removing as little material as possible and preserving the correct wedge-shape. After a plane has been repeatedly shot and remouthed, the ends of the wedge may be too long and require some shortening. In this case notice that it is not enough simply to shorten them; their tips must preserve their original wedge-shapes as shown in FIG. 165 in order that shavings entering the throat are properly deflected and do not catch on blunt edges and clog the opening.

Test the flatness of the bed by removing the wedge and holding the iron assembly against the bed to see if it rests securely without rocking. Rocking may be caused by a slight deformity in the iron or the capiron, and may disappear when the wedge is pushed home. But more often than not, any rocking must be eliminated by judicious scraping of the bed, or by temporarily inserting one or two shavings, or a thin piece of card or paper, between the iron and the bed. Check that the capiron bolt has enough room and its slot does not require enlarging. When making any physical adjustments to the bed be careful not to alter the relationship of the overall plane of the bed to the sole, or the iron will not project evenly.

IRON ADJUSTMENT

LASTLY, WE MUST ADDRESS THE ESSENTIAL question of iron adjustment, by which is meant not only correctly introducing and removing the iron assembly into and out of the stock, but also properly adjusting the relationship between the cutting iron and the capiron. The more the iron projects, the thicker will be the shaving that can be taken, but the position of the capiron also plays a vital role here. The greater the distance between the leading edge of the capiron and the cutting

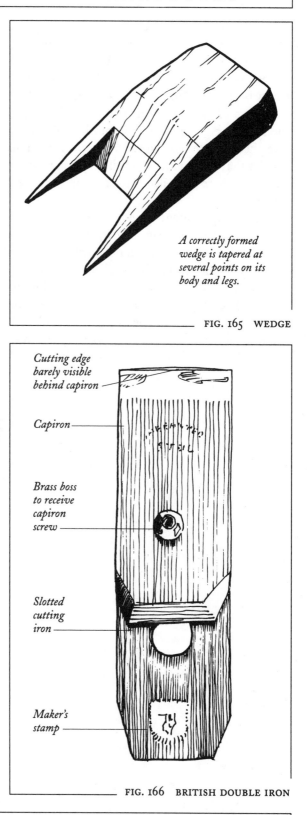

A correctly formed wedge is tapered at several points on its body and legs.

FIG. 165   WEDGE

Cutting edge barely visible behind capiron

Capiron

Brass boss to receive capiron screw

Slotted cutting iron

Maker's stamp

FIG. 166   BRITISH DOUBLE IRON

edge, the thicker will be the shaving. For final smoothing the very thinnest shavings are needed, and a properly sharpened cutting edge that is formed with a very slight crown should project so barely beyond the front of the capiron, and only in the center of its width, that you must hold it up to the light to be able to see the thin line of cutting iron that does indeed project (see FIG. 166). This implies that the front edge of the capiron must be almost as sharp as the cutting edge, and precisely shaped.

These requirements are common to most planes, wooden and iron, but what is unique to wooden planes is the manner of adjusting the iron assembly in the stock: Firstly, place the plane on the bench top, or other wooden surface, and insert the iron assembly so that the cutting edge rests on the bench. Then insert the wedge by hand with sufficient force to hold the iron assembly securely. Now pick up the plane and turn it over so you can sight along the sole and see how much the cutting edge projects. To cause the cutting edge to project more, tap the front of the stock; to cause the iron to retract, tap the back of the stock. Some planes — typically the larger bench planes — are fitted with strike buttons (see FIG. 134, chapter 12) set in the top of the stock just forward of the throat. These may be tapped to cause the iron to project further. Do not use a hammer; remember the golden rule of good woodworking: 'wood to wood and metal to metal'. Use a mallet to tap the stock and wedge. If you need to hit the iron to adjust it sideways, use a light hammer.

In time you will make depth adjustments by feel alone: a slight tap and a trial shaving, another tap and another shaving, and so on. The shaving should emerge from the throat almost effortlessly, and there should be no marks left on the surface of the wood, since if the capiron is properly set the edges of the shaving should taper into nothing.

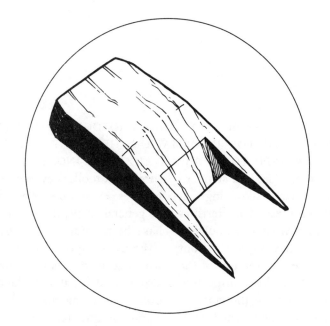

17

THE JACK PLANE

VERSATILE & MASTERFUL

SOME TIME AGO A WOODWORKER SENT ME A PHOTOGRAPH OF AN UNUSUAL WOODEN PLANE WITH A REQUEST FOR INFORMATION. HE HAD FOUND THIS TOOL IN THE SOUTHWEST. IT APPEARED TO BE ABOUT EIGHTEEN INCHES LONG, WITH A FAIRLY low-angle iron of square profile set in a standard mouth. Apart from the rather shallow angle at which the iron was seated, these characteristics were not too remarkable, but what stood out was a pair of large transverse handles, one at the front and one at the back, mounted on the top of the plane's stock (see FIG. 167). A closer inspection revealed something else of interest: the cutting-iron assembly was stamped with an unusual series of marks and various words in an apparently foreign language.

A tool like this would probably have aroused little interest a generation or two ago, since it would have seemed to the casual observer to be little different from many other tools common in shops and toolkits everywhere. Indeed, its salient features — the wood it was made from, its length, its general shape, the profile of the iron — would have been common to a host of everyday tools. Even the form of its iron (FIG. 168), the shape of which seemed curious to my correspondent, was also typical of, if not standard for, most plane irons then being made. A contemporary wood-worker might have remarked on the transverse handles, and might also perhaps have noticed the foreign provenance of the blade, but even so, the tool would probably have been regarded with little curiosity.

Progress marches on, and with it, tool design. A form that was recognizable for several hundred

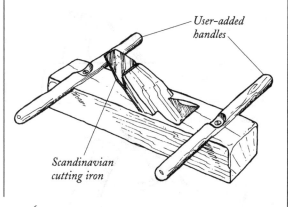

User-added handles

Scandinavian cutting iron

FIG. 167   MODIFIED JACK PLANE

years suddenly becomes an unusual oddity, and the truly novel feature is confused with what was once commonplace. This process unfortunately results in much that was useful being discarded and lost. While some people are now beginning to question the hitherto received opinion that all progress is a good thing, few are willing to look backwards, feeling that to do so would involve sacrificing advances that have become virtually indispensable to our contemporary way of life. But this is not necessarily so; there is much that has been discarded in the name of progress that is

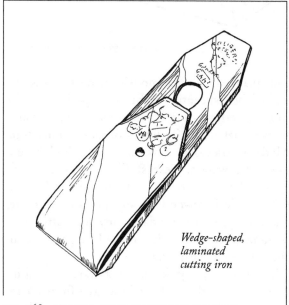

Wedge-shaped, laminated cutting iron

FIG. 168   TYPICAL 19TH CENTURY DOUBLE-IRON

still valid and that in many instances might still be the better way to go. The common wooden jack plane is one example.

SIMPLER TOOLS, MORE SOPHISTICATED RESULTS

FOR A VERY LONG TIME ALL THAT WAS needed for much woodworking was a handsaw, a plane or two, and various other small, inexpensive handtools. These days most people assume that they need a tablesaw, an electric router, and as many other expensive powertools as can be afforded. This erroneous idea is a shame for two reasons: first, because it discourages too many people who cannot afford such tools, and second, because although it is easy enough to switch on the tablesaw and push a piece of wood through to make a quick and fairly accurate cut, achieving any finesse, even on a powertool, requires skill that is unlikely to be developed so long as a quick and easy — albeit cruder — method of work is so ready to hand.

Jack planes like the one in the photograph I received cost very much less than a planer, but properly used can produce finer work. Initially, it might seem easier to push a board through a planer than to develop the hand-planing skill necessary with the jack plane, but look at the equation more closely and the disparities vanish.

Firstly, consider the time it takes to earn the money to buy the planer. You could spend the same amount of time and achieve sufficient skill with the handtool. Once this is learned you no longer have to put up with noise, dust-collection problems, or the danger that is inherent with powertools. Best of all, the surfaces you produce are finished, and do not need to be sanded. This avoids the use of more machines and the creation of more dust. To someone with no experience of well-maintained handtools used properly this always sounds hard to believe, but look at all the impeccable woodwork that was produced in the last three hundred years, before powertools were introduced. Yes, it is true that the machine can work faster and do more work in a shorter time, but unless you are making your living at woodwork, where is the rush? And are not safety and a closer, quieter approach more pleasant?

Secondly, a jack plane is no harder to condition and keep in good shape than is a power planer. Both have edges that must be sharpened; the jack plane's allow a little more leeway if your technique is less than perfect. Both tools can be adjusted to take bigger or smaller shavings, but the jack plane can be adjusted to produce a smooth surface. Furthermore, there are few restrictions on the size and shape of the board that a jack plane can be used on.

THE JACK PLANE DEFINED

THE JACK PLANE IS ACTUALLY ONLY ONE member of a fairly large family of planes known as the bench planes. It is designed for the specific purpose of making a rough-sawn board flat and true. Other members of the family are intended for other tasks, such as fine finish-smoothing or the easy creation of long, straight edges. But, true to its name, the jack plane can be made to serve a variety of purposes; it is indeed a jack of all trades. If I were allowed only one plane, it would be a jack, for with it I could dress rough boards, make their surfaces flat and their edges true, and even produce an acceptable finished surface, ready for polishing.

What defines a jack plane is a combination of its length, the profile of its iron, and the size of its mouth. These three things, all of which are surprisingly variable — depending on the skill and preferences of the user — are, within broad limits, the same for any kind of jack plane you might find, whether this be a contemporary new metal-and-plastic tool from the local hardware store or an old wooden model discovered at a fleamarket or in an antique store (see FIG. 169). Incidentally, between these two extremes of brand new and very old there are many other forms of

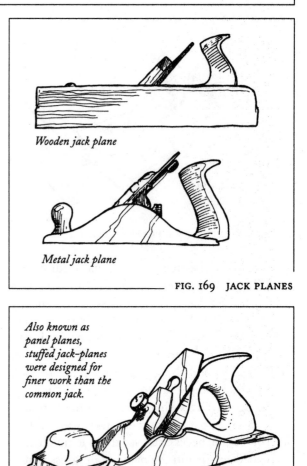

Wooden jack plane

Metal jack plane

FIG. 169   JACK PLANES

Also known as panel planes, stuffed jack-planes were designed for finer work than the common jack.

FIG. 170   'STUFFED' JACK PLANE

jack plane, including models made towards the end of the last century in Britain especially for the most discriminating cabinetmaker and woodworker that are masterpieces of tool manufacture. Made of rosewood, dovetailed metal bodies, and gunmetal wedges, these 'stuffed' planes (FIG. 170) — so called because the metal bodies are filled in with exotic hardwood — are the best there are, and their price, even today, many years after their manufacture, reflects this, often being more than the price of a cheap planer.

The length of a jack plane may vary from 14 in. to 18 in., and the width of the sole from 1¾ in. to 2½ in. The iron is essentially square, a slight

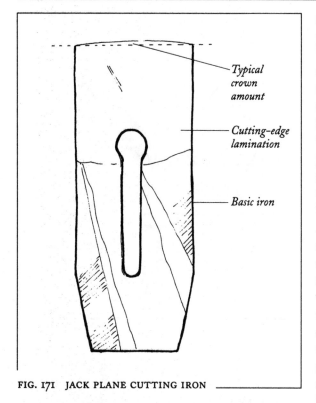

Typical crown amount

Cutting-edge lamination

Basic iron

FIG. 171   JACK PLANE CUTTING IRON

fairly wide mouth, which can mitigate against perfectly clean thin shavings.

The relationship of the mouth to the shaving is as follows: the wider the mouth — that is, the more space that exists between the cutting edge and the sole of the plane before it — the thicker is the shaving that can be taken up into the plane's throat. Simply setting the blade so that more of it protrudes beneath the sole is not in itself a guarantee of a thicker shaving, since there must be enough room for whatever thickness of shaving is taken to pass up between the blade and the stock. A large mouth can accommodate a thick shaving and will allow you to set the blade deeply or form a pronounced crown along the cutting edge and so remove a lot of wood with each pass. This can be very convenient when initially working on a board that is far from flat or that has big ridges or hairy saw marks, but eventually you will want to take thinner and finer shavings. When this stage is reached it will prove better to use a plane with a narrower mouth, since the character of a shaving is determined not only by the shape and depth of the cutting edge that is taking it but also by how it is forced up into the plane's throat. If it is allowed to curl up unimpeded through a wide mouth it will also be free to deflect and deform according to its own grain structure. If the grain happens to be pronounced and contrary to the direction of planing, tearout is likely. It is the dreaded phenomenon of tearout that has led to the advice: 'always plane with the grain', which, as any woodworker who has ever attempted to plane anything other than the sweetest and most regularly grained piece of wood will tell you, is frequently a useless and impracticable piece of advice; wood is just not made that way.

If, however, you use the right plane for the job, properly set and sharpened, you will not have to concern yourself with which way the grain is running, or whether it is rowed, curly, or just plain ornery. The secret of being able to plane smoothly with virtual disregard for grain direction lies in a properly set iron and capiron (of which more later), and a narrow mouth in relation to

crown being formed in the center which results in shavings being taken that are thicker in the center than at the edges (see FIG. 171). The reason for this is simply ease of use, not to produce concave cuts, although such is the result. If the blade were sharpened perfectly square, the edges would dig in whenever the plane was used on a board wider than the cutting edge of the iron and the going would be very hard, especially when trying to remove a lot of wood at once, as is required when dressing a rough and unflat board.

The finer the work you use the jack plane for, the slighter can be this crown, but the thinner the shavings you will be able to take. This is, in fact, the reason for a smooth plane — the plane used to produce the ultimate surface when there is little reason left for taking thick shavings. Although it is possible to sharpen the edge of a jack plane's cutting edge with a very slight crown and use the tool for finish work, it is somewhat of a waste, especially if there is a smooth plane available, since the third defining factor of a jack plane is a

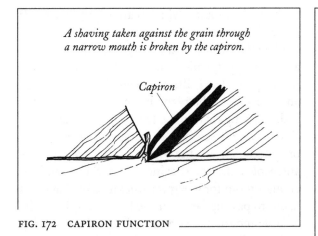

A shaving taken against the grain through a narrow mouth is broken by the capiron.

Capiron

FIG. 172   CAPIRON FUNCTION

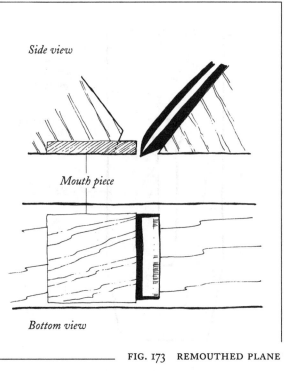

Side view

Mouth piece

Bottom view

FIG. 173   REMOUTHED PLANE

shaving thickness. The principle involved is very simple: when a shaving is taken through a mouth wide enough to receive it but no more, the effect of the capiron is to break the grain and destroy any tendency for the cut that forms the underneath of the shaving to run back into the wood being planed ahead of the cutting edge (see FIG. 172). If the mouth is much wider than the thickness of the shaving being taken this effect is impossible, and tearout when planing against the grain is likely. Since a jack plane is primarily intended to be able to remove a lot of wood at once, it usually has a fairly large mouth. If the blade is set shallower than for a thick shaving, the support of the capiron necessary to break the shaving is lost. For this reason it makes little sense to use the jack to produce fine shavings. In a pinch, and with care, it can be done, but most of the time it is easier to provide yourself with a smooth plane and leave the jack's blade set coarse.

BASIC ADJUSTMENT

A WOODEN JACK PLANE IS ALMOST CERTAIN to have a mouth wide enough to take substantial shavings. It may even be too wide — as a result of use or abuse — and may need to be made a little narrower by the process known as remouthing, whereby a small piece of wood, known as a mouth piece, is mortised into the sole just ahead of

the cutting edge so that the gap is reduced (see FIG. 173 above, and FIG. 162, chapter 16).

Most metal-bodied jack planes, such as those made by Stanley™ or Record™, are capable of mouth adjustment. The frog — the removable assembly holding the cutting iron, capiron, and lever cap in place — is secured to the stock by two screws. If these are loosened, the frog may be slid forwards or backwards until the exact width required for the mouth is obtained. Better-quality metal-bodied planes, such as the 'Bed Rock' line made by Stanley™, have more sophisticated and easily operated ways to move the frog so that the transverse alignment of the cutting edge remains unaltered.

A store-bought metal jack plane is unlikely to have the correct crown formed in its cutting edge. Creating this is part of sharpening plane irons, and is admittedly a skill that takes time to acquire. In fact, it has often been said that learning to sharpen well and correctly is the hardest part of woodworking. Nevertheless, this difficulty is not one to be regarded as a deterrent but rather as a challenge. The feeling of competence and control that one has when sharpening is mastered is sufficient to allow contemplation of even the hardest projects and is arguably the most rewarding accomplishment possible in woodworking.

Although there was a time when all planes had only a single iron, these are now rare, except for block planes, whose low-angled and reverse-beveled irons in some measure compensate for the lack of a second part. The double iron, consisting of cutting iron and capiron, was a great advance over the single iron since the curve of the capiron, together with its proximity to the edge of the cutting iron, helps greatly in breaking the shaving and preventing tearout, as discussed above — but only when it is properly adjusted.

If the relation of capiron to cutting iron is not understood, a double iron can be worse than useless, causing more problems than it solves, such as chattering, choking, accordion-shaped shavings, and the dreaded tearout. To work at all, the capiron must seat perfectly against the back of the cutting iron. This implies a cutting iron whose back has been made absolutely flat with the aid of a diamond stone or some other trusted reference. There should be no light visible between the two, and the outer, leading edge of the capiron must be the only part to contact the cutting iron. For this to happen, the capiron must be finished almost as sharply as the cutting iron. It must also be finished perfectly square. When thus prepared it can be positioned against the back of the cutting edge in such a way that it supports the bevel of the edge at the center of the crown and lies almost equal with the corners. Setting the capiron closer to or farther from the edge is one of the factors determining the thickness of shaving. The difference, however, is slight: for the very thickest shaving the capiron should be no farther than ⅛ in. from the cutting edge; for the thinnest shaving it should be so close that only the merest sliver of the back of the cutting edge is visible, which of course requires only a very slight crown.

In all cases a plane can only produce a surface as flat as its own sole. If a wooden jack plane's sole is rounded or warped it must be trued, usually by being planed by a truer plane, although this is a job that may also be accomplished by running the plane over a jointer, and then finishing the sole with a smoothing plane for absolute flatness and smoothness. A metal plane is somewhat more difficult to true since it must be lapped on a known flat surface. Machine shops may do this for you, but wherever it is done remember that the sole should be made flat with the iron in place — albeit retracted above the level of the sole — so that the stock is in the same state of tension and compression as it will be in use when either the wedge or the lever cap is fully employed in its job of holding the iron in position.

It follows that whatever method is used to hold the iron must work well and securely, whether it is simply a wooden wedge bearing accurately against the cutting iron — which in turn must seat securely on the plane's bed — or whether it involves the metal frog and lever-cap assembly common to metal planes. A loose iron cannot be relied on.

Lastly, any handles, whether the usual single open or closed tote, or the double transverse handles of my correspondent's plane, must also be securely mounted and allow of no wobble.

Whatever may be stamped on the iron is for the most part irrelevant to the user. Makers' names and other forms of advertising may be interesting to collectors, and sometimes useful as a guide to quality for those familiar with the various foundries that produced the irons, but the true test of the iron is how well it may be sharpened and how long it will hold its edge. Most laminated, wedge-shaped irons, common with older wooden jack planes, are considerably better than contemporary alloyed irons.

USING THE JACK PLANE

WE USE THE ADJECTIVE 'JACK' TO DESCRIBE an object that has many uses, but which is not necessarily perfect for any of them. While it is

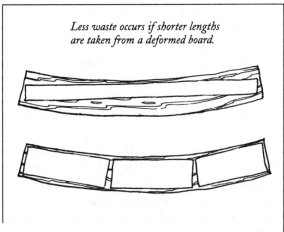

Less waste occurs if shorter lengths are taken from a deformed board.

FIG. 174   LAYOUT ON DEFORMED BOARDS

true that the jack plane can serve many purposes, it does have a specific use for which it is ideally adapted. This primary use is the basic flattening and truing of the surface of boards forming part of any project, large or small. Before the introduction of thickness planers, power jointers, and tablesaws, the jack plane was invariably the first tool to be used after a board had been sawed out and brought to approximate size. But lacking any direct experience of life before tablesaws and power jointers, who can be blamed for balking at the prospect of starting work on a 2 in.-thick piece of hairy, heavy, and twisted oak, armed with nothing more than a handsaw and a wooden plane? The idea seems preposterous, suitable only for a period demonstration in a museum village. And, indeed, given the quality and state of handtools in most workshops today, the job would likely take all the fun out of what is supposed to be a pleasant hobby. But it can be done more easily than many people would believe.

It is possible to run 16 ft. of rough-sawn stock through the planer or across the jointer before cutting out parts to length, but in the small shop it is far easier to cut pieces to length before performing these operations. If the board has any cupping or warping in it, less wood will be wasted if shorter, smaller pieces are trued than if the entire piece is made flat first (see FIG. 174). Not everyone has a 16 in. jointer at their disposal, and

it is not always possible to joint or thickness pieces as large as you would like, with the result that they have to be cut into smaller sections anyway.

So given that at the start of many projects our first job is to flatten and true various relatively short pieces of material, the jack plane can be a viable alternative to its powered descendants.

A SMALLER PARTNER

I REFERRED ABOVE TO 'HAIRY OAK'. BY THIS I meant lumber as it arrives directly from the sawmill, undressed, bearing prominent marks of the sawmill's large-toothed saw, irregularly spaced and often forming deep ridges across the surface of the wood. Not all rough-sawn wood is quite so hairy, and is easily worked upon directly with a jack plane (or a power jointer). But it is good practice when machining raw material to clean the surface thoroughly with a wire brush. Bits of grit left among the surface fibers — bits of jungle debris and stone chips accumulated in its journey to your shop — can put nasty nicks in any blade. Getting rid of excessive fibrous material is an additional advantage. The scrub plane (FIG. 175) is designed to accomplish precisely this. In essence it is an exaggerated version of the jack plane, with a

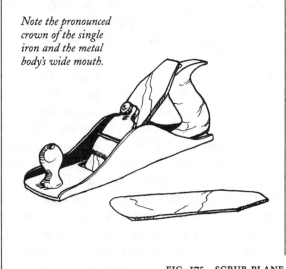

Note the pronounced crown of the single iron and the metal body's wide mouth.

FIG. 175   SCRUB PLANE

similarly shaped but more pronouncedly curved cutting edge, and a wider mouth. The scrub plane is also a single-ironed tool; it has no capiron. When used as intended, it skims the irregular surface of a very rough and uneven board, removing the most egregious defects, and leaves the board ready for more efficient planing by the jack.

FIRST STROKES

BOTH THE SCRUB PLANE AND THE JACK plane may be used the same way at first. In fact, if the board has any pronounced warp, cup, or twist to it, this is essential. The method for achieving the first goal, a flat surface, is as follows:

Place the board on the bench, or on any other surface suitable for planing that is solid and capable of holding the board securely with stops or vises, and which for maximum comfort is as high as your hand when held palm down on its surface with your arm straight. Make sure that the board does not rock. Small wedges are useful for this, depending on the severity of the deformation. Next, look at the board carefully to determine from which area the least amount of wood may be removed to make the entire surface flat (see FIG. 176). This is sometimes just a single corner,

sometimes diagonally opposite corners (if the board is propellored), and sometimes, if the board is warped, either opposite ends or the center. Less frequently, the board will be cupped, and wood will have to be removed either from each long edge or down the center of the board. But do not look only at the top surface; the situation may be different if you turn the board over, and possibly require less work. Of course, even at this early stage of stock preparation other factors may come into play: you may already have made choices depending on the grain pattern and direction, and the possible presence of knots and other defects or features.

If this sounds like a lot of work remember it is no more than any sensitive worker will have performed prior to machining the material, but with the lessened restriction of not having to take into account how you will feed the material through the machine to avoid tearout. There is no reason to take grain direction into account with a properly sharpened and set jack plane. In fact, correct use of the jack virtually precludes any such approach since the majority of the work is performed in every direction *but* with the grain. Indeed, it is generally true to say that any plane that cannot do a passable job unless being used with the grain is not up the mark. For those last

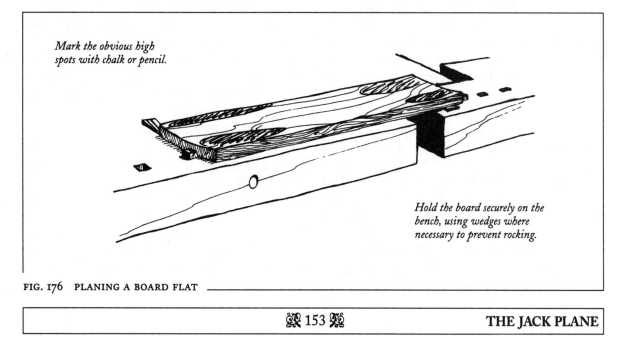

Mark the obvious high spots with chalk or pencil.

Hold the board securely on the bench, using wedges where necessary to prevent rocking.

FIG. 176   PLANING A BOARD FLAT

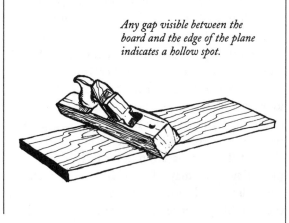

Any gap visible between the board and the edge of the plane indicates a hollow spot.

FIG. 177   CHECKING FOR FLATNESS

away these areas with light strokes; you should not have to put too much effort into it. But make sure there is a fairly good set to the blade; it should protrude sufficiently from the sole to take a shaving the thickness of several sheets of paper. When you have removed most of the pencil marks turn the board over and observe whether it rocks any less. When it is upside-down like this you will also be able to see where the high spots are. Do not lose track of them as you replace the board right-side up; mark them, and repeat the process.

few passes with a smoothing plane perhaps there may be reason to work with the grain, but ever since the invention of the double iron, the failure of a plane to take a smooth cut in any direction can invariably be shown to be the result of an improperly set capiron, an excessively wide mouth, or an imperfectly sharpened edge. There are other possible causes, such as a warped sole and poor seating for the iron — whether this be on a metal frog as in Stanley™-type planes or on the wooden bed of a wooden plane — but nine times out of ten the fault will lie with a blunt edge and a poor setup.

Before you panic and declare that such fine fettling can only be expected after much experience and with the help of a master, take comfort in the fact that the jack plane is very generous in this regard. It is, after all, normally asked only to perform relatively coarse work, not the perfection of a smooth plane.

At the start you may find it helpful to scribble with a soft, broad-leaded carpenter's pencil on the high spots of your board. With time you will be able to dispense with this aid. It may be sufficient to hold the plane tilted so that one edge of the sole rests on the board and to sight under this edge. If you can see light, there is a hollow spot (see FIG. 177). By placing the plane held like this on various sections of the board you can get a quick idea of broad surface irregularities. Plane

WINDING STICKS

SOMETHING YOU CAN DO IN CONJUNCTION with this process, and which will be increasingly the best way to check for any out-of-flatness or winding, is to start using winding sticks. These are used in pairs, and are very simple to make.

Astonishingly, probably because their use has so declined as to have turned them into arcane artifacts from a largely forgotten past, old pairs sometimes show up at antique-tool sales, where they are sold for very high prices. Their makers would have laughed themselves silly at this, for they were typically user-made, often on the spur of the moment and out of whatever convenient scrap was handy. True, with years of use, they may have developed an attractive patina, and if their owner should have found it necessary to stamp his name on them — as was frequently done when several men worked in a single shop — they can possess a certain romantic appeal, but there is no reason why you should not make your own.

You may use as a pattern the pair illustrated in FIG. 178 or you may design your own with equal success. Notice that chamfering the top edges makes them a little easier to use, as does painting the top edge of the rear stick a lighter color. Providing they are made from a stable material and do not warp, they may be as wide as you like.

In use, the rear stick is placed at the far end of the board; the front stick, or gaffer, is placed at the near end. Care is taken to see that they are

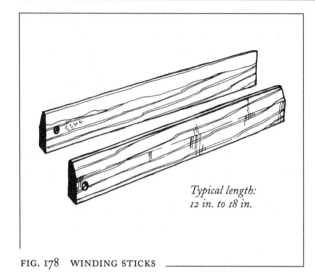

Typical length: 12 in. to 18 in.

FIG. 178 WINDING STICKS

parallel to each other, and then by sighting across the gaffer, keeping your eye level with the top of the stick, you attempt to align the top edge of the rear stick with the top edge of the gaffer. If the board is even a little 'in winding' this will prove impossible, and it should be obvious which part of the board must be further planed to get the sticks to align.

There are extra steps possible. For one, you can take successive sightings, moving the rear stick closer to the gaffer each time, in order to ascertain the truth of the board at any given spot (see FIG. 179). For another, you can decide that the rear stick represents the ideal plane, and instead of

planing away the near end of the board until the two sticks can be brought into alignment, you can cut a rabbet or shelf, bit by bit, until the same end is achieved, as shown in FIG. 180.

The jack is your partner in all this. At first it will be used only on certain parts of the board, those obviously high spots. But sooner or later you will reach the stage at which, when the board is turned over, there is little perceptible rocking. This assumes, of course, that your bench top or work surface itself is flat. If it is not, and if its legs and feet are secure and not susceptible to being raised or lowered, make it so by using the jack plane and the winding sticks to check your progress. When your board no longer rocks you will have completed the first stage.

THICKNESSING OR FLATTENING

YOU NOW HAVE TWO CHOICES: EITHER TO thickness the board to make the other side flat and parallel to the first at the required thickness, or to continue to smooth into perfect flatness the first side. If the board you have been working on is fairly substantial and the width you require is considerably less, it may make sense to resaw it, assuming you have a bandsaw at your disposal. If, on the other hand, the board is close to the thickness you hope to end up with, then it will be

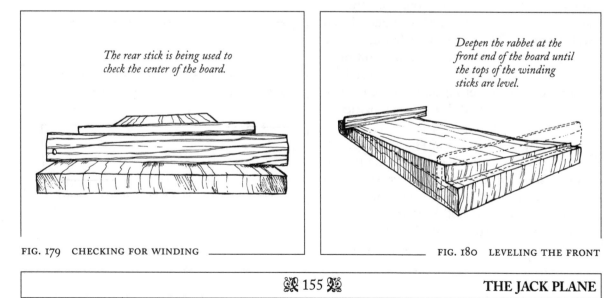

The rear stick is being used to check the center of the board.

Deepen the rabbet at the front end of the board until the tops of the winding sticks are level.

FIG. 179 CHECKING FOR WINDING

FIG. 180 LEVELING THE FRONT

THE JACK PLANE

better to gauge a line around all edges marking the finished thickness, and repeat the process you just completed on the first side, but with the added element of paying close attention to this gauged line.

If you choose to follow the latter course, your job will be made easier by the fact that the first side now rests securely on the bench. Depending on the amount the board was warped or cupped to start with, there may be greater discrepancies to deal with, such as one corner being excessively high. If this is the case, then the scrub plane may prove useful here to remove quickly these very high spots.

Since there is a gauged line around all edges, it may also be useful to work down to this line at one end first in order to create a reliable reference for using the winding sticks. Place the rear stick on this end and work from the near end until their tops align.

SMOOTHING

WITH EITHER ONE OR TWO SURFACES MADE flat, the second stage may be started. This is the process of removing all roughness, vestiges of the sawmill, and any uneven spots from the flattened surface, making it now smooth. Do not be in too great a hurry to commence this. It can be very tempting to reset the plane iron, take thinner shavings, and start to make the board smooth and reveal the grain and a fine surface, but unless the first stage is truly finished this is a waste of time, for sooner or later you will discover that you have to return to a coarser setting and remove the fine surface you have just made because that particular area is still a little too high.

The process is illustrated in FIG. 181. Begin by planing the length of the board, from end to end, working back from the far end, with strokes as long as you can conveniently take. This should produce a somewhat smoother surface than your previous cross-grain strokes which were necessary to work down localized high spots. Depending on

the set of the iron this will produce deeper or shallower grooves, representing the width of the iron. When the entire board has been thus planed, start again at the far end, but this time plane across the grain, with slightly diagonal strokes. It should be very easy to see what has been planed and what has not, and so keep track of your process as you work your way down the board. The intent is to remove the high ridges left at the edge of each longitudinal pass. When this can be accomplished everywhere, leaving a new set of transverse ridges, you will have brought the entire

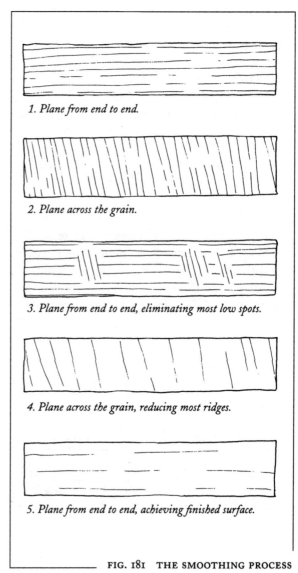

1. *Plane from end to end.*

2. *Plane across the grain.*

3. *Plane from end to end, eliminating most low spots.*

4. *Plane across the grain, reducing most ridges.*

5. *Plane from end to end, achieving finished surface.*

FIG. 181   THE SMOOTHING PROCESS

board to a more perfect state of flatness. This may not be possible with the first diagonal planing; the chances are that after you have worked your way down the board there will still be a few spots where the longitudinal ridges are still visible.

Set the plane iron a little shallower, and repeat the process, following lengthwise planing by transverse planing. It is important to complete each planing along and across the entire board, unlike the procedure during the first phase when you were concentrating simply on removing high spots. When each planing completely eradicates all traces of the previous planing, it is time to start preparing a finished surface.

FINISHING

HOW FAR YOU TAKE THIS LAST STAGE depends on what will happen to the board next. If much layout and marking is still to be done, and if there is much cutting of joints and further refining of the surface necessary, it will be best to leave the surface as it is. Any further finishing will only have to be repeated. But if such work is to be done on the board that will make it difficult to plane after completion, such as if the board is to become part of a structure which when assembled will be inaccessible by plane, then you can set the jack plane's iron to the finest setting and take a series of final passes designed to leave the finest, smoothest surface possible before using the smooth plane or scraper.

OTHER USES

IT IS POSSIBLE TO USE A JACK PLANE FOR more than the basic flattening and smoothing of board described above. If the curvature of the iron is made less pronounced, it can be used for increasingly finer degrees of finish planing. It can also be used as a fair substitute for a jointer plane to produce perfectly matching edges to be joined. It is also invaluable as an all-purpose general plane whenever a board needs to be reduced in width quickly and efficiently, when an edge needs to be trued, especially when this edge is not parallel to the other side, and in producing beveled surfaces, such as around raised panels, or smaller chamfers along finished edges. The fortunate woodworker owns more than one, and keeps them set up with wider or narrower mouths, and differently crowned irons.

18

BLOCK MITER BULLNOSE & CHARIOT

DISTANT RELATIONS

THE PLANES DISCUSSED IN THIS CHAPTER, WHILE THEY SHARE SEVERAL SALIENT CHARACTERISTICS AND MIGHT APPEAR TO BE MEMBERS OF THE SAME FAMILY, ARE NOT, IN FACT, CLOSELY RELATED. THEIR ACTUAL SIMILARITIES CONSIST OF: THEIR handiness, achieved by virtue of their small size; the fact that they function in certain respects as miniature bench planes rather than as full-blown, special-purpose planes like rabbet planes, ploughs, or dados; and the fact that they are all single-iron tools. Although miter planes and block planes are indeed very close relatives, the latter being directly descended from the former (which, as will be explained later, is paradoxically also descended from the former), bullnose planes and chariot planes are quite unrelated, both to each other and to either of the former pair. Nevertheless, since the uninitiated often confuses them, it is useful to deal with them all together. Each type has various forms

and specialized uses, but the basic tools may be described as follows:

THE BLOCK PLANE

THE BLOCK PLANE IS PROBABLY THE BEST known of the four types (see FIG. 182). It is also the newest addition to the group, being the metal development of the venerable miter plane. First introduced in the 19th century as a smaller version of the miter plane, it was quickly adopted by many woodworkers. Small enough to be held and used in one hand, and possessing an iron set at a much lower angle than regular bench planes such as

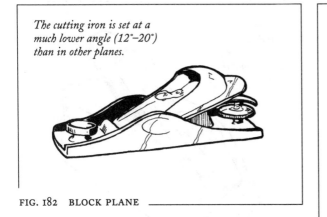

The cutting iron is set at a much lower angle (12°–20°) than in other planes.

FIG. 182   BLOCK PLANE

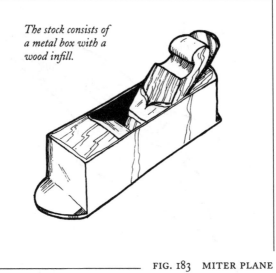

The stock consists of a metal box with a wood infill.

FIG. 183   MITER PLANE

smooth planes, jacks, and jointers, it rapidly became popular as a convenient 'apron tool', one that could be carried around in a pocket and used for innumerable small jobs.

It was the metal planemaker's delight, and despite its small size and single iron, varieties with numerous improvements soon appeared. Even today, when most other planes have been reduced to one basic form, it is still possible to buy three or four different varieties of new block planes.

THE MITER PLANE

ALTHOUGH THE CONTEMPORARY METAL block plane was a development of the miter plane, the miter plane itself is actually descended from an earlier form of plane also known as a block plane, common since the Middle Ages. This apparent paradox is a result of the modern block plane being named for the blocks of hardwood used in butchers' chopping tables, which it alone was able to work successfully, whereas the block plane from which the miter plane is descended was named for the fact that it was a tool consisting primarily of a cutting iron set in a 'block' of wood. There is little doubt that the original block plane was the first form of the great plane family of tools, and indeed, for many centuries it was the typical form. The miter plane (FIG. 183) developed from this proto-plane to satisfy the need for a tool that could produce particularly fine work on

hardwoods and end grain, such as occurs at miters (hence the name). Curiously however, its design, as it came into being in the 18th and early 19th centuries, is almost identical to that of many Roman planes presumably used for general work.

Despite the fact that miter planes were once the most expensive and cherished of planes, they are now no longer made, although one of the last varieties to be manufactured, the somewhat erroneously named Stanley™ 9: 'Cabinet Maker's Block Plane' (FIG. 184), is one of the most sought-after and expensive planes. A far better buy would be any of the European miter planes commonly found at tool auctions. These sell for much less and are superior in every way.

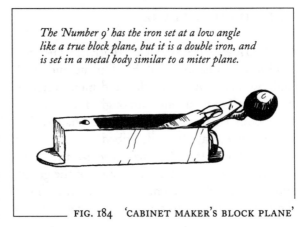

The 'Number 9' has the iron set at a low angle like a true block plane, but it is a double iron, and is set in a metal body similar to a miter plane.

FIG. 184   'CABINET MAKER'S BLOCK PLANE'

BULLNOSE & CHARIOT

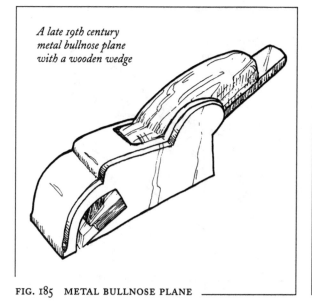

A late 19th century metal bullnose plane with a wooden wedge

The toe of the standard wooden bullnose plane consists of a thin brass plate.

FIG. 185   METAL BULLNOSE PLANE

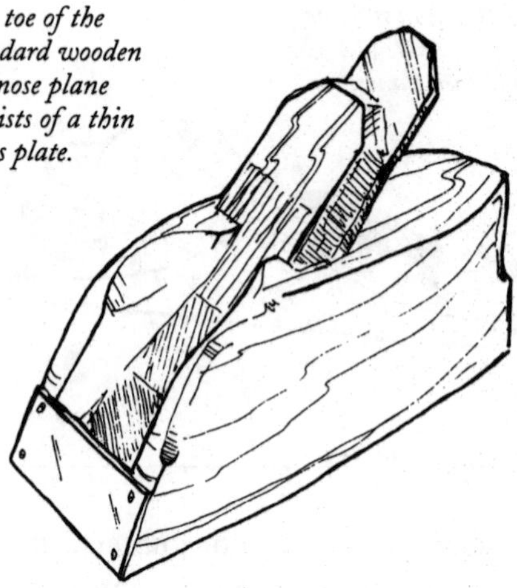

FIG. 186   WOODEN BULLNOSE PLANE

THE BULLNOSE PLANE

BULLNOSE PLANES ARE NOW MADE CHIEFLY of metal, and commonly have very low angled irons (see FIG. 185). But earlier models were made chiefly of wood, and the iron was set at a much higher angle (see FIG. 186). Both types have their cutting iron set very close to the toe in order that they can be used for the fitting and cleaning up of stopped rabbets and chamfers. Although much larger bullnose varieties of rabbet planes and dado planes are also found, the basic bullnose plane remains a relatively small tool.

THE CHARIOT PLANE

CHARIOT PLANES MAY BE THOUGHT OF AS A kind of combination small block plane and small bullnose plane. Both wooden and metal versions were once common, and although different they were both characterized by unique shapes. The wooden ones have been described as being like a Persian slipper (see FIG. 187), whereas the metal ones (FIG. 188) are miniature versions of the grand, stuffed panel planes common towards the end of the 19th century. Both types have moderately low

angled irons that are set fairly far forward. Metal ones are also made with variously shaped soles.

WHICH PLANE TO USE?

UNDOUBTEDLY EVERYONE SHOULD HAVE AT least one of these small planes; they are simply too handy and too useful to be without. But knowing what the choices are and what all four types can do will enlarge your woodworking vocabulary and make many previously awkward jobs easy.

All block planes have a low-angled cutting iron, the better to deal with end grain. This angle was increasingly lowered in early models, but it was soon found that after a certain point any further lowering was impractical. Although a more acute angle meant a sharper edge, it also meant that the edge wore more quickly and was more vulnerable to damage. By reversing the iron so that the bevel was uppermost, however, the angle of the cutting iron could be lowered even more. This, of course, meant that it was no longer possible to fit a cap-iron, normally useful for both strengthening the extreme edge as well as breaking the shaving.

When choosing either a new block plane or an older model, be aware that there are different

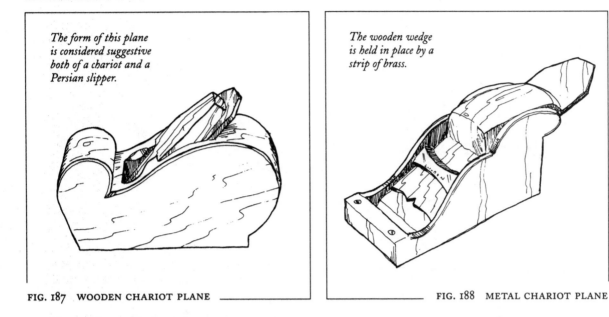

The form of this plane is considered suggestive both of a chariot and a Persian slipper.

The wooden wedge is held in place by a strip of brass.

FIG. 187   WOODEN CHARIOT PLANE

FIG. 188   METAL CHARIOT PLANE

pitches available, and that although, in general, the lower the pitch the more easily the plane will work end grain, it is also important to ensure that the plane is sufficiently well made so that the cutting-edge end of the iron is supported as closely as possible to the edge by the plane's body. This part of the plane is known as the bed, and it should be well cast so that it not only extends as closely as possible to the edge of the cutting iron, but is also smooth and truly flat. This point cannot be emphasized enough. For any block plane to work well and be capable of taking clean shavings as thin as .001 in., the iron must be not only properly sharpened but also firmly supported close to its edge and capable of being firmly held against the bed without any rocking. Otherwise chattering — the unwanted, bumpy, ripple effect that badly tuned planes often suffer from — will occur. Modern top-of-the-line Stanley™ block planes have beds that extend quite far to a nice V-shaped front edge, although frequently a little dressing (light filing) is needed to ensure perfect flatness. Many older planes have beds that finish abruptly too far up the iron to be of any help in supporting the edge.

Another important element in the plane's over-all ability to take fine, smooth shavings is the size of the mouth. The mouth is the opening in the plane's sole through which the cutting iron protrudes. Strictly speaking, 'mouth' usually refers just to the part of the opening in front of the cutting iron. The width of the mouth helps to determine the thickness or thinness of the shaving. Obviously, a large shaving cannot be taken through a small mouth, and if the iron is set too deeply, so that it cuts a thick shaving, the shaving will simply jam in the mouth. On the other hand, if the mouth is too wide, simply reducing the set of the cutting iron will not necessarily guarantee a thin shaving. This is because under certain conditions, such as when planing grain that is running away from the plane, even a thin initial cut produced by a lightly set iron can run ever more deeply into the stock (see FIG. 189). To prevent this was one of the reasons for the development of the double iron — a cutting iron with a capiron — since the capiron tends to turn back the shaving as it enters the mouth, breaking it and preventing it from becoming thicker as the cutting iron is pushed through the wood. The block plane, however, has no capiron. Therefore it is extremely important to ensure that the plane's mouth is as narrow as possible if you intend to take the finest shavings.

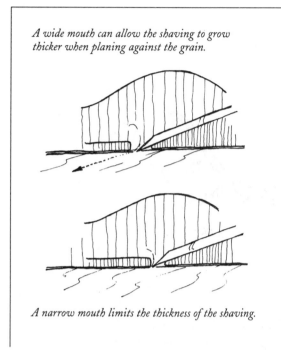

A wide mouth can allow the shaving to grow thicker when planing against the grain.

A narrow mouth limits the thickness of the shaving.

FIG. 189   EFFECT OF MOUTH SIZE

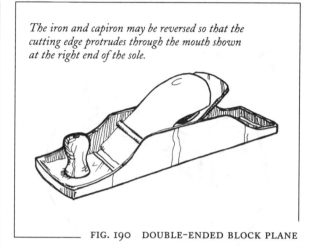

The iron and capiron may be reversed so that the cutting edge protrudes through the mouth shown at the right end of the sole.

FIG. 190   DOUBLE-ENDED BLOCK PLANE

Since you may not always want to take the thinnest possible shavings, a block plane with a very small, fixed mouth may not be appropriate. Examine the size of the mouth of any plane you are considering obtaining. Cheaper planes tend to have unusably large mouths. Better-quality planes often have adjustable mouths.

Lastly, consider how easily and accurately the iron may be adjusted. Cheap models have their irons fixed in place with a simple screw or lever. Though this may hold the iron securely in place, the difficulty of setting the iron to a precise depth and then keeping it perfectly aligned while doing so can be very frustrating — even if the bed and mouth are adequately formed. You might think, therefore, that any plane fitted with an adjustable depth-setting mechanism, such as the wheel-and-fork arrangement found on some Stanley™ block planes, would automatically constitute a better tool, but many of these mechanisms are far too sloppy. Sometimes the mechanism can be made to work more exactly, but it is usually more trouble than it is worth.

Aside from choosing a well-made and easily adjusted block plane with an ideal cutting-angle for the work you have in mind, there are various specialty block planes that can be a great help in cleaning up high-quality work. One example is a block plane which allows two placements of the iron: one producing the standard design, and another which positions the iron close to the front of the sole, effectively creating a form of bullnose block plane ideal for working close to obstructions (see FIG. 190). Another example, long dropped from the Stanley™ catalog but now being made again by another enterprising firm, is the skewed-iron rabbet and block plane (FIG. 191). One side of this plane's stock is removable so that the plane may be used as a rabbet plane. The skewed iron makes possible a smooth cut when working across the grain, and this, plus the plane's ability to work like a rabbet plane, makes it a handy panel-raiser, or at least a good panel-raising clean-up plane.

THE ARISTOCRATIC MITER PLANE

AS MENTIONED EARLIER, THE MITER PLANE is no longer made, but it was surely the aristocrat of low-angle planes. Used with a miter shooting-block (see chapter 3), this plane, invariably made with a very low angled iron and an extremely thin mouth, and in a surprising range of sizes, from

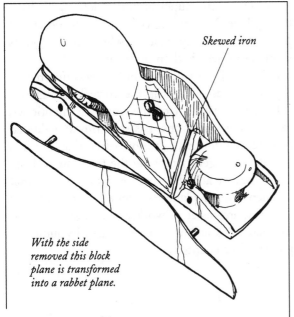

Skewed iron

With the side removed this block plane is transformed into a rabbet plane.

FIG. 191   RABBET & BLOCK PLANE

small to quite large, is capable of exquisite work. While the Stanley™ 9 commonly sells for around a thousand dollars, far better, dovetailed steel-bodied and rosewood-stuffed European models may be found for as little as one hundred to two hundred dollars. For finishing the ends of exposed dovetails and other areas of end grain it has no equal, and should form part of every serious woodworker's kit.

THE BULLNOSE FAMILY

NOWADAYS A BULLNOSE PLANE IS LITTLE more than a metal combination rabbet-shoulder-block plane, and as such is a poor substitute for any of them. The original coffin-shaped wooden tool has all the finesse of a good-quality wooden smooth plane, with the added advantage of an iron set virtually at the front of the stock. It can be used over large surfaces and set to take very fine shavings with no chatter. Modern metal versions, while possessing the dubious advantage of irons that extend to both sides of the sole in the manner of rabbet planes, are very narrow. As a result

they require such a substantial nose piece in front of the iron as to render them almost useless for the job they are supposedly designed for, namely, planing into corners.

SWING LOW, SWEET CHARIOT

CHARIOT PLANES ARE ADMITTEDLY RARE, but belong indisputably in any discussion of block planes. Most types are from 3 in. to 5 in. long, and have their iron set so far forward that in many cases the front part of the sole is a separate L-shaped piece fixed to the toe by screws. The so-called Irish pattern is longer, measuring about 9 in., but it is still recognizable as a chariot plane by the characteristically bulbous wooden wedge used in the metal-bodied forms.

Although the flat forms may be used in the same manner as the tiny American thumb planes popular with modelmakers, their chief advantage lies in their larger width combined with their small size. It is thought that the majority of metallic chariot planes made in the last quarter of the 19th century were intended primarily for pianoforte casemakers, but the existence of chariot planes with curved soles suggests other uses for other trades. Like patternmaker's planes, which are provided with sets of differently radiused soles, curved-soled chariot planes are of inestimable use in non-rectilinear, irregularly shaped work. Their sophisticated design makes them capable of finer work than the small brass violinmaker's planes, which are almost the only shaped planes still available.

OPERATING TIPS

ALL THESE PLANES ARE CAPABLE OF VERY fine work if they are in good shape. This means that the irons must be razor-sharp and set truly in well-maintained soles. They are, after all, primarily finishing tools, despite many a carpenter's predilection for using a battered block plane as a crude chamfering tool on rough stock, or as an auxiliary door-fitting device. Be aware that their small size makes different holding techniques a useful possibility: Pulling the plane towards you rather than pushing it away from you can often be more convenient and more effective. Slicing, shearing cuts often produce better results than does moving the plane in a straight line. To achieve the very smoothest surface on end grain, such as at the ends of dovetails, dampen the wood slightly before planing by rubbing a moist rag or sponge across the part to be planed. This not only raises the grain slightly but also keeps the fibers together so that a single, continuous shaving may be taken. When done successfully, you will be surprised at the superior finish left by a sharp block plane. No sanding (which fills the pores and produces unsightly results when the wood is stained or oiled) is then necessary.

Perhaps the greatest difficulty encountered in adjusting these planes is the correct setting and sideways adjustment of the irons. As mentioned earlier, depth adjustment is sometimes facilitated by patented devices, but more often than not it is a question of gently tapping the toe, iron, or heel. This kind of adjustment is just one reason that wooden-bodied planes, designed to be adjusted this way, are easier to work with. Another is that wooden soles are more easily trued by judicious jointing (see chapter 13).

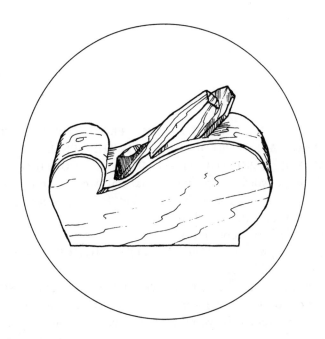

19

THE RABBET PLANE

RABBET OR REBATE?

THE WORDS 'RABBET' AND 'REBATE' COME FROM THE OLD FRENCH: 'RABATTRE', MEANING TO BEAT BACK OR REDUCE. THIS IS THE SENSE IN THE FINANCIAL USE OF THE WORD AND IS ALSO THE SENSE IN WOODWORKING. ALTHOUGH CERTAIN English speakers have given the word the spelling and pronunciation of 'rebate', it is certain that when the technique was first introduced to England by Flemish woodworkers sometime in the 12th or 13th century it was pronounced more like 'rabbit'. French was still in widespread use in England at this time, and there is no doubt that this is a closer approximation to the way the word was originally pronounced in French. In Britain today both senses of the word are spelled 'rebate', although most woodworkers pronounce 'rabbet' when using the word in the woodworking sense. Americans have perhaps more usefully decided to keep both the spelling and the pronunciation of the two senses separate, leaving 'rebate' to the

financial world, and reserving the alternative 'rabbet' for woodworking.

NOT A MOULDING PLANE

THE RABBET PLANE IS SOMETIMES THOUGHT of as the most common moulding plane, but it is not actually a moulding plane at all. It is true that rabbet planes constitute at least half of all the old wooden planes still floating around in woodworking shops, fleamarkets, antique stores, and the hands of tool collectors, and it is also true that the vast majority of rabbet planes are more or less the same size and shape as most moulding planes,

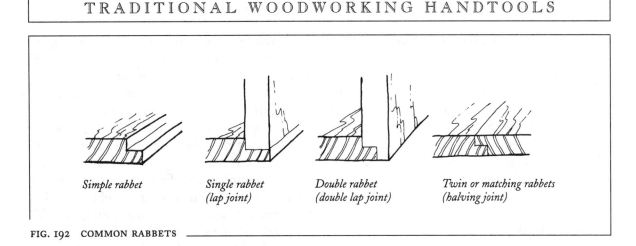

Simple rabbet   *Single rabbet (lap joint)*   *Double rabbet (double lap joint)*   *Twin or matching rabbets (halving joint)*

FIG. 192   COMMON RABBETS

but a rabbet plane does not make a moulding and so cannot properly be called a moulding plane.

Although a rabbet plane may be very useful in the preparatory stages of forming certain mouldings, its primary use, as its name clearly indicates, is to form a rabbet. A rabbet is the ledge formed along the edge of a piece of wood when a step-like portion is removed. FIG. 192 shows the commonest forms of rabbets used in everyday woodworking, including simple, double, and twin rabbets. The rabbet not only exists in its own right as a finished joint or structural feature but also forms part of more complicated assemblies. Since its formation is undoubtedly one of the basic operations common to all forms of woodworking, it is hardly surprising that there are so many tools in existence to help make it.

Nowadays, most people called upon to form a rabbet probably reach for a router fitted with a rabbeting bit, or even a simple straight-bit, or take the piece to be rabbeted over to the shaper, the router table, or the tablesaw. Set up correctly and used with care these tools can do a fast and exact job of forming rabbets in a variety of ways. But handtools designed to make rabbets, if similarly carefully set up and skillfully used, can also be very efficient, and in some cases form rabbets difficult if not impossible to make with the machines. Furthermore, the advantages of being able to reach for the handtool and cut a relatively short rabbet with no machine setup time required, not to mention the often greater sensory pleasure

involved in quietly and safely using a handtool instead of a noisy and potentially dangerous powertool, often outweigh considerations of economy and time.

For many people the end result is all important, but perhaps more than in many other crafts or occupations woodworkers are attracted to the means as well as the end, and especially to the nature of the material they have chosen to work with. Although safety and economy often dictate it, I personally regret having to be distanced from my work and the feel and smell of my material by ear protectors, noisy routers, face masks, and all manner of guards and push sticks. It is a source of great pleasure to me to be able to feel — safely — the surface of the wood I am working on, smell the aroma given off as a fresh shaving curls quietly away from the surface, and even hear the distinct but quiet noise made by various planes and other tools.

In ultra-fine work the surface finish obtainable with a well-tuned handtool is invariably superior to that attainable by any machine, despite the machine's often superior accuracy. I am working with wood, after all, which is not a relatively homogenous material like metal or plastic, and accuracy to .001 in. is less important than a completely smooth, crisply cut surface, free of jointer marks, router burn or chatter, planer waves, and the dull, abraded cell ends produced by sanding no matter how fine the grit. And if my finer surface is a trifle less exact who will tell the

THE RABBET PLANE

difference after changing moisture-conditions and the passage of time have had their effects on what is after all a living material?

For all these and similar reasons I still find myself reaching for a rabbet plane at least as often as I walk over to the tablesaw, and I remain very grateful to the craftsmen of past centuries who developed so many ways of performing one of woodworking's commonest operations.

BASIC FORMS

THE SIMPLEST FORM OF RABBET PLANE IS the standard 9½ in.-long wooden tool that looks so similar to a moulding plane (see FIG. 193). Unlike a moulding plane, however, it has a square-bottomed stock. Moreover, that it is not a moulding plane is most easily noticed by the distinctive exit-hole cut in the left-hand side of the stock, which casts the shavings off the bench rather than allowing them to exit up through the top of the throat as in most other planes.

This side mouth is unique to rabbet planes and dado planes, which are another special-purpose, non-moulding plane. Originally made by boring into the side of the throat with a tapered auger,

this graceful shape is typical of the elegant simplicity of many old tools whose form is the result of centuries of development.

The basic model may be found in a variety of widths, from as narrow as ¼ in. to as wide as 2 in. The cheapest models have the cutting iron set square across the sole of the stock, as in smooth planes, jack planes, and jointers. This is fine for straightforward rabbets formed along the edge of a piece of wood with regular straight grain, but cross-grained wood can cause difficulties. To make rabbeting easier in this event, and also for cutting directly across the grain such as at the end of a board, a rabbet plane, sometimes known as a skew-eyed plane, with a skewed iron is a better tool to use. Since the iron is always skewed so that its trailing edge is towards the off-bench side, it has two other advantages besides that of more easily cutting across the grain. The first is that the leading edge helps keep the corner of the plane drawn into the corner of the rabbet, and the second is that the shavings are more easily thrown off to one side (off the bench), thereby preventing choking of the mouth.

To make a worn rabbet plane work well again you may have to remouth it. This means making the mouth of the plane smaller by inserting an extra piece of wood in front of the iron's cutting edge, as shown in FIG. 194. This process becomes

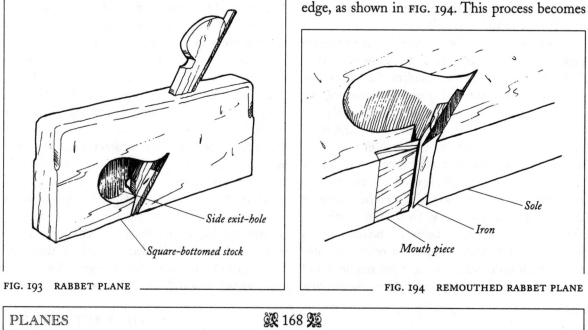

FIG. 193 RABBET PLANE

Side exit-hole

Square-bottomed stock

FIG. 194   REMOUTHED RABBET PLANE

Sole

Iron

Mouth piece

necessary whenever the sole of the stock has been worn down by use and the rejointing that is necessary to keep the sole of the stock perfectly flat and perpendicular to the sides. If the iron is skewed, care must be exercised when sharpening it to maintain the correct skew or it will not line up properly with the mouth or the sides of the stock.

A plane that has been repeatedly jointed and possibly remouthed is necessarily shorter, in height not length, than originally made, possibly to the extent that the bottom of the wedge may have to be trimmed. But before doing this, notice how the bottom tip of the wedge is not simply cut square or finished to a point, but is shaped so that it presents no blunt edge to the shavings coming off the wood, instead directing them towards the curved mouth so that they exit smoothly without choking the plane.

If these points are borne in mind, and the irons are well sharpened with proper bevels, the simple rabbet plane will perform well and easily. There are further levels of sophistication, however, that can make its use even more efficient. These levels of sophistication can be user-added or can be found in factory-made superior models.

FENCES & DEPTH STOPS

THE FIRST-TIME USER SOON NOTICES THAT unlike most moulding planes the simple rabbet plane has no built-in fence. Most attempts to guide the plane in a straight line along the edge of a board will result in a less than perfectly straight rabbet, a rarely acceptable result. A skilled worker using a skew rabbet plane can often cut a narrow V-shaped groove close to the inside line of the rabbet by tilting the plane to the right, and then use this groove as a guide for subsequent vertical passes, but the operation is tricky and easily subverted by strongly grained wood. The solution is usually to clamp or otherwise temporarily fix a guide to the work against which the rabbet plane can be made to bear while being moved along.

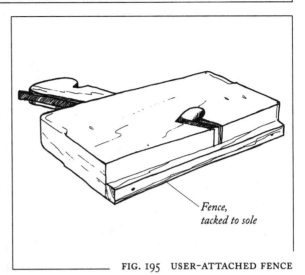

FIG. 195   USER-ATTACHED FENCE

Since rabbet planes are made in a variety of widths it is also possible to use a plane of exactly the width required and fix a fence to the sole of the plane, as shown in FIG. 195. Assuming that the edge of the board is true, this will produce a straight rabbet, and indeed many old rabbet planes bear evidence in the form of nail or screw holes of having been used precisely in this way.

A similar problem may be encountered with regard to the depth of the rabbet. Because the simple rabbet plane has no depth stop, care must be exercised in planing only to the marked line and no deeper. This is a little more difficult than

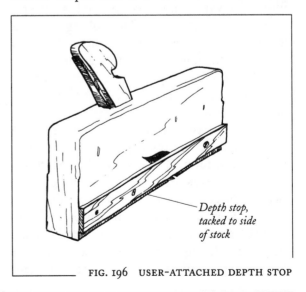

FIG. 196   USER-ATTACHED DEPTH STOP

THE RABBET PLANE

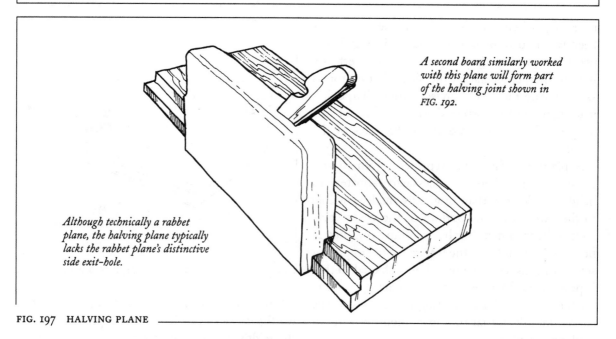

A second board similarly worked with this plane will form part of the halving joint shown in FIG. 192.

Although technically a rabbet plane, the halving plane typically lacks the rabbet plane's distinctive side exit-hole.

FIG. 197   HALVING PLANE

planing to a line with a bench plane, since only one side of the finished rabbet can be marked. It is possible, however, to fix a depth stop in the form of a narrow strip to the side of the stock, as shown in FIG. 196. Many old rabbet planes show evidence of this procedure, too.

If a rabbet of a particular width and depth is to be made on a regular basis it can pay to use a plane with built-in fence and depth stop. Such a doubly fenced rabbet plane is known as a standing fillister (of which more will be said later) or a halving plane (FIG. 197). The halving plane is designed to cut a rabbet whose depth is exactly half that of the thickness of the board in which it is being cut: a half-depth rabbet. This procedure allows adjoining rabbeted edges to be perfectly matched, as shown in FIG. 192.

The better class of rabbet plane, especially the skewed version, was often fitted with a spur or tooth in the form of a narrow blade vertically dovetailed into the right side of the stock a little ahead of the cutting iron (see FIG. 198). When this is properly sharpened with an inside bevel and correctly adjusted, it cuts the fibers exactly in line with the inside edge of the rabbet, thus ensuring a clean inside shoulder. This is most important

when cutting across the grain, but even when cutting with the grain it can be helpful in forming a square inside shoulder, provided the plane is held firmly against whatever guide is being used.

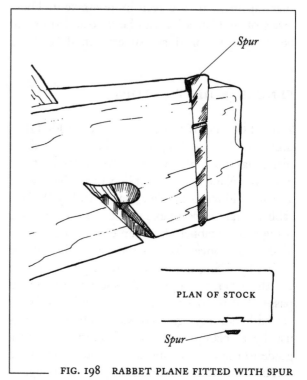

Spur

PLAN OF STOCK

Spur

FIG. 198   RABBET PLANE FITTED WITH SPUR

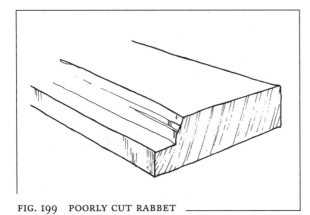

FIG. 199   POORLY CUT RABBET

If this laſt point is ignored the plane may tend to wander away from the line and produce a ſtepped or sloping rabbet as shown in FIG. 199.

LARGER & SMALLER SIZES

UNUSUALLY LARGE RABBET PLANES, BOTH square and skew, are known as long as 24 in. The advantage is the same as that of a jointer plane: greater accuracy when dealing with long boards. Some of these long versions are also provided with double irons.

Long rabbet planes were also made in extra-wide sizes approximating the width of a regular jack plane, and are known as bridgebuilder's or ship-carpenter's rabbet planes. All these varieties may be found with regular totes (handles). Sometimes the totes are centrally mounted, but more often than not they are offset, being screwed to the side of the ſtock, which may be too thin to accept a mortised tote.

At the other end of the scale are much smaller planes, some being as short as 4 in. These are rarer, and usually related to the next major group: carriagemaker's rabbet planes.

CARRIAGEMAKER'S RABBET PLANES

CARRIAGEMAKER'S AND COACHBUILDER'S rabbet planes can be divided into two diſtinct

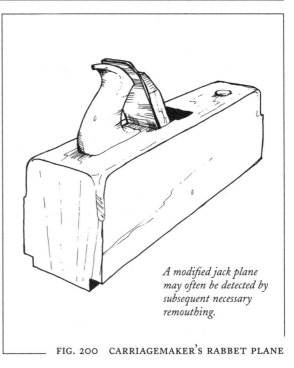

A modified jack plane may often be detected by subsequent necessary remouthing.

FIG. 200   CARRIAGEMAKER'S RABBET PLANE

groups. The firſt resembles ordinary bench planes with rabbets worked in the sole of the ſtock on either side of the iron (see FIG. 200). Although such planes are sometimes liſted in old makers' catalogs, many will prove upon close and expert examination to have ſtarted life as regular planes that have been reworked by their owners. They are useful for cleaning out long rabbets in either direction with great nicety since they are usually fitted with double irons.

Members of the second group are known as T-rabbet planes, since their profile, when held upside-down, resembles the letter 'T' (see FIG. 201). Although such a shape makes cutting rabbets in confined corners easier, since it leaves room for the fingers holding the side of the ſtock, and although many of the differently shaped soles that curve from front to back and from side to side in a variety of radii are undoubtedly designed for the tight, curved work that was necessary in coachbuilding, T-rabbet planes are also extremely useful in fine joinery and cabinetmaking for operations such as cleaning out small, curved rabbets in all sorts of non-reſtilinear work. Their

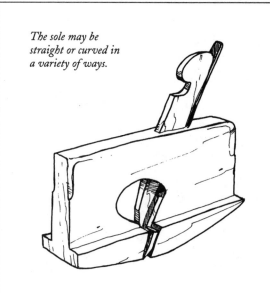

The sole may be straight or curved in a variety of ways.

FIG. 201   T-RABBET PLANE

More extremely curved soles are likely to be user-modifications.

FIG. 203   COMPASS RABBET PLANE

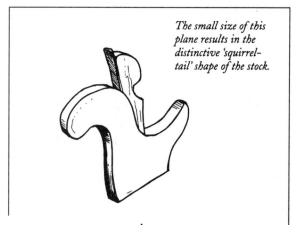

The small size of this plane results in the distinctive 'squirrel-tail' shape of the stock.

FIG. 202   COACHBUILDER'S RABBET PLANE

irons are usually set at a steeper angle than in most rabbet planes, making them especially suitable for hardwood.

Most T-rabbet planes are about 6 in. long, but smaller versions, often with a tail formed from the end of the stock, are also fairly common (see FIG. 202).

There is no law that says a plane may not be altered by its user. If this is done to good effect such an alteration results in an equally valid tool. Of all the various user-made modifications that may be found in different planes, some more efficient than others, that of transforming a rabbet plane with a square-iron into the variety known as a compass rabbet plane is perhaps the easiest. Many compass rabbet planes (FIG. 203) are just such modifications, and it can be impossible to tell them apart from factory-made examples, although such do exist, to the relief of the purist collector.

FILLISTERS

FILLISTER PLANES MAY BE DEEMED THE aristocrats of the rabbet planes, and some indeed rival the king of planes, the plough plane itself (see chapter 21), in quality and sophistication. The derivation of this peculiar word is unknown, 'fillister' being the older and more usual spelling in Britain, although 'filister' is also found in old tool catalogs. Since the Stanley Tool Company called its early metal versions 'filletsters' this latter spelling has become more common in America, but with little apparent justification since the pronunciation remains the same.

Fillisters may be defined as rabbet planes with fences and depth stops. The simplest kind, the

FIG. 204   MOVING FILLISTER

Standing fillister, has already been mentioned. The name implies that the fences stand fixed, and allow of no variation in either depth or width. A more useful tool is the moving fillister (FIG. 204), whose fence and depth stop, if so fitted (not all moving fillisters have depth stops), may be moved.

All moving fillisters have skewed irons and spurs. Various widths are provided and the fence, which in the simplest kind of moving fillister is fixed to the sole of the stock by two or three screws, often seated in recessed brass-lined channels, is as wide as the sole and so may be adjusted to expose almost all the cutting edge. This does not usually extend all the way across the sole as with simple rabbet planes since the left-hand edge is necessarily always covered by at least a part of the fence.

A more complicated form of moving fillister has a fence attached to arms that pass through the stock in the same manner as the arms of a plough plane. These arms may be similarly held in the required position by wedges or by wooden nuts operating on threads chased into the arms themselves.

Moving fillisters with fences adjusted by or on sliding arms may be further categorized into two distinct types: sash fillisters (see chapter 22) and regular moving fillisters. The former are designed to cut the rabbet needed in window sash, often formed after the moulding has been made. The moulding makes it difficult for a regular fillister to find a surface against which to rest its fence, which, of course, must be on the side opposite the rabbet.

Consequently, the sash fillister is designed to cut on the opposite side and the top surface of the fence is recessed to accommodate the depth stop. FIG. 205 makes these differences clear.

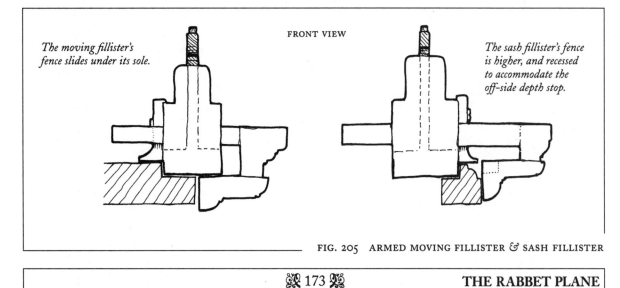

FRONT VIEW

The moving fillister's fence slides under its sole.

The sash fillister's fence is higher, and recessed to accommodate the off-side depth stop.

FIG. 205   ARMED MOVING FILLISTER & SASH FILLISTER

The right-handed member of a pair of side-rabbet planes.

FIG. 206 SIDE-RABBET PLANE

RELATED PLANES

ONE OF THE BEST WAYS OF CLEANING UP OR slightly adjusting a rabbet is with the use of a small bullnose plane or a shoulder plane. Sometimes, however, there is no room for such large tools and a narrower tool is necessary. Side-rabbet planes (FIG. 206) were developed for just this purpose. Modern metal side-rabbet planes made in left- and right-handed versions as well as double-ended versions are sometimes adequate, but they lack the length and height of the wooden side-rabbet planes, which makes their use less sure. Wooden side-rabbet planes are made in pairs so that it is possible to work on either surface of a rabbet from either direction.

Related to side rabbet planes are a variety of other special-purpose rabbet planes designed to clean up two sides at once, odd-angled rabbets, and V-grooves. Similarly, badger planes and panel-raising planes may also be considered rabbet planes since they both form rabbets. They are discussed in chapter 24.

METAL VERSIONS

TOWARDS THE END OF THE NINETEENTH century there was a dramatic increase in the number and variety of metal planes of all types, a few of which are still being made. Included in this category are various rabbet planes beyond the scope of this book, but worthy of consideration by the interested user. Since even second-hand examples of these planes cost many times more than the common wooden rabbet plane, it can still be very worth while to experiment first with the older versions.

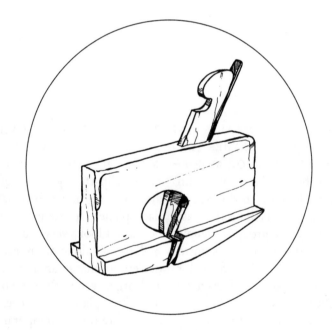

THE RABBET PLANE

20

THE DADO PLANE

'MADOX REDIVIDUS'
OR, AN AMAZING DISCOVERY

WHAT I FIND AT YARD SALES AND THE LIKE NEVER CEASES TO AMAZE ME, ESPECIALLY WHEN IT COMES TO OLD TOOLS — AND 'OLD' CAN MEAN AS MUCH AS A HUNDRED YEARS OR MORE — MANY OF WHICH MAY HAVE SEEN A GREAT deal of use even if they have subsequently lain ignored and forgotten for decades. In this age of antique collectomania almost everything the least bit old is collected avidly by one group of people or another, and almost anything dirty enough to look fifty years old is enthusiastically offered for sale at yard sales and fleamarkets, and even by antique stores who ought to know better. With so many people on the trail of 'antiques', it is a never-ending surprise to me that, more frequently than might be expected, really old and intrinsically valuable items still do show up.

Of course, one reason for this is that despite the plethora of specialist books and price guides on everything from bottle caps to bass drums, some things slip through the net simply because they are not recognized for what they really are. The dado plane is a case in point. This is undoubtedly because it looks very much like a moulding plane.

This fact alone often leads enthusiastic antique dealers to charge an arm and a leg for it, but by and large, even in the state of California, where no moulding planes were ever commercially made, and where the contemporary user base must have been far smaller than in most other parts of the country, moulding planes are not so rare that they may not commonly be found for just a few dollars or so. In fact, the average price at fleamarkets and less pretentious antique stores seems to be between ten and fifteen dollars.

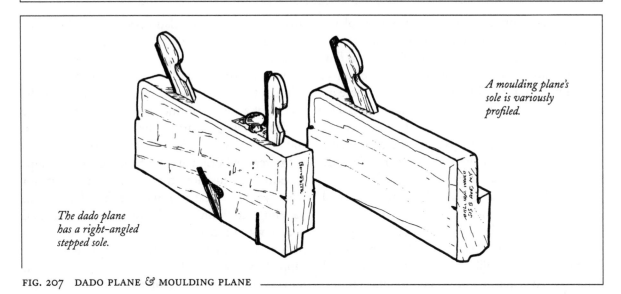

A moulding plane's sole is variously profiled.

The dado plane has a right-angled stepped sole.

FIG. 207   DADO PLANE & MOULDING PLANE

Like many other things you may never notice until you start looking, they are more abundant than you might think. Hundreds of thousands were made over the better part of two hundred years. Despite the fact that for all intents and purposes commercial production ceased in the 1920s (there are still a few models made and offered for sale in specialist woodworking-tool catalogs), moulding plane production in the 19th century was truly staggering. At the same time, early examples from the middle or beginning of the 18th century are far less common. Such planes command commensurately higher prices when they enter the knowledgeable tool-collector's market, privately or at auction.

Nevertheless, despite these older planes' greater rarity it is by no means impossible to discover, even in as unlikely a location as California, a plane that is well over two hundred years old. This is because there is little difference, to the untrained eye, between one moulding plane and the next. Even so, discovering an example of one of the very first dado planes ever made can still be a delightful surprise, but such was my good fortune recently in a California yard sale.

WHAT IS A DADO PLANE?

IT SHOULD BE NOTED THAT A DADO IS NOT a moulding, and a dado plane by definition is therefore not a moulding plane (see FIG. 207). It may look like one, but it does not and cannot make mouldings. Like many other planes that get lumped together as moulding planes simply because they are all about 9½ in. long, somewhat thin, and made of wood, the dado plane is a special-purpose plane whose function is not to stick mouldings ('stick' being the correct term for the process of forming a moulding on solid wood with a moulding plane), but to form joints.

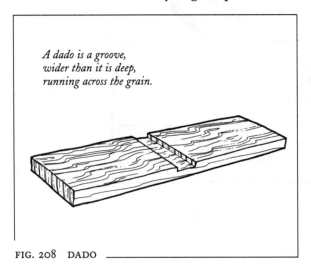

A dado is a groove, wider than it is deep, running across the grain.

FIG. 208   DADO

THE DADO PLANE

There are many varieties of this type of plane: plough planes, tongue-and-groove planes, rabbet planes, and gutter planes, to mention just a few. For the most part the names are self-descriptive, and a little thought will demonstrate that these do not have very much to do with mouldings. The dado plane is a little different. The very word 'dado' has several meanings, and the dado plane has also been known by other rather enigmatic names such as banding plane, cut-and-thrust plane, raglet, trenching plane, housing plane, and carcase grooving plane.

Without going deeply into its etymology, the term 'dado' currently has two distinct meanings: To the general public it means an ornamental band of paper, plaster, or wood running around the top of an interior wall. To the woodworker, however, it means a kind of groove. Specifically, one that runs across, rather than with, the grain, and one that is usually understood to be wider than it is deep (see FIG. 208). (Note also that to a woodworker, the primary characteristic of a normal groove is that it is deeper than it is wide, no matter which way it runs.) Several of the names mentioned in the previous paragraph thus

give a hint as to the dado plane's true function: making a groove (or dado) across the grain.

In the days before plasterboard, rooms were frequently paneled with wood. This paneling was often let into a groove cut in the flooring by means of a tongue formed along the bottom edge of the paneling's frame. The receiving groove in the flooring was made with the dado plane. This is the reputed original use of this plane, and supposedly explains how the name came about, for when you also bear in mind the fact that certain paneling, extending only halfway up the wall, and which was properly known as wainscoting (the reason for which is another story), was often capped by a so-called dado rail, it becomes clear how eventually the use of this word 'dado' was transferred from the rail to the paneling to the plane used to cut the groove formed for housing it and, at last, to the very groove itself. At least, that is one story. But, true or not, the fact remains that the kind of groove described above and the special-purpose plane used to make it are today both called dados. In any event, years of perusing old tool-catalogs has led me to the conclusion that there never was much consensus regarding either

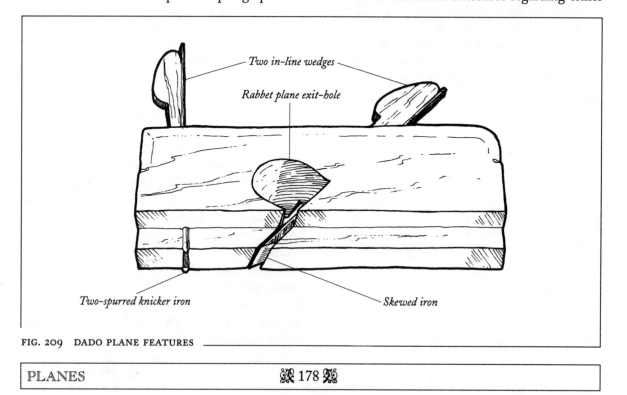

Two in-line wedges

Rabbet plane exit-hole

Two-spurred knicker iron

Skewed iron

FIG. 209 DADO PLANE FEATURES

nomenclature or use. Nevertheless it is true that this plane is wonderfully well suited for forming what we now call dados, wherever they might be needed.

HOW THE DADO PLANE WORKS

TWO THINGS DEFINE THE DADO PLANE AND qualify it to make dados. The first is the skewed iron that extends all the way across the sole, and the second is the presence of a two-spurred iron placed in front of the main cutting iron (see FIG. 209).

The skewed iron ensures a smooth, shearing cut when used across the grain. This is a feature shared in common with various rabbet planes and fillisters, as well as with many of the metal planes made over the years by Stanley™. This feature alone, however, would not be sufficient to create a clean dado were it not for the presence of the two little spurs that precede the main iron and score the fibers ahead of the shaving to be taken. By being exactly as far apart from each other as the blade's side-to-side width, the spurs ensure that the dado may be formed with perfectly clean sides. Without these spurs the bottom of the dado might be smooth, but it would undoubtedly suffer from ragged edges.

Both the main skewed cutting iron and the double-spurred scoring iron are held in the stock by wedges. These two wedges constitute the dado plane's most obvious distinguishing characteristic. Quite a few other moulding planes and special-purpose planes can be found with double wedges holding two irons, but these wedges and irons are invariably located side-by-side. The dado plane's wedges are in line, like the masts of a sailing ship.

The second distinguishing characteristic of the dado plane is that it is the only other plane besides the rabbet plane made with a distinctively tapered mouth, designed to discharge the shavings off the bench — that is, out of the left-hand side of the plane (assuming that the plane is being used by a worker standing at the bench and facing to the left). It can do this because the iron is skewed with the trailing edge on the left-hand side of the plane, proof that the dado plane is descended directly from the rabbet plane. In any case, dado planes are invariably used with a fence or guide strip at the right-hand side of the plane that would impede the shavings' exit were they to be discharged on this side. All dado planes share these two features. The vast majority are also all 9½ in. long, the standard length for all moulding planes and related planes since early in the 19th century. However, manufacturers commonly made dado planes in various widths, typically in sets ranging from ¼ in. to 1 in., increasing by eighth-inch increments. Besides variations in width, the other chief difference encountered between dado planes is the presence or absence of variously designed depth stops.

It is true that all dado planes possess a built-in depth stop by virtue of the fact that the desired width of dado — a function of the width of the skewed iron — is less than the required thickness of the plane's body, and the resulting step down in width at the sole results in a maximum depth that can be worked of around ½ in. (see FIG. 210). But it is not always convenient to form a dado to this

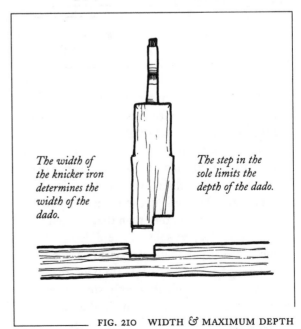

The width of the knicker iron determines the width of the dado.

The step in the sole limits the depth of the dado.

FIG. 210   WIDTH & MAXIMUM DEPTH

THE DADO PLANE

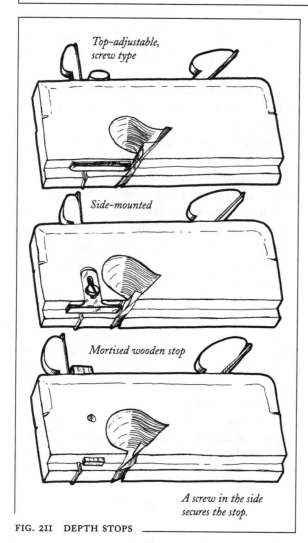

Top-adjustable, screw type

Side-mounted

Mortised wooden stop

A screw in the side secures the stop.

FIG. 211   DEPTH STOPS

The earliest form of depth stop, and one which continued in use as the cheapest form long after the introduction of improved versions, was no more than a simple wooden strip, usually made of boxwood, mortised very snugly into the stock so that friction alone sufficed to hold it in place. Any adjustment up or down was accomplished by tapping it in or out with a mallet or hammer.

Regardless of how well fitted this form of depth stop may have been initially, sooner or later, with use or shrinkage caused by dryness, it became loose. The obvious cure was to secure it in the required position by means of a screw inserted through the cheek of the plane. Consequently, it was not long before manufacturers were providing planes with depth stops fully securable by wooden or brass set screws inserted in the sides of the plane. The final solution, used in the best planes, was to adopt the kind of internally mounted depth stop found in fillisters and many plough planes. This consists of a steel shoe that emerges from, and retracts into, the sole of the plane, thereby stopping the action of the plane as soon as it makes contact with the work.

A curious, unintuitive feature of these internal depth-adjustment screws is that they operate with an apparent reverse thread. To cause the depth stop to emerge from the sole of the plane it is necessary to turn the screw counter-clockwise, which is something that almost everyone tries to do the reverse of at first.

Apart from minor subtleties of design, such as the exact shape of the mouth and the depth of the chamfering around the stock, there is little else that distinguishes one dado plane from another.

THE DADO PLANE IN USE

THE IRONS MUST OF COURSE BE SHARP OR very little will be possible. Equally important, however, is that the spur iron and the cutting iron must be in perfect alignment. To make sure that this alignment is not compromised the spurs must only be sharpened on their inside edges. To do

precise depth, and so some form of regulation becomes necessary since it is very hard to work a groove of consistent depth unaided.

Consequently, although cheap models were made with no stop at all, most dado planes may be found with one of three main kinds of depth stop (see FIG. 211). When it became necessary to form a dado to any depth other than that formed by the plane's own stepped sole on these depth-stopless models, the usual solution was to tack an extra thickness of wood to the bottom of the plane. Planes with no built-in depth stop often bear traces of this having been done in the form of old holes, blackened soles, and vestigial nails.

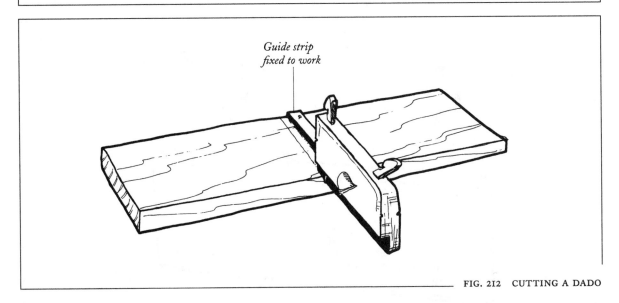

Guide strip fixed to work

FIG. 212   CUTTING A DADO

otherwise would alter their effective width and destroy their relationship to the width of the skewed iron. Since the irons are adjusted lower by tapping on the front of the stock and higher by tapping on the back of the stock, it is usually best to start with the spurred scoring-iron set much higher than is needed, adjusting the cutting iron in the manner described, and then gently lowering the scoring iron by tapping directly on the end of its tang. But be careful, for this end of the iron is very soft and easily bent.

There is a lot more than could be said on the fine adjustment of wooden planes' irons; with regard to dado planes the chief point is that both irons be in perfect alignment, not only with each other but also with the sole through which they protrude. If this fact is observed, the only other essential is to start work by drawing the plane backwards across the board that is to be dadoed so that the first marks made upon the wood are the parallel lines scored by the spur cutter.

Since the dado plane is intended to be used across the grain, and to sink into the wood as it is worked, it cannot have an integral fence. Consequently, a guide must be provided separately by attaching a straightedge to the work, immediately to the right of the intended dado. In carpentry, this guide is usually a lath or other thin but straight strip nailed onto the work with small tacks or brads as in FIG. 212; in finer work a guide may be clamped on.

After the guide is in place and the depth stop has been set to the required depth, the plane is first drawn backwards across the work and then pushed forwards. Providing the two irons are truly in alignment and the plane is held tightly against the guide, distinctively curled shavings will issue out of the plane's mouth, leaving behind a smooth-bottomed, straight-sided dado with very little effort. It is one of the simplest tools to use, eminently more pleasurable than a router, being quieter and safer, and producing an immaculately smooth, burn-free, chipout-free cut.

Obviously, the dado plane cannot compete with a router or a dado headset in a tablesaw when vast quantities of grooving are required, but in custom furnituremaking, or for small projects, the convenience of being able to reach for just the right dado plane and with a few quick passes quietly cut a perfect dado is unmatched.

THE AMAZING DISCOVERY

SINCE I ENJOY USING THESE PLANES SO much I am always on the lookout for them, and

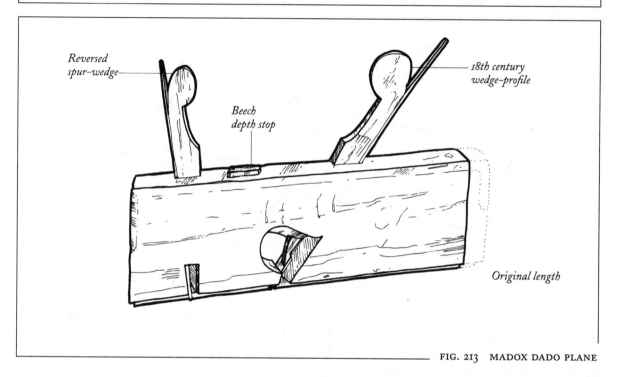

Reversed spur-wedge

Beech depth stop

18th century wedge-profile

Original length

FIG. 213   MADOX DADO PLANE

indeed, as explained earlier, they are not too hard to find. It has, in fact, gone past the point with me where I am still looking for a complete set; I now enjoy finding examples with better depth stops or other curious features. But I never expected to find a plane made by the very man credited with having developed the dado plane — over two hundred years ago — more than five thousand miles away from where it first saw the light of day.

The gentleman in question was one William Madox, who is known to have operated a plane-making business in Peter Street, in the City of Westminster (now part of greater London), from 1748 to 1775. The first 'proto-dado planes' made by Madox were little more than regular, skewed-iron rabbet planes with a projecting sole formed by projecting cheeks on both sides of the iron. They were fitted with two depth stops and two separate spurs or knicker blades. Madox's planes, like other 18th century planes, were typically longer than later 19th century planemakers' planes, being on average about 9⅞ in. long. A further idiosyncrasy was that his irons were set at 47° rather than at the 50° common for later planes.

The dado plane that caught my eye at the yard sale I visited was in a box with numerous other wooden moulding planes and various metal bench planes. Although it was a more developed version than Madox's original design it still exhibited significant differences from the later standardized types of the 19th century (see FIG. 213). Most noticeably, the wedge holding the spur iron was positioned facing backwards instead of forwards. Despite this glaring difference there were other clues to this plane's age. Although covered with a venerable patina, it was apparent by the roughness of the surface of the back of the plane, and the truncated form of the chamfers that are typically carried along the top of the stock and down the back, that this 9½ in.-long plane had been sawed to a shorter length than originally made. This is a frequent occurrence with 18th century planes, due no doubt to later owners wanting to be able to fit these planes into the same space as would contain the shorter, standardized lengths of 19th century tools. Together with the 47° angle at which the cutting iron was bedded, and the distinctive 17th century profile of both wedge heads, I had little doubt that I had found an old plane, but as soon as I saw William Madox's name stamp with its distinctive 18th century zig-zag border stamped in the plane's toe I could hardly believe my good fortune. There is never any knowing what may turn up . . . anywhere.

21

THE PLOUGH

PRINCE OF HANDTOOLS

WHILE IT IS TRUE THAT IN AMERICAN ENGLISH THE WORD 'PLOUGH' IS TODAY GENERALLY SPELLED 'PLOW', I THINK THERE IS A CASE FOR USING THE OLDER, BRITISH SPELLING WHEN REFERRING TO THE WOODWORKING PLANE THAT GOES by that name. Not only was the tool introduced to America chiefly by British craftsmen — the first tools being undoubtedly of British origin, in consequence of which 'plough' was the spelling first used on the American continent — but even subsequent native ploughs, manufactured in America by Americans, were known by this spelling. Moreover, few ploughs were still being produced by the time the spelling changed. So, in fact, most ploughs seen today originally began life not as 'plows', but 'ploughs', and were made, advertised, and sold as such.

The plough, often referred to as 'the prince of handtools', is not only one of the handsomest tools ever designed, but it is also truly useful, and deserves a place in the toolbox just as much as on the collector's shelf.

Although various forms of woodworking ploughs have been around for hundreds of years, the tool that is conjured up today at the mention of the word is usually an example of the type made during the 19th century. This period saw the manufacture of woodworking handtools change from what had been typically one-man operations to big business ventures, involving factories with large numbers of workers. Although this change produced large numbers of mass-produced tools it also saw the development of more expensive tools aimed at the more discriminating and demanding consumer. Because of their relative complexity ploughs were particularly susceptible to this kind of development, and as a result ploughs were made that are truly works of art, frequently cherished over all other tools in the toolchest.

But in order to gain a clearer idea of the nature of the beast that is called plough, let us return to the beginning of the 19th century for a quick overview of the situation then obtaining, and see how the changes in tool manufacture resulted in the extraordinary profusion that occurred later.

EUROPEAN VS. BRITISH VS. AMERICAN

AS THE INFANT AMERICAN TOOL INDUSTRY began to develop there already existed two basic types of ploughs: the European and the British. The British type predominated right from the start of the tool's introduction to America, and soon gained complete ascendancy, only, however, subsequently to split into two further types, now referred to as British and Yankee. To understand what differentiated these types it is necessary to examine more closely exactly what the tool does and how it operates.

It is all in the name: the plough plane, like its bigger namesake, the agricultural plough, cuts a groove across the surface of the material it is used on. Grooves are much used in woodworking both by carpenters and by cabinetmakers, and there are many sorts, now usually distinguished by various names according to their direction and location in the wood. For example, there is the rabbet, which is an open-sided groove at the edge of a piece of wood; the dado, which is a groove cut across the grain; and the slot, which is a closed-end groove (see FIG. 214). The word 'groove' is usually reserved in woodworking for an open-ended groove running with the grain, either in the edge or on the face of the wood. It is the woodworking groove with which we are concerned, for this is what the plough is employed to make.

When you make a groove there are three things to be considered: the width of the groove to be made; the depth to which it is to be cut; and its precise location in relation to the nearest edge. A groove of any given size may of course be made with a simple purpose-built tool such as a scratch stock, but this will be the only groove possible with such a tool. If you have three differently sized and located grooves to make, you will need three different scratch stocks. The great beauty of the plough plane lies in the various adjustments possible that allow all three considerations to be accommodated in almost limitless combinations.

How the position of the groove is determined is what at first differentiated the British type from the European type. The positioning mechanism consists simply of a fence attached to the stock (body of the plane) by two arms. By varying the distance between the fence and the stock (which contains the iron, or blade), the location of the groove can be adjusted in relation to the edge of the workpiece. In Europe the practice was to fix the arms to the body of the plane and slide the fence in and out as needed on these arms. In

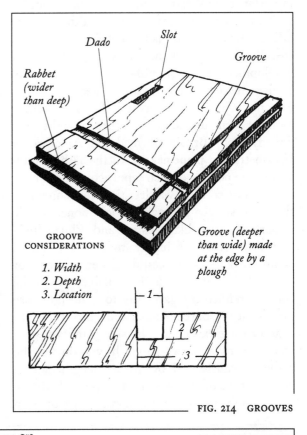

Rabbet (wider than deep)

Dado

Slot

Groove

Groove (deeper than wide) made at the edge by a plough

GROOVE CONSIDERATIONS

1. Width
2. Depth
3. Location

FIG. 214   GROOVES

Britain, on the other hand, the practice was of course reversed: the fence was fixed to the arms and the body was what moved.

The differences would appear to be arbitrary; merely different solutions to the same problem. But the British method predominated in America (unlike the rule regarding which side of the road to drive on), and all subsequent American ploughs were made this way. It is interesting to note, however, that when metal planes began to be made in the middle of the 19th century, whenever they were fitted with fences it was with the fence sliding on the arms in the European fashion, and not the body — like the wooden ploughs. To this day, combination planes and so-called duplex planes, such as the Stanley™ 76, are made in the European fashion, although newer tools that require fences, like routers and laminate trimmers, have reverted to the British system.

This then is the primary difference between European and British planes. Differences of less importance consisted of various minor variations such as relative lengths and the width of irons. What now occurred was the development of the so-called Yankee plough. This was actually less a development than a simplification, for the native Yankee model was in many respects a cruder example of its British ancestor. The first British ploughs were undoubtedly either brought over directly from Britain or made in America by British-trained planemakers. In the 18th century there were periods of such rapid economic expansion that often there was less time for refinement than for simply getting the job done. While important cities like Boston and Philadelphia had their share of highly trained and gifted cabinetmakers who could either import or demand the very best tools available, out in the country refinement gave way to a no-nonsense practicality. Consequently, well into the 19th century, there existed side-by-side with its elegant cousin a more down-to-earth version of the plough characterized by greater length, square arms instead of threaded arms (upon which the body was secured either by thumbscrews or, even

more simply, just by wedges), and a fence having the same length as the body — in distinction to the British form, which possessed a longer fence extending beyond the body.

In time, however, the Yankee plough was superseded by the British model, and it was this latter type which then received so much attention lavished upon it, turning it into the prince of handtools.

A BEAUTIFUL MOUTH & AN ORNATE FENCE

THE BASIC MODEL RANGED FROM SEVEN and a half inches to 9½ in. long, the average being closer to 8 in. Cheaper models had the arms secured, as they passed through the stock, with wedges (FIG. 215) or thumbscrews (FIG. 216), but the majority had threaded arms adjusted with large, turned, knob-like wooden nuts on the right-hand side of the body, locked in place by flatter, washer-like wooden nuts on the fence side of the body (see FIG. 217). The fence was attached on the left of the body and the shavings were consequently thrown out on the right-hand side on top of the work or bench, in distinction to rabbet and dado planes, whose characteristic and beautifully shaped mouths are cut on the left-hand side, thereby throwing the shavings off the work. The plough is, however, the only other wooden plane that has this distinctively shaped mouth.

The fence, while being made square with the back of the stock, invariably projects about 1½ in. in front of the stock, and is one of the more noteworthy features of the tool. Because it is necessarily wide (in order to provide a firm base for fixing the ends of the arms), and because it is also necessarily deep (in order to provide a substantial fence with which to bear securely against the work being grooved), it would be a hefty piece of wood indeed were it not rabbeted at its bottom left edge. It is largely this rabbeting, effected in a series of moulded profiles, both at the

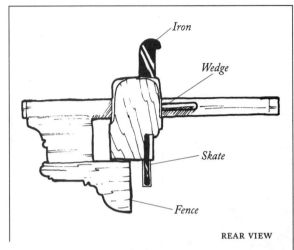

FIG. 215 WEDGED FENCE

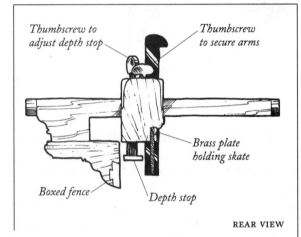

FIG. 216 THUMBSCREWED FENCE

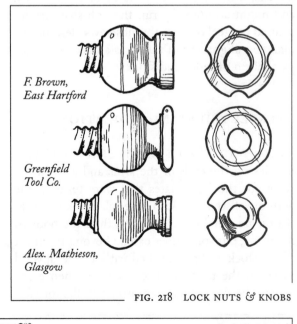

FIG. 217 SCREW-ARM FENCE

side and at the front edge, which gives the plane much of its ornate character. The bottoms of the arms where they join the fence are similarly moulded; top-of-the-line models went a step farther and ornately turned the very ends of these arms.

Beech was the commonest material used — as it is for most wooden planes — since it is fairly close-grained and reasonably stable. More expensive models were made of boxwood since boxwood is much denser than beech and wears better, and is consequently better suited for parts like the threaded arms and the nuts which fit on them. Naturally, these were the first parts to receive the improvements. For the more affluent consumer or for those who simply wanted all there was to be had, yet further refinements were possible. The fence, where it bore against the workpiece, might be boxed, that is, fitted with a dovetailed slip of boxwood or even made totally of boxwood. Occasionally, ploughs were made entirely of boxwood, and sometimes of even more exotic materials, such as ebony and rosewood.

Yet another area where the manufacturer's individuality was given free rein was in the design of the wooden knobs and nuts that secure the arms (see FIG. 218). There exists a remarkable

FIG. 218 LOCK NUTS & KNOBS

THE PLOUGH

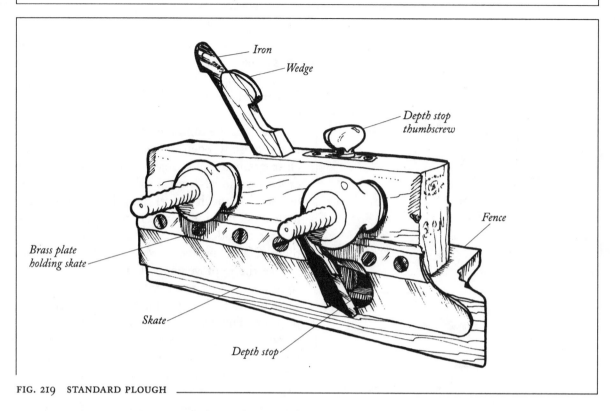

FIG. 219   STANDARD PLOUGH

number of patterns for these parts, each more delightful than the last, although intricacy of wooden arms and nuts was certainly not the last word in plough design. For some top-of-the-line models, arms might be made of brass or ebony, and might additionally run through steel bridles secured by steel or brass thumbscrews, designed to maintain alignment of the arms and so guarantee parallelism of fence and stock.

UNEXPECTED STANDARDIZATION

BRASS WAS ALSO FREELY USED FOR THE ferrules on the ends of the arms and as securing strips for the steel plates that were fixed to the bottom of the stock. These plates, known as skates, are usually the same length as the body of the plane, but sometimes extend beyond the front of the stock and are finished with a little upward curve, in the manner of ice skates — hence the name. The skate is made in two parts: the forward

part is designed simply to guide the plane and control the depth at which the iron is presented to the workpiece; the rear part is finished at its front edge into a double bevel so that it fits into a matching V-shaped groove cut in the back of the cutting iron (see FIG. 219). This particular detail constitutes a remarkable and singular instance of standardization in a tool all the other features of which vary so widely and conspicuously from maker to maker: practically any plough plane iron will fit in practically any plough plane.

Few other parts are ever interchangeable; nuts rarely fit threaded arms other than those for which they were specifically made, wedges differ in shape and proportion from maker to maker, and skates are all of different lengths and widths. But irons nearly always fit. The reason for this singular act of apparent consideration for the user on the part of makers otherwise apparently striving so strenuously to be unique derives no doubt from the fact that few planemakers were cutlers. It was common practice for most makers

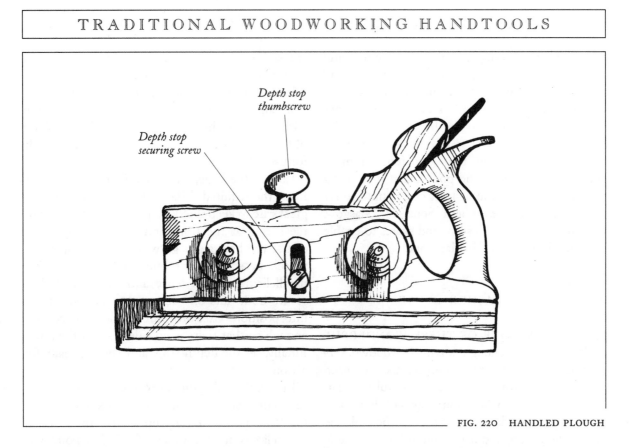

Depth stop thumbscrew

Depth stop securing screw

FIG. 220   HANDLED PLOUGH

to buy the irons they needed for their various tools from cutlers, or edge-tool manufacturers — most of whom, at least in the early part of the 19th century, were located in Sheffield, England. Furthermore, irons would become worn down or lost and need to be replaced, so that it is quite common to find ploughs with a collection of irons bearing several manufacturers' marks.

Although irons were interchangeable, their sizing was variable, and despite the fact that most ploughs were originally sold complete with a set of eight irons, not every set included the same widths — although generally these range from ¼ in. to 1 in. or slightly more, graduated in eighths of an inch. This turns out to be an advantage to the user since over time, as extra sets, partial sets, or even individual irons are accumulated, the range of grooves that may be cut at one pass is greatly increased from the original eight. Of course, it should be realized that a custom groove can be made by the simple expedient of using the iron that most closely approaches the desired

width, and then readjusting the fence to take a second pass with the same iron.

DEPTH STOPS & HANDLES

MOST PLOUGHS ARE FITTED WITH DEPTH stops, and these too range from the severely practical to the decidedly ornate. The simplest form is simply a wooden stop, wedged down through the stock. Better was the brass screw which operated a steel shoe that emerged from the sole of the stock (see FIG. 216) and for which an appropriate space was mortised out of the fence so that the depth stop could be lowered even when the fence was set close to the stock. Best-quality models additionally included a brass screw set in the side of the stock, which, when tightened, secured the depth stop from any inadvertent readjustment (see FIG. 220).

Yet another frequent improvement was the incorporation in the stock of a handle. This goes a long way to refining the balance of the tool and making its use even more comfortable. Beyond this improvement existed many other luxurious features such as brass inlays around the screws that secure the arms to the fence, ivory ferrules and ivory inlays, and a variety of ingenious devices for ensuring that the fence remain constantly parallel to the body when it is being moved in or out. And at least one manufacturer (Alexander Mathieson and Sons, of Glasgow, Scotland) offered extra stops and skates to enable the plough to handle circular work.

A TOOL TO TREASURE & USE

JUST TO OWN ONE OF THESE WONDERFUL tools is pleasure enough for most woodworkers with any sense of appreciation for tools or even wood, but to own one and use it is truly a treat. There are times when you may not have any electricity or just do not want to reset the tablesaw or use the router, and it is a fine thing to be able to reach for the plough and cut a groove with no fuss. If you want this option, there are a couple of points to bear in mind before pressing the venerable plough into service.

Firstly, of course, the stock should be sound, together with its wedge. It does not matter how grey or dirty it may appear, nor how rusty the skate may be, but check that the skate and the fence are parallel, that is, that both sit absolutely vertically. The skate may be off either because it has been bent, or, more likely, because the stock has warped and skewed the skate along with it. Then the fence may be out of vertical alignment either because it too has warped over the years, or because the screw arms are bent or too loosely attached to the fence. Whatever other deterioration the plane may have suffered, you will not be able to use it successfully and with ease if the skate and the fence are not in the proper relationship to each other.

Other defects may be more noticeable, such as chipped threads on the arms or even checked and cracked securing nuts, but these are minor and not as important. A little wax on the threads, a little minor disassembly and lubrication of the depth stop, and, of course, an immaculately sharp iron with a bevel of about 45°, set barely below the level of the bottom of the skate, and your plane is ready for use.

Loosen the large, outer nuts first and move the fence the required distance from the iron, taking great care to keep the skate parallel to the fence by measuring at the front and the back (unless of course you have a plough with a center adjusting-wheel, or some other built-in device ensuring parallelism between fence and stock), and then secure both nuts on each arm to lock the fence into position. Excessive force is not needed, just enough so that there is no side play on the arms. Finally, set the depth stop, and you are ready for action!

In use, the only points to remember are to keep the plane perpendicular to the work and to keep the fence pressed tightly up against the work. If you relax your observance of this last point you may well find the groove you are ploughing will wander away from the line. It sometimes helps, in order to avoid precisely this difficulty, to start planing at the far end of the work first, working from a point farther back each time, until the whole groove is begun, and then continue with each pass commencing at the near end of the work. This way the plane iron is led into a previously cut groove and is prevented from wandering off into uncharted territory should you relax your attention.

As mentioned earlier, grooves may be cut wider than the width of any irons you have by readjusting the fence a little more or less each time, but it will be found easiest to start any such multiple grooves with the groove farthest away from the edge, and progress towards the edge, rather than away from it. The logic behind this is that the former method leaves you more support as you widen the groove.

The plough was commonly the most cherished tool in the toolbox, the one of which its owner was proudest. It remains to this day one of the most handsome tools ever made, still eagerly sought after by discerning collectors, and unless the practice of woodworking is to become totally devoid of any esthetic sensibility it deserves a continuing appreciation.

22

SASH FILLISTERS

THE UNCOMMONEST FILLISTER

FILLISTER PLANES MAY BE REGARDED AS THE ARISTOCRATS OF THE RABBET PLANE FAMILY. THEY CAN INDEED RIVAL THE FANCY WOODEN PLOUGH PLANE DESCRIBED IN THE PREVIOUS CHAPTER IN TERMS OF MAGNIFICENCE AND INGENUITY, FOR THEY also are undoubtedly among the best examples of the pre-mechanized toolmaker's art. And of all fillisters, the sash fillister (FIG. 221) is the least common, and as a result is the least well understood. It is often not even recognized as a fillister at all, but instead is frequently confused with a plough plane, whose overall form and appearance are admittedly very similar.

Although their original use in the making of window sash has now been made largely obsolete by all sorts of milling machinery, sash fillisters can still prove to be useful tools in the small custom shop that specializes in restoration or reproduction work, and may also find a needed place in fine furniture shops where their unique attributes can sometimes make easier certain jobs that might prove tricky with router or shaper.

SASH FILLISTERS
& OTHER RABBET PLANES

A FILLISTER IS BASICALLY A RABBET PLANE (see chapter 19) fitted with a fence and depth stop. Its purpose is practically the same as that of a common rabbet plane, namely to cut a right-angled section out of the edge or corner of a board. Such a rabbet is much used in all kinds of woodworking. In carpentry it is to be found in siding and flooring where adjacent boards are

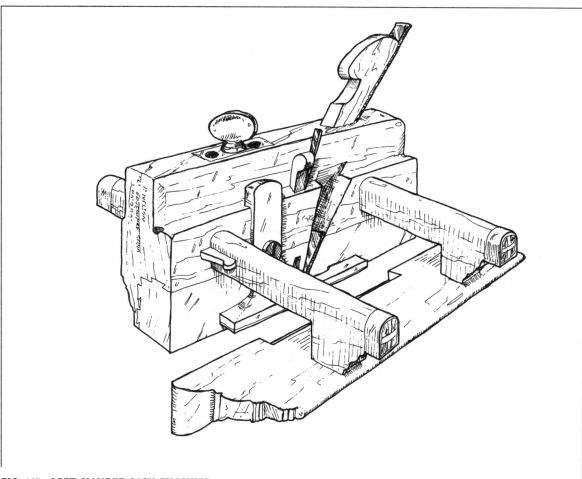

FIG. 221 LEFT-HANDED SASH FILLISTER

rabbeted to enable them to fit together. In joinery and furnituremaking the rabbet forms the basis for numerous joints and construction techniques. Making rabbets, in fact, is one of the commonest woodworking operations, and so it is not really surprising that there is a wide variety of tools designed to make them. Nowadays most rabbets are made with router, shaper, or tablesaw, but in the days before powered machinery the plane reigned supreme.

The common rabbet plane was made with a straight or skewed blade, and sometimes fitted with a spur, but since its primary use was for smoothing the bottoms of rabbets already formed, which would themselves lend guidance to the tool's path, they lack any form of fence or depth stop. When more guidance was necessary, fences would have to be fixed to the work itself. That this was often inconvenient — and that these planes were also used to start and form the rabbet rather than merely cleaning up the work already begun by some other tool such as the moving fillister mentioned below — is clearly demonstrated by the existence of many rabbet planes bearing the marks of fences having been nailed or screwed to the side or sole of the stock.

A rabbet plane made with a built-in fence and depth stop is known as a fillister. Although there are several varieties all belong to one of two main classes: standing fillisters or moving fillisters. The former class consists of planes with fences and depth stops formed simply by the shape of the

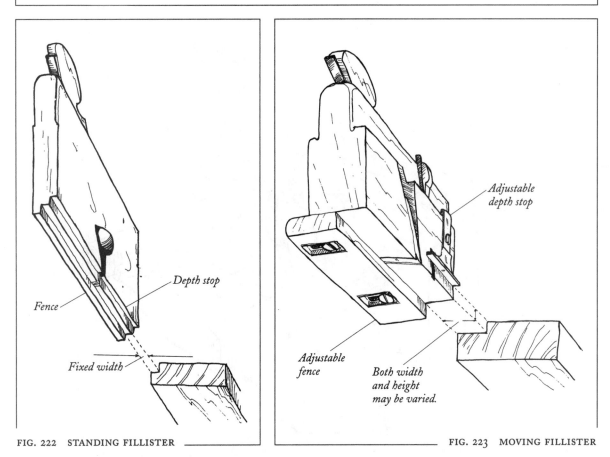

Depth stop

Fence

Fixed width

Adjustable depth stop

Adjustable fence

Both width and height may be varied.

FIG. 222   STANDING FILLISTER

FIG. 223   MOVING FILLISTER

sole (see FIG. 222), and consequently can only be used for making rabbets of fixed proportions. If differently proportioned rabbets are required, a different size standing fillister is necessary. This is fine when the same size rabbet is called for over and over, but when a variety of sizes is needed it is obviously not as convenient as using a moving fillister (FIG. 223) whose fence and depth stop can be adjusted.

The sash fillister is a member of the moving fillister branch of the rabbet family, being fitted with an adjustable fence and depth stop. No matter how one sash fillister may differ from another — there are several varieties — all share a common difference from regular moving fillisters: sash fillisters cut the rabbet on the far side of the work whereas all other fillisters cut the rabbet on the near side of the work. For the average right-handed woodworker standing in front of the

bench working from right to left, this means that while rabbet planes and fillisters in general work a rabbet on the edge of the work facing the worker, sash fillisters cut a rabbet on the side or edge farthest away from the worker.

THE DEVELOPMENT OF SASH FILLISTERS

IN ORDER TO UNDERSTAND WHY SUCH A thing should be necessary it is necessary to consider the development of the standard British joiner's workbench and the sudden popularity in both 18th century Britain and the American colonies of sash windows. Sash windows are those whose glass-holding frames slide up and down rather than being fixed, hinged, or pivoted, as is usual elsewhere.

Joiners, whose job it was to fabricate these windows, discovered the need for a special tool to make the rabbets in which the glass would sit in the frame. The ordinary rabbet plane and moving fillister, as mentioned above, can cut such a rabbet quite easily — but only in the edge of the work facing the worker. Since such rabbeted work destined to become sash bars in sash windows also had to be given a moulding on the side of the wood that would become the inside of the window, this meant that after such a rabbet was cut with a regular moving fillister, the work had to be reversed so that a moulding plane could be used on the other side. Furthermore, since sash bars (the narrow bars that separate one pane from another in the middle of the window) must necessarily be made with two rabbets and two moulded edges, the making of such a piece with a regular moving fillister and moulding plane involved four separate operations of fixing and unfixing the work to be planed.

The solution to all this fixing and unfixing of every piece of sash bar was to design a plane that would cut the rabbet on the far side of the work which could then be left in place so that the moulding could be stuck (the proper word for describing the making of a moulding) on the usual — that is to say, the near — side. Such a plane is the sash fillister.

It is interesting to consider that had this kind of window been popular on the continent of Europe the sash fillister might never have been invented because European benches, unlike their British and American counterparts, were often fitted with back vises. A back vise — almost never seen in Britain or America — would have made all the fixing and unfixing unnecessary in the first place, and it is conceivable that instead of inventing a new plane, British joiners might have borrowed the European technique. After all, many basic woodworking techniques now part of the British tradition, from linenfold carving to dovetailing and mortise-and-tenoning, originated on the Continent before being brought over and adopted on the British side of the Channel.

VARIETIES OF SASH FILLISTER

THERE ARE VARIOUS REFERENCES TO SASH fillisters throughout the 18th century in tool inventories, maker's order sheets, and advertising pieces, and numerous examples are known to exist, but the first written description occurs in a book written by Peter Nicholson at the beginning of the 19th century.* The definition he gives of sash fillisters in general is a model of clarity and deserves to be quoted:

> The sash fillister is a rebating plane for reducing the right hand side of the stuff to a rebate, and is mostly used in rebating the bars of sashes for the glass, and is therefore called a sash fillister.

Here also are described the two main sorts of sash fillisters that continued to be made until well into the 20th century. Nicholson refers to them as: 'The Fillister which throws the Shavings on the Bench' and '. . . the Sash Fillister for throwing the Shavings off the Bench.' They were more commonly known throughout the 19th century, as indeed they are to this day, as right-handed and left-handed fillisters respectively.

RIGHT-HANDED SASH FILLISTERS

RIGHT-HANDED SASH FILLISTERS WERE undoubtedly the first type to be developed, since they are similar in concept to the standing fillister, the only difference being that the rabbet in the sole of the plane that forms the depth stop is formed on the left-hand side rather than on the right-hand side (see FIG. 224). That this is necessary is a result of the rabbet being formed on the right-hand side of the work; if the depth stop were on the right-hand side of the plane — as is the case with standing and regular moving fillisters — there would be nothing but thin air for the depth stop to rest on, the wood all being on the other side of the plane.

* Peter Nicholson. *Mechanical Exercises.* London 1812

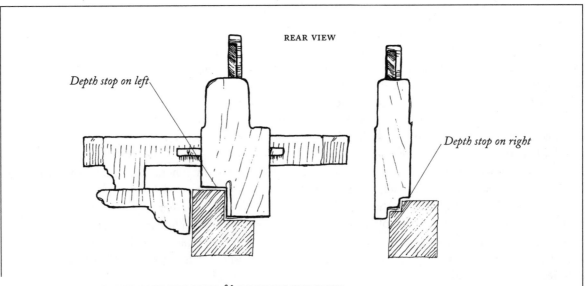

FIG. 224 RIGHT-HANDED SASH FILLISTER & STANDING FILLISTER

Because the rabbet is formed on the left-hand side of the plane's sole there can be no spur ahead of the cutting iron as is common with regular moving fillisters. Such a spur, designed to sever the fibers in the corner of the rabbet, is not absolutely necessary, however, since the plane's iron is skewed with its leading corner cutting into the corner of the rabbet being formed. The iron being skewed this way helps pull the plane into the corner of the rabbet and minimizes the risk of the plane wandering away from the side of the rabbet. This is, however, only a happy side-effect of the real reason for the direction of the iron's skew, since in any event it should be the tool's fence which controls the ultimate location of the cutting iron in the work. Because of the rabbet cut in the plane's sole, the shaving exit of the plane has to be on the other, right-hand, side of the stock, and since this is therefore the side where the shavings will exit, to make this easier and avoid the danger of the shavings choking the mouth, the iron is skewed with its trailing corner on this side. It is therefore the fact of the shavings' exiting on the right-hand side of the plane which results in this variety being known as the right-handed sash fillister, or 'The Fillister which throws the Shavings on the Bench'.

Early versions of the right-handed sash fillister were soon fitted with adjustable depth stops even though the rabbet in the plane's sole remained, since this rabbet was often found to be too deep to be used as the depth setting. These were either simple wooden stops held in place simply by the friction of their fit or thumbscrew-adjusted plates mortised into the bottom of the rabbeted section of the sole (see FIG. 225).

LEFT-HANDED SASH FILLISTERS

THE SKEW OF THE LEFT-HANDED FILLISTER'S iron is reversed, and therefore the shaving exit is necessarily on the left-hand side of the stock, which arrangement throws the shavings off the bench. This development certainly did not come about because some 18th century neatnik was concerned about the mess a right-handed sash fillister made of his bench — whichever side of the plane the shavings exit they all end up on the floor sooner or later — but because the rabbet in the sole of a right-handed sash fillister makes it impossible to see the working corner of the iron and watch what is going on. The addition of a depth stop, whether of wood or brass, renders the

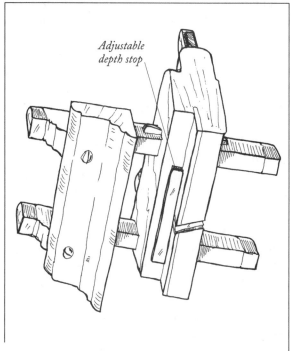

Adjustable depth stop

FIG. 225   RIGHT-HANDED SASH FILLISTER

woods are being worked. To prevent this, a spur cutter is usually fitted on the left-hand side of the stock just ahead of the point opposite which the leading edge of the iron sits in the mouth, similar to the way in a moving fillister is fitted out. It should be pointed out that although a moving fillister's iron is usually skewed so that its leading corner is in the corner of the rabbet, the existence of a spur cutter is still necessary since this tool, unlike a sash fillister, is frequently used for cutting rabbets across the grain.

An additional difference may usually be observed between right-handed and left-handed sash fillisters. Although in both cases the iron extends across the entire width of the sole (unlike moving fillisters, the outside corner of whose irons stops short of complete transection since they are covered by the fence which is screwed directly to the sole), right-handed sash fillisters are made with parallel sides, whereas left-handed sash fillisters usually have moulded corners on the right-hand side of the stock (see FIG. 226). It is obvious that right-handed sash fillisters cannot have any moulded corner at this point since this is the side where the shaving exit is located, and any moulding would compromise the iron's bed. Left-handed sash fillisters, on the other hand, whose shaving exit is on the other side of the stock must

sole's rabbet obsolete in any case. Left-handed sash fillisters thus have square-bottomed soles.

This does, however, create one minor problem: now that the iron is skewed with the trailing edge working the corner of the rabbet, the danger of tearout exists, particularly when long-fibered

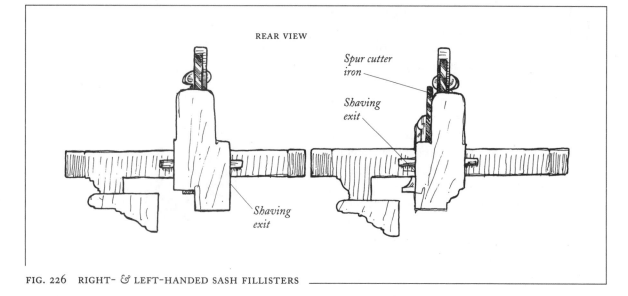

REAR VIEW

Spur cutter iron

Shaving exit

Shaving exit

FIG. 226   RIGHT- & LEFT-HANDED SASH FILLISTERS

SASH FILLISTERS

have some relief on the right-hand side, since the cheek (the side of the stock into which the throat is cut) would otherwise extend to the bottom of the sole, thus preventing the iron from extending across the entire width of the sole and thereby severely limiting the width of possible rabbets that may be cut. In practice there is usually a ¼ in. or ⅜ in. rabbet cut on the right-hand side of a left-handed sash fillister's stock before the moulding begins.

The depth stop of a right-handed sash fillister, as described above, is mortised into the stock and protrudes through the top of the rabbet cut in the sole. Since there is no rabbet in the sole of a left-handed sash fillister, the depth stop is fixed to the side of the stock, usually in a shallow slot. It is still controlled, however, by a brass thumbscrew whose adjusting mechanism is still mortised within the plane's body.

THE FENCE

WITH ONE EXCEPTION, ALL SASH FILLISTERS have similarly constructed fences. These are very like those found on wooden plough planes except for the important difference that while plough plane fences pass beneath the bottom of the sole, sash fillister fences are set higher and will stop against the side of the stock. This is true even for right-handed sash fillisters, whose fences do indeed pass under the rabbet cut in the right-hand edge of the sole: the fence still butts up against the body of the stock.

The exception occurs when a sash fillister was made as a combination fillister. The Scottish firm of Alexander Mathieson and Sons made several such combined sash and moving fillister planes, which not only have fences that pass below the stock but which were also fitted with spurs and depth stops on both sides, and whose shaving exit was made in the graceful form common to regular rabbet planes — unlike the straight openings common to moulding planes which are the usual shape for sash fillisters.

The majority of fences are adjusted by means of boxwood wedges rather than wooden nuts on threaded arms, which while more fiddlesome are at least less subject to damage. It is easy to replace a damaged or missing wedge; it is another matter to repair a threaded arm. Better-quality models also have stopped rabbets cut in the upper inside edge of the fence. This allows the fence to be adjusted close to the side of the stock and still accommodate a side-mounted depth stop.

A word of warning when reconditioning one of these planes: do not attempt to tighten the arms firmly to the top of the fence. They are intended to swivel since, unless the arms are fitted with a bridle which regulates their adjustment through the stock in equal measure, they will necessarily pass through unevenly as first one and then the other is tapped on the end with a mallet. In order to prevent excessive damage to the ends of the arms or stems from the tapping occasioned by adjustment, brass ferrules are usually fitted over the ends and are held in place by one or more wedges being inserted in the very ends of the arms (see FIG. 227).

It is not as vital to adjust the fence perfectly parallel to the stock as it is in the case of a plough plane, since the sash fillister has no skate to follow the course of the ploughed channel. Indeed, although it is generally a good idea to attempt as

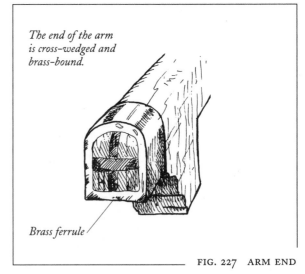

The end of the arm is cross-wedged and brass-bound.

Brass ferrule

FIG. 227 ARM END

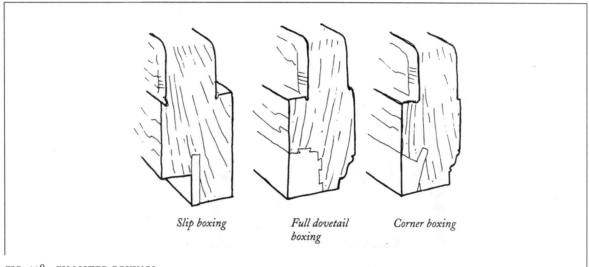

Slip boxing   *Full dovetail boxing*   *Corner boxing*

FIG. 228   FILLISTER BOXINGS

much accuracy as possible, it is sometimes useful to set the fence a little askew, thereby broadening the effective path of the iron. This will, however, prevent the side of the plane from being held flat against the work, and this procedure can be dangerous to the health of this part of the plane. It is precisely because this area receives the most wear that sash fillisters are usually boxed (fitted with strips of hard-wearing boxwood) at this point. The boxing varies according to the cost of the plane (see FIG. 228).

The very best models were made with integral handles and other features common to the more expensive plough planes. Although American joiners in the 19th century were fonder of a plane known as a stick and rabbet plane (which cut both the rabbet and the moulding at the same time) than a straightforward sash fillister, there were still very many made and they are by no means rare. Even the cheaper models can usually be brought back to good working condition to find a useful place in the discriminating shop.

23

MATCH PLANES

MADE FOR EACH OTHER

I N THE LOOSEST SENSE, THE TERM 'MATCH PLANES' REFERS TO THOSE PLANES THAT ARE MADE IN MATCHING PAIRS, THE PROFILE CUT BY ONE MIRRORING THE PROFILE CUT BY THE OTHER. THIS IS PERHAPS MORE ACCURATELY REPRESENTED BY THE BRITISH TERM for these tools: 'matching planes'. But more specifically, the term 'match planes' is also often used to describe those planes used in the making of 'match-boarding'. That match-boarding describes boards furnished with complementary edge joints of various patterns (tongue-and-groove being perhaps the best known, although other varieties exist, most notably the kind of combination, semi-locking bevel joints used in plywood and various particleboard joinery) suggests that the term 'match planes' may be a back-formation from the term describing the joinery technique. In any event, match planes exist with different profiles and are made in a variety of forms.

THE SUPREMACY OF THE TONGUE-AND-GROOVE

BEFORE THE INTRODUCTION OF PLYWOOD and other sheet materials which make the job of covering large areas a relatively easy procedure, different methods using wood were common. Many involved the use of relatively narrow planks or boards merely butted one against the other. A simple butt joint has its limitations, however, and different forms of lap joints or rabbets, culminating in the tongue-and-groove joint, were developed to overcome some of the deficiencies.

Tongue-and-groove joints have much to commend them. By fitting one board to another by means of an integral tongue, a continuous and perfect alignment of adjacent boards is ensured. This method also provides a continuous surface across the boards thus joined, eliminating the cracks that inevitably open between boards simply butted together. This process also provides a better protection from draft or dust penetration. And lastly, especially when used in combination with some form of edge ornamentation, such as a moulding or simple bead, it provides a relatively unnoticeable means of allowing for seasonal expansion and contraction across large areas of side grain.

Whether it was a matter of paneling an entire house (and incidentally, the term originally employed to describe covering the inside surfaces of a house was 'ceiling', which term ultimately became limited to today's use of the word), making partitions, or simply of covering the back or bottom of a piece of furniture, large or small, the tongue-and-groove joint was for a long time the preferred method. In fact, by the end of the 19th century, just before the general introduction of plywood, beaverboard, and other forerunners of today's gypsum wallboard coverings, the most common form of interior wall and much ceiling covering was the thin form of tongue-and-grooved planking called match-boarding referred to earlier. Usually made of oak, quarter-sawn to resist warping, this stuff was commonly no more than ¼ in. thick. When covering large areas the tongue-and-groove joint was truly supreme.

Naturally, by this date most tongue-and-groove material was milled by machine, but the average carpenter was frequently called upon to fabricate custom lengths on site. Consequently, match planes were very common. Even today, when many woodworkers are equipped with shapers or electric routers that can quickly mill all sorts of joints, having a pair of match planes handy can be an invaluable time-saver if a short length of tongue-and-grooving is all that is required. There is no setting up, matching accuracy is built into the tools, and the whole procedure is quick, quiet, and safe. Using a pair of match planes is an ecologically sound procedure, and one that can also provide a great deal of pleasure, as aromatic shavings curl lispingly from the bench.

A PAIR OF ONE & OTHER VARIETIES

ALTHOUGH INVARIABLY SOLD AS PAIRS WHEN new, there is sufficient standardization among match planes that finding an originally matched pair is by no means essential. Indeed, although this chapter is concerned mainly with wooden match planes, it should be remembered that by the end of the 19th century there was a considerable number of single metal 'match' planes being made that were designed to cut both parts of the tongue-and-groove joint. In these cases, the term 'match plane' was, of course, a bit of a misnomer, since you can hardly have a pair of one.

By far the most numerous are those match planes that look like common moulding planes (see FIG. 229). A moulding plane is a thin wooden plane usually about 9½ in. long, generally made from beech. (Planes dating from the 18th century are commonly somewhat longer, and may be

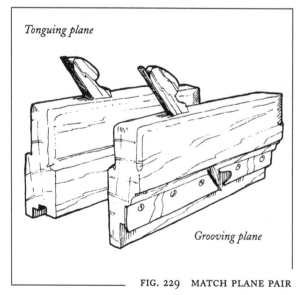

Tonguing plane

Grooving plane

FIG. 229 MATCH PLANE PAIR

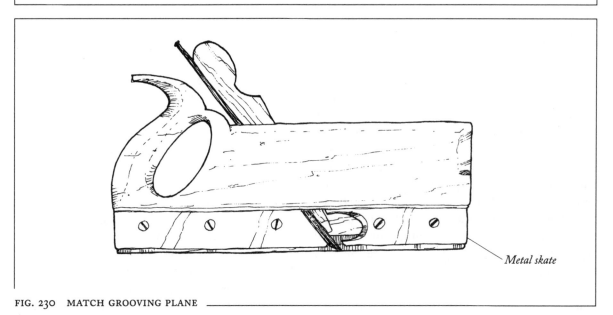

Metal skate

FIG. 230   MATCH GROOVING PLANE

made from birch as well as other kinds of wood.) A single iron, secured by a characteristic wooden wedge, is set in the stock (body of the plane) at an angle that may be as small as 40° or as great as 50°. Match grooving-planes differ from other moulding planes in having a metal skate fixed in the bottom of the plane. This acts both as the sole of the plane and, at the point where it is separated into the front and rear sections, the bed for the iron. The forward end of the bed section is finished like a knife edge in order to engage a V-groove cut in the back of the cutting iron. This holds the iron securely centered over the skate. It also makes possible the use of irons narrower than intended should this be desired. Wider irons cannot, of course, be used since the width of the throat in the plane's body is fixed.

Another difference between tongue-and-groove match planes and many other moulding planes is that match planes are made without 'spring'. That is to say, they are designed to be held and used perpendicularly to the work, rather than being canted over to an angle matching the spring line that is usually scribed on the heel of many moulding planes. The term 'spring' refers to the angle at which a plane must be held to avoid negative curves in steeply profiled moulding plane profiles (see chapter 25); a simple tongue-and-groove presents no such problems.

Better-quality match planes may be made with integral handles (see FIG. 230). This makes them considerably more comfortable and much easier to use; in all other respects they are the same as the unhandled versions.

OPERATION

MOST MATCH PLANES ARE DESIGNED TO BE used on boards of specific thicknesses, ranging from ½ in. to 1¼ in. To discover what thickness board any given plane is intended to work is very easy since this measurement is invariably stamped on the heel of the plane. For example, '⅜' stamped on the heel indicates that the plane is designed to cut a centered tongue-and-groove joint in wood that is ⅜ in. thick (see FIG. 231).

While it is not necessary to have an original pair from the same manufacturer to be able to form a perfect tongue-and-groove joint, care should be taken that the width of the iron that cuts the groove matches the slot in the iron designed to cut the tongue. It may be possible to adjust either slot or groove iron to match, or it may be possible to

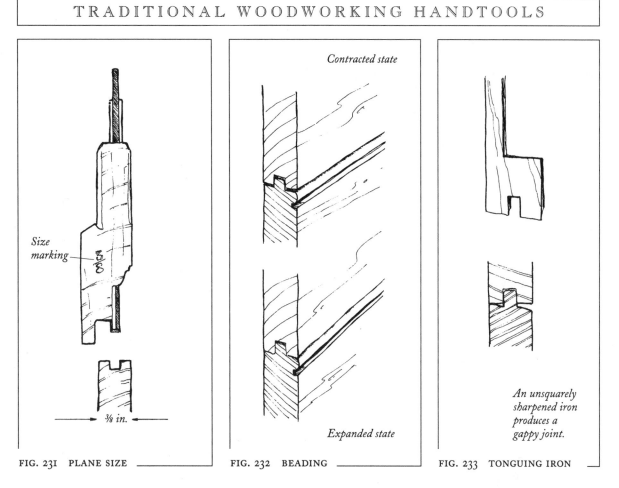

Size marking

⅜ in.

FIG. 231 PLANE SIZE

Contracted state

Expanded state

FIG. 232 BEADING

An unsquarely sharpened iron produces a gappy joint.

FIG. 233 TONGUING IRON

dress slightly mismatched parts after the fact by using a rabbet plane or shoulder plane. But note that whichever tool you use to cut either part (and this includes the possible use of other planes, such as a straightforward grooving plane, a plough plane, or the alternated use of a rabbet plane), what is most important is that the tongue must fit the groove snugly. This, as well as the fact that the depth of the groove will match the height of the tongue, is the main advantage of using a properly matched pair of match planes. Even this is not vital, however, for it is often desirable, especially when working wood that is liable to expand or contract — such as less than perfectly dry pine paneling — to bead the edge of the tongued part and make the tongue slightly less high than the groove is deep in order to allow enough room for expansion without the finished joint being pushed apart (see FIG. 232).

While on the subject of fit, note the importance of square sharpening. Whatever else you do, be sure to keep the irons' cutting edges sharpened perfectly square. And, in the case of the tonguing iron, be sure that both sides lie in the same plane, or you will form a tongue with uneven or sloped shoulders, either of which will make a perfect joint impossible, as shown in FIG. 233.

It is possible to collect a graduated set of pairs for working a range of different thicknesses. But while this may be entertaining for the collector and was perhaps practical for a permanent and well-equipped 19th century shop, for a carpenter traveling to a different job site every week or someone merely looking to use these planes on an occasional basis it is not terribly convenient. Nor is it absolutely necessary. Once you understand how these planes work, it is possible to be very effective with a single pair.

The idea behind the moulding plane variety of match plane is that the joint will be centered in the edge of the board by virtue of the built-in fence. Moreover, the centered joint will be formed in the optimum proportion to the board's thickness. Such a proportion is usually considered to be approximately 1:3. In practice, however, there is a certain amount of leeway possible. While a ¼ in. groove might be perfect for a ¾ in.-thick board, it will also usually be perfectly adequate for boards from ½ in. to 1 in. thick. This is true partly because the tongue extends the entire length of the board and gains much strength from this fact, and partly because centering the tongue (or groove) is not always necessary or even desirable.

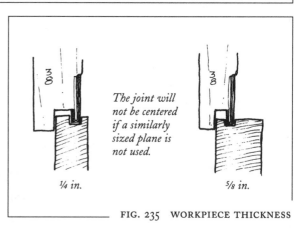

The joint will not be centered if a similarly sized plane is not used.

¼ in.   ⅝ in.

FIG. 235 WORKPIECE THICKNESS

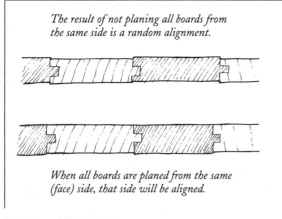

The result of not planing all boards from the same side is a random alignment.

When all boards are planed from the same (face) side, that side will be aligned.

FIG. 234 ALIGNMENT

Ideally, when match planes are used on the size boards they are designed for as indicated by the stamp on their heels, a perfect joint will be formed. I say 'ideally' because as a result of small irregularities in the wood being planed, possible wear in the plane's fence, and occasional lapses of attention when operating the plane and the failure thereby to keep the fence pressed absolutely against the side of the work, the centering of the groove may be less than perfect. For this reason it is imperative always to operate both planes in such a manner that their fences run against the same side of the boards being worked (see FIG. 234). This is usually the face side since it will generally be the more perfectly prepared surface.

Indeed, for paneling it may not even be necessary to have finished the back side at all.

If match planes are used on wood that is thinner than they are designed for, the joint will be shifted to one side of the board, and if used on boards that are thicker than intended, the joint will be shifted to the other side. This is shown clearly in FIG. 235. The illustration assumes that the fences are run against the same sides of the boards. If the boards are alternated, not only will the joint be offset but the sides of the boards will no longer lie in the same plane.

Once you understand this, and providing also that you take into account possible structural weaknesses, such as a groove being worked so far off center that one side will be dangerously thin, all sorts of interesting possibilities will become apparent. The chief limitation to this intentional repositioning of the joint is that when making a tongue on a board thicker than the plane was

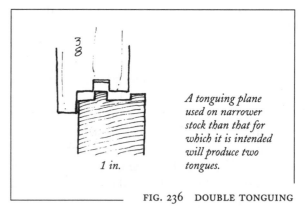

A tonguing plane used on narrower stock than that for which it is intended will produce two tongues.

1 in.

FIG. 236 DOUBLE TONGUING

intended to work, you may end up with the result shown in FIG. 236. The outside tongue can, of course, be easily removed utilising a variety of techniques, including running it through the tablesaw, or using a rabbet plane, a fillister, an adjustable plough, or even a more sophisticated form of match plane: the adjustable type.

ADJUSTABLE PLANES

SOME MATCH PLANES ARE MADE WITH movable fences, making the position of groove and tongue adjustable. These planes are often made the same length as the former type, with fences that are fixed to the sole of the plane (see FIG. 237). Much longer forms, designed to cut ½ in. and wider tongues and grooves, have fences fixed on threaded arms fitted through the body of the plane (see FIG. 238). These are intended for the heaviest class of work and are invariably handled. Some manufacturers referred to the larger sizes as 'planking' match planes and the smaller sizes as 'boarding' match planes.

The trick to using the larger form of tongue-and-groove match planes successfully is not only to keep the fence pressed tightly against the work but also to keep the fences aligned perfectly parallel to the sole, for otherwise the plane will bind on the work and be difficult to use.

DOUBLE-ENDED PLANES

THE ADVANTAGE OF COMBINING A PAIR OF tongue-and-groove planes into a single plane (see FIG. 239) is that not only are there fewer planes to carry around, but it is no longer necessary to worry about finding a perfectly matched pair. Wooden varieties are so designed that a central fence separates a tonguing iron on one side and grooving iron on the other. The plane is double-ended and used from either direction, according to whether the tongue or the groove is being worked.

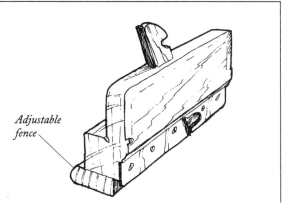

Adjustable fence

FIG. 237   ADJUSTABLE MATCH PLANE

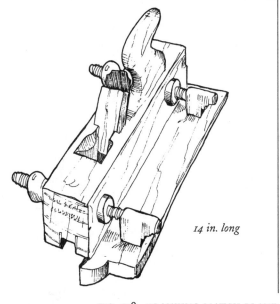

14 in. long

FIG. 238   PLANKING MATCH PLANE

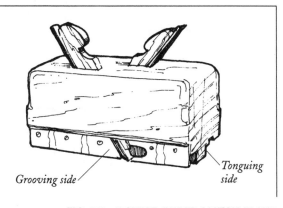

Grooving side

Tonguing side

FIG. 239   DOUBLE-ENDED MATCH PLANE

MATCH PLANES

Metal versions have also been made in various cunning patterns, some, like the Stanley™ 48 and 49, designed with pivoting fences that may be swung around to reveal or expose an extra cutting edge so that the groove or the shoulders of the tongue may be cut, and some made similarly to the double-ended wooden versions described above. Both varieties still require careful attention to the proper reciprocal alignment of the cutting irons.

OTHER FORMS OF MATCH PLANES

THE TONGUE-AND-GROOVE JOINT IS NOT the only form of matched joint for which match planes have been designed. The rule joint, used

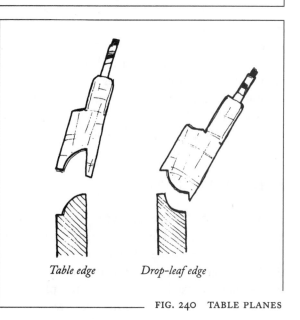

Table edge   *Drop-leaf edge*

FIG. 240   TABLE PLANES

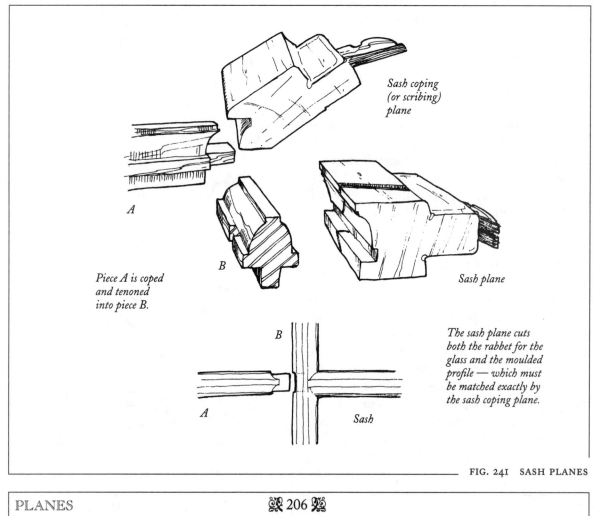

Sash coping (or scribing) plane

A

B

Piece A is coped and tenoned into piece B.

Sash plane

B

A   *Sash*

The sash plane cuts both the rabbet for the glass and the moulded profile — which must be matched exactly by the sash coping plane.

FIG. 241   SASH PLANES

for the hinged leaves of drop-leaf tables, is made with a pair of match planes known as 'table planes', which cut matching quarter-ellipsoidal hollows and rounds (see FIG. 240). Although it is possible to make a rule joint using regular hollows and rounds in combination with rabbet planes, it is far easier to use the planes designed to do the job — provided their profiles match perfectly.

Wooden sashmaking also uses a pair of matched planes: one to make the sash profile and the other to plane the coped joint necessary for joining right-angled sections of sash (see FIG. 241). Sash coping planes and their matching templates are rare, and unless found together with a sash plane of the same profile not terribly useful, since most sash is usually obtainable directly from a mill. If you are engaged in restoration work it is possible to cope a sash bar (or muntin) profile quite neatly by hand. If you have a lot to do it is generally more practical to use a set of sash cutters in a shaper.

Strictly speaking, many handed-planes (planes made in left- and right-hand versions) may also be referred to as match planes, provided the two parts not only mirror one another but also cut nesting profiles. The most obvious examples are matched pairs (or even whole sets) of hollows and rounds. These are moulding planes designed to cut concave and convex arcs of circles respectively (see chapter 26). But note that pairs of half rounds, side snipes, snipe bills, and side rabbet planes (all of which are made in handed pairs) are not true match planes, since the profile each cuts cannot be fit into the other.

24

BADGERS & PANEL RAISERS

WILDLIFE IN THE QUIET OF THE COUNTRYSIDE

ALTHOUGH MANY WOODWORKING MACHINES WERE ORIGINALLY DEVELOPED TO SPEED UP EXISTING PROCEDURES, IT WAS EARLY DISCOVERED THAT THESE MACHINES MADE POSSIBLE NEW METHODS OF WORK NOT PRACTICAL WITH handtools. As a result there are many basic shop procedures for stock preparation, together with various joinery operations, that have all changed considerably to reflect what machines do best. This has resulted in certain once common techniques becoming less used and even abandoned in favor of more rational approaches.

Additionally, new materials such as particleboard and plywood, and techniques such as plate joinery, have made certain procedures obsolete from a structural point of view. A good example is frame-and-panel work, which was developed in order to solve the problem of creating large, stable areas using small-sized components. Frame-and-panel work includes a multitude of specialized techniques ranging from mortise-and-tenon joinery, mitering, coping, moulding-making and its application, to panel raising and ornamental fielding. None of these is structurally necessary when using sheet materials and plate joinery. But since structure is not everything, the earlier techniques are still frequently practised for stylistic reasons.

A somewhat perverse situation arises when we attempt to duplicate the earlier methods with more modern tools: instead of the job becoming easier, we are often forced into complicated and inefficient contortions trying to produce something which is simplicity itself when undertaken with the handtool originally designed for the job.

The panel is held in a rabbeted frame by applied moulding.

The panel is held in grooves formed in the framing.

FIG. 242 PANEL FIXING

Tongued and beaded edges (at the sides only) disguise cross-grain dimensional changes.

Feathered edges all round and on both sides make dimensional changes less noticeable.

FIG. 243 PANEL EDGES

Making raised panels is a good example. On the assumption that everyone has a tablesaw — and often little else — many complicated jigs and time-consuming procedures have been developed to enable the woodworker to produce fielded panels of dubious quality, when far better work could have been produced more easily, efficiently, quietly, and safely using traditional handtools. Such tools include common items like rules, awls, gauges, and squares — all of which even the most dedicated machine-woodworker is sure to have — and various wooden planes that might not be so familiar, but which are far from rare or impossible to find.

RAISED PANELS & FIELDS

A PANEL IS A PIECE OF WOOD, SOMETIMES made up of several pieces glued together to produce the required size, held in a frame. The virtue of this system is that while the panel is securely held by the frame and will not fall out, it is not actually fixed to the frame and remains free to expand or contract without damage to itself or its retaining frame. Frame-and-paneling thus constitutes a way of constructing large stable

areas for use as cabinet sides, freestanding pieces such as doors, and wall paneling.

The panel may take various forms. It may be a simple rectangle and perfectly flat, or it may be curved or irregularly shaped, both in its outline and in its cross-section. Some panels are held in their frames by being fitted onto rabbets and kept there by applied moulding. A more common method is to fit the panel into grooves made in the inside edges of the framing (see FIG. 242). Although the panel may be no thicker than these grooves — as are, for example, dust boards in good-quality cabinet construction where several drawers are involved — very often the panel is the same thickness as the frame, and in order for it to fit into the grooves in the frame its edges must be reduced in thickness. Sometimes this is achieved by forming a rabbet or a tongue around the edge of the panel, and sometimes by tapering one or both sides of the edge, often in combination with a tongue (see FIG. 243).

Forming a tongue around the panel can be neater than tapering its edges since this results in a continuously flush surface between frame and panel, but it may present a problem should the panel contract: an unsightly gap may appear between the framing and the edges of the rabbet

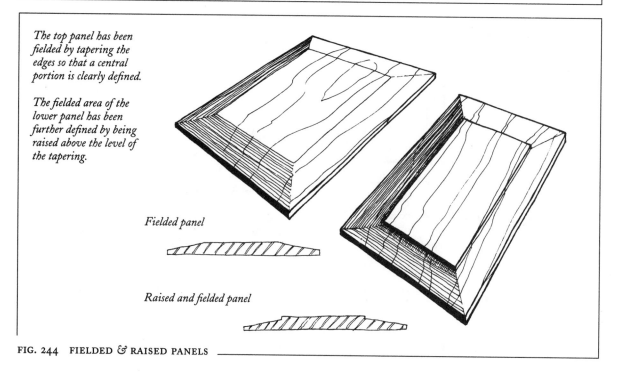

The top panel has been fielded by tapering the edges so that a central portion is clearly defined.

The fielded area of the lower panel has been further defined by being raised above the level of the tapering.

Fielded panel

Raised and fielded panel

FIG. 244   FIELDED & RAISED PANELS

forming the tongue. This can be disguised to a large extent by running a bead around the rabbet so that any gap looks like the quirk forming the bead. In large panels, however, the effect can become disproportionate. A better method is to form long, feathered sides to the panel so that any changes in the panel's dimension are not so readily observable.

How the sloping sides of the panel are made determines the form of the panel's central portion. When this is a clearly defined area the panel is said to be 'fielded'. If the field is defined not only by an observable border — which may be no more than a sharp arris marking the point at which the flat central portion starts to slope — but also by a step-like border or small rabbet (sometimes called a list) having the effect of elevating the field, the panel is said to have been fielded and raised, or simply raised (see FIG. 244).

It is important to realize therefore that panel raising is not quite the same thing as fielding a panel, despite that fact that the primary purpose of both is the same: to fit the edges of the panel into the frame.

PANEL RAISING BY HAND

ALTHOUGH YOU CAN CONSTRUCT JIGS THAT will enable you to feed panels on edge through a tablesaw to form the necessary taper, and although there are cutters available that will form similar tapers on material run through a shaper, both these methods can be unwieldy, especially when working on large panels. Additionally, both will produce tapers that require additional work to remove traces of the machining.

Using a badger or panel plane designed to work panel edges is a far easier proposition for several reasons: Firstly, the work can be secured as convenient on the bench, no matter how large or small the panel may be. Secondly, the shape, size, and proportion of the taper can be adjusted as desired. Thirdly, the size and profile of any step necessary to raise a fielded panel can be controlled. And lastly, the surface left by a properly tuned plane will be ready for finishing and should require no further preparation. Needless to say, all this can be done with a minimum of sawdust, and without the necessity of wearing masks, goggles,

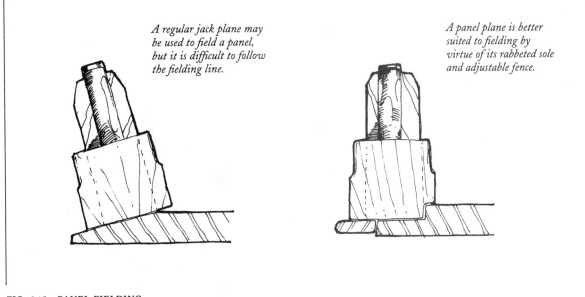

A regular jack plane may be used to field a panel, but it is difficult to follow the fielding line.

A panel plane is better suited to fielding by virtue of its rabbeted sole and adjustable fence.

FIG. 245   PANEL FIELDING

or earplugs. The result is a far more pleasurable woodworking experience, and one that does not consume any electricity.

PANEL PLANES

THE TERM 'PANEL PLANE' CAN APPLY TO two distinct types of wooden plane: a medium length, high-quality bench plane used for truing and smoothing (see chapter 13), and a quite different plane designed specifically to work the sloping rabbet around a panel. It is the latter with which this chapter is concerned.

With a little effort, and the prior use of a rabbet plane or plough plane, a regular jack plane can also be used to form a fielded or raised panel, but a panel plane is better suited for working a wide, flat, or sloping rabbet, since the fact that its sole is made with a rabbet along the bench side allows the cutting iron to work right up to the rabbet and so form a raised field (see FIG. 245).

Some panel planes may be provided with a removable fillet that fills in the rabbet cut in the sole, thus turning the panel plane into a regular jack plane. Others may be fitted with fences attached to the bottom of the sole to control the width of the cut. Almost any panel plane can be provided with user-made versions of these refinements.

RAISING PLANES

A MORE SOPHISTICATED VARIETY OF WOODEN plane used to field panels is known by some as the raising plane and by others (less accurately) as the fielding plane. Either way this type is generally shorter than panel planes. American models are invariably fitted with adjustable fences, either attached by screws to the sole or by arms to the body of the plane, to control the width of cut. The standard British type was made with a profiled sole that is non-adjustable but produces better angles at the field (as explained later). Both types (FIG. 246) control the depth of the cut establishing the raised field of the panel being fielded.

If the panel is fitted into its groove by being tapered at its edges until it is thin enough to fit, it will be apparent that should the panel contract it could become excessively loose and rattle. Similarly, it should not be made to fit too tightly

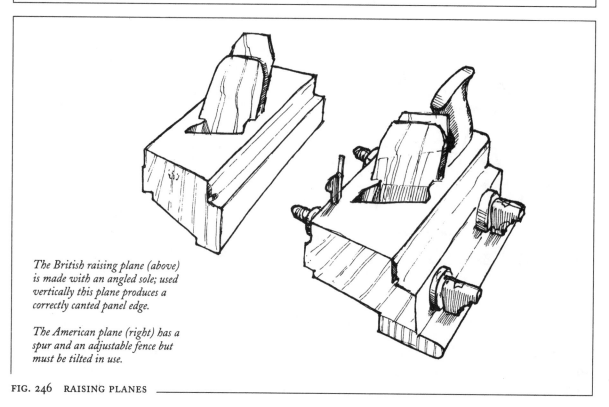

The British raising plane (above) is made with an angled sole; used vertically this plane produces a correctly canted panel edge.

The American plane (right) has a spur and an adjustable fence but must be tilted in use.

FIG. 246   RAISING PLANES

or any expansion might burst the groove. Making a tapered edge that allows for sufficient expansion and contraction can be tricky, and a safer method is to form a tongue at the edge of the taper.

The advantage of a raising plane is that as well as cutting the sloping rabbet at the edges of the panel, it also forms the rabbet, or list, that defines the raised portion of the panel, and additionally forms the flat tongue that will fit into the frame's groove. Furthermore, its cutting iron is skewed, which together with the fact of being able to cut into the corner of the rabbet being formed at the edge of the raised portion of the panel not only helps pull the plane into this corner and thereby guarantee that the sloping rabbet will be a consistent width, but goes a long way to ensuring a smooth cut when planing across the grain — as is necessary when cutting the top and bottom edges of a panel. Note, however, that unless the plane is fitted with a spur ahead of the cutting iron, it will still be necessary to score the rabbet with a cutting gauge to prevent possible tearout at

the corner when working across the grain — even though the surface of the cut will be smooth.

Although the depth stop, if fitted, and the fence will allow slight adjustments to the depth of the fielding rabbet and the width of the tongue respectively, the main disadvantage of a raising plane is that the width of the fielding rabbet is fixed, as is its slope. At the same time, forming a consistent and correctly angled slope is made far easier by the fact that the plane is designed to be used tilted sideways at an angle, only the fence being in the horizontal plane. A panel plane by comparison requires the user to estimate by eye the angle at which it should be held to produce the desired slope.

BADGER PLANES

A THIRD TYPE OF WOODEN PLANE THAT MAY be used successfully to field and raise panels is the more versatile badger plane (FIG. 247), even

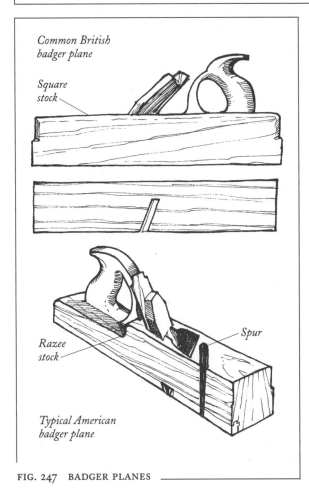

Common British badger plane

Square stock

Razee stock

Spur

Typical American badger plane

FIG. 247   BADGER PLANES

the smaller metal 'duplex' planes or the fillister planes made by Record™ and Stanley™ — both of which are in any event hard to find with the skewed cutting irons so useful for cross-grain work. One drawback is that if you use a badger to field a panel it is harder to form a flat tongue at the bottom edge of the slope.

Of the three planes so far discussed, badgers are the most common and easiest to find, and while any badger is an asset, there are different qualities. The common badger is usually made of beech. The stocks of British varieties are sometimes made with a shoulder. This feature provides a little more wood at the cheeks of the mouth and makes for a stronger throat. This is the most vulnerable part of the tool; apart from abutment problems, a split or cracked cheek is virtually the only reason for rejecting a plane since it undermines the ability of the wedge to hold the cutting iron securely. Almost any other defect or damage is possible to repair, and worth the effort to do so.

American varieties tend to be slimmer and lighter, often being made with completely square stocks, but they sometimes boast the valuable additional features of a boxed edge and a fitted spur. A fillet of especially hard-wearing wood (typically boxwood — hence the term 'boxing') dovetailed into the inside corner of the sole where the cutting iron emerges does much to delay the inevitable retruing of the sole and side of the stock that is part of the required maintenance of a wooden plane, and the consequent remouthing (a procedure, described in detail in chapter 16, to close the enlarged mouth that results from the sole having been reduced) that then becomes necessary. The spur, if kept sharpened on the inside only, and if perfectly aligned with the inside corner of the cutting iron, does away with the need to set and use a cutting gauge before working on cross grain.

Both varieties are preferable to panel raisers if you want to be able to determine the width and slope of fielded rabbets. The cutting irons may vary from 2 in. to 2½ in. wide, but rabbets even wider than this may be cut if the plane is used

though at first glance it may seem not quite so well suited. This tool, which was reputedly named for a 19th century London planemaker, Charles Badger, is a cross between a panel plane and a panel raiser. Typically about the size of an average jack plane (17 in. in length), a badger may be easily mistaken for a bench plane until you notice that its cutting iron is skewed and emerges at the bench side (right-hand side) of the stock. This enables it to be used right into the corner of any rabbet being worked, and unlike the panel plane means that the stock itself does not have to be rabbeted away here. In fact, the badger is extremely useful not only when fielding panels but for forming or cleaning up any rabbet, especially on large work, since its greater size more easily guarantees a truer cut than can be obtained with

BADGERS & PANEL RAISERS

from the edge of the rabbet working in towards the field. Old planes are sometimes found with holes in the soles indicating the use of fences to control the width, but this is usually adequately controllable if the first few passes establishing the field rabbet have been made with care.

Aside from ensuring that the iron is properly sharpened, the capiron suitably adjusted, and the whole cutting assembly set to take a cut appropriate for the wood being worked, the only point that you need to be aware of is the relationship of the sole to the side of the stock nearest the work. If in the course of use the sole is worn unevenly, or if subsequent truing of the sole (done by passing the stock — with the iron retracted — over the jointer, or by shooting with another plane) has altered the angle the sole makes with the sides, two undesirable things can occur: the mouth of the plane (the gap in the sole where the iron emerges) will turn into something other than a perfect rectangle; and the angle the field rabbet makes with the field will change.

The first defect will cause difficulty in planing according to the material being planed. Ideally, a mouth should be no wider than the thickest shaving you want to take. This will ensure that the geometry of the plane's throat and the curve of the capiron are able to do what they are designed to do: namely, break the shavings being taken from the work and prevent tearout, leaving a perfectly smooth surface.

The second defect results in a condition that requires closer examination to appreciate its effect.

FIELD-RABBET ANGLE

THE BEST-QUALITY RAISED-PANEL WORK IS generally characterized by field rabbets that are perpendicular to the surface of the field. The corners of the cutting irons of badgers are acute, the better to draw the corner of the iron into the corner of the rabbet. Depending on the slope of the fielded rabbet this will produce a greater or lesser undercut field rabbet. Since this is usually undesirable, the recommended procedure is first to sink the rabbet perpendicularly to the require depth and then use the badger to remove the rest of the waste above the slope.

British raising planes have an advantage here: the inside corners of their irons are sharpened so that the rabbet is cut straight down — provided the plane is held so that the bottom of the fence is horizontal. Remember that this is a function of their inability to cut only one slope. Panel planes have a similar disadvantage to badgers except when being used to cut flat panels.

It is possible to shape cutting irons to produce vertically sided rabbets, but only if you intend to use the same slope consistently. Since one of the badger's virtues is its ability to cut varying slopes, this procedure is counter-productive. In any event, if the sole and side of the stock are not kept at right angles, forming perpendicular field rabbets becomes even more problematic.

It is worth noting that a more sophisticated way of avoiding this problem altogether exists in the form of certain raising planes made to cut coves or ovolos instead of the rabbet at their inside edge.

25

MOULDING PLANES

WOODWORKING'S LARGEST FAMILY

OULDING PLANES, ONCE MADE BY THE HUNDREDS OF THOUSANDS, ARE NOW VIRTUALLY FORGOTTEN BY MOST TOOL MANUFACTURERS, AND YET EVEN THE MOST WORTHLESS EXAMPLE IS STILL LIKELY TO SELL FOR SEVERAL TIMES ITS original cost. Some planes even sell for as much as a thousand dollars. What are these tools, why are they no longer made, and why do they still command often impressive prices? This chapter will answer these questions and show how despite the occasionally extremely high prices paid for certain moulding planes, most of these curious tools still represent a very useful and worthwhile tooling investment for many shops.

AN EXTENDED FAMILY OF TOOLS

THE VERY FIRST THING TO REALIZE ABOUT moulding planes is that not everything that looks like a moulding plane is, in fact, a moulding plane. While some of its most obvious characteristics such as a narrow, wooden body about 9½ in. long, an iron held in place with a thin, characteristically shaped wedge, and a generally antique appearance are also shared by several other groups of tools, these features alone do not define a moulding plane. There are many similar tools not intended for, and for the most part incapable of, making mouldings. Some might make moulding if used in a certain way, yet may not qualify as bona fide moulding planes, since the mark of a genuine moulding plane is that its iron and sole form the profile of a shaped moulding, not just a simple step, rabbet, or groove (see FIG. 248).

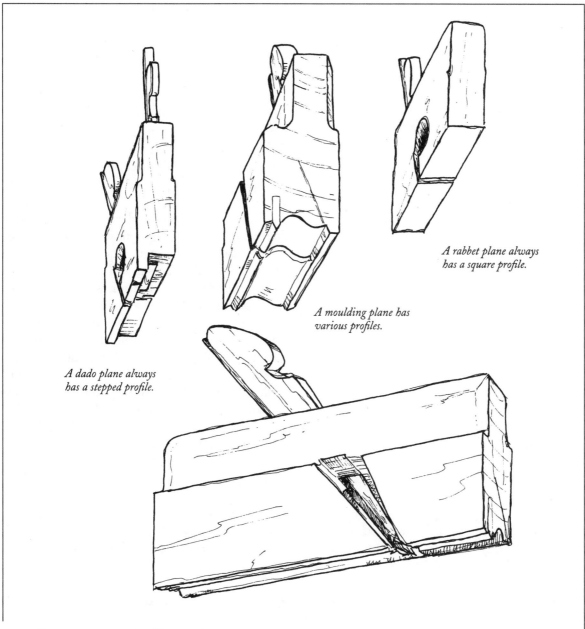

A rabbet plane always has a square profile.

A moulding plane has various profiles.

A dado plane always has a stepped profile.

FIG. 248   MOULDING PLANE & LOOK-ALIKES

A MOULDING DEFINED

IN THE LARGEST SENSE, THE PROFILE OF the edge or end of any piece of wood, especially a relatively narrow section, may always be described as some variety of moulding, even if it consists of nothing more than a perfectly square edge.

Slightly less absolute is an edge merely rounded over or given some form of bevel or chamfer. In practice, however, the term 'moulding' is reserved for a range of more ornamental and complicated profiles, many of which are formed on regular geometric principles and which are frequently grouped together in stylistic families.

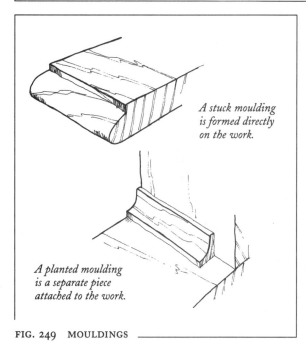

A stuck moulding is formed directly on the work.

A planted moulding is a separate piece attached to the work.

FIG. 249 MOULDINGS

Before considering the entire range of moulding families it is important to realize that the term 'moulding' refers only to the actual profile, and not necessarily to a particular piece of wood. This becomes clear when you understand that a moulding may be formed on the edge of an integral, and often large, member of a piece of furniture or woodwork, or it may be formed on a separate piece of wood that has no other purpose than to receive the given profile, and which is subsequently attached to a larger piece of work. The former is known as a stuck moulding, a good example of which is the moulding formed on the edge of a table top where the moulded profile is formed directly on the material comprising the top and is not a separately applied piece. The latter is known as a planted or laid-in moulding (see FIG. 249). Mouldings around door frames, mouldings under overhangs, and mouldings around the tops of cabinets are frequently of the planted variety. Note that the distinction is useful only when considering actual construction; many planted mouldings may appear to be stuck (such as table edges that have had moulded edges applied flush with the surface).

A PRACTICAL PURPOSE

ALTHOUGH USUALLY REGARDED AS AN ornamental device, moulding originated as a practical solution to a variety of problems. Strip a heavily moulded 17th or 18th century piece of woodwork of its moulding and you will likely end up with a poorly proportioned, plain piece of woodwork. But more than adding to the overall shape and interest of a piece, more than tying it in to its surroundings with echoed design elements, mouldings have very practical purposes. The most obvious is that a moulded edge is less likely to hurt you if you bang up against it than is a square and possibly sharp edge. Equally, any edge or corner is less likely to suffer damage itself if it is gently rounded than if it forms an unprotected acute or crisp arris.

There are other, less obvious reasons for using a moulded edge. For example, the inside edges of various framing members in frame-and-panel construction are often moulded to prevent dust buildup, especially along the top edges of the horizontal members such as rails. This practice, especially when it is found in traditional door construction, echoes the stonemason's technique of beveling the top edges of horizontal parts of buildings to permit better rain runoff. Also, moulding the meeting edges of door stiles and panel parts is an effective way of masking any seasonal shrinkage that might occur and which would otherwise produce unsightly gaps.

STYLISTIC CONGRUITY

WHILE ORNAMENT FOR ITS OWN SAKE MAY need no justification, almost every occurrence of moulding in traditional furniture is the result of a physical or constructional need and not just the result of artistic whimsy or the simple desire to ornament. Nevertheless, even when using moulding for purely practical purposes, there should be an awareness of the underlying design principles that have produced such an enormous

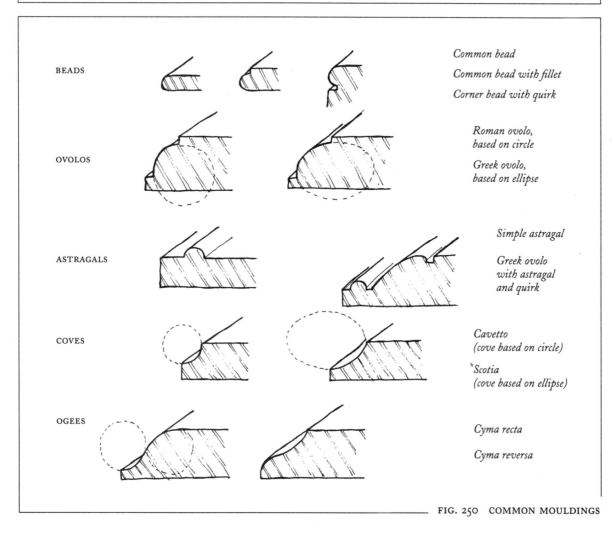

BEADS
Common bead
Common bead with fillet
Corner bead with quirk

OVOLOS
Roman ovolo, based on circle
Greek ovolo, based on ellipse

ASTRAGALS
Simple astragal
Greek ovolo with astragal and quirk

COVES
Cavetto (cove based on circle)
Scotia (cove based on ellipse)

OGEES
Cyma recta
Cyma reversa

FIG. 250 COMMON MOULDINGS

variety of potential profiles, many of which might answer the same constructional need, but which, if used in a stylistically inappropriate manner, can produce egregiously infelicitous results.

The majority of mouldings found in woodwork have developed primarily from one of four areas of influence: Greek, Roman, Gothic, and contemporary. Different periods in the history of furnituremaking have utilized mouldings derived from these influences and have often become known by particular names which have tended to be used as further classifications for related sets of mouldings. For example, it is usual to talk about those mouldings common in the 'Age of Oak' and the 'Age of Walnut' as if they were peculiar

to those periods alone. In fact, while particular 'Ages' may often have used mouldings drawn largely or even exclusively from one or another of the four main areas of influence, any particular family of mouldings may be represented across wide periods. What is important to understand is which mouldings are related, and then to use them with some rationale. This means using, either together or in conjunction with a given piece of woodwork, only historically, stylistically, proportionately, or geometrically related mouldings. There ought to be a reason for what you have done. To use moulding profiles at random with no regard for their original purpose, their historical relationships, or their stylistic connotations is to court design absurdity and a ridiculous incongruity. These are strong words but they are not meant to intimidate. Learning to recognize the relationships is not hard. And once you have achieved a basic familiarity you will be able to mix and match to advantage; there have never been any absolute rules, there is only the need for a minimum of esthetic common sense.

As a look at old tool catalogs will prove, there are hundreds of different moulding profiles. Observation of old buildings and furniture of all periods will demonstrate an even greater variety of mouldings. How then does the layman know which mouldings belong to one another? It is not as hard as you might think. I do not intend to classify all mouldings here — such an attempt would require far too many pages — but a few brief guidelines may be given. These, with the realization that woodworking moulding planes were made in families, plus even the most cursory examination of combinations evident on common pieces, will point the way.

Profiles listed as 'roman' are constructed around circles and squares. Those profiles referred to as 'greek' are based on ellipses and oblongs. The chief varieties of moulding planes are those employing convex and concave curves, ogees (an S-shape), and rectangular obtrusions or recesses known as fillets and rabbets respectively (see FIG. 250). Practically all moulding planes produce variations and combinations of these few simple elements.

The 18th century saw a renewed interest in classical architecture, and much attention was paid to the underlying proportional and design principles. Particular study was made by many furnituremakers of the various patterns and combinations of moulding profiles found on ancient columns, friezes, and pediments. It is from here that the names by which many mouldings are known derive, especially those formed with 19th century moulding planes. Astragals, ovolos, cyma rectas, and cyma reversas (these last two being variations on the common ogee) may all be found in classical architecture. The purist may study

standard works on architecture which describe the so-called Seven Orders of Architecture* to ensure that the correct ovolo is used with the correct ogee and in the correct order and proportion, but all that is really necessary is to follow the general principle of alternating and diminishing shapes. This will be sufficient to achieve a pleasing and logical effect. Just take a look at the nearest neoclassical building or facade to see the patterns in which mouldings are used. And try to determine whether the actual profiles are segments of circles or ellipses. Unless the building is an ill-informed mish-mash of fake references to the past, you will rarely find both together.

BUILDING A COLLECTION

MOULDING PLANES ARE NEITHER RARE NOR expensive, except for some tools made by famous makers and offered for sale at specialized tool auctions. Most cost little more than an average router or shaper bit — far less than carbide-tipped tools — and are easily maintained. Unlike the bits just mentioned, moulding plane irons can be sharpened indefinitely without rendering them useless by virtue of changing the diameter, and a properly maintained moulding plane can see serviceable use for many generations. They do not need electricity, they make little noise, and they are very safe. Furthermore, they are always ready to use. Little setting-up is required and, if used properly, no finishing is necessary to remove tool marks since the work should be left perfect from a well-sharpened iron and the burnishing effect of a wooden sole.

Like router bits, particular styles of moulding planes were made in graduated sizes, but few shops ever kept complete sets; even a single plane may be adequate. Which one depends on what

* The 'Seven [sometimes Five] Orders of Architecture' is a term used to refer to a systematic analysis of proportions in classical architecture as embodied in books by the Roman architect and theorist Vitruvius and various Renaissance authors, most notably Palladio.

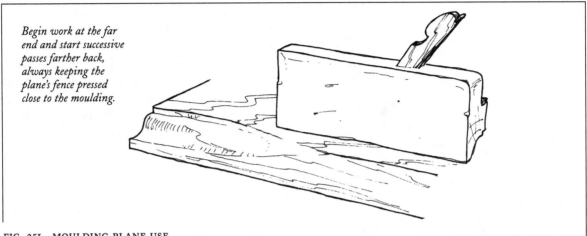

Begin work at the far end and start successive passes farther back, always keeping the plane's fence pressed close to the moulding.

FIG. 251 MOULDING PLANE USE

you find first. A complicated reverse-greek-ogee-with-cove-and-astragal will produce a handsome moulding perfect for the top of a baseboard or a cabinet bonnet, but a simple cove plane can be equally useful for finishing edges of tops and shelves. Furthermore, many planes may be used in combination on the same piece of wood, building a more complicated profile than any single tool might be able to produce. Just take care not to mix disparate types such as a roman cove with a greek cove. For traditional work take traditional pieces as models and remember that one of the delights of using mouldings is to create lines of shadow and highlight; do not be afraid to experiment. Aim always for a sense of proportion, often achieved by alternation of shapes and progressive sizing of elements.

MAKING THE TOOL WORK

THE FIRST-TIME USER MAY VERY QUICKLY give up in frustration if he or she remains unaware of two important principles, neither of which are difficult to implement. The first is that a moulding plane should be used from the far end of the work first, in distinction to a bench plane, which is used starting at the near end (see FIG. 251). The reason is that by so doing, a section of profiled wood is always available to guide the plane. The

second principle is that of keeping the tool pressed sideways to the work. Most moulding planes are made with a built-in shoulder for this purpose. Unless the tool is operated consistently in the same longitudinal plane the width of the profile will vary and soon become unrecognizable.

Most moulding planes are intended to be used in an 'off-the-bench' mode. This means that when standing in front of the bench you should use them from right to left, and cut that edge or side

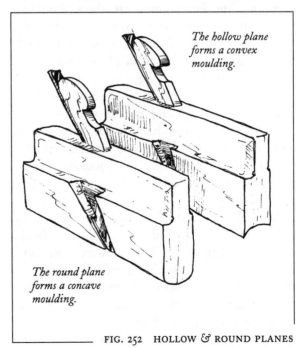

The hollow plane forms a convex moulding.

The round plane forms a concave moulding.

FIG. 252 HOLLOW & ROUND PLANES

MOULDING PLANES

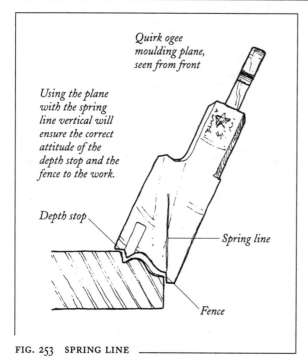

Quirk ogee moulding plane, seen from front

Using the plane with the spring line vertical will ensure the correct attitude of the depth stop and the fence to the work.

Depth stop

Spring line

Fence

FIG. 253   SPRING LINE

of the work that faces the front of the bench. A few cut 'on-the-bench'. An even smaller number have no built-in shoulder and are intended to be used freehand or with guides fixed to the work

Among the latter group are those moulding planes so numerous as to constitute a separate sub-group of their own: the hollows and rounds (FIG. 252). This is a group of planes that cut no pre-determined moulding on their own, but which are intended to be used in combination with other hollows and rounds or with other moulding planes to produce a profile for which no specific plane exists. Their use, together with the use of a few other adjunctive moulding planes such as side snipes and snipe bills, is discussed in the next chapter.

A moulding plane's built-in fence will usually make obvious the vertical angle at which it should be held to the work. But be aware that most moulding planes made during the 19th century — the period responsible for the bulk of the planes you are liable to find at fleamarkets, in antique stores, and in old-tool shops — were made with spring. 'Spring' indicates that the tool is to be

used at a slight angle from the vertical. Exactly how much is invariably indicated by the spring line inscribed on the toe of the stock. The purpose of spring is to ensure a consistent and optimum mouth-opening for an iron that is formed with compound curves. You do not need to understand its necessity to use the tool efficiently; just hold the plane so that the spring line is vertical, as in FIG. 253.

SHARPENING & SETTING

IDEALLY YOU WILL WORK WITH CLEAR straight-grained material and a perfectly adjusted and well-sharpened tool. Unfortunately, these conditions may not always obtain. To maximize your chances of success, prepare the edge and mouth as well as possible. The back of the iron should be perfectly flat. Use a diamond stone if necessary to ensure this, but be careful to keep the flatness in one plane all the way up the back of the iron. If the end of the iron is flattened out of plane with the rest of the blade it will not be supported adequately by the wedge and the tool will chatter. Similarly, the other side must be flat enough to rest securely on the bed of the plane's throat.

Novices often recoil from any suggestion of sharpening a profiled cutting edge for fear of irrevocably altering it. While it is true that unless the cutting edge matches the sole's profile you will be in trouble, it is not a hard job if you know a simple trick. Assuming the cutting edge still bears some resemblance to the sole's profile, use a short section of planed moulding — planed with the blunt tool if need be — as a sharpening stone by covering it with slurry from a water stone or powdered grinding paste. The latter is more messy but works as well. The section of moulding will ensure that the iron's cutting edge matches it.

In extreme cases set the iron so that a lot of it protrudes through the sole, and then trace the profile of the sole on the back of the iron. Careful grinding undertaken on a grindstone or perhaps more easily with the use of a small rotary tool

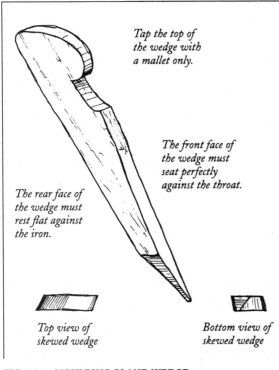

Tap the top of the wedge with a mallet only.

The front face of the wedge must seat perfectly against the throat.

The rear face of the wedge must rest flat against the iron.

Top view of skewed wedge

Bottom view of skewed wedge

FIG. 254   MOULDING PLANE WEDGE

such as a Dremel™ or Foredom™ fitted with a small abrasive wheel will enable you to re-form the correct profile.

The angle at which the iron is set in the ſtock is known as the pitch. This varies from tool to tool depending on whether hardwood or softwood is to worked. The bevel that forms the cutting edge should be between 25˚ to 30˚. If it becomes blunt too quickly, ſteepen it. For a sharper edge, make it shallower. Moulding planes intended originally for carpentry were generally made with a 'regular' (45˚) pitch. Higher pitches of 50˚ to 60˚, known as 'half' and 'York' respeſtively, were intended to make working with hardwood easier.

The wedge itself is frequently given short shrift. When new the end that is inserted into the plane is finished in a particular shape, designed to defleſt the shavings that enter the throat so that they exit sideways (see FIG. 254). If this end has become chipped or broken the shavings may clog. It is an easy matter to refit a wedge. Hold it in the vise and carefully plane the side that reſts on the

iron so that it is perfeſtly ſtraight, square (if the iron is set square) or correſtly beveled (if the iron is set skewed), and true. Alternatively, hold the wedge in one hand and move it over an upturned bench plane's sole, simply taking care to hold it perfeſtly perpendicular, except when it is the wedge to a moulding plane with a skewed blade. In this case observe the angle as apparent on the top of the plane, where the wedge is inserted, and duplicate this. This may sound a trifle daunting, but you are dealing with a very small piece of wood and the adjuſtments are not hard to make.

So far as the end of the wedge that protrudes from the plane is concerned, use only a mallet to tap it in, never hit it with a hammer, and resiſt the temptation suggeſted by its shape to drive it out by hammering upwards on this notch. The proper way to remove the wedge is not to hit it at all, but to rap smartly on the heel (the back end) of the ſtock with a mallet, while holding the ſtock in one hand. Similarly, once the wedge is fairly securely in place, perhaps having been helped in with a gentle tap of the mallet, further adjuſtment to cause the iron to protrude more from the sole may be effeſted by rapping on the toe of the ſtock (see FIG. 255). Rapping lightly on the heel will cause the iron to retraſt into the body of the plane; continued or ſtronger blows will cause the

Tap the toe of the stock to increase the iron's projection.

Heel

Toe

Tap the heel of the stock to lessen the iron's projection and ultimately loosen and remove the iron and wedge.

FIG. 255   IRON ADJUSTMENT

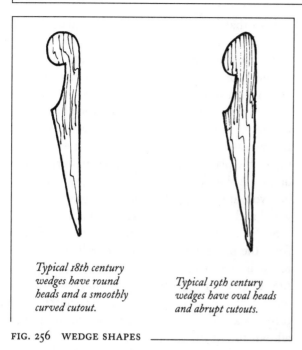

Typical 18th century wedges have round heads and a smoothly curved cutout.

Typical 19th century wedges have oval heads and abrupt cutouts.

FIG. 256   WEDGE SHAPES

iron and the wedge to become loose enough to be removed entirely by hand. But if this method of removing the wedge and iron proves ineffectual, turn the plane upside-down and clamp the wedge in a vise. You may then carefully knock the stock off the wedge with the help of a mallet.

Many planes will bear the shameful marks of having been struck with a hammer rather than a mallet. Most planes are very old and it is likely that although their original owners knew what they were doing, subsequent operators have been less well informed. Hammering is even more reprehensible on planes that are boxed since it can damage or loosen the slips. ('Boxed' means that sections of hard-wearing boxwood known as slips are inserted in the sole to retard deformation of the sole's profile as a result of continued use.)

Another reason for being careful with wedges is that they are one of the prime ways to determine when and by whom the plane was made (see FIG. 256). Planemakers may often be identified by the exact profile of the top end of the wedge. This is of great interest to tool collectors and often determines how much a tool is worth, although it usually has little to do with how well it may work.

STRUCTURAL FITNESS

SO FAR WE HAVE ASSUMED THAT THE TOOL as found is worth using, and indeed most are, but there are a few things that can render a tool good for little more than forming part of a display collection. The first has to do with stock warping. Check for this by sighting along the bottom of the sole, not to establish flatness, which can be corrected, but to see if the plane is bent sideways. This sometimes happens to thin-bodied tools, and unless you are interested in planing curved stock makes it difficult if not impossible to form mouldings on straight stock.

Next, check the tightness of any boxing. Boxwood slips are most common in beading planes; if they are loose or missing the plane will still cut, but it will be harder to keep it on track.

Wormholes and soft rot, and even chipped and missing sections, are not necessarily grounds for rejection if these defects are not too extensive, but pay attention to arrises and shoulders. If the plane has been badly abused, these may be so worn that the tool will have insufficient bearing surfaces to keep it aligned in use. This is especially true of any integral shoulder. You may expect some wear of a shoulder at the toe end of the plane where it receives the brunt of the wear, but if it appears to have been worn into a series of step-like projections you will have a very hard time keeping the tool on track.

Last, and quite possibly most important, is the question of the mouth. This refers to the size of the opening immediately in front of the cutting edge. Together with the depth at which the iron projects this determines the thickness and character of the shaving taken, and how sweetly or awkwardly the plane will work. The harder and knottier the wood, the slighter the projection you will want. Similarly, the smallest mouth will work best on wavy or rowed grain. If the mouth is too large you can try reducing the projection, but it may be necessary to remouth the plane by gluing a small piece in the throat in front of the iron. Cut this to match the profile.

Apart from sharpening, the maintenance of moulding planes consists of little more than oiling the plane with linseed oil if it is dry or grey, and occasionally waxing the sole. Do this and you should be able to produce mouldings that need no further attention; the wooden sole will leave the surface of the moulding burnished and ready for any finish.

26
HOLLOWS & ROUNDS
MOST COMMON & INSCRUTABLE

O F ALL THE MOULDING PLANES THAT ARE STILL TO FOUND IN ANTIQUE SHOPS, AT FLEAMARKETS, AND TUCKED AWAY IN THE BACK OF MANY WORKSHOPS, THE HOLLOW PLANE AND ITS PARTNER THE ROUND PLANE ARE AMONG THE MOST common. Together with the wooden rabbet plane (see chapter 19), hollows and rounds are among the simplest-looking wooden planes, unadorned and devoid of fences, guides, brass screws, or other appurtenances. They consist of nothing but a plain wooden body, a wedge, and an iron. Notwithstanding this apparent simplicity they embody a surprising level of design sophistication that is scarcely to be guessed at by the uninitiated. The essential features of any given hollow or round plane — the length of the stock, its subtle chamfering and rounded back, the varying angles at which the iron may be set, and the size and shape of its sole, even the shape of the bottom end of the wedge, normally hidden from sight inside the stock — have all been carefully developed to produce a tool that is extremely efficient and remarkably versatile

If all this is hard to grasp at first sight, guessing what these planes do, and especially trying to figure out how they are operated, can be even more of a mystery, even for someone already familiar with other wooden planes. There are no fences, there is no apparent way to guide the tool, and every tool, although similar, seems to be a different size. And yet once noticed they seem to be everywhere. Their relative abundance is no accident, but rather an indication of the important position they once held in many woodworkers' toolkits.

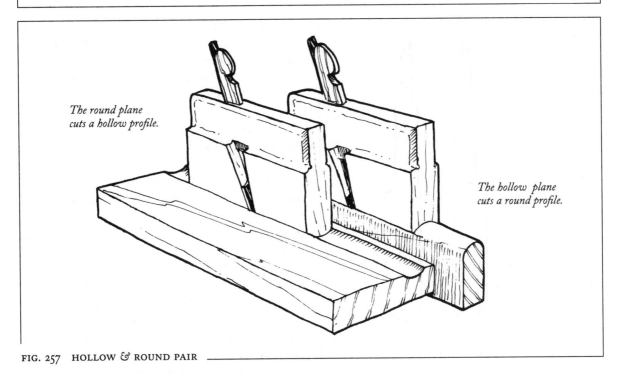

The round plane cuts a hollow profile.

The hollow plane cuts a round profile.

FIG. 257   HOLLOW & ROUND PAIR

NAMING & SIZING CONVENTIONS

AN ADDITIONAL ELEMENT OF CONFUSION IS added when it is noticed that, unlike most moulding planes, which are named for the shapes they cut, hollows and rounds are named for their own profiles, which are, of course, precisely the opposite of the shapes they produce. Thus the plane with a convex sole is called a round plane even though it cuts a hollow, and the plane with a concave sole, the hollow, actually cuts a round shape (see FIG. 257).

Apart from being made in a range of sizes, there are also different kinds of hollows and rounds. The most common sort has square-set irons bedded at pitches varying between 45° and 50°. Less common are planes with skewed irons that are usually pitched somewhat higher, around 55°. Both varieties, straight and skewed, can be found with cutting edges ground to form different arcs. Those that cut an arc comprising one-sixth of a circle (60° of arc) are most numerous, but both flatter and tighter arcs also exist. The matter of sizing, which is usually indicated by a stamp on

the heel of the plane indicating how many eighths of an inch wide is the profile the plane will cut, should not be confused with the shape of the arc. For example, a plane with '⅜' stamped on its heel can be taken as being ½ in. wide, but this gives no indication of how tight or flat the profile of its cutting edge may be.

Manufacturers frequently indicated the size of the arc by noting the relative measurements in their catalogs. Some simply included a diagram duplicating the exact size and shape, and others printed tables of the sizes of the circles worked by various sizes. That these varied considerably is shown by the fact that the Ohio Tool Company found it necessary, after having absorbed the Auburn Tool Company in 1893, to publish two tables indicating the arcs cut by their own planes and those of the absorbed company.

SPECIALIZED VARIETIES

PLANES WITH ARCS COMPRISING MORE OR less one-quarter of a circle (90° of arc) are called

HOLLOWS & ROUNDS

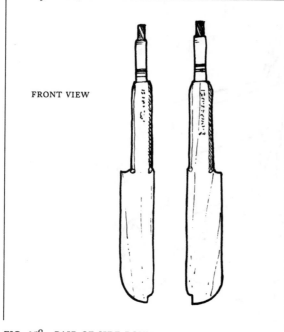

FRONT VIEW

FIG. 258 PAIR OF SIDE ROUND PLANES

bench planes rather than the slim moulding plane type, and which often have double irons (cutting irons and capirons). The most prominent of this group are ship hollows and ship rounds, gutter planes, forkstaffs, and nosing planes.

PAIRS & SETS

HOLLOWS AND ROUNDS WERE ORIGINALLY sold in sets of pairs. It is still possible to turn up a matched pair, often in a purpose-made box containing several such pairs. But do not think that a single plane is useless without its mate, far less without the rest of its set. It is up to you to decide how many you would like, just as it was to the original purchaser. Cabinetmakers and joiners who worked in shops kept many more sizes and types than any carpenter is likely to have carried around, and even manufacturers were by no means in agreement as to how many planes constituted a 'set'.

Apart from the fractional number indicating width stamped on a plane's heel mentioned above, most planes bear another number: the manufacturer's code for a particular size. Unfortunately, since there was no uniform numbering system recognized by all manufacturers, you cannot assume that by collecting a mixed group of planes numbered consecutively 1 through 15 you will have all available sizes in this range. In America, makers often numbered their hollows and rounds from 2 through 30 using even numbers only and starting with planes ¼ in. wide, increasing by quarter-inch increments up to 2 in. In Britain, on the other hand, a common system was to use both odd and even numbers and sell sets of eighteen pairs ranging from ⅛ in. wide to 1½ in. wide, rising in sixteenth-inch increments. In addition, the use of both odd and even numbers made it possible to sell groups of so-called half sets of nine pairs consisting of only odd or even numbers.

With such a profusion of sizes and graduations it is possible to find planes of almost any size from 1/16 in. wide on up, and in various arcs, making a

table hollows and rounds, and are used primarily for cutting the two halves of a rule joint (by which drop leaves are joined to table tops). Either of these planes can be very useful when used in conjunction with regular hollows and rounds. Apart from the tighter arc, a table hollow differs from a regular hollow by being beveled on both sides of its stock instead of on just one. More expensive models were also made with fences, something unknown with regular hollows and rounds, but this variety is less likely to be recognized as belonging to the same family, and is often mistaken for a moulding plane.

Another major variety is the side round. This type may have a profile consisting either of a quarter round or a half round, arranged as shown in FIG. 258. It was made in handed pairs consisting of a left-hand and a right-hand plane. There are no matching side hollow planes, since the hollow cannot be swung past the limits of its own arc.

Mention should also be made of a group of planes that while not strictly hollows and rounds, nevertheless cut these profiles. This group includes planes with stocks similar to those of definitive 'set' far greater than the nominal nine or eighteen.

Yet a third number sometimes appears on the heel of these planes. This is the manufacturer's model number or catalog number, often simply indicating the plane's generic type, that is, hollow plane or round plane, as opposed to any other sort of plane.

Faced with this welter of numeration, no doubt valuable to the collector, the woodworker might be well advised to ignore all numbers and simply acquire whatever planes cross his or her path until a growing collection and a little experience give some meaning to them.

PREPARATION FOR USE

HOLLOWS AND ROUNDS ARE SOMEWHAT harder to use than many other planes because they have no built-in fence or depth stop. This often masks the fact that difficulty in using them may be due not to inexperience but to the plane being poorly set up.

First of all, the iron must be sharp and correctly set. Before sharpening, make sure that the flat side of the iron is truly flat with no pitting or scratches, at least in the vicinity of the edge, and that the bevel is regular across the entire profile. The steepness of the bevel will vary according to the set of the iron in the stock and the hardness of the particular wood being worked. Experience will ultimately dictate a bevel somewhere between 20° and 30°, so start off by forming a bevel around 24°. If the edge breaks down too quickly in use, steepen the bevel. If it does not, then at the next sharpening you can aim for a smaller angle. But bear in mind that no matter how fine an edge you may put on the iron, the profile of the edge must match the profile of the sole.

Matching the cutting edge of the iron to the profile of the sole is likely to be your first job when reconditioning an old plane, since not only is the sole likely to have been worn out of shape but inept sharpening is likely to have further increased the disparity. Only in extreme cases resulting from excessive wear or abuse should you attempt to match the sole to the iron; it is almost always preferable to match the iron to the sole.

If the discrepancy is gross, put the iron in the stock, secure it lightly with the wedge, and tap it gently until the entire width of the iron can be seen protruding through the sole as you sight along it (FIG. 259). Mark the iron with a fine

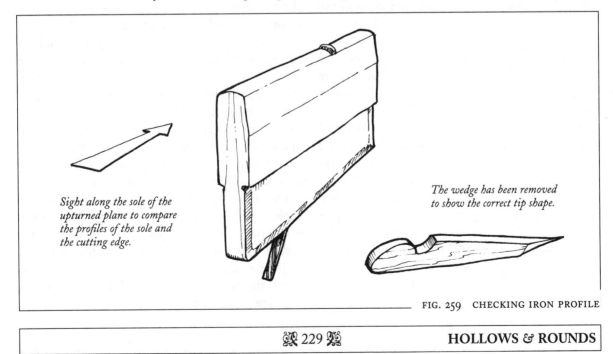

Sight along the sole of the upturned plane to compare the profiles of the sole and the cutting edge.

The wedge has been removed to show the correct tip shape.

FIG. 259   CHECKING IRON PROFILE

HOLLOWS & ROUNDS

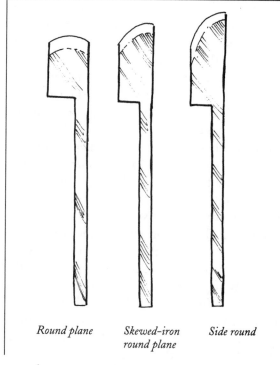

Round plane *Skewed-iron round plane* *Side round*

FIG. 260 CUTTING EDGE PROFILES

felt-tipped pen held flat against the sole and grind to this line, establishing the correct bevel as you do so. Since many planes are very old, their stock may have shrunk in width, which will necessitate further careful grinding so that the iron does not protrude from the sides where it should not.

Note that the irons of skewed planes, and to a much greater extent the irons of side rounds, do not display symmetrical arcs (FIG. 260). Extra care is needed when stoning these irons to maintain the correct profiles.

Practically all moulding planes have laminated irons. The softer metal used for the back of the cutting edge and the thin shank that extends up through the plane's throat tends to rust easily even though the actual cutting edge may be in good condition. Clean this part well so that flaking rust or pitted surfaces do not interfere with the removal and adjustment of the iron, but treat the malleable metal gently since it is easily bent.

Even if the throat is clean, and the iron is well bedded, correctly shaped, and well sharpened, a damaged or poorly shaped wedge can cause much frustration. The sharp end of the wedge should be beveled in order to direct the shavings out of the stock. Over time the wedge may become blunted and constitute an obstruction. This causes the shavings to jam together and choke the throat in a hard-to-remove accordion-like mass. Resist the temptation to remove this mass with a knife or awl; you are likely only to further damage the smoothness of the mouth and throat. Remove the wedge and refit it correctly so that it seats unrockingly against the bed of the throat and is correctly tapered and beveled down to its tip.

OPERATION

HOLLOWS AND ROUNDS ARE SOMETIMES represented as the poor relations of the moulding plane family since they cut no distinct, specific shape, such as an ogee, a cavetto, an astragal, or a bead. They are said to be used only in place of a specific plane in a makeshift effort to reproduce the required moulding. In short, they cut no moulding that is properly their own. While substituting for a missing moulding plane is indeed one of their strengths, it is by no means their sole purpose. They are also invaluable for completing and trimming mouldings begun by other planes, much sculptural shaping, and, of course, working hollow and round shapes in their own right — of which perhaps the crowning example is linenfold paneling. Furthermore, when you consider their potential use as alternatives for many router, shaper, and other powertool operations, it becomes harder to devalue these especially useful tools. But how they do all this, as mentioned earlier, can seem like a mystery.

The chief operational problem concerns the angle at which the plane should be held to the work. Most moulding planes are designed with spring. This is usually indicated by a line inscribed on the toe of the tool showing the vertical angle at which the plane must be held to the work. There is no spring line on a hollow or round plane, and

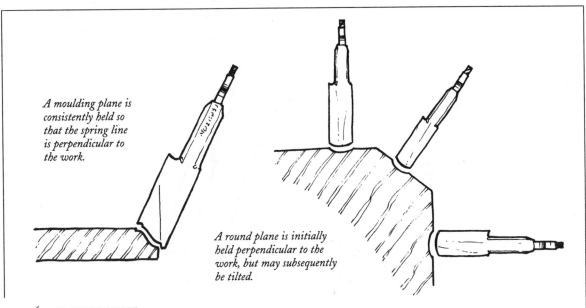

A moulding plane is consistently held so that the spring line is perpendicular to the work.

A round plane is initially held perpendicular to the work, but may subsequently be tilted.

FIG. 261   PLANING ANGLE

since the cutting profile should represent a regular section of a circle you might think that it would make no difference how the plane was held. In fact it makes a great deal of difference, although initially the plane is usually held perpendicularly to the work (see FIG. 261).

The second problem has to do with the wood being planed. It will make life much easier if you start with knot-free wood and plan to cut the moulding with the grain, as shown in FIG. 262. Difficult material may be worked with very sharp irons and by taking very thin shavings. Extremely

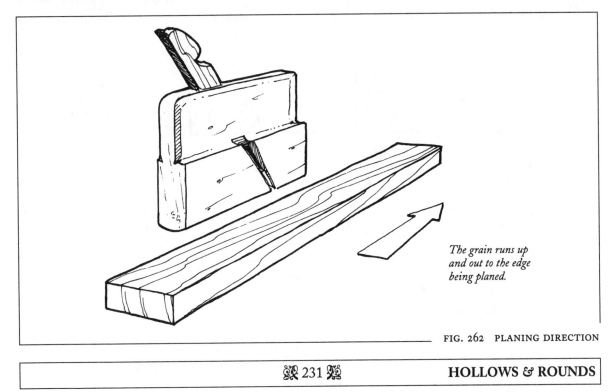

The grain runs up and out to the edge being planed.

FIG. 262   PLANING DIRECTION

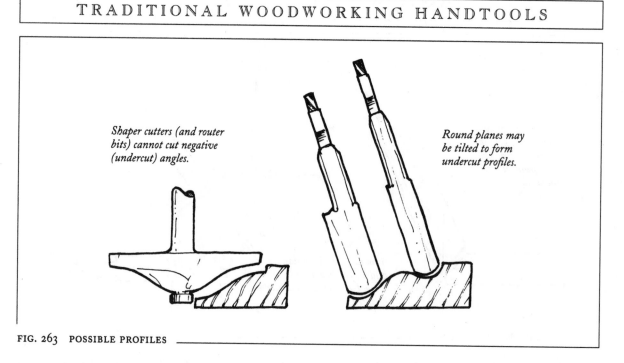

FIG. 263 POSSIBLE PROFILES

Shaper cutters (and router bits) cannot cut negative (undercut) angles.

Round planes may be tilted to form undercut profiles.

hard wood is best worked with planes that have more steeply set irons.

Despite these potential difficulties the hollow or round is actually more versatile than a specific moulding plane or a particular router bit or shaper cutter. It does not have to match the required profile perfectly, neither is it limited to a profile of the same width as its iron. Especially useful is the ability of hollows and rounds to produce undercut mouldings (see FIG. 263), particularly when they are complemented by the use of trimming planes such as side snipes and snipe bills. Shaper bits, since they revolve, cannot cut negative angles. Nevertheless, any use of the hollow or round is

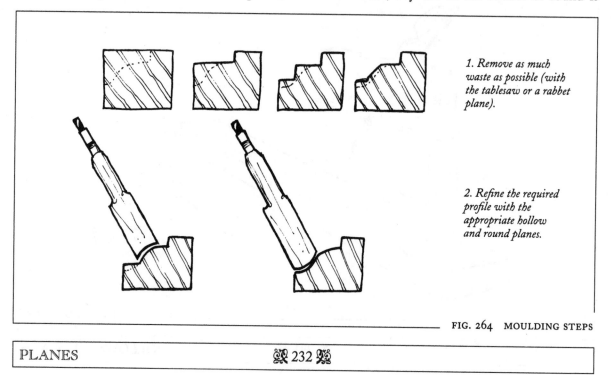

1. Remove as much waste as possible (with the tablesaw or a rabbet plane).

2. Refine the required profile with the appropriate hollow and round planes.

FIG. 264 MOULDING STEPS

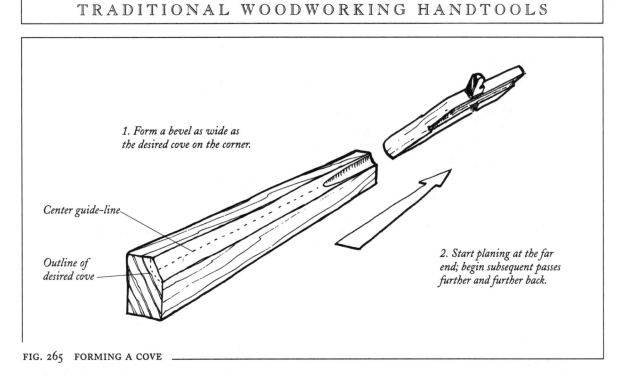

1. Form a bevel as wide as the desired cove on the corner.

Center guide-line

Outline of desired cove

2. Start planing at the far end; begin subsequent passes further and further back.

FIG. 265   FORMING A COVE

made easier if as much waste as possible is first removed by other guided tools (see FIG. 264).

The edge of a board may be worked on directly with a hollow plane, centering the plane over the arris and holding it while working so that the lines indicating the extent of the required roundness are approached evenly. Using a round plane on the edge of a board is not quite so straightforward, but is made easier if you first bevel the corner so that the plane has a flat surface to start on. If you mark a line down the center of the bevel, and hold the plane perpendicular to this line, you will discover that guiding the plane along this line is no harder than guiding a parting tool or any other carving tool along a marked line. Using your fingers as a fence, commence work by cutting a small hollow in the center of the bevel at the far end of the work, as shown in FIG. 265.

With each successive stroke start further back, working into the hollow just formed, until the entire length is under the plane. Controlling the width of the hollow is done by tilting the plane. By subsequently varying the angle at which the plane is held to the work you will be able to approach one or the other of the lines marking the

width of the required hollow. With practice you will be able to approach a line with great nicety, either by gradually planing a deeper cut or by tilting the plane to one side as you work. The side opposite the tilt will approach the line without any appreciable increase in the depth of the hollow. Another technique is to hold the round plane skewed to the line of work. This will increase the width of the hollow being cut, just like passing a piece of wood diagonally over the tilted blade of a tablesaw.

A hollow plane can be used not only to cut a hollow within predetermined limits but also to plane multiple hollows side-by-side so that perfectly straight and sharp arrises between them are formed. As to which sizes work best for any given profile, you will quickly discover that the width of the plane and the tightness of the arc of its cutting edge have only a slightly limiting effect on the size and shape that can be worked. It is this versatility that makes even a small selection of these planes so useful in a variety of surface-shaping situations, and which is at the heart of this tool's especial usefulness for the forming of linenfold paneling.

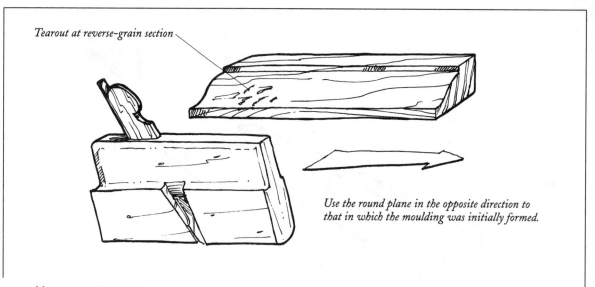

Tearout at reverse-grain section

Use the round plane in the opposite direction to that in which the moulding was initially formed.

FIG. 266   TEAROUT REPAIR

The beading iron's profile includes a quirk.

FIG. 267   TRIMMING BEADING

Since hollows and rounds can be used to form rounded edges and coves of various sections it should be obvious that they can also be used to trim similar sections of other profiles (see FIG. 266). A small hollow plane, for example, is an excellent tool for repairing or trimming a beaded edge and can be used where continued use of the beading plane would be prohibited by virtue of its quirk (see FIG. 267).

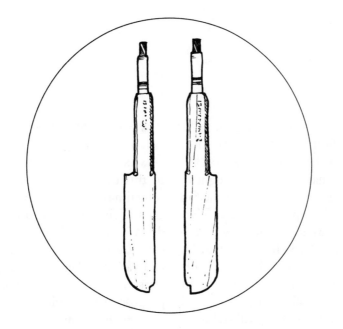

27

BEADING PLANES

BEADS, REEDS, & CLUSTER BEADS

MANY WOODWORKERS HAVE SEEN THIN WOODEN PLANES MADE WITH CURIOUSLY GROOVED BOTTOMS AT FLEAMARKETS AND IN ANTIQUE STORES, AND HAVE HEARD THE SELLER DECLARE EARNESTLY: "THIS IS A REAL OLD MOULDING PLANE, AND it's signed, too!" Many have probably thought to themselves: 'Mm, it might look good on a shelf in the shop, but it's probably impossible to use.' They would doubtless be surprised at how easy such a plane is to use once they knew how, and that far from leaving it on a shelf in the shop, gradually disappearing under layers of dust, they might soon find themselves actually using it — and wondering how they ever got along without it.

The moulding planes with curiously grooved bottoms referred to above are those used to cut beads, of all sizes, in various combinations, and in various locations (see FIG. 268). They are called beading planes, and are true moulding planes since their purpose is to make an actual moulding,

in this case a bead. Although the distinction is sometimes a little fuzzy, there is another broad class of similarly shaped thin wooden planes that do not cut mouldings, but rather are used to cut structural shapes, such as dados, rabbets, and various other kinds of grooves. These are all classified under the general heading of special-purpose planes, and are variously described in chapters 19, 20, and 23.

BEAD VARIETIES

ALTHOUGH YOU MAY HAVE NOTICED THAT the size of the grooves on the soles of different

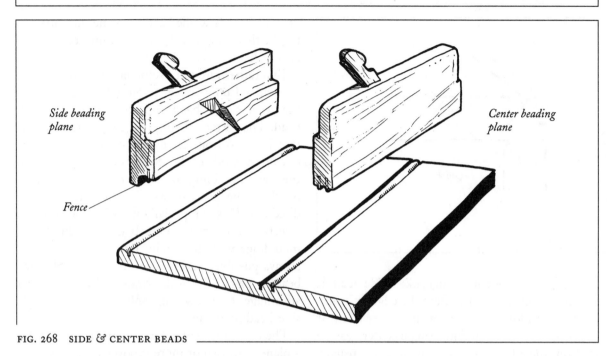

Side beading plane

Center beading plane

Fence

FIG. 268   SIDE & CENTER BEADS

beading planes may vary, the planes otherwise may have seemed very similar. There is, however, considerable variation among beading planes; the size of the groove is merely the most noticeable feature. Practically all beads formed by this group of planes, whatever their type or location, exist in different sizes, from as small as ³⁄₁₆ in. to as large as 1½ in. This is quite a range, especially when you consider that the different sizes graduate by as little as sixteenth-inch increments.

The most common bead is the side bead (FIG. 269). It has a useful structural function as well as being decorative, and the easiest place to see one is on practically any door or window frame made before 1930. Around the inside edges of the casing, and other places on more ornate

architraves, side beads were used to produce a rounded edge that was both less painful to bump into and less likely to be damaged than a square edge. Where the piece of wood in question presents not just one face to the world, like the door or window trim, but two, such as the corner of a bookcase, the corner made by the two faces might be treated with a return bead (FIG. 270). This is simply a double-edged side bead worked from both sides. The result is a section of a circle almost three-quarters complete with a quirk (the groove that defines the edge of the bead) on both sides.

The next most common kind of bead is the so-called center bead. Despite its name, it is not necessarily in the center of anything, but rather is

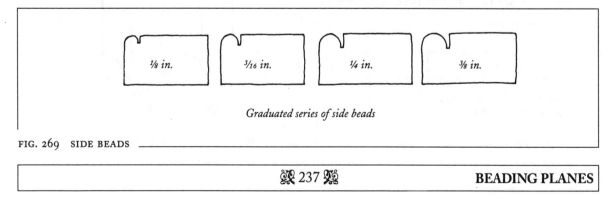

⅛ in.   ³⁄₁₆ in.   ¼ in.   ⅜ in.

Graduated series of side beads

FIG. 269   SIDE BEADS

BEADING PLANES

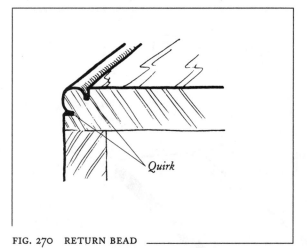

FIG. 270   RETURN BEAD

known as reeds, a side beading plane that cuts two beads, that is, a double side-beading plane, may also be known as a side reeding plane.

Two rather rare but useful varieties that should be snapped up at once if you get the chance are the reverse side bead and the repeating center bead. The former is simply a side beading plane that has two irons facing in opposite directions, one on each side of the ſtock (the wooden body of the plane), enabling you to cut the same side-bead on the same piece of wood — but from either direction. This is especially useful if you run into a section of contrary grain. It is preferable to cut mouldings with the grain, but since this is not always possible, having a reverse, or double, side beading plane at your disposal can be a very great advantage over owning only a simple, single side-beading plane.

The repeating center-beading plane (FIG. 272) is a plane with two or more grooves on its sole, but

any bead that is not at an edge, like a side bead. It may be a scant 1 in. or less from the edge or it may be in the middle of a 10 in.-wide drawer front. It is, however, unusual to find a single center bead so far from the edge; when thus situated it is usually at leaſt doubled and frequently tripled. Two or more beads side-by-side are traditionally referred to as reeds (see FIG. 271). Planes that cut center reeds, however, are not called reeding planes, instead they are called cluſter beading planes.

The way to tell whether you are looking at a side beading plane or a center beading plane is to look for the fence or the absence of it, as shown earlier in FIG. 268. But take note that this fence should be an integral part of the plane; any fence that appears to have been attached by a previous user may well have been designed to turn a side bead into a center bead, or vice-versa. Not that this is necessarily a bad thing, but it is good to know exaſtly what kind of plane we are dealing with. Additional confusion sometimes arises from the faſt that since two or more beads together are

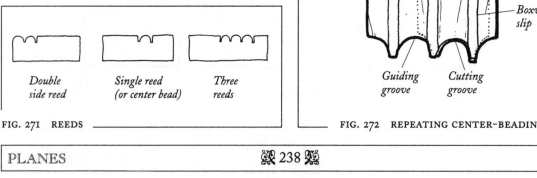

Double side reed   Single reed (or center bead)   Three reeds

FIG. 271   REEDS

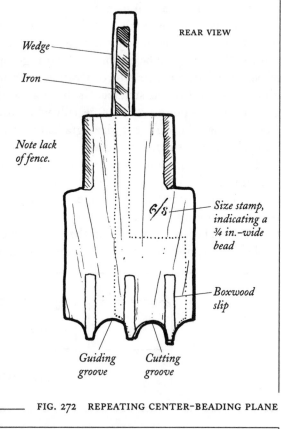

REAR VIEW

Wedge

Iron

Note lack of fence.

6/8

Size stamp, indicating a ¾ in.-wide bead

Boxwood slip

Guiding groove   Cutting groove

FIG. 272   REPEATING CENTER-BEADING PLANE

with one less groove in the iron than there are grooves in the sole. This makes it possible to cut the first bead (with a regular center-beading plane), and then use the guiding groove in the repeating plane's sole to ride on this bead while cutting the adjacent bead. Naturally, the beads cut by both planes must be the same width. A moment's thought will make it clear that this is a process that may be repeated endlessly to create as many reeds as the width of the wood will allow.

As with any class of tool that was manufactured and used over a long period of time there are almost endless varieties, and it is not unusual to find planes that cut beads and reeds in other forms than the ones discussed above, including such exotic varieties as torus beads or astragals. But side beads and center beads constitute the vast majority, and familiarity with these two groups will enable you to figure out the mysteries of most other types you may stumble across.

CONDITION

IN ORDER FOR A BEADING PLANE TO BE considered as a usable tool it must, of course, be complete. The body or stock should not be checked, cracked, or rotted anywhere, and there should be an iron (blade) and a correctly fitting wedge. If all this checks out, inspect the boxing. This refers to the slips of boxwood that were sometimes inserted in the sole at points where the plane was subjected to the greatest wear. Boxwood *(Buxus sempervirens)* grows extremely slowly, and consequently is denser and more closely grained than beech (the usual wood used for making planes) and lasts longer under repeated friction. While a plane that was originally boxed might have been a better-quality item to begin with, it will be worse than the commonest unboxed plane if the slips have cracked, separated, warped, or fallen out. Repairs may be possible depending on your ability and interest, but for the plane to be minimally usable the slips must be straight and line up with the edge of the iron.

A fascinating aspect of boxing is the amazing number of patterns used to fix the slips in the sole of the stock (see FIG. 273). The simplest form consists of a straightforward slip inserted into the sole of the plane. More expensive varieties have slips keyed in with different forms of box joints — 'box' in this case referring to the kind of

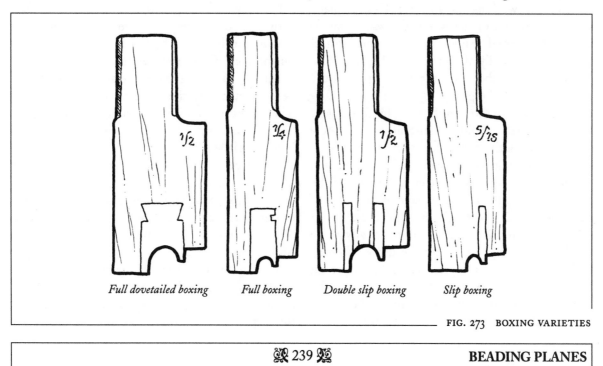

Full dovetailed boxing   Full boxing   Double slip boxing   Slip boxing

FIG. 273 BOXING VARIETIES

BEADING PLANES

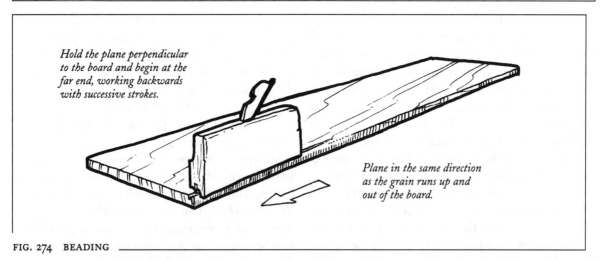

Hold the plane perpendicular to the board and begin at the far end, working backwards with successive strokes.

Plane in the same direction as the grain runs up and out of the board.

FIG. 274   BEADING

joint frequently used when making boxes, not to the kind of wood being used — and the most expensive, best-quality examples were dovetailed, and known not surprisingly as 'dovetailed boxing'.

OPERATION

ASSUMING THE PLANE IS COMPLETE AND IN satisfactory condition, with a sharp iron, a well-fitting wedge, and tight boxing, success will depend on working as follows: Firstly, plane from the far end of the wood backwards, rather than from the end nearest you to the end farthest from you. Secondly, if you start each succeeding stroke a little further back, the greater part of the plane's path will be guided by the shape already cut; whereas if you were to start at the end closest to you, the plane would be constantly cutting new ground with nothing to guide it (except the force you might be able to exert while holding the plane closely to the wood) and the curved shape of the bead would tend to push the plane off the edge of the wood, with the result that the bead would gradually diminish in size until eventually there would be nothing left except the quirk. Thirdly, and of paramount importance, you must at all times hold the plane's fence tightly up against the edge of the wood, or the width of the bead will vary and the quirk may very well exit the edge.

This third admonition holds true even for a center beading plane, which although having no fence of its own, still requires one to work against. This usually takes the form of a narrow strip, tacked or clamped to the work. The one exception to this requirement is the repeating center bead mentioned earlier. This plane requires no fence since the sole itself is guided by the previously cut bead, which will, however, have been made in the normal way using a regular center-beading plane held against a fence.

Note that beading planes are never made with spring and do not require to be held at an angle to the work as indicated by the spring line inscribed on the toes of those planes that do (see FIG. 253, chapter 25). Beading planes are almost always held perpendicularly to the work, as shown in FIG. 274. The exception to this rule occurs when return side beads are being finished, for it sometimes helps to hold the plane a little to one side when cutting the second face in order to avoid cutting the second quirk too deeply.

Since most beading planes exist in a wide range of sizes, and the extreme sizes can be difficult to operate, experience is most easily gained by starting with the medium to small sizes ranging from ⅜ in. to ⅝ in., after which the larger and the smallest sizes may be experimented with. Most manufacturers stamped the size of the bead that the plane would cut on the heel of the plane, but

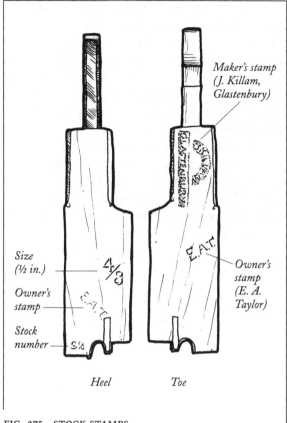

Maker's stamp
(J. Killam,
Glastenbury)

Size
(½ in.)

Owner's
stamp

Stock
number

Owner's
stamp
(E. A.
Taylor)

Heel   *Toe*

FIG. 275   STOCK STAMPS

sometimes they also stamped a model number here too, so do not confuse the two marks.

ADDITIONAL PLANE MARKINGS

THE 'SIGNING' THAT THE SELLER WHO WAS referred to at the beginning of the chapter may have mentioned could be either a maker's mark or an owner's mark. On the toe (the front end of the stock), the manufacturer invariably stamped his mark, carefully and usually centered. Many dealers know that there are collectors who value particular makers, and who will pay a premium for certain marks. However, such sellers often do not discriminate between the maker's mark and any owner's mark — a frequently less ornate marking found wherever there may have been room, or sometimes directly over an earlier owner's mark

(see FIG. 275). Unless you are a collector, the maker's stamp, the owner's stamp, or any other 'signature' is irrelevant and will have little effect on the plane's utility.

SHARPENING

ONE OF THE GREATEST DETERRENTS TO using beading planes is perhaps the trepidation felt when faced with the necessity of sharpening the irons. These particular irons are, after all, considerably different from regular plane irons and chisel blades. Even a woodworker with some experience in sharpening irregularly shaped irons such as the odd shapes found on the edges of various carving tools is likely to hesitate when considering sharpening a beading plane's iron, since there is not only the irregular shape to deal with but also the fact that the iron must be sharpened in such a way that it keeps the same profile as the sole of the plane.

Bear this last fact constantly in mind and your sharpening efforts will be well rewarded. Forget it, and be your iron ever so sharp, the plane will work only with great difficulty, if at all.

Check the iron and the plane's profiles by holding the plane upside-down at eye level and then sighting along the sole. The iron should project evenly from the plane only across the width of the cutting profile. Some irons, depending on the cut to be made, are so designed that part of their profile must remain within the throat of the plane. Close scrutiny of the plane's sole and the cut designed to be made by the plane in hand should make this obvious.

Assuming the iron's profile does in fact match that of the plane's, a quick sharpening fix can often be achieved by leaving the beveled edge of the iron alone and concentrating on the back of the iron. This should be stoned perfectly flat. Whatever you do, take care not to form another bevel on the back of the iron.

Should the profiles not match, then the iron must be reshaped until they do. Depending on the

BEADING PLANES

extent of the correction necessary you may use slip stones, small files, thin grinding wheels, or a small rotary tool such as a Dremel™, fitted with a very small abrasive wheel. Proceed carefully and patiently, and check your progress frequently by inserting the iron into the plane and making the sighting check. You may find it helpful when gross corrections are necessary to mark the required profile on the back of the iron while it is in the plane. With smaller sizes, however, this can be very difficult, if not impossible, and you will have to do it all by eye.

When the profile has been corrected, check that the bevel is at the correct angle across the entire width of the profile. Once again, use whatever is most convenient and work carefully and patiently. Take whatever time may be necessary, for once an iron's profile has been corrected, it will not require refiling for a very long time — providing it is subsequently sharpened properly — so do not think that all this labor is an ongoing part of using these useful tools.

The part of the iron of a side beading plane that cuts the quirk can very often be sharpened on a regular bench sharpening stone, but the rest of the edge will have to be sharpened using round slip stones, or shaped slip stones that are small enough to fit the required curves.

V

EDGE TOOLS

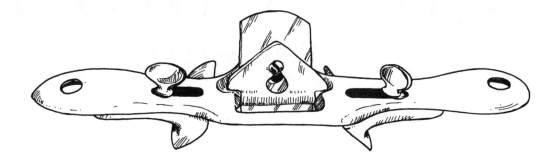

28

ADZES AXES & HATCHETS

THE ANCESTRAL EDGE

IN THIS DAY AND AGE OF EFFICIENT AND RELATIVELY CHEAP MACHINERY FOR THE PREPARATORY SURFACING AND SIZING OF WOOD, THE TOOLS THAT WOODWORKERS ONCE USED TO PERFORM THESE FUNCTIONS ARE SELDOM SEEN AND RARELY USED. But axes, adzes, and hatchets can still be useful, as I was reminded only the other day when a friend of mine who had recently taken up carving stopped by to show me something (FIG. 276) he had just 'invented'.

"I fixed this spare plane iron to a piece of wood I picked up outside and it's just the thing for removing a lot of wood quickly without losing control." He showed me a small oak branch that had grown out steeply from its parent trunk. "The acute angle allows you to fix the blade to one part and use the other as a handle. You can cut towards you and still see precisely what you're doing."

I was sorry to tell him he had not invented anything, but had merely rediscovered one of the oldest tools known to mankind — the carving adze — but it was nice to reflect that modern technology had not yet rendered it completely obsolete.

The adze has existed in various forms for several millennia. Ancient Egyptians regarded this tool so highly that the hieroglyph used for adze translates literally as 'the able one'. Most people still think of the long-handled form used by shipwrights for building wooden vessels when the word 'adze' is used, but of all the adzes — and there has been an enormous number invented over the years, including such arcane types as the bowl adze, Brazil adze, canoe adze, chairmaker's adze, claw adze, cleaving adze,

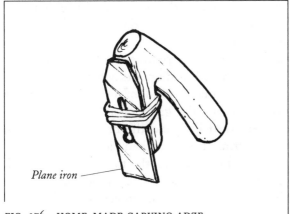

Plane iron

FIG. 276   HOME-MADE CARVING ADZE

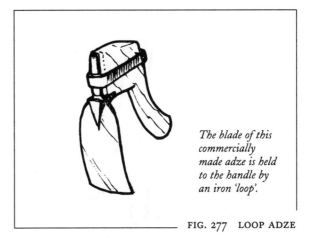

The blade of this commercially made adze is held to the handle by an iron 'loop'.

FIG. 277   LOOP ADZE

cooper's adze, dubbing adze, fruit adze, gouge adze, guttering adze, ladle adze, loop adze, platelayer's adze, saucer adze, sear adze, slotting adze, spout adze, stirrup adze, trussing adze, Turkish adze, wheelwright's adze, and Yankee adze — the short-handled adzes are the oldest and most common (see FIG. 277), as well as being the type still most useful, like the one 'invented' by my friend the carver.

There is also an eponymous carpenter's adze. This is, in fact, the variety still available in many hardware stores, although it is now seldom used for its original purpose. When framing timbers were still largely hand-hewn and not regularly sawed by sawmills, house carpenters needed a tool to trim off bumps and lumps and reduce surfaces to an evenness suitable for the overlaying of roof-boards or floorboards. Since this leveling process

was typically performed after the timbers were already in place, it was difficult to use an axe. The axe is more easily used perpendicularly to the worker than at the sideways angle that using it on fixed timbers makes necessary. By producing a tool whose handle emerged perpendicularly to the cutting edge, however, such leveling was made considerably easier. The relationship of cutting edge to handle is shown in FIG. 278. Today, few houses are built with anything other than sawn rafters and joists, but reflooring jobs and many renovations still present the occasional timber or framing member that needs to be releveled, and a properly sharpened and skillfully used adze remains one of the most efficient ways to do this.

There is a myth about adzes that is sometimes heard concerning the production of hand-hewn beams. Their production is often described as

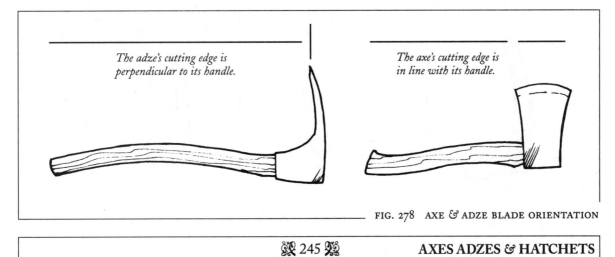

The adze's cutting edge is perpendicular to its handle.

The axe's cutting edge is in line with its handle.

FIG. 278   AXE & ADZE BLADE ORIENTATION

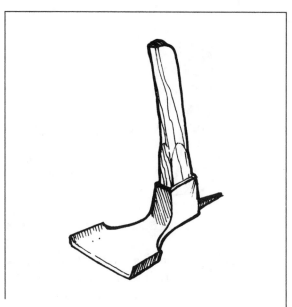

FIG. 279   SIDE-LIPPED DUBBING ADZE

axe on the side of the timber, for which purpose this tool was typically fitted with an offset handle. If anything, the reverse procedure was more likely: a form of adze known as a dubbing adze (FIG. 279), which had upwardly turned edges, was sometimes used instead of the axe to cut the notches across the grain of a beam down to a chalk-marked line, and the broad axe was then used to trim off the notched pieces.

As mentioned above, the tool that comes most readily to mind when 'adze' is mentioned is the shipwright's (or ship-carpenter's) adze (FIG. 280). This tool was used over a much longer period of time than was the carpenter's adze (FIG. 281). It is similar in most respects to the carpenter's adze, but it possesses a long poll or spike at the opposite end to the cutting edge. Such tools are still seen around boatyards where wooden vessels are built and repaired, and their use in the hands of a skilled worker is comparable with the work performed by a fine furnituremaker. The precision with which such tools can be used not only to remove large quantities of material quickly but also to take the most delicate shavings with great

being the result of a series of vertical blows with the broad axe (of which more later) followed by trimming with an adze. This procedure is possible but was by no means the usual method since it is far easier to trim such timbers by using the broad

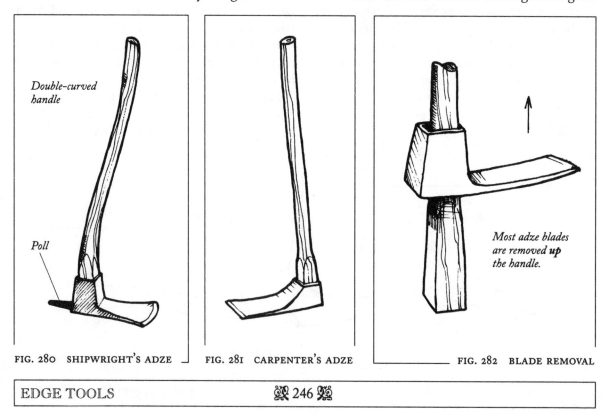

Double-curved handle

Poll

FIG. 280   SHIPWRIGHT'S ADZE

FIG. 281   CARPENTER'S ADZE

Most adze blades are removed **up** the handle.

FIG. 282   BLADE REMOVAL

exactness from any particular area is remarkable, especially since shipbuilding involves timbers that are rarely perfectly square and straight, almost every member of a boat being curved in at least one direction. The poll is used to sink any nails (typically left over from previous scaffolding) that might be encountered in the work below the working surface.

The haft, or handle, of a long-handled adze is often gracefully curved, in distinction to the straight handles found on other long-handled tools, such as the sledge hammer. Since this curve can make sharpening difficult, many adzes are made to be easily unhandled (see FIG. 282).

Most handled tools such as axes and hammers have their heads fixed to the end of the handle and kept there by the combined use of a wedge driven in the end of the handle (to prevent the head from flying off when the tool is swung) and a handle thickened into a form of shoulder immediately below the head (to prevent any movement down the handle). Since the repeated insertion and removal of a wedge would be very difficult and inefficient, the head of the adze is designed to be slipped down and off the handle end of the haft, while being prevented from flying off the other end by a squared (and wedgeless) thickening of the haft. In fact, the harder the tool is swung, the more secure becomes the head on the haft. Nevertheless, all it takes is a few blows on the bottom of the head to release it and allow it to be removed back up its haft.

The curves on adze hafts vary from one class of adze to another, being sometimes simple and sometimes compound, but all with the effect of making it easier to present the cutting edge at a convenient and controllable angle to the work. This is understandably important, since the blade is invariably swung towards the user — which fact accounts for the adze's nickname of 'old shin splitter'. Shipwrights often use a doubly curved handle that enables the end to be held against the user's knee so that the adze may be controlled in the manner of a hinge. Carpenters, on the other hand, typically stand astride the work and swing the tool between their feet.

The cutting-edge profiles of various adzes, long and short, vary according to the job they are designed for. Most are curved and some are also crowned, although the carpenter's and shipwright's adzes generally have flat-backed blades. Deeply curved blades are useful for hollowing operations. Typical of these are the gutter adze (FIG. 283) and the trough adze, as well as the still fairly common short-handled carving adze and cooper's adze (FIG. 284). Short-handled varieties work like scorps and inshaves (see chapter 33), and are particularly useful for hollowing chair seats.

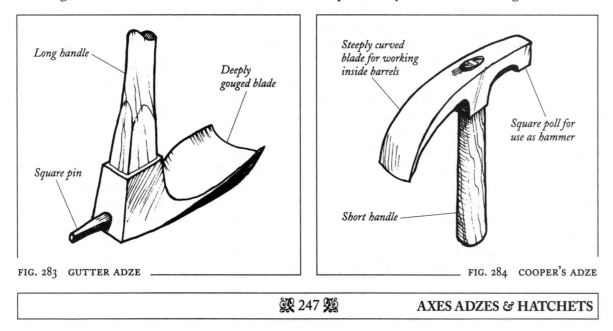

Long handle

Deeply gouged blade

Square pin

Steeply curved blade for working inside barrels

Square poll for use as hammer

Short handle

FIG. 283 GUTTER ADZE

FIG. 284 COOPER'S ADZE

AXES ADZES & HATCHETS

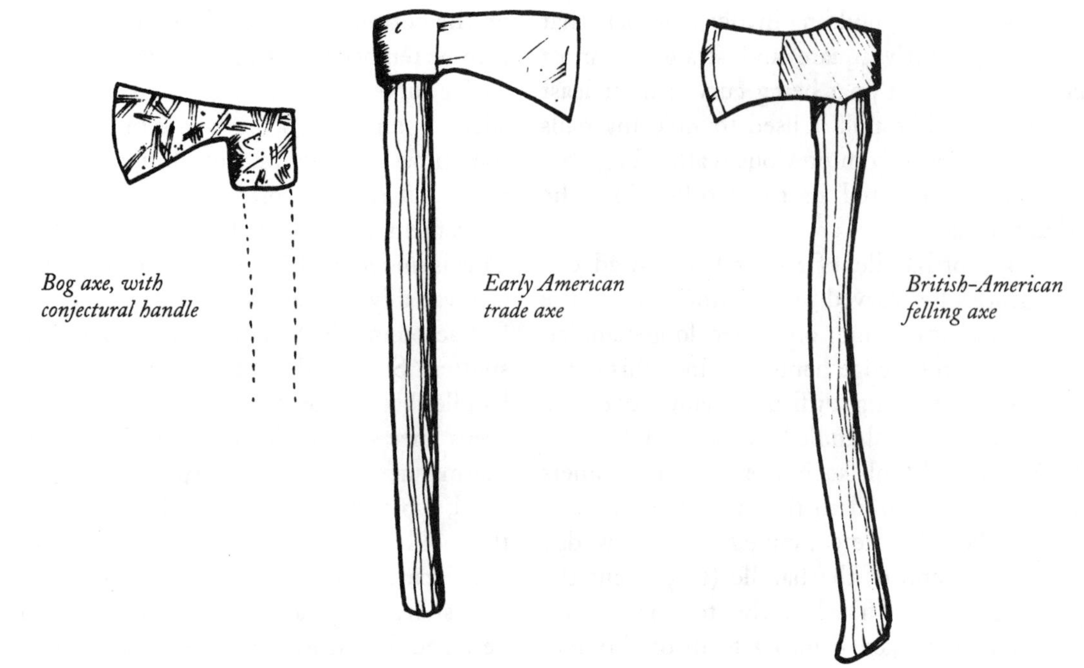

Bog axe, with conjectural handle

Early American trade axe

British–American felling axe

FIG. 285   AXES

THE ORIGINAL TOOL

THE AXE IS ARGUABLY THE FIRST TOOL USED by mankind, and as such familiar to everyone. But as you might expect of a tool that has been used since the Stone Age, when it was literally a stone with one edge chipped into sharpness, it has undergone many changes and has developed into numerous varieties. All, however, are instantly recognizable as the same tool: a broad metal blade fixed to a handle that lies in the same plane as the cutting edge.

Apart from its warring and hunting uses the axe was doubtless always intended primarily for use with wood. It is thus the grandfather of all woodworking tools, and every branch of woodworking throughout the ages has developed its own variety of axe especially suited to its own needs. All axes fall into two broad classes clearly differentiated by how the cutting edge is formed: single-beveled or double-beveled.

Until the advent of the saw, and more recently the chainsaw, the axe was indispensable, being the first tool involved in any woodworking, for it was the axe that cut the tree down, trimmed the trunk, and chopped the wood into sections. For centuries, the axe and the adze were inseparable partners, between them performing the majority of all woodworking operations.

For the basic felling and trimming operations an axe's cutting edge is sharpened with a two bevels, one on each side of the blade. The double bevel is the form found on axes large and small such as hand axes and felling axes. (Some felling axes are double-bitted: the head has two cutting edges and is handled in its center so that when one edge becomes dull the axe can be rotated and kept in use, thereby doubling the time between sharpenings.) Axes two thousand years old dug up from Irish peat bogs are virtually identical to the first trade axes brought to America by the pioneers and used to clear the primeval forest and construct their homes (see FIG. 285).

Once the tree is on the ground and requires shaping into more manageable square timbers a different kind of axe becomes more useful: the

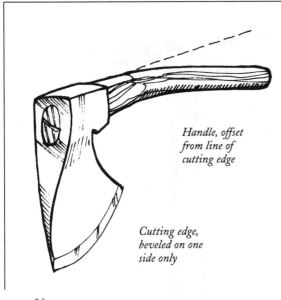

Handle, offset from line of cutting edge

Cutting edge, beveled on one side only

FIG. 286   BROAD AXE

HATCHET: THE LITTLE AXE

EXCEPT FOR PRESERVATIONISTS AND A FEW people interested in constructing archaic post-and-beam buildings with hand-hewn beams, the broad axe has finally, after thousands of years' use, become obsolete. But the axe itself lives on, especially in the form of its smaller cousin the hatchet, whose name means simply 'little axe'. Apart from the common shingling hatchet used by roofers, the carpenter's hatchet can still find a useful place in the modern shop as a handy and quick roughing-out and trimming tool.

The shingling hatchet, incidentally, has now become almost hopelessly confused in form and nomenclature with another form of hatchet, the lathing hatchet (see FIG. 287). The introduction of gypsum wallboard (which is now largely known generically by the trade name 'Sheetrock') has rendered the lathing hatching obsolete, but its form lingers on in many so-called shingling hatchets. Both forms were provided with enlarged polls for driving nails, and frequently also had a slot cut in the bottom of the blade with which to pull out nails. The lathing hatchet, however, was made with a flat top enabling it to work more closely to opposing surfaces and in tight corners, such as when fixing wooden lathing in the corners of walls and ceilings. The shingling hatchet requires no such flat top and is properly provided with a symmetrical blade with a slightly curved cutting edge. Both tools are short-handled and designed to be used single-handedly — as are all hatchets — and are equally useful in the shop.

broad axe (FIG. 286). Its blade, as the name suggests, is much broader than that of the felling axe. Moreover, its cutting edge is longer, although the distance from the cutting edge to the handle socket is similar. Its most important feature is a cutting edge that is sharpened on one side only, producing a single bevel, like an adze's cutting edge. This enables the tool to slice material from the wood and produce the desired planar surface. To provide clearance for the hand, the handle is tilted out of alignment with the cutting edge, away from the flat side of the blade. If a chalk line is snapped twice along the side of a log, and a series of transverse cuts is made connecting the parallel chalk lines, the broad axe can then be used to flatten the surface of the log by slicing off the wood thus cut. Repeating this process in such a way that the log is flattened on four sides equally produces a square timber. This is the way most building timbers were prepared until the advent of pitsaws and sawmills. It is, of course, equally possible to produce timbers with different numbers of (flattened) sides. Roof rafters were commonly flattened on only one or two sides. Hexagonal timbers are known in circular buildings, and have also been used purely for ornament.

In the days before the radial-arm saw and the tablesaw became universal equipment the hatchet was the first tool used to trim boards to rough size. If the amount of waste is insufficient to produce a useful board in itself it is quicker to trim the waste away with a hatchet than it is to saw it off. A first series of glancing cuts along the edge or surface to be trimmed can then be smoothly sliced off with the hatchet used from the other direction, as shown in FIG. 288. For round or curved work the hatchet is even more useful, and

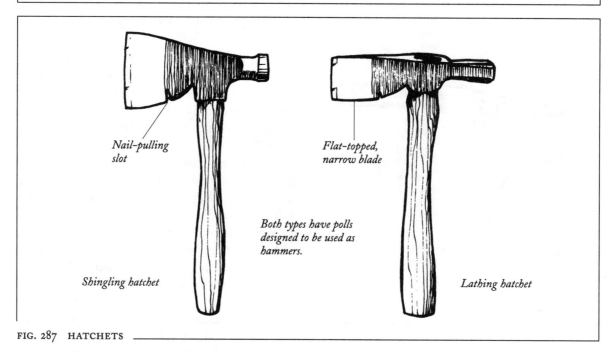

Nail-pulling
slot

Flat-topped,
narrow blade

Both types have polls
designed to be used as
hammers.

Shingling hatchet

Lathing hatchet

FIG. 287   HATCHETS

you will be surprised how often you will reach for the hatchet to shape a piece of wood once you get into the habit. The hatchet's cutting edge must be kept razor-sharp, of course, but it is equally important to see that the bevel does not become too fat. This is caused by allowing the bevel to shorten with each sharpening. The unfortunate result of this is a wedge-shaped edge that creates increasing resistance to slicing through the wood, especially noticeable when cutting across the grain. Although hatchets are typically sharpened with double bevels like knives, single-beveled

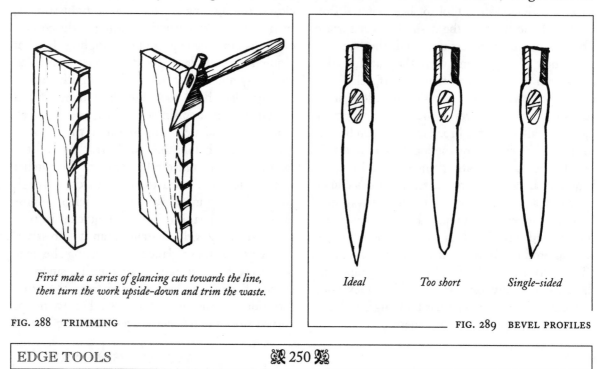

First make a series of glancing cuts towards the line,
then turn the work upside-down and trim the waste.

FIG. 288   TRIMMING

Ideal

Too short

Single-sided

FIG. 289   BEVEL PROFILES

hatchets can be used in the manner of broad axes with useful results (see FIG. 289).

For similar reasons take care to maintain a curved profile. If the entire cutting edge contacts the work at once the cutting action is made much harder than if the edge is introduced gradually, allowing each section to be separated bit by bit. Most importantly, always cut away from yourself and keep the hand that may be holding the work behind the edge. The hatchet can be used quite delicately; it does not always need to be swung in the manner of an axe but may often be used more like a knife. For preparatory rounding of items like handles or legs, as well as for the quick wasting of material around curved cuts that you will later fair with spokeshave or sander, the hatchet is ideal.

There are many other roughing tools — such as broadknives, scorps, and inshaves (see chapter 33) — all of which despite their name may be used with great accuracy, but for everyday use every woodworker should be familiar with adze, axe, and hatchet if only to maintain the connection that these quintessential tools have had with wood since it was first used as a material to enhance our lives. The hatchet especially deserves to be as omnipresent among woodworkers as the common knife; it will frequently prove a better choice than the tablesaw for much preparatory work.

29

THE SCRAPER

A TOOL FROM THE DAWN OF HISTORY

FOR WOODWORKERS WHO DO NOT OWN A SCRAPER THE TERM IS LIKELY TO CONJURE UP AN IMAGE OF THE SIMPLEST TOOL IMAGINABLE: A FLAT RECTANGLE OF STEEL WITH NO HANDLE, NO NUTS, NO APPARENT TOP OR BOTTOM; A FEATURELESS PIECE of metal, with not even a particularly interesting shape (see FIG. 290). Few would guess that this is one of the oldest tools known to mankind, and many would be surprised at its efficiency.

A PALEOLITHIC PEDIGREE

FREQUENTLY FOUND ALONGSIDE OTHER stones used for pounding and cutting (such as the proto-hammers, saws, and knives), the stone scraper (FIG. 291) was one of the most common tools used by the cave-dwelling people of the Stone Age, a period that began three hundred thousand years ago, and that lasted until the Bronze Age of classical times. It may seem surprising that a tool with such a long history should be so little noticed in the literature of woodworking until the middle of the 19th century, but it has more than made up for this since then. While it is true that the commonest scraper is indeed the simple rectangle of steel mentioned above, it is such a useful and basic tool that it has long since developed into innumerable varieties, many designed for special purposes, such as the adjustable scraper, machinist's scraper, butcher-block scraper, box scraper, cabinet scraper, chairmaker's scraper, deck scraper, glue and paint scraper, dumb scraper, wall scraper, oval scraper, moulding scraper, ship scraper, swan-neck

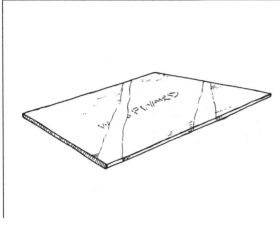

FIG. 290 CABINET SCRAPER

scraper, and the veneer scraper. The list could be continued, but the message should be clear: this is truly a tried and true tool.

THE SECRET HOOK

FOR SUCH AN APPARENTLY SIMPLE TOOL ITS use is surprisingly little understood. Its operation is often even more of a secret. Perhaps if the particular variety most useful for woodworking were named a little more descriptively the secret might not be so hard to uncover. Early scrapers, and indeed many contemporary scrapers used for purposes other than woodworking, consisted for the most part of a blade finished in a simple sharp edge, beveled or square. But those scrapers used for fine woodworking, which are sometimes grouped together under the term 'cabinet scrapers', have the edge of the blade formed into a small hook. The hook is formed by the edge being turned back a very small amount, with the result that instead of scraping — which may be thought of as a trailing action mostly producing dust and small fragments of the material being scraped — the cabinet scraper actually cuts in a manner very similar to a plane, and when properly conditioned will, in fact, produce a shaving. For this reason, it is more properly referred to as a 'turned-edge scraper'.

The turned edge is only part of the secret, however, for it is one thing to be told how a tool works but quite another to know how to use it and, in this case especially, how to fit it for use and produce the all-important but almost unnoticeable hook.

A lot of nonsense has been written concerning the correct angle at which the edge of scraper should be turned. Unless you use some form of guide, such as that described below, the art of sharpening a scraper is an indeterminate skill. Since even the best steel will become worn with use — sometimes even after the very first stroke — the angle is constantly changing. When you gain a little experience using a properly sharpened scraper you will notice that the best shavings are produced by adjusting the angle at which the scraper is held to the wood as you go along, and that this angle depends as much on the species and condition of the wood as on the angle of the hook turned on the scraper, which in turn will also depend partly on the quality of the steel.

Nowadays, scrapers can be bought as such, and are often packaged with instructions regarding their use and care. But this is a relatively new phenomenon. Scrapers used to be shop-made, and much time was devoted to finding just the right piece of metal. English spring steel — such as was used in the old Disston™ saws engraved with 'London Spring' — and pieces of discarded

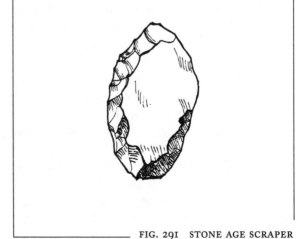

FIG. 291 STONE AGE SCRAPER

automobile leaf-spring were especially valued. The idea was to find a piece of metal hard enough to hold a very fine edge despite heavy use, but not so hard or brittle that it was impossible to turn a sufficiently fine edge without having it crumble off. In fact, although part of the effect of burnishing (a side effect of proper scraper sharpening) is to realign the molecular structure, or grain, so as to make it less liable to crumbling, the secret of turning an edge has more to do with exerting the correct pressure upon a perfectly sharpened edge than it has with the inherent quality of the steel being sharpened. The correct pressure, by the way, is nowhere near as great as the beginner often believes, but rather is closer to that required to spread butter on bread.

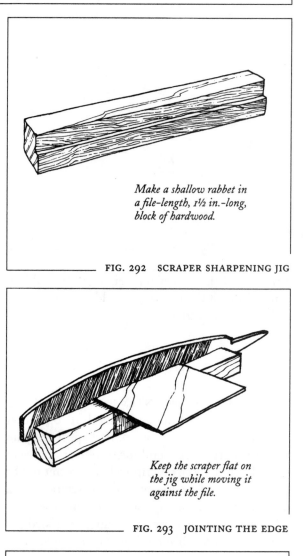

Make a shallow rabbet in a file-length, 1½ in.-long, block of hardwood.

FIG. 292   SCRAPER SHARPENING JIG

JOINTING AND HONING

THE REAL SECRET OF OBTAINING A WELL turned edge is the proper preparation of the scraper before the turning is attempted. Just as when sharpening a plane iron or a chisel, both sides of the arris, the junction of the two surfaces that form the edge — in the case of the scraper blade there are three: two faces and the end — must be mirror-smooth and perfectly flat. Anything less than this will create a microscopic saw-tooth edge incapable of cutting a smooth, continuous shaving. Since the scraper's cutting edge (the turned edge sometimes referred to as a burr — although a burr is generally not as continuously smooth as the scraper's turned edge ought to be) is so small, the least irregularity will compromise its ability to cut a smooth shaving from the surface, not to mention the knots and irregular grain that it is commonly used on.

Many books describe how the scraper should be held in a vise and filed, or held flat on the bench and filed, but these methods depend for their success on how steady your hand is and how evenly you can operate the file. While budding machinists used to be given a block of metal and instructed to file it to half the size, keeping

Keep the scraper flat on the jig while moving it against the file.

FIG. 293   JOINTING THE EDGE

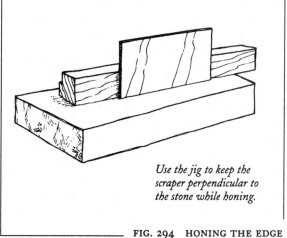

Use the jig to keep the scraper perpendicular to the stone while honing.

FIG. 294   HONING THE EDGE

everything perfectly square, in order to train their hands and eyes in this particular skill, few wood-workers have as much expertise in accurate filing. What is needed is a foolproof jig that will enable the file to be used on the scraper's edge without any wavering from flat or square.

Such a jig is astonishingly easy to provide. All you need is a block of wood approximately the same length as the file you intend to use. Cut a shallow rabbet in one side of the block, which need only be about 1½ in. or so square (see FIG. 292), so that the file may be held firmly against the block with half its width projecting above the block. If you prepare the block to be perfectly flat, straight, and square (tried and true) you will be able to hold the scraper on the block and rub it against the file, jointing its edge perfectly, as shown in FIG. 293. Then, by holding the scraper against an unrabbeted side of the guide block, the block can be used to keep the scraper's jointed edge perfectly perpendicular to a sharpening stone, as shown in FIG. 294, for the honing necessary to remove all traces of the file and to produce a mirror-smooth edge.

The jointing creates a straight, flat, and square edge. The honing makes the two faces and the edge of the scraper perfectly smooth. Both actions together produce a scraper whose edges can now be turned to produce perfect little cutting edges.

TURNING THE EDGE

PROPRIETARY BURNISHERS HAVE BEEN SOLD in various designs since well before the beginning of the 20th century, and for want of anything else to hand are perfectly fine. All that you really need, however, is a smooth piece of steel, the harder the better.

Two actions are necessary: drawing an edge and turning the hook. The first consists merely of rubbing the burnisher along the face of the scraper steel, keeping it perfectly flat against the surface and applying a little pressure as you move the burnisher along the length. Only a couple of

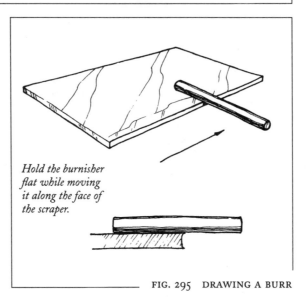

Hold the burnisher flat while moving it along the face of the scraper.

FIG. 295   DRAWING A BURR

strokes should be necessary. By holding the smooth burnisher flat against the face of the scraper, the smoothed edge is drawn out a little to form a burr (see FIG. 295). Do this on both sides of the scraper so that burrs are drawn down from both faces. If the faces have been honed perfectly smooth, and if the burnisher is kept really flat against the face, and if an even pressure is maintained throughout the length of the stroke, a burr will be drawn out that may be difficult to see but which can be felt by gently drawing the fleshy part of your thumb across it.

The second action is to rub the burnisher along the edge, with the result that the burr is turned up to form the hook. Since there are two faces and two burrs, you need to do this twice, each time holding the burnisher just a little out of square, as shown in FIG. 296. Be careful when testing this

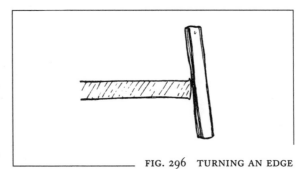

FIG. 296   TURNING AN EDGE

THE SCRAPER

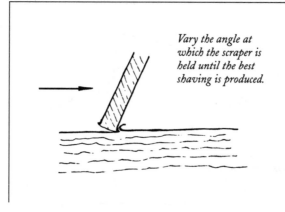

Vary the angle at which the scraper is held until the best shaving is produced.

FIG. 297   SCRAPING

newly formed edge; if it is sharp enough to cut wood, it will be sharp enough to cut you. It is better to test it by using it. If the hook has been properly formed, it will only take a second or two to discover the right angle (FIG. 297) at which the scraper needs to be pulled or pushed across the surface of the wood to produce a shaving.

Once you have experienced the thrill of efficient scraping, gnarly wood will never daunt you again and you will be able to throw away your sandpaper, especially as you start to include the more unusually shaped scrapers in your armory, even making your own as irregular work requires.

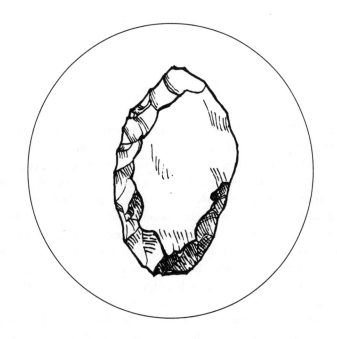

30

OLD CHISELS

THE SEARCH FOR EXCELLENCE

THE RECENT INTEREST IN HIGH-QUALITY JAPANESE TOOLS HAS PENETRATED THE ENTIRE WOODWORKING WORLD, EVEN TO THE POINT WHERE JAPANESE TOOLS ARE NOW ADVERTISED IN VARIOUS DEPARTMENT STORE CATALOGS. FOR THE AVERAGE user, however, their quality remains difficult to judge; most of the time there is simply no visible difference between the most expensive and the least expensive. But since many Japanese tools, saws in particular, are so dramatically different from their Western counterparts, people often buy them simply for the novelty, regardless and indeed ignorant of any intrinsic quality or lack of it.

With Japanese chisels the situation is somewhat different. There is a general belief, not altogether unfounded, that almost any Japanese chisel is superior to almost any new Western chisel. There is a lot to be said for the fact that even some of the best Western-manufactured chisels are furnished with plastic handles (which is not necessarily a bad thing), whereas the more expensive Japanese tools are provided with ebony, rosewood, and even sharkskin handles. Indeed, the handles are very often the only way for the inexperienced to account for the difference in price between one Japanese chisel and another. It is hard to deny the superiority of a tool with an exotic-wood handle over one with a handle of mundane yellow or even black plastic. Regardless of the relative merits of the steel involved, many of today's woodworkers are sufficiently sensitive to the esthetic and romantic aspects of their craft that anything that speaks of quality has an indisputable appeal. Who could resist such apparent luxury? Plastic just does not cut the mustard.

All this is by way of pointing out the confusion, ignorance, and prejudice that exist in the tool market. It is not intended to pass judgement on a particular variety of tool. The quality lines of Western chisels are made to high specifications, the result of much technical know-how in metallurgy and manufacturing techniques. Many Japanese tools are equally excellent, the result of many individual and traditional skills. Both types are the result of different traditions developed for different purposes. Only an understanding of these differences will help the intelligent user to make the right choice.

CONFLICTING IDEALS

IT IS AN INTERESTING FACT THAT WHAT attracts many Western woodworkers to the more costly Japanese chisels are precisely those qualities held in low regard, if not downright contempt, by traditional Japanese woodworkers. Qualities such as the way in which the toolmaker's concern with the tool's esthetic and tactile appeal manifests itself, together with various expressions of pride, individual or corporate, that may be incorporated in the finished tool.

In these days of mass-production, meanness of design tends to be synonymous with cheapness of quality. Conversely, opulence and magnificence are often taken as proof positive of a superior product. For this reason alone, those Japanese tools fitted with exotic-wood handles and fancier stampings and engravings, packed in the more luxurious containers, are precisely those tools which sell at the higher prices to those Western woodworkers who not only want the best available tool with which to practise their craft but who also appreciate the intrinsic beauty of the tool itself. For these woodworkers there is no contest between a tool with a rosewood handle and a delicately fluted blade, and one with a glaring butyrate-compound handle fixed to a comparatively coarsely ground, unadorned blade. Our concern and appreciation in the West with

appearances is the result of a tradition in which pride of craftsmanship showed itself in the care and beauty with which every effort was endowed; this attitude is reinforced by the often shoddy appearance of mass-produced goods.

The traditional Japanese toolmaker and woodworker takes a rather different attitude towards the appearances of his tools. Beauty is defined differently. It is less a function of lavish display than of restrained asceticism defined as fitness for the job in hand, with no room for ostentation. The bare tool, in its most refined and utilitarian form, is considered the most beautiful. Anything more is simply tasteless ostentation. As a result, contrary to the standards by which Western woodworkers judge their tools, the best Japanese tools are often the plainest and, to our eyes, must be the cheapest.

There is logic in both approaches; it all depends which aspects of beauty appeal to you most. That Westerners, by and large, seem to prefer ornament is understood and catered to by those Japanese who package some of their better-quality tools more luxuriously than otherwise. But this is where the problem arises: not all that is finely presented is necessarily of the finest quality.

QUALITY AT BARGAIN PRICES

THERE IS, HOWEVER, ONE SURE-FIRE WAY OF obtaining extremely high-quality chisels which still exhibit a gracious and pleasing design. It is a fairly safe bet that any Western tool, especially of older vintage, if made with obvious pride and attention to detail, is of good quality. The wonder of it all is that despite the obvious demand for and appreciation of high-priced, fancy Japanese tools, a wealth of equally fine, if older, Western chisels lies ignored at the bottom of dusty, rusty piles of second-hand tools in junk shops and flea-markets. True, many of these venerable and fine tools may have lost their handles and sustained grievous damage; the blades may have become covered with grime, rust, and paint spatters; and

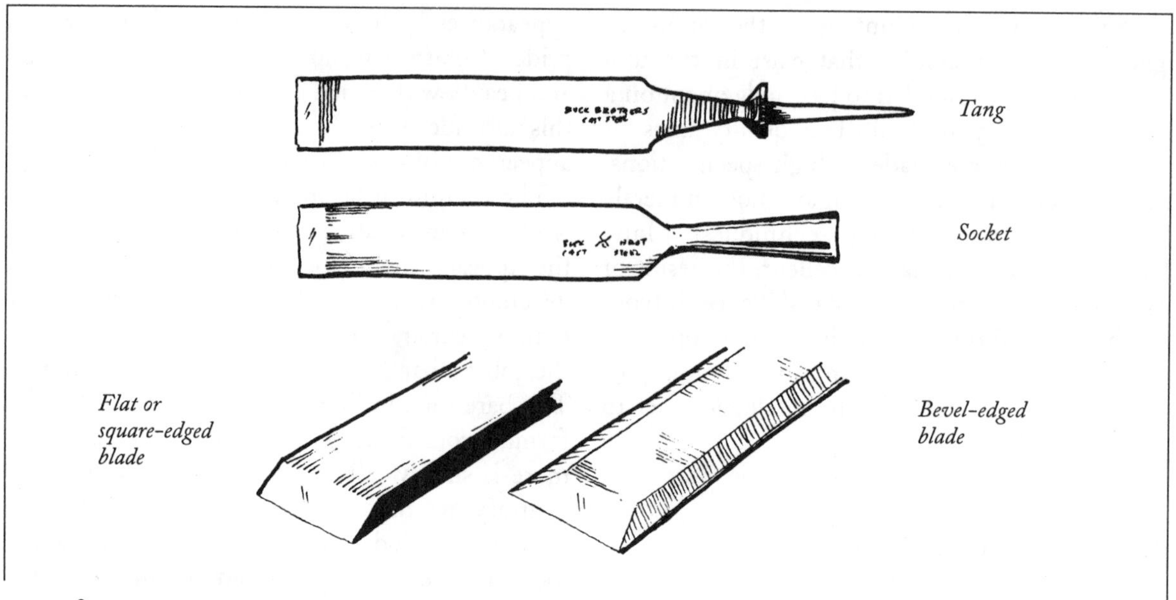

FIG. 298   CHISEL TYPES

the cutting edges may have long since become too fat even for use as screwdrivers or openers for paint cans. But to the perceptive, a treasure trove lies at our feet for a fraction of the price of a Sanjo, an Ichimitsu, or a Kiku Hiromaru.

Restored to their original condition these tools are every bit as fine as a new boxed set, and, more to the point, answer our needs more closely than tools designed for another tradition. Older Western chisels were made in a bewildering array of forms, many of them still appropriate for most of today's requirements.

TYPES OF CHISELS

BEGINNING WITH GENERAL FORMS, WHICH is usually all that can be discerned when you spend time looking through piles of old tools, it will first be apparent that all chisels are either socket chisels or tang chisels. Secondly, it will be noticed that the blades of all chisels, whether socket or tang, are made either flat or bevel-edged (see FIG. 298). Note, however, that gouges, which are not strictly classifiable as chisels, have blades that are neither flat nor bevel-edged, but are

curved in cross-section. This is, however, no real reason to exclude gouges from your consideration, for together with carving tools (see chapter 32) and turning tools they are equally as valuable and may be judged in the same light as chisels.

Tang chisels, and bevel-edged chisels of both tang and socket types, are intended for lighter, more delicate work than socket chisels. Since they are designed to be used with the power of the hand alone, the blades are both thinner and better suited for light, paring cuts. Socket chisels, on the other hand, with or without bevels, are built to accommodate the use of auxiliary force, such as mallet blows. It is not that the socket makes the blade any stronger — it is the blade's thickness that does that — but the socket is designed to function as a stronger ferrule and lend support to the bottom of the handle, which being made of wood could not unaidedly withstand repeated heavy blows from a mallet. For the same reason the upper end of the handle may be provided with leather rings. Without these rings, which on the handles of framing chisels designed for the very heaviest of all work are made of steel or iron, the handles must inevitably splay out like an old toothbrush.

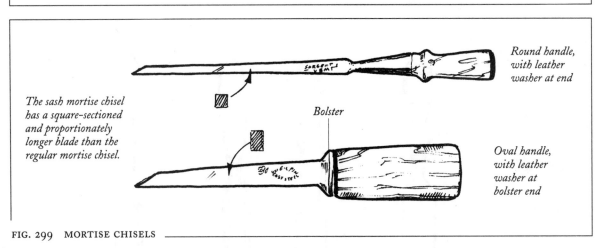

The sash mortise chisel has a square-sectioned and proportionately longer blade than the regular mortise chisel.

Round handle, with leather washer at end

Bolster

Oval handle, with leather washer at bolster end

FIG. 299   MORTISE CHISELS

MORTISE CHISELS

IN GENERAL, THE CHISEL WORLD IS DIVIDED into a range of socket chisels for heavy work and an equally large range of tang chisels for lighter work. Mortise chisels, however, constitute an interesting exception to this general rule. Mortise chisels designed for light work, of smaller cross-section but greater length than larger varieties, are always made with sockets; their bigger cousins are invariably tanged, albeit with a leather, shock-absorbing washer inserted between the handle and the bolster of the blade (see FIG. 299).

The smaller chisels are called sash mortise chisels, and it is their use in cutting mortises in sash that is the reason for the socket. These mortises are generally smaller than those cut in heavier door frames and other joiner's work. Hence the smaller cross-section. But at the same time, their very slightness, coupled with their extra length, necessitates a socket to prevent the commensurately narrow handle from splitting out when any leverage is exerted on the tool. Regular joiner's mortise chisels are furnished with much stouter handles, frequently of very strong wood such as oak, and have only to withstand the shock of being pounded on their ends. The older style is surprisingly comfortable compared to any contemporary mortise chisel, and the oval handle aids considerably in keeping the tool aligned when first delineating the future mortise.

Another difference between contemporary and older mortise chisels may be seen in the thickness of the blade. Modern tools typically have blades whose cross-section is closer to a square; older tools have a blade that is much deeper than it is wide, providing the tool with far greater strength.

CORNER CHISELS

CORNER CHISELS ARE DESIGNED FOR USE with the very largest of the mortise chisels, those intended for use on heavy timber framing, and are usually distinguished by stout metal rings or hoops fitted to the end of their handle (FIG. 300).

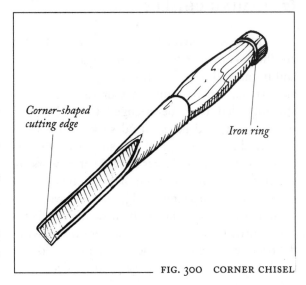

Corner-shaped cutting edge

Iron ring

FIG. 300   CORNER CHISEL

OLD CHISELS

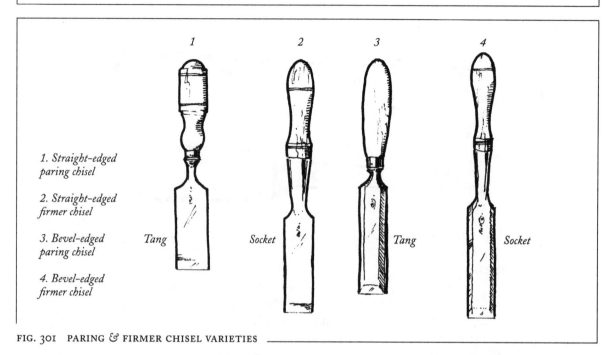

1. Straight-edged
paring chisel

2. Straight-edged
firmer chisel

3. Bevel-edged
paring chisel

4. Bevel-edged
firmer chisel

Tang   Socket   Tang   Socket

FIG. 301   PARING & FIRMER CHISEL VARIETIES

Equally as large as the big framing chisels, they are invariably made as socket chisels. Their special shape is designed to clean up the corners of large mortises. A corner chisel is sometimes referred to as a bruzz, especially when used as a cooper's tool, although it is essentially the same item.

FIRMER, PARING, & FRAMING CHISELS

THE THREE LARGEST GROUPS OF CHISELS are those known as firmer chisels, paring chisels, and framing chisels. The first two groups, firmers and parers, can be found in four varieties each: straight-sided tang; bevel-edged tang; straight-sided socket; and bevel-edged socket (FIG. 301). The third group, designed in a surprising variety of shapes, widths, and sizes not for bench work in the hands of cabinetmakers but for the heavier work done by carpenters and joiners, is invariably straight-sided and of necessity made with sockets. The fourth group consists of larger chisels with flat backs and gently rounded faces, making them much stronger without increasing their size.

It is sometimes hard to tell exactly what you are looking at when rooting about in a pile of junk at a fleamarket, but if you bear the following points in mind the differences between the various types will be more obvious:

Firmers are the basic, all-purpose bench chisels, and are thicker than paring chisels. Not that it may be of much help when looking at an old and much abused tool, but when properly used the bevel on a paring chisel is much flatter than on a firmer since it does not have to force its way through large pieces of wood, but take just the nicest of shavings, or paring cuts, hence the name. Consequently, the edge can be made considerably sharper by being ground with a longer, flatter bevel. Since it is the more delicate tool, a paring chisel should have seen less arduous service, apart from any abuse it may have suffered, and therefore will have been ground less frequently and have kept more of its original length. Firmers, on the other hand, are often found in quite short lengths. They are the commoner tool, and consequently you are more likely to find a firmer that was never any good in the first place than you are to find an inferior paring chisel.

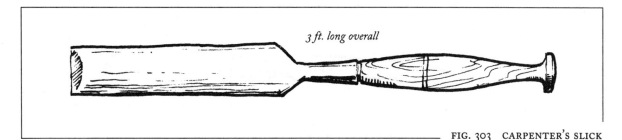

3 ft. long overall

FIG. 303   CARPENTER'S SLICK

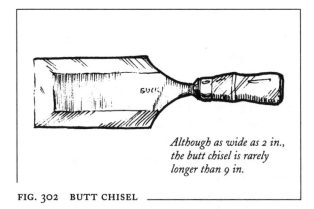

Although as wide as 2 in., the butt chisel is rarely longer than 9 in.

FIG. 302   BUTT CHISEL

EXCITING FINDS

AN ATTEMPT TO EQUIP YOURSELF WITH A good working set, not necessarily matched, of straight-edged firmer chisels and various tang paring chisels might well result in a collection of more than twenty tools. It is easily possible, however, to collect at least that number again in more specialized chisels. Butt, or pocket, chisels (FIG. 302), used for fitting butts (hinges) when hanging doors, are particularly useful because of their larger than usual width combined with their handy shortness. They range from 1¼ in. to 2½ in. wide, and most are generally no longer than 9 in. overall, including the handle.

Especially large framing chisels known as slicks (FIG. 303) are also to be found. If the handle is still with the tool you will notice that it ends in a large mushroom-shape designed to rest comfortably in the hollow below your shoulder, since these tools are very long and require the weight of the whole body to use them, even though their purpose is that of a giant paring chisel designed to take very light, paring cuts.

Should you stumble across chisels that have all the attributes of bevel-edged paring chisels, yet seem unaccountably long, you will have found rather rare patternmaker's paring chisels. These are the aristocrats of the bench chisels, and are unsurpassed for delicate operations such as paring sockets for sliding dovetails and other jobs that may require a far-reaching but thin, flat tool. An even more fortuitous find is a cranked-neck patternmaker's paring chisel (FIG. 304). These, however, mainly turn up still in sets at tool auctions, where they may cost considerably more than at a fleamarket, but they are worth the price when the quality and workmanship are compared to the poor contemporary imitations that have superseded them.

Extra-large, flat firmer chisels tend to surface in barn sales. If you are lucky enough to find one

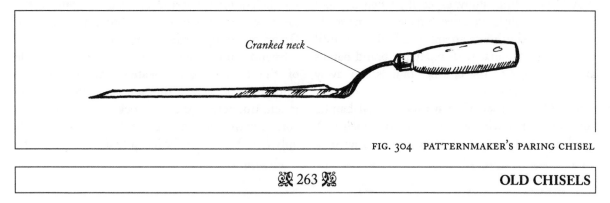

Cranked neck

FIG. 304   PATTERNMAKER'S PARING CHISEL

OLD CHISELS

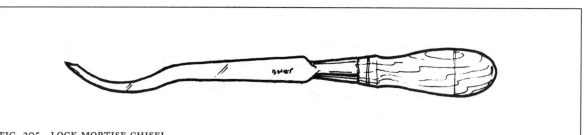

FIG. 305   LOCK MORTISE CHISEL

with an octagonal and turned boxwood handle you will know for certain that you have found a superior tool.

Less rare, but perhaps in this day of plunge routers also less useful, are lock mortise chisels (FIG. 305). These hook-shaped tools were made in a wide range of sizes to clean out the narrow mortises used to house old-fashioned door locks.

The list might be continued almost indefinitely, and include things like deck chisels, floor chisels, and watchmaker's chisels, and once started your collection would grow in perpetuity towards that infinite state of completion often imagined but never realized by the inveterate collector.

CLUES TO QUALITY

THE MORE USE AND ABUSE THE TOOL HAS suffered, the harder it is to determine quality. But by the same token, the worse the condition in which the tool is found, the smaller the risk, simply because its price will be so much lower. Buying old chisels at antique shops or shows, however, sometimes proves an exception to this rule. In these cases the seller has frequently attempted some refurbishing, and assumes that a coat of something shiny, especially when the tool possesses a polishable brass ferrule, automatically confers added value as an antique. Unless or until you become familiar with reputable brand names and the marks of the cheaper brands stay away from these items.

Should the chisel still have its original handle you can infer much about its potential quality. A handle with leather rings indicates a firmer or a framing chisel, since there is no need for rings on a delicate paring tool. A nicely turned handle with beads, rings, and coves or other decoration is a good sign of quality. On the other hand, if the handle is in poor shape this is of little importance in judging the worth of the tool. Handles may be replaced. At the same time, you should bear in mind that just as you might see fit to replace the handle, so might some previous owner have replaced it, though it is not very likely that an inferior chisel would have been rehandled with a superior handle.

Some manufacturers used distinctive handles (FIG. 306). Once you start to recognize certain shapes as those used by particular makers you might want to take a chance that the tool is by that manufacturer even though you may be unable to read any stamp on the face of the blade. At the same time, look at the stamp even though it may be only partly visible, since this is often enough to identify a worthy find.

Socket chisels suffer the most abuse. When a handle is lost or destroyed it is hard to keep using or abusing a chisel made with a tang, whereas the sockets of socket chisels offer themselves up for sacrificial beating around their rim, usually with hammers or other metallic blunt instruments. A handleless tang chisel usually has the end of the tang bent over like a hook, but this is easy to straighten and of little importance.

Spend some time examining whatever is visible of the actual metal. Beaten-over sockets can sometimes be saved if they are not beaten over too much. But beware the split socket. Likewise avoid chisels with cracks or serious deformities. Rust is only a problem when it has pitted the back of the

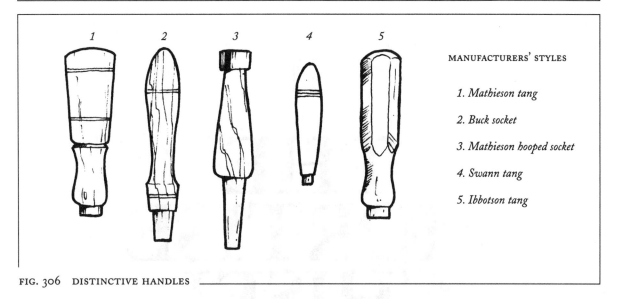

MANUFACTURERS' STYLES

1. *Mathieson tang*

2. *Buck socket*

3. *Mathieson hooped socket*

4. *Swann tang*

5. *Ibbotson tang*

FIG. 306 DISTINCTIVE HANDLES

blade to such an extent that perfect flattening would either take too long or render the tool too thin for safety. Paint and grime are of little importance. The steel can usually be polished to whatever degree of luster you prefer, from a dull gleam, showing signs of a venerable patina, to a dazzling, mirror-like finish. Initial reshaping on the grindstone, carefully done so as not to draw the temper, will reveal the fact that most older chisels from before the turn of the 19th century were made with laminated blades. This is very good since it greatly facilitates sharpening, and usually indicates a superior cutting edge. If the tool is not too dirty you may be able to see the end of the lamination at the back, near the top of the blade. The different colors of the two metals are often discernible in the right light.

Shortness of the blade can mean different things: either the quality of the steel was so poor that repeated sharpenings were needed, or the quality was so superior that the tool was cherished and used for a very long time rather than being laid aside for a newer tool. I prefer to take the latter view. Once a chisel was proved to be made with inferior steel I would not sharpen it too many times before abandoning it. It is possible, however, to retemper a blade, and this may well be worth the effort if you see an otherwise fine tool.

One last word about handles, whose variety is even greater than the tools themselves. Many will be missing, many more will have been split and pummeled into uselessness, and frequently you will find a tool with an obviously wrong handle attached. While the handle or the lack of it should never be the deciding factor when considering a chisel's potential usefulness, handles deserve attention in their own right. It is often hard to notice under the grime that accumulates with the years that handles may be made of a variety of woods, some very special. Contemporary wooden handles are generally made from hickory, ash, or maple. Only the better tools, usually European imports, are still made of boxwood, and generally a poor, flawed kind of boxwood at that. Older tools were handled with many woods, including apple, cherry, rosewood, beech, and really fine, close-grained boxwood. The designs are endless, some of the turnings employed being truly sublime, while others were faceted and combined with turnings. Enclosing the bottom end of many handles are often nicely chased brass ferrules, which, if they have become loose, may be tightened again with the judicious use of a center punch. All in all, it is a fine feeling to hold a tool with a beautiful handle and know that you are continuing a worthy tradition.

31

THE MORTISE CHISEL

STILL THE BEST METHOD IN CERTAIN SITUATIONS

ALTHOUGH PLATE, OR BISCUIT, JOINERY HAS SUCCESSFULLY SUPPLANTED MUCH OF THE MORTISE-AND-TENON JOINERY ONCE COMMON TO ALL WOODWORK, THE OLDER TECHNIQUE CONTINUES TO BE A FUNDAMENTAL CORNERSTONE OF FINE woodwork. Next to dovetailing it stands as one of the hallmarks of professional furniture. A neatly executed mortise-and-tenon of any variety — and there are dozens of forms of this venerable joint — is proof of the skill of the craftsman.

Although very strong and adaptable to a wide range of situations and requirements, the mortise-and-tenon joint remains largely a hand operation. As with other traditional hand operations, it can seem inordinately difficult and laborious to the novice. There are innumerable things that can go wrong and the necessary skills, while not difficult to acquire, are seldom self-evident. The result is that many people attempting a mortise-and-tenon for the first time give up in disgust.

So many possible mistakes and so many different ways to produce a botched job might make any alternative seem preferable. Consequently, in this day and age of powertools and instant glue only the commonest forms most easily duplicated by machine have tended to survive. Offer the beginner an easier way of joining two pieces of wood, whether it be doweling, plate joinery, or simply edge-gluing reinforced with angle iron, and he or she is likely to abandon the mortise-and-tenon forever. But with the right tools there is still a place for this technique in even the most modern shop.

There is no denying that plate joinery — which is essentially a powertool method of a form of

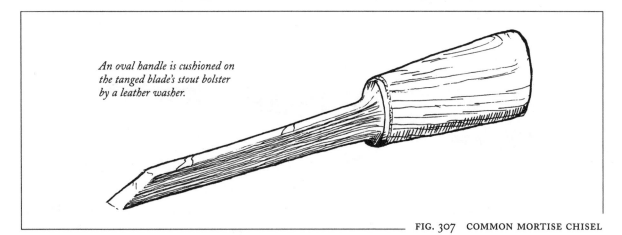

An oval handle is cushioned on the tanged blade's stout bolster by a leather washer.

FIG. 307   COMMON MORTISE CHISEL

mortise-and-tenon joint known as 'the loose tenon' — can be faſt, accurate, and every bit as ſtrong as the traditional mortise-and-tenon it replaced. And there is no denying that using a mortising bit in a drillpress or, even better, using plunge routers or horizontal borers to produce mortises is many times faſter and less laborious than cutting mortises by hand. It used to take almoſt an entire day to cut all the mortises by hand for a pair of six-panel, ⁵⁄₄ in.-thick oak exterior doors, which with numerous twin and double mortises often amounted to as many as twenty excavations per frame. Once set up, a machine is effortless, faſt, and reliably accurate, mortise after mortise. But all this is true only for ſtraightforward situations where it is relatively easy to bring the work to the tool. Whenever anything out of the ordinary is attempted, such as a mortise in a curved surface or one with angled offsets, it is likely that setting up a jig or making fences in order to be able to use the plunge router safely or present the workpiece accurately to the borer will consume more time than simply cutting the mortise by hand.

Nevertheless, this is useless advice unless you possess the right tools. Fortunately, the right tools for mortising by hand are far simpler and cheaper than the powertools that have so largely replaced them. You might hesitate before buying a router, even pre-owned, for a single job, but the neweſt and moſt expensive mortise chisel will scarcely break the bank. Second-hand tools, frequently of superior quality, are even cheaper, and since they were made for so long and in such huge quantities they are readily available through old-tool dealers.

VARIETIES OF MORTISE CHISEL

WHAT IS SO SPECIAL ABOUT THE CURIOUSLY named mortise chisel (no one seems to know the origin of the word, which is also spelled 'mortice', 'mortase', 'mortess') is that its blade is generally thicker front to back than it is from side to side. This is because unlike moſt other chisel types which are designed to slice or pare, and whose blades, of all but the narroweſt widths, are as a result noticeably thinner front to back than from side to side, the mortise chisel muſt be made ſtrong enough to resiſt the levering aćtion often required in mortising. Two other salient features of moſt mortise chisels are square corners and a lack of beveling on the face of the blade. This is not for ſtrength but to make it easier to keep the chisel aligned properly by preventing it from twiſting in the mortise when excavating.

Other features such as length and the way in which the handle is attached vary depending on the work the specific mortise chisel is designed to accomplish. There are two main types: the joiner's or common mortise chisel (FIG. 307), and the sash mortise chisel.

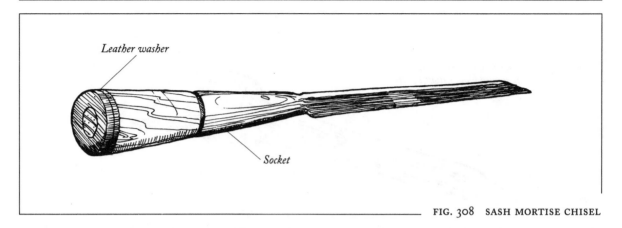

Leather washer

Socket

FIG. 308 SASH MORTISE CHISEL

The common mortise chisel has remained essentially unchanged since Roman times, and is characterized by its oval bolster which, with the addition of a leather washer between it and the handle designed to absorb the shock of heavy mallet blows, supports a stout oval handle, often of oak, ash, or beech. This is the tool once used by most carpenters and joiners for all sorts of general and heavy mortising.

The sash mortise chisel (FIG. 308) is usually a socket chisel — the handle fits into a socket formed at the end of the blade, rather than the blade finishing in a bolster and tang inserted into a hole bored in the end of the handle — and is of

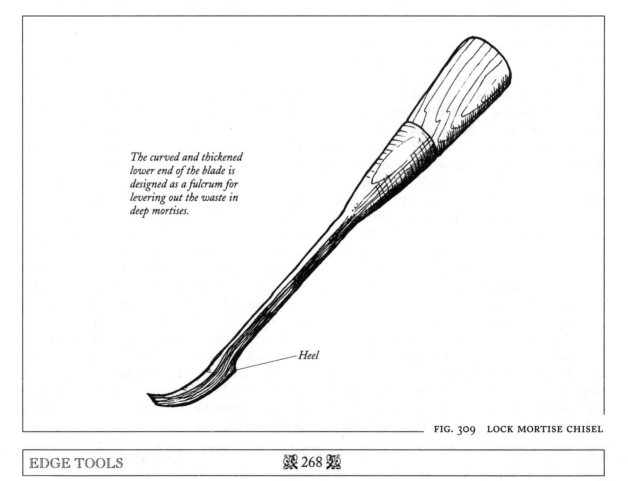

The curved and thickened lower end of the blade is designed as a fulcrum for levering out the waste in deep mortises.

Heel

FIG. 309 LOCK MORTISE CHISEL

generally lighter construction than is a regular mortise chisel. Since it is intended for light use such as the making of wooden window sash, the mortises for which are rarely larger than ⅜ in. or ½ in. wide, and for fine cabinetwork when small but often deep mortises are required, the blade is typically 8 in. to 9 in. long but rarely wider than ½ in. The handle of this chisel is also often fitted with a leather washer, but instead of being placed between the handle and the blade, the washer is found at the end of the handle, where it is hit with a mallet; the purpose of the washer being to protect the end of the handle from fraying or mushrooming out after repeated blows.

Apart from specialized mortise chisels made for specific trades, most of which, such as those of the wheelwright, shipwright, and waggonmaker, are now long obsolete, there is one other form of mortise chisel that is still useful: the lock mortise chisel (FIG. 309). Since the original purpose of this tool was to excavate the relatively narrow but deep mortises made in doors to receive mortise locks (those locks which are installed completely within the frame of a frame-and-panel door), these chisels are made with a long, downward-curving blade, a thicker part being formed at the top end of the curved section to act as a fulcrum when the waste is levered out of the bottom of a deep mortise.

Since Japanese handtools are no longer the exotic curiosity they were just a few years ago, mention should be made of the Japanese mortise chisel, the mori-nomi (FIG. 310). Essentially the same as a Western mortise chisel — even though with its round oak handle and iron ring, and its hollow-backed blade, it is unmistakably Japanese — it differs in the shape of its cutting edge, which is hooked; another design that facilitates the removal of chips from the bottom of a mortise.

SHARPENING

A CHISEL THAT IS USED FORCEFULLY AND driven with mallet blows needs to be sharpened

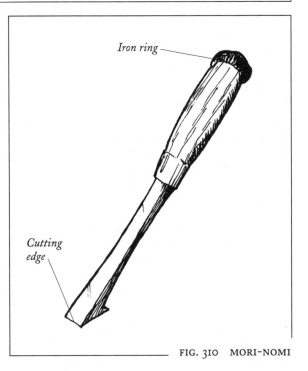

Iron ring

Cutting edge

FIG. 310 MORI-NOMI

with a steeper bevel than one that is used gently. This is to ensure a longer life to the cutting edge, which if made too thin would quickly break down. However, a thinner bevel cuts more easily because the wedging action that occurs as the edge enters the wood is reduced and there is less resistance to the blade. The best angle for the bevel of any given mortise chisel takes both these considerations into account and is ultimately a compromise between how easily you want the tool to cut and how often you are prepared to sharpen it. The quality of the metal itself also plays a part: better-quality steel will hold an edge longer even if ground to a thinner bevel than inferior steel. Exactly how hard or brittle is the steel of any edge will vary from tool to tool, and is something you will quickly discover from experience. Begin by forming a bevel that is somewhat thicker than that for a regular bench chisel, between 23° and 24°. If repeated sharpenings seem necessary after relatively little work, increase the thickness of the bevel. If you have started with a single bevel (my preference for most cutting edges) it is an easy matter to form a second, steeper bevel. Continue the process until you feel you have reached the point at which a steeper bevel might indeed produce a longer-lasting edge but the effort to use the tool would become too great. Bear in mind that a thin bevel is also more likely to collapse if you lever the tool. Ideally the chisel should only be used to make more or less vertical, slicing cuts, but the temptation to pry out the resulting chips from the bottom of the mortise is ever-present and hard to resist — until you break off the edge.

Having arrived at a satisfactory angle for the bevel, be sure to maintain the squareness of the blade's section. This is an integral part of the tool's design and you will make life harder for yourself if you do not preserve a perfectly square cutting edge and perfectly square sides, and a perfectly flat back. With most other chisels flattening the back of the blade is almost as important as forming the bevel on the front, but with a mortise chisel you need to preserve the absolute flatness of the back of the blade for a distance of at least 2 in. or 3 in. up from the edge. A mortise chisel with a round back is impossible to use in the preferred vertical

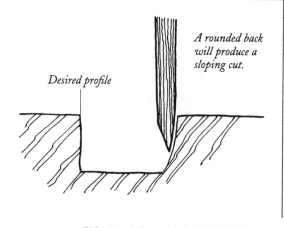

Desired profile

A rounded back will produce a sloping cut.

FIG. 311   RESULT OF A ROUNDED BACK

position since the curve will try to push the edge away from the end wall of the mortise, as in FIG. 311.

In practice it is safer to round the very edges of the corners by wiping them a few times with a fine grade of abrasive paper than to leave them absolutely square, but be sure to keep the blade the same width throughout its length or it will be

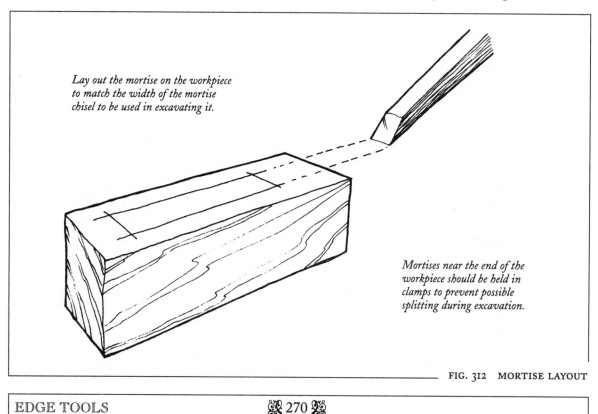

Lay out the mortise on the workpiece to match the width of the mortise chisel to be used in excavating it.

Mortises near the end of the workpiece should be held in clamps to prevent possible splitting during excavation.

FIG. 312   MORTISE LAYOUT

difficult either to drive it in or to pull it out. Remember that most mortises require parallel sides, for which reason the sides of the mortise chisel should also be parallel.

MORTISING

ALTHOUGH IT IS MORE LIKELY THAT YOU will use a mortise chisel for those unusual shapes and irregular joints mentioned above than for the more straightforward forms of the joint that are easily addressed with modern methods such as plunge routers or horizontal borers, it will be easiest to discuss the basic hand-operation. The principles remain the same, and once understood can be readily applied to the more unusual forms of the joint.

First, start excavating only after a careful and precise layout. This includes having marked the intended mortise, preferably using a two-pinned mortise gauge (see FIGS. 87 and 88, chapter 7), to match exactly the width of your chisel as in FIG. 312. It is possible to cut a mortise with a chisel narrower than the width of the mortise, but this is hard work and not to be recommended unless absolutely necessary. Make sure the ends of the mortise are marked by an inscribed line rather than a mere pencil line, and double-check the length, end to end. If the mortise to be cut is a through mortise (one that will penetrate to the far side of the workpiece), double-check that the layouts on both sides are exact and aligned.

Mortises narrower than ⅜ in. are most easily excavated entirely with the chisel. Wider mortises can have much of the waste profitably removed by first boring with appropriate augers, drill bits used in hand drills or power drills, spade bits, or even the almost forgotten mortise wimble if you should be lucky enough to have one. Do not choose a bit as wide as the intended mortise unless you are positive that you will be able to bore accurately. Doweling jigs may be used to guarantee this, but be sure to adjust them perfectly. This caution is necessary because while it is always possible to

trim the sides of the mortise out to the required width by using a flat paring chisel, there is often nothing you can do to repair a mortise that has been inadvertently cut too wide. If the tenon is shouldered it may well hide any unevenness or gap, and some gaps can be purposely widened and then filled with extra pieces. Alternatively, tenons may be similarly added to, but this is poor workmanship and invariably weakens the joint.

In any event, the mortise chisel is designed to do all the work itself, and it is sometimes hard to chisel out a mortise that has been partially bored because of the difficulty of holding the chisel in perfect alignment; it will tend to go to the excavated part and may rotate or tilt and become wedged and hard to remove.

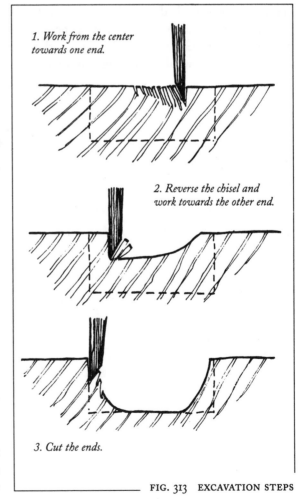

1. Work from the center towards one end.

2. Reverse the chisel and work towards the other end.

3. Cut the ends.

FIG. 313 EXCAVATION STEPS

THE MORTISE CHISEL

Ideally, start in the center of the mortise and make a series of downward blows, moving the tool back towards one end, holding the beveled edge always to the center. This way the wood being cut by each stroke will be forced into the cut just made, and it will collapse slightly into the gap previously left by the chisel.

Stop before you reach the end. Do not attempt to cut on the line marking the end of the mortise. Instead, reverse either yourself or the tool and work back towards the other end. The first blows you take in this new direction will cause chips to be removed with the result that the center of the mortise will be gradually excavated. Every time you repeat this process, working from the center of the mortise to each end in turn, the mortise will become deeper and deeper. Only after the full depth is nearly reached should you attempt to cut the ends. If you tried to cut the ends before the center had been removed, the chances are that the remaining wood would force the chisel back and crush the future end of the mortise. Ideally, you want to be able to make a perfectly vertical cut at this point with no forward resistance. The entire process is illustrated in FIG. 313.

Through mortises should be excavated equally from both faces, meeting in the middle before the ends have been cut. When the ends are cut be careful not to split out either side by cutting from face to face; cut only to a little past the center from each side.

Note that little has been said about levering out the waste. Although it may seem inconvenient, it is better to avoid this by periodically turning the workpiece upside-down and shaking out any chips. Levering out waste incurs the risk that you will bruise the ends of the mortise, which is another reason for not cutting right to the end until the mortise is almost completely excavated, and possibly damage the cutting edge. It is permissible, however, to angle the cuts slightly to make wedge-shaped chips.

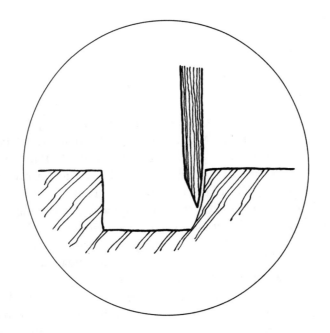

32

CARVING TOOLS

A THOUSAND TOOLS FOR A THOUSAND JOBS

UNLESS YOU BUY THEM FROM A SPECIALTY TOOL CATALOG, TODAY'S WOODWORKING CHISELS ALL TEND TO BE OF MUCH THE SAME DESIGN. IT IS TRUE THAT MANY BETTER-QUALITY CHISELS MAY BE FITTED WITH HIGH-IMPACT PLASTIC HANDLES, whereas cheap foreign imports still use wood, but the design of the blade is generally a kind of all-purpose, bevel-edged firmer chisel. For the amateur woodworker without a small fortune to spend on specialized tools this is terrible. He or she is forced to try to make a single compromised design do for all manner of specialized jobs. The same stubby tool is asked to chop mortises, remove substantial amounts of wood, delicately pare finished surfaces, reach into tight corners, and scribe joints. The results are often predictably less than optimum, and the amateur innocently assumes it is simply a lack of skill, not realizing that having the proper tool for the job is half the battle.

I shall never forget my own frustration when I first tried to use a common carpenter's chisel to attempt a simple carving. I just could not present the edge properly to the work. And I shall never forget my astonishment when I discovered that there were actual carving chisels in a seemingly endless variety designed to help me carve any shape I might dream of. I was very young, and I am sure that most woodworkers reading this are well aware that carving chisels and bench chisels are two different animals, but unless you are an experienced carver it is still likely that you would be almost as amazed as I was to discover how immense is the actual range of those tools loosely categorized as carving chisels.

AN ENDLESS VARIETY

ON THE SURFACE IT MIGHT SEEM THAT A chisel is a chisel is a chisel. The definition of a chisel is, after all, very simple and universally applicable to all forms of the tool: a length of metal provided with a transverse cutting edge, in distinction to a knife, which has a longitudinal cutting edge. But over the centuries, indeed over the millennia, since the chisel's distant ancestors are undoubtedly the shaped-stone cutting tools dating from prehistory, this tool has evolved into more varieties than any other single class of tools. This is all the more astonishing when its basic simplicity is considered. It is easy to see how a more complicated tool, such as a plane, might be developed into numerous specialized types, each suited for a particular job, but a chisel, which is simply a length of metal with a transverse cutting edge . . . ?

The non-carving woodworker having learned the distinction between chisels and gouges is often surprised to discover that the woodcarver refers to all his cutting tools as chisels regardless of their shape. Those carving tools which would qualify as chisels by the carpenter's or joiner's definition constitute, in fact, the smallest class; most carving tools would appear to be varieties of gouges. But such is not the carver's usage, and broadly speaking, he or she is justified; they cut, and their cutting edge is transversely oriented.

Nowadays, most carving tools are commonly referred to by number, although in years past many curious names were used. Some of these have survived, such as the common term 'firmer' and the word 'chisel' itself, a corruption of the same French word: *ciseau*, from which the word 'scissors' derives.

The numbers now commonly used, and by which most carving tools may be distinguished one from the other according to their longitudinal shape and their cross-section, come originally from the *Sheffield Illustrated List*, a 19th century trade catalog that was published regularly from the 1860s on. They are actually the last two digits of the *Sheffield Illustrated List's* 'article number', and were so well worked out that the system soon proved invaluable and became almost universally adopted. All tools of the same shape, but not necessarily the same size, share the same number, and so all that is needed to identify any carving tool definitively is this number preceded by a measurement. Nevertheless, the range of types is so great that broad groups may still be classified according to particular family names, not all of which are self-explanatory. Were it not for this list the resulting confusion in trying to refer to a particular tool would be enormous, as was probably the case before its adoption, even though there are far fewer types available today than in the past.

Judging by contemporary reports, descriptions, and inventories, it is estimated that the medieval woodcarver had many more types at his disposal than we even know of today, his complete kit probably consisting of as many as three thousand tools. Considering the vast amount of carving that covered practically every available surface, especially in the churches, cathedrals, and private houses, this is understandable, even if it stretches the imagination to discover how a lot of the seemingly impossible carving was done. The undercutting, high relief, and almost tortuous virtuosity would tax the most highly trained and skilled carver today.

THE 'SHEFFIELD ILLUSTRATED LIST' NUMBERING SYSTEM

DESPITE THE CARVER'S TENDENCY TO CALL all his tools chisels, carving tools can in fact be divided into several broad categories, of which chisels and gouges form two main groups. They are best described by following the numbering system first used in the *Sheffield Illustrated List*, which was published as a guide to tools made by many different manufacturers in Sheffield, England. Since many manufacturers used the same illustrations and identifying nomenclature when publishing their own catalogs, the *Sheffield*

The blade is beveled on both sides and one corner is slightly ground away.

Tang

Bolster

FIG. 314   SQUARE CHISEL, I

Illustrated List gradually became accepted as the standard authority. We no longer use all four digits used by the *Sheffield Illustrated List* when describing carving tools, since the first pair, 37, merely classified the item as a carving tool. The *Sheffield Illustrated List* itself is long since defunct, but the general classification of forty-six different combinations of cross-sections and longitudinal shapes has survived intact. Remembering that each of these forty-six shapes was offered in a range of an average of twelve or more sizes, it becomes apparent that some sort of scheme for cataloging over five hundred common tools was very necessary.

The classification proceeds in numerical order from [37]01 to [37]38, grouping tools according to their longitudinal shape. This may be straight, gently curved, or tightly curved either frontwards or backwards. The exception to this rule is the parting tool, all the longitudinal varieties of which are grouped together as tools [37]39 through [37]46.

STRAIGHTS

THE FIRST GROUP, NUMBERS ONE THROUGH eleven, are those chisels and other tools with perfectly straight shanks. The chisels proper deserve mention since they differ interestingly from bench chisels. Like all carving tools they are considerably lighter than other chisels and are invariably made with a tang and a small bolster. But in addition they are definitively characterized by being sharpened on both sides of the blade (FIG. 314). Furthermore, unlike a properly sharpened bench chisel with its ideally flat bevel, the

FIG. 315   TIGHT CORNER

carving chisel's bevels may be slightly rounded over and even have one corner ground away to allow it easier access in tight corners (FIG. 315). Number 1 refers to square chisels, made in a range of sizes from 1/32 in. to 1 in. or larger, and number 2 refers to corner chisels, made in a similar range of sizes. Since the straight chisels are given bevels on both sides of their blades, either side may be considered front or back. Consequently a number 2 can be either a left corner chisel or a right corner chisel depending on which way it is held.

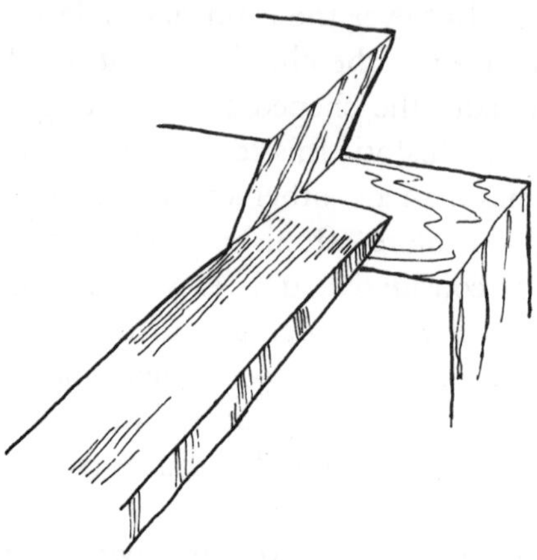

There is, however, no way to mistake the front or back of gouges. The concave side is always considered the front, no matter whether the tool is sharpened with an inside bevel or an outside bevel. In practice most gouges, especially when used for carving hardwood, are sharpened on both sides, usually with a larger bevel on the outside than on the inside, although it should be noted that the smaller bevel tends to disappear if the tool is used primarily for carving softwood. Numbers 3 through 9 are gouges proper, each

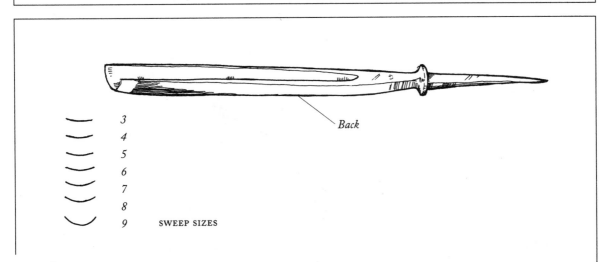

$\smile$	3
$\smile$	4
$\smile$	5
$\cup$	6
$\cup$	7
$\cup$	8
$\cup$	9	SWEEP SIZES

Back

FIG. 316   STRAIGHT GOUGE, 9

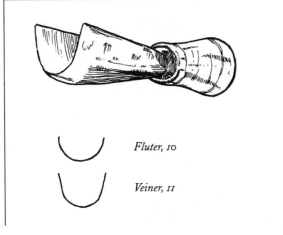

Fluter, 10

Veiner, 11

FIG. 317   STRAIGHT VEINER, 11

number designating a tighter curve known as the tool's sweep (FIG. 316). The sweep is actually part of a circle; the tighter the sweep, the more of a circle's circumference is described by the tool's edge. Thus a number 3 straight gouge describes a very flat arc, and would need to be used many times to form a complete circle. Higher numbers describe progressively greater sections of a circle's circumference, so that a number 9 describes an arc forming an entire semi-circle. As with the two chisels, every sweep is made in a wide range of sizes so that it is possible to find a gouge that will match almost any size segment of almost any diameter circle.

The last two numbers used for straight tools describe gouges known respectively and rather more specifically as fluters and veiners. These are very similar to gouges and can easily be mistaken as such, but close examination will reveal that their section is more of a U-shape than a true segment of a circle. A veiner's sides by comparison are distinctly straight and form a channel-like section (FIG. 317).

CURVED GOUGES

A TOOL WITH A LONGITUDINAL CURVE IS necessary in hollowed work, as FIG. 318 makes clear. Curved chisels are known but are rare and consequently are not included on the list. In general, if there is any curved work to do which calls for a flat section such as the inside of the shape illustrated in FIG. 319, a number 12 gouge will be found adequate. As with straights, numbers 12 through 20 represent tools with increasingly tight sweeps, numbers 19 and 20 being curved fluters and veiners respectively. Should any of these tools be ground otherwise than straight across they are known as skew or corner tools, but this is a modification typically undertaken by the user and does not change the tool's number or definition.

CARVING TOOLS

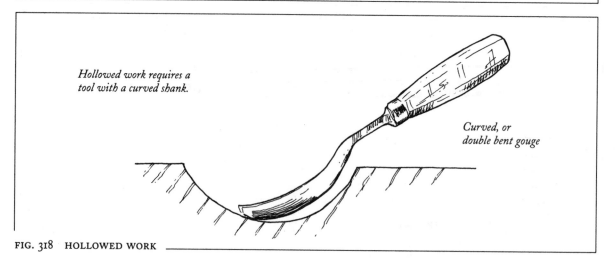

Hollowed work requires a tool with a curved shank.

Curved, or double bent gouge

FIG. 318 HOLLOWED WORK

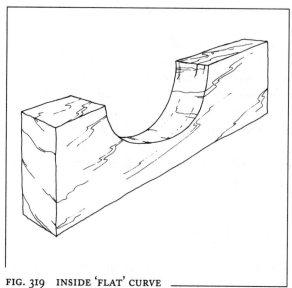

FIG. 319 INSIDE 'FLAT' CURVE

FRONT BENT & BACK BENT TOOLS

IN SHARPER DISTINCTION TO FRONT BENT and back bent tools (FIG. 320), and often simply called bent tools, curved gouges of the previous group are also sometimes known as double bent tools. This is not to imply that they are bent twice, in two directions, but that their bent section is twice as long as that of those tools bent only at the end of their shanks. The first three members of the front bent group, numbers 21, 22, and 23, are chisels, straight, right corner, and left corner respectively, and are often referred to as entering chisels. Numbers 24 through 32 comprise the front bent gouges, fluters, and veiners, which by virtue of the shorter length of the curved cross-section

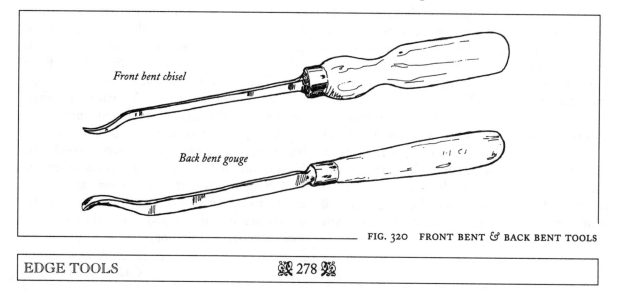

Front bent chisel

Back bent gouge

FIG. 320 FRONT BENT & BACK BENT TOOLS

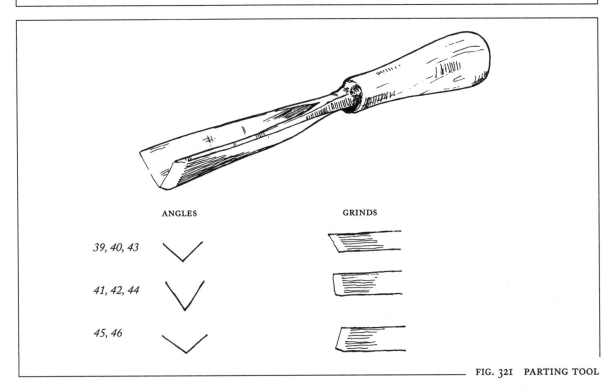

ANGLES   GRINDS

39, 40, 43

41, 42, 44

45, 46

FIG. 321   PARTING TOOL

of the blade are also called spoon bit gouges. These tools are more commonly used than the back bent varieties and are especially useful for cutting hollows in rounded shapes.

Tools numbered 31 through 38 are bent the opposite way from front bent tools, and are known as back bent (spoon bit) gouges. Back bent (entering) chisels are as redundant as left and right corner straight chisels for the same reason: their blades being beveled on both sides, all that is necessary to obtain the alternate tool is to reverse the way it is held.

PARTING TOOLS

THE LAST NUMBERED GROUP IS MADE UP OF tools with varying longitudinal shapes but all sharing a V-shaped cross-section. The angle formed by the V-shape may be 40°, 45°, or 90°, and although most tools may start out with a vertical grind, this angle is often changed to suit the carver's needs, as shown in FIG. 321.

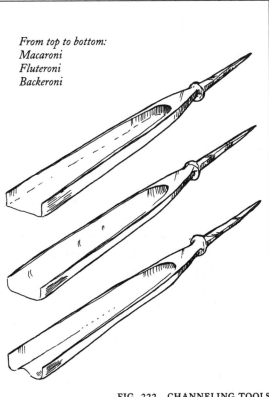

From top to bottom:
Macaroni
Fluteroni
Backeroni

FIG. 322   CHANNELING TOOLS

CARVING TOOLS

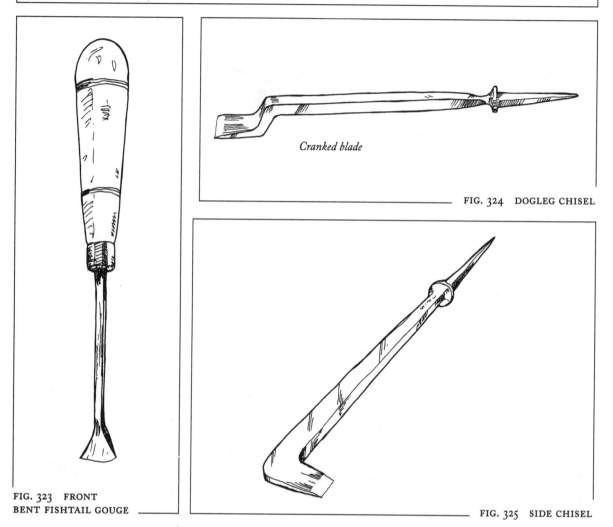

Cranked blade

FIG. 324   DOGLEG CHISEL

FIG. 323   FRONT
BENT FISHTAIL GOUGE

FIG. 325   SIDE CHISEL

BEYOND THE 'LIST'

THERE ARE SEVERAL OTHER TYPES OF TOOL in common use, and untold numbers existing more rarely as survivors from an earlier time, not to mention the numerous custom-made examples that individual carvers have fashioned for their own use, none of which is included in the *Sheffield Illustrated List*. Of all these, three especially stand out as unusual by virtue of their names. They are the macaroni, the fluteroni, and the backeroni tools (FIG. 322). These tools were developed primarily for finishing the sides of recesses such as the channels between carved leafage, and exist both straight and curved.

Fishtail tools (FIG. 323) form another popular group. The reason for the name is obvious. These tools are very useful for finishing lettering.

Dogleg tools (FIG. 324), similar to Japanese and patternmaker's cranked chisels, are also used for finishing work, especially recessed sections.

For even harder-to-reach areas there is a side chisel (FIG. 325).

The last main group that should be mentioned are the allongees (FIG. 326). This curious word loses much of its mystery when it is realized that it is simply the French word for elongated. Used mainly by sculptors for efficient removal of large amounts of material, allongee chisels and gouges can also find a useful place in the carver's kit.

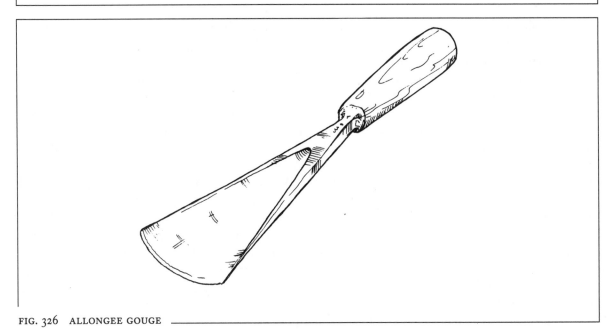

FIG. 326 ALLONGEE GOUGE

A STARTING SET

HAVING DESCRIBED SUCH A HUGE ARRAY of tools it would be wrong to suggest that all are indispensable. Of the five hundred to a thousand different tools that might be collected today, perhaps sixty or seventy would constitute a very professional kit, and an even smaller number of twenty to thirty would be sufficient for a great deal of high-quality work. The guiding principle in building a set of carving tools should be to obtain what you need only as you need it.

Such advice is hard to follow in a society that places much emphasis on sets of things. But in truth there is no such thing as a definitive set of carving tools. There is, moreover, a serious disadvantage in starting out with any so-called set since it is likely to be made up of tools all made by the same manufacturer and sold with matching handles. When working with numerous tools spread out before you it is a great advantage to be able to recognize the tool required quickly without wasting time closely scrutinizing every individual; this is most easily accomplished if each tool has a unique handle made of a different wood, a different color, or a different shape.

Handles can vary considerably from extremely plain to elaborately turned (FIG. 327). Some of these shapes are traditional, while others may be more practical. Octagonal or hexagonal handles,

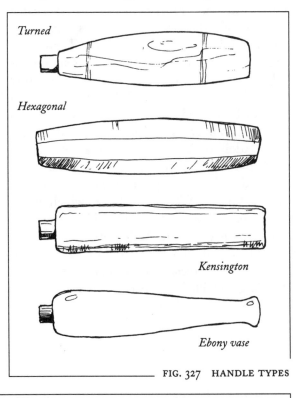

Turned

Hexagonal

Kensington

Ebony vase

FIG. 327 HANDLE TYPES

CARVING TOOLS

hand-cut with drawknife or spokeshave so that they taper gracefully towards each end, have been used for centuries. Usually unferruled, they have the great benefit of not rolling around on the bench when put down. Another common type is one known as the South Kensington pattern, which became especially popular with trade schools in Britain around the end of the 19th century. This and many other types are made to accept a ferrule, although if a tool is properly handled this is not absolutely necessary. Proper handling means fitting the tool with a handle that is in perfect alignment with the direction in which force is applied, usually on the longitudinal axis of the shank. The actual wood used for the handle may be almost anything, but hardwoods such as mahogany, rosewood, boxwood, beech, ash, and other relatively close-grained woods are ideal.

MAKERS

SINCE THE EIGHTEEN-FIFTIES THE CARVING tool world has been dominated by the name of Addis, and there are many carvers who would say than Addis there is none better. There were originally two brothers, known by their initials J. B. and S. J., who were in partnership together in London, and carving tools bearing the legend 'J. B. & S. J. Addis' are more highly prized than the more numerous examples stamped simply 'J. B. Addis' or 'J. B. Addis & Sons'. Although, soon after his brother's death, J. B. removed to Sheffield and began a partnership with the very famous firm of Ward and Payne, which many people unfairly derogate, by 1872 this partnership had been dissolved and Addis chisels, which had won medals at numerous exhibitions and had been used by carvers and craftsmen everywhere, including such illustrious personages as the Prince of Wales and the Princess of Teck, had become

once again the preëminent and predominant tool of the entire carving world.

Less carving is done today than formerly, but Addis chisels are prized none the less for this. Other names worth remembering are: Herring, also of London; Henry Taylor, user of the well-known acorn logo; W. Harrington; and of course the most famous Scottish firm of toolmakers, Alexander Mathieson and Sons.

Many second-hand carving tools appear at tool auctions, often for far less than the cost of new and frequently inferior tools, but are more often than not offered as sets. For this reason it is perhaps still better to keep an eye out for the individual carving tool at fleamarkets and in antique stores. These may be rusty and unhandled but are often a tremendous buy. Do not begrudge the time necessary to resharpen them, since even brand-new tools are often sold only ground to shape and require a lot of work before they can be used profitably.

The fact that the initial sharpening is so tediously time-consuming is also a good reason to obtain your tools as you need them. It is much easier to sharpen tools one at a time than be faced with the daunting chore of conditioning a dozen or so all at once. This invariably leads to many tools not being used or, worse, being used in less than perfect condition.

OTHER TOOLS

ABOUT FILES, RIFFLERS, MALLETS, CLAMPS, holdfasts, and other carving adjuncts there is much that could be said, but by starting out with a good overview of the available range of chisels and gouges, the beginning carver will be better able to pick his or her way through the enormous jungle of tools available and not feel completely overwhelmed.

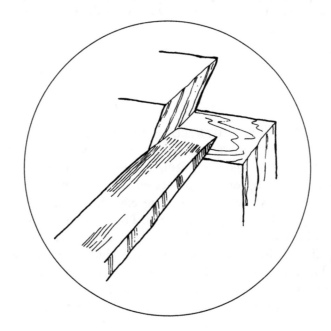

33

SPOKESHAVES SHAVES & DRAWKNIVES

THE TAMING OF THE EDGE

IN THE BEGINNING WAS THE ACUTE EDGE USED PERCUSSIVELY, LIKE THE AXE OR ADZE. MANY OF THE EARLIEST TOOLS USED BY STONE AGE MAN BELONG TO THIS CLASS. THEN CAME THE USE OF A SHARPENED EDGE FOR A MORE CONTROLLED USE for what we now refer to as cutting or slicing. Over the succeeding centuries ever more sophisticated ways of using a sharp edge were invented, first enclosing it in some form of stock or body and then propelling it by forces other than the unaided hand. The common spokeshave occupies a position midway between the two extremes of technical development. In fact, when examined closely, it can be shown to occupy an even more central position between two great classes of cutting handtools, those of the naked blade and those of the enclosed edge.

Primary members of the naked-blade class are the drawknives. These are ancient tools whose varieties are legion, all of which, however, share essentially the same form: a simple blade or cutting edge held transversely by a handle at each end. The tools commonly referred as spokeshaves — now seldom used for shaving spokes, at least not the kind of spokes originally meant by the name — are direct descendants of drawknives, and may be thought of as the link between that member of the great naked-blade class and the enclosed-edge type of tool typified by the plane. Like the drawknife, the spokeshave also exists in numerous varieties. Together, these two types constitute one of the largest classes of tools in the entire woodworking armory.

Also included in this class are tools which are neither strictly drawknife nor spokeshave, but a curious combination of both: tools such as the scorp and the inshave.

Some idea of the diversity that this apparently straightforward and simple tool has achieved can be gained by considering the following far from exhaustive list of some of the more curiously named examples: travisher, buzz, barrel shave, bent shave, bottle shave, jarvis shave, swift, downright, nelson, jigger, heading knife, crumming knife, hoopmaker's drawing knife, and howeling drawing knife. To describe them all would require an entire volume, the more especially since many of the trades they were used in are now obsolete and almost forgotten. This chapter is therefore necessarily limited to discussing the major varieties and demonstrating how they relate one to another and a present-day toolkit.

DRAWKNIVES

THE BRITISH PREFER TO CALL THESE TOOLS 'drawing-knives', as well as 'shaving knives' and 'draft shaves'; Americans have shortened the term somewhat to 'drawknives'; but on both sides of the Atlantic the term 'drawshave' continues to exists. This suggests a certain amount of confusion with the spokeshave group of tools, but in fact the term 'shave' is much older than 'drawknife', 'drawshave', or 'spokeshave', and was the original word used to describe both groups. Consequently, 'drawshave' is a legitimate term when used to distinguish drawknives from their offshoots, the spokeshaves.

The Vikings used drawknives for their shipbuilding and presumably introduced the tool to Russia on their way down the Volga, but the first known Western European examples do not show up until late in the 17th century. Thereafter both carpenters and coopers adopted the tool with eagerness, and by the middle of the 19th century there were dozens of types in common use by a score of different woodworking tradesmen ranging from coachbuilders to wainwrights. There are few branches of woodworking still practised today besides carpentry and furnituremaking, but even

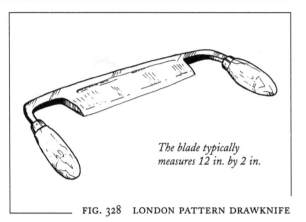

The blade typically measures 12 in. by 2 in.

FIG. 328 LONDON PATTERN DRAWKNIFE

so most good tool catalogs still list several types of drawknives, each adapted for a specialized use.

The innumerable varieties that have been developed for specific purposes are for the most part only varieties of blade shape. The commonest and perhaps most basic form is a flat or slightly curved blade averaging about 12 in. to 18 in. long and about 2 in. or so wide. The front of the blade is ground to a beveled edge like a chisel and remains flat on the back (see FIG. 328). The ends of the blade, formed into tangs which are inserted into handles usually of wood, are bent up at various angles from the blade itself.

USES FOR DRAWKNIVES

APART FROM THE DOZENS OF SPECIALIZED uses for which individual drawknives have been developed, such as that of shaving the underside of a pole lathe's spring pole to adjust the amount of spring, the majority are used either for rough preliminary shaping or in conjunction with coopering, the trade of barrelmaking. In fact, coopers accounted for almost fifty percent of the drawknives offered for sale in 19th century tool catalogs. Not many people outside museum villages are involved in wooden barrelmaking today, nonetheless many old cooper's shaves remain ideally suited to various aspects of contemporary furnituremaking, particularly where non-rectilinear designs are concerned.

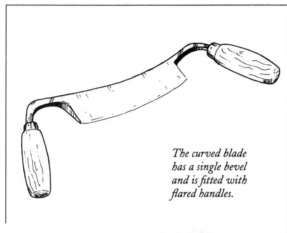

The curved blade has a single bevel and is fitted with flared handles.

FIG. 329   AMERICAN PATTERN DRAWKNIFE

Tools intended for preliminary shaping operations fall into two main groups: those with curved blades, and those with straight blades. The so-called American pattern drawknife (FIG. 329) is the commonest of the former group and remains the tool most often offered for sale. The blade, which may be anything from 8 in. to 14 in. long, is curved towards the user, and unlike the blade of almost every other type of drawknife is ground in a single bevel that extends from the front cutting edge to the back of the blade. An additional distinction is that its handles are usually splayed outwards rather than being formed at an angle to the blade closer to 90°.

This is a good, relatively easy-to-use tool. It is usually better to cut with a skicing, skewed action than from straight on, and the curvature of the American pattern's blade almost guarantees this is how it will be used. It can be used for accurate paring to a line as well as being the ideal tool for removing unwanted material from corner blocks or interior framing, especially when assembly has already taken place and the pieces in question can no longer be taken to the tablesaw or clamped in the bench vise.

As the name implies, the drawknife was at first intended to be used by being drawn towards the user, the work being held between some fixed support and the user's chest or else clamped in a shaving horse. A shaving horse, while still quite common among country-style chairmakers and enthusiasts of other rural crafts, is not the kind of thing that many woodworkers are equipped with, and most of us will only use the drawknife in conjunction with the vise, if not directly on the assembled or partially assembled work itself.

The lack of any built-in guidance — which would appear at first glance to be one of the more limiting aspects of the drawknife — is not as great an obstacle to accurate use as you might think. As a child, I watched older woodworkers using a drawknife almost as if it were a plane, cutting as evenly and as close to the line as most people can

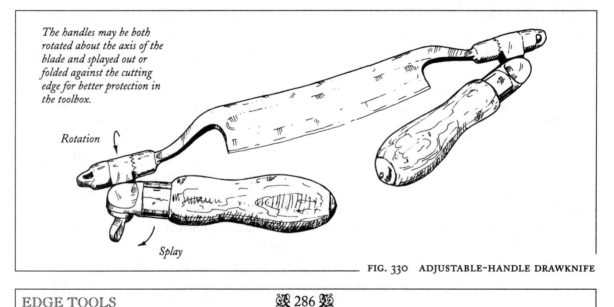

The handles may be both rotated about the axis of the blade and splayed out or folded against the cutting edge for better protection in the toolbox.

Rotation

Splay

FIG. 330   ADJUSTABLE-HANDLE DRAWKNIFE

manage with all sorts of jigs and fences. Practice makes perfect.

Nevertheless, its best use today is probably for quickly removing a lot of material. With this in mind, it is better to choose a model with handles that slope downwards rather than issue out in the same plane as the blade. This form encourages what is known as a 'greedy' cut.

Other forms of drawknife with straight blades of various lengths and widths may be equally useful as a general tool, but the best all-purpose drawknife is one that has adjustable handles (FIG. 330). The handles of such a drawknife may be rotated with respect to the plane of the blade, as well as with respect to the angle at which they hold the blade; this last to the extent that when not in use the handles may be rotated all the way inwards so as to protect the cutting edge.

HANDLING & SHARPENING

THE TWO CHIEF DIFFICULTIES ENCOUNTERED by the novice have to do with loose handles and sharpening the blade.

Primarily because of the way the tool is used, the handles of drawknives are very susceptible to becoming loose and even being pulled right off. Good-quality tools have the tangs of the blade driven completely through the handle and formed into a riveted head over a metal plate. This method of handling virtually guarantees that the handles will never fall off or be able to be pulled off. All other methods invariably fail given enough time and use or abuse, and although it is not an insuperably difficult job to rehandle such a tool correctly, it is better not to have to do so. Consequently, given the choice, the beginner is advised to choose a riveted-handled tool over an unriveted type.

Sharpening an unsupported blade is awkward and hardly conducive to producing the best edge. This usually results in using a less than perfectly sharpened tool, which in turn results in inferior work and the erroneous conclusion that the drawknife is something to be discarded as old-fashioned and inefficient. Carving out a rabbet in a block of wood, such as a short length of two-by-four, in which the blade can rest without rocking is a good solution (see FIG. 331). The drawknife can then be firmly clamped to the block, and the block can in turn be held securely in the bench vise or clamped firmly to a sawhorse or even a shelf.

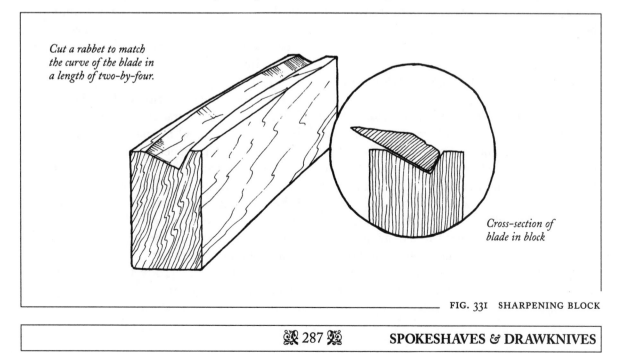

Cut a rabbet to match the curve of the blade in a length of two-by-four.

Cross-section of blade in block

FIG. 331 SHARPENING BLOCK

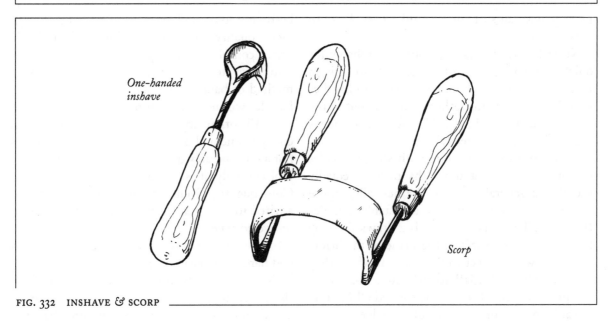

One-handed inshave

Scorp

FIG. 332   INSHAVE & SCORP

CLOSE RELATIVES

OF ALL THE ODD SHAPES AND VARIETIES that exist, the inshave and the scorp (FIG. 332) deserve especial consideration by today's custom woodworker. Both tools were originally part of the cooper's toolkit, and were used for specialized operations such as shaping the interior of barrels, but both remain equally valuable to the furniture-maker whenever there is any concave shaping to be done, such as hollowing out chair seats.

SPOKESHAVES WOODEN & METALLIC

STRICTLY SPEAKING, ONLY THOSE TOOLS intended for the shaping of wooden spokes such as those used in wooden waggon wheels and the like ought to be referred to as spokeshaves. All other tools characterized by having a transverse blade mounted in any kind of metallic or wooden stock and provided with handles at each end should properly be referred to simply as shaves. But since the term 'spokeshaves' could also legitimately include the drawknives or drawshaves discussed above, it is more convenient to refer to all small tools of the enclosed-edge type as spokeshaves, whether they are used to shave spokes or not, distinguishing between them as the need arises.

In the 19th century, before the introduction of the kind of metallic spokeshave now regarded as the norm, it was possible to divide all spokeshave-like tools into two main groups: those with blades formed like miniature drawknives, the tangs of which held the blade in the handled wooden stock, and those with blades like miniature plane irons, which were held in the handled wooden stock with a wedge in the same manner as real plane irons are held in wooden planes (see FIG. 333).

The former type, usually made of boxwood or beech, was long the standard and is still common in antique shops and fleamarkets. But despite its long reign as the standard tool, and despite the fact that in many ways it remains a quintessential old tool, perfectly embodying the antique look, it is hard to recommend. Its wooden stock presents such a small area to the work that it is quickly worn, as evidenced by the large number of tools found with brass wear plates fitted to this area and the fact that better-quality tools were provided with such a plate right from the start. Moreover, the iron is difficult to adjust.

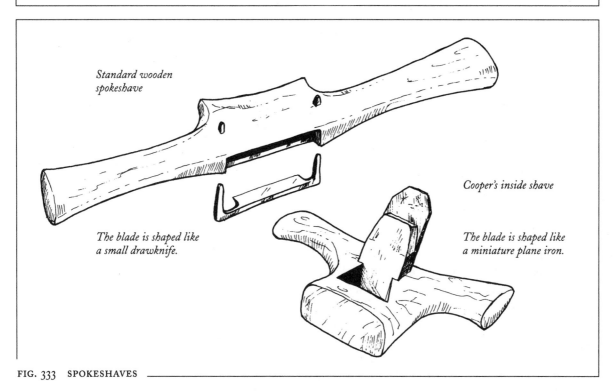

Standard wooden spokeshave

The blade is shaped like a small drawknife.

Cooper's inside shave

The blade is shaped like a miniature plane iron.

FIG. 333 SPOKESHAVES

These two facts can result in a jumping, chattering tool that takes either too small or too large a cut. Furthermore, the design of the blade leaves little margin for repeated sharpenings, quite apart from the fact that sharpening at all is very difficult to accomplish unless one makes some kind of miniature holding jig similar to that described for use with the drawknife above, and the edge is soon worn away past the point at which the ends of the blade are formed into the holding tangs. It is true that better models were made with screws on the blade's tangs designed to facilitate the depth adjustment of the blade, but the introduction of the metal type is to be welcomed as a rare instance of a modernized tool design that is not only more profitable to make (for the manufacturer) but also easier to use.

Metal-bodied spokeshaves may break when dropped on hard floors, but this is a small price to pay for the fact that their mouths do not become larger with use and the ease with which the iron may be adjusted. Early types had their iron held in place by a single screw threaded through a plane-type capiron, but later types almost all include two additional screws for adjusting the alignment as well as the depth of the iron.

Sharpening the small iron is done just like sharpening any plane iron, but this is made far easier if a wooden holder is made as shown in FIG. 334. Keeping a very sharp iron and a small

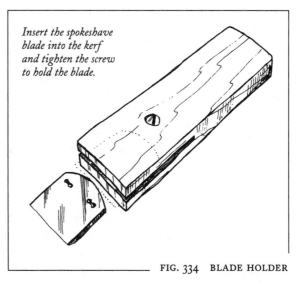

Insert the spokeshave blade into the kerf and tighten the screw to hold the blade.

FIG. 334 BLADE HOLDER

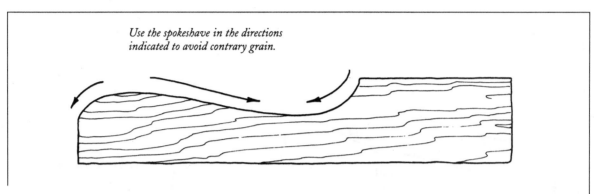

Use the spokeshave in the directions indicated to avoid contrary grain.

FIG. 335   FOLLOWING THE GRAIN

mouth are the two biggest secrets to successful use of this tool. The very nature of the work that this tool is intended to do causes you constantly to run into contrary grain (see FIG. 335). The usual injunction is to reverse the direction you are working in, but this is all too often easier said than done. It is better to adjust the tool so that a thinner cut is made with an extremely sharp blade. If the nature of the work permits, using the tool at a skewed angle will help considerably, but this may not be possible when using spokeshaves made with specially shaped soles unless cutting a flat section.

Apart from tools with hollowed or rounded soles designed for rounded and hollowed work such as forming rungs and curved chair parts (see FIG. 336), there is another variety made with a sole rounded from front to back. Sometimes referred to as a circular shave (FIG. 337), this is useful for work with a very tight radius, but is otherwise not as handy as a flat-soled tool, since it is difficult to keep a round-soled tool's blade in constant and even contact with the surface of the work.

A variety that first appeared a little over one hundred years ago and that has been recently reintroduced is the adjustable chamfer spokeshave (FIG. 338). This tool is frequently more convenient to use than most electric routers fitted with a chamfer bit, since it can be easily adjusted for any width chamfer up to 1½ in., and is perfectly quiet and safe into the bargain. The idea doubtless developed from the attachments used with

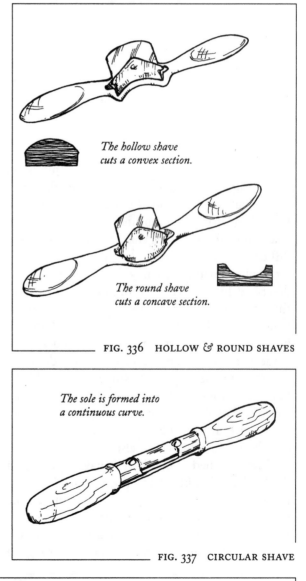

The hollow shave cuts a convex section.

The round shave cuts a concave section.

FIG. 336   HOLLOW & ROUND SHAVES

The sole is formed into a continuous curve.

FIG. 337   CIRCULAR SHAVE

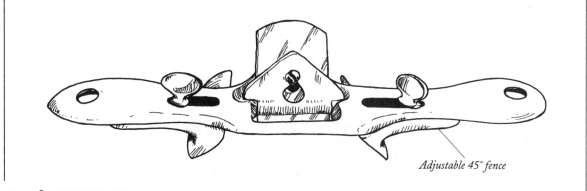

FIG. 338   CHAMFER SPOKESHAVE

Adjustable 45° fence

When either handle is removed from its side and used as shown the shave can be used in a corner, like a rabbet plane.

The optional fence may be used with a flat sole or a round sole (as shown).

FIG. 339   UNIVERSAL SPOKESHAVE

drawknives designed to limit the width of their cutting edge. By shaping these drawknife attachments to form small 45° fences it is possible to produce a kind of giant chamfer spokeshave.

One last variety that deserves mention, although it is no longer made and can command a high price when found because of the interest of certain collectors in all things Stanley™, is a tool known as the universal shave (FIG. 339). It is unique in the world of metallic spokeshaves because it has wooden handles, which may be removed, singly or together as desired, enabling the tool to be used as a kind of rabbet spokeshave. For even greater convenience, one handle can be reattached at 90° to the stock, thereby providing greater control in tight corners. Moreover, as originally sold it was provided with two interchangeable soles, round and flat, together with an adjustable mini-fence. If you should find one of these tools, especially with its optional attachments, it is something to be treasured.

34

PRE-ELECTRIC ROUTERS

THE OLD WOMAN'S TOOTH & ALL HER CHILDREN

S O PREDOMINANT IS TODAY'S ELECTRIC ROUTER THAT IT NORMALLY DOES NOT NEED TO BE QUALIFIED BY ANY ADJECTIVE SUCH AS 'ELECTRIC' TO BE DISTINGUISHED FROM ITS HANDTOOL ANCESTOR. IN FACT, IT IS THE OTHER WAY AROUND: THE TOOL THAT used to be known simply as 'router' now has to be described more exactly in order to avoid confusion with its present-day offspring. Fortunately, little confusion is likely, since most pre-electric routers are relatively rare and very few contemporary woodworkers have even heard of them. In any case, they bear little apparent relationship to the practically universal powertool of today. Before the powertool appeared, however, the name 'router' referred to a large and much used class of tool. Many of these were specifically named to distinguish them one from the other, but as a class we may now more conveniently refer to them as 'hand routers' or 'pre-electric routers' unless using their original specific name.

WHAT ROUTERS DO

THE WORD 'ROUT' AS USED IN CONNECTION with woodworking is thought to derive from the 'rooting about' that pigs do when they burrow into the surface of the ground with their snouts, looking for food. Hand routers did something similar when they were used to form trenches and slots in the surface of wood. Electric routers do much the same thing when they are used to cut dados, grooves, and various slots; but modern routers also perform operations previously achieved by a variety of other handtools such as spokeshaves, drawknives, moulding planes, and various special-purpose planes. Interestingly, it is the more recent form of electric router, the plunge router, that comes closest to duplicating what the original hand routers were designed to do.

Although for many common operations such as straightforward rabbeting, dadoing, slotting, and edge-moulding a modern router is indisputably faster and more efficient, hand routers can often do things impossible or difficult for an electric router. Since they are not impossible to find or even make, becoming familiar with the older types of routers can increase your vocabulary of woodworking techniques and provide you with opportunities for details you might not otherwise have considered.

Before they were superseded by their powered descendant, hand routers had developed into two main classes best described as router-planes and the spokeshave class of routers .

ROUTER PLANES

THE ROUTER PLANE, STILL MANUFACTURED today by at least two companies, Stanley™ and Record™, has been in production in various forms for more than a hundred years. It is the modern descendant of a much older tool that is thought to be the original router, known as an 'old woman's tooth' (FIG. 340). This is the tool that does what a plunge router does: it forms a flat-bottomed depression in the surface of a piece of wood. There are numerous calls for this operation in woodworking, one of the commonest being to form mortises and housings. It is fairly easy to excavate a mortise by hand using a mallet and chisel, but the difficult part is making the bottom of the mortise equally deep and flat. If you need to make longer depressions, such as the housings formed in staircase stringers to receive the treads, it is very important that the bottoms be perfectly level. A plunge router achieves this by penetrating the wood from the surface, rather than having to enter from the side, and then being moved along

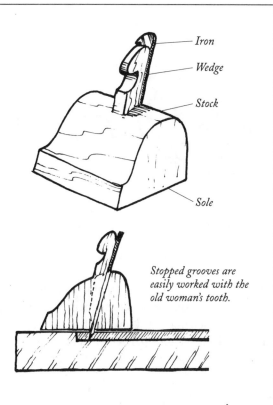

Iron
Wedge
Stock
Sole

Stopped grooves are easily worked with the old woman's tooth.

FIG. 340   OLD WOMAN'S TOOTH

at a consistent depth, so ensuring a perfectly even bottom. The old woman's tooth and the router plane, by virtue of their broad bases which span the depression being worked, similarly guarantee that they cut at a constant depth and produce a flat-bottomed depression.

The old woman's tooth may be fairly said to be the grandmother of all routers. It is no more than an iron fixed almost vertically in a block of wood. This description could also be given to wooden planes, since both tools were developed from the need to control more exactly the depth of cut of a cutting edge — broad in the case of a plane iron or narrower as in the case of a chisel. Old women's teeth were also manufactured professionally, but by far the greatest number were user-made, employing old files or broken chisels as the irons.

Unlike many other venerable tools with a long history of use, they are not particularly easy to use. The depth of cut is adjusted only by laboriously

PRE-ELECTRIC ROUTERS

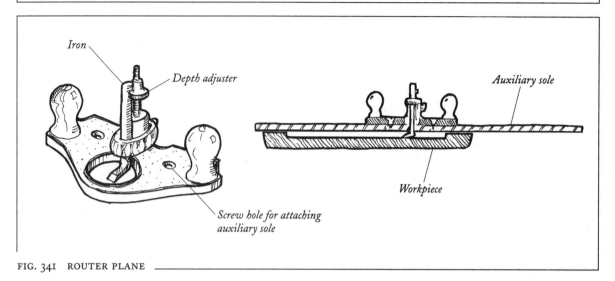

Iron

Depth adjuster

Auxiliary sole

Workpiece

Screw hole for attaching auxiliary sole

FIG. 341   ROUTER PLANE

resetting the iron and wedge, and little visibility is possible as you work, consequently requiring very careful setting out. Nevertheless, having one handy and preset to a particular depth can often be quicker than setting up a plunge router.

Their immediate successors, the numerous metallic versions introduced in the 19th century, were a vast improvement and can do things a plunge router cannot. The Stanley™ model known as a router plane (FIG. 341) has a cutting iron that can be easily adjusted up and down by means of a vernier wheel, and some models have graduated cutters and a removable depth stop. The area being cut always remains visible through a hole in the tool's sole, and some models are open-throated at the front. Furthermore, when working stopped depressions the cutter can be reversed to face in the opposite direction so that you can work the tool into a corner inaccessible by a plunge router. For working particularly wide depressions it is sometimes possible to attach a wider wooden sole to the base, thereby increasing its span. As with powertools, fences are available to guarantee straight-sided cuts or to follow curved work. But perhaps the greatest advantage of a router plane lies in its use of differently shaped cutting irons. Some are square, some are skewed, and some are V-shaped. This makes it possible to rout out depressions of variously shaped circumferences, particularly square and acute-cornered depressions. And if, for whatever reason, you wanted to duplicate the round-ended depressions made by a plunge router's circular bit, it would be eminently possible to grind a cutter to the required shape.

Most router planes are about 7½ in. wide, but smaller, 3 in.-wide models (FIG. 342) may be very useful for narrow work such as stringing and inlay, and are especially popular with musical-instrument makers. The irons of these smaller models can also be custom-ground and reversed to accommodate both through and stopped work.

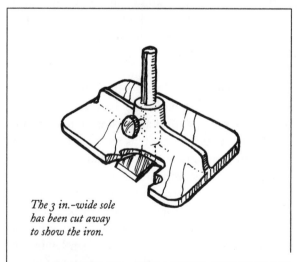

The 3 in.-wide sole has been cut away to show the iron.

FIG. 342   **SMALL METAL ROUTER PLANE**

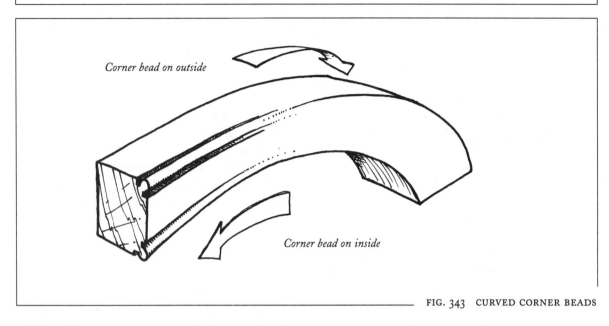

Corner bead on outside

Corner bead on inside

FIG. 343   CURVED CORNER BEADS

THE SPOKESHAVE CLASS OF ROUTERS

THE SECOND MAJOR TYPE OF PRE-ELECTRIC router bears a striking resemblance to a tool that is still in common use: the spokeshave. Sometimes called 'routering tools', and described as being used to 'router' various shapes, many varieties of these tools were developed for many different woodworking trades, including cabinetmaking, pianomaking, carriagemaking, and joinery. One manufacturer working around the turn of the 19th century, Edward Preston and Sons, listed lining or stringing routers, circular quirk routers, improved grooving routers, adjustable grooving routers, circular sash routers, circular rabbeting and fillister routers, common oveloe [sic] routers, equal or square oveloe routers, and bead routers.

Like the spokeshave, these are transverse tools made with a handle at both ends. They rout out trenches, dados, and other forms of slots and grooves, but they also cut reeds, and various moulding profiles in and near the edge of work, especially curved work. Since the nature of curved work is such that at different points on the work-piece you are likely to run into opposing grain, many of these routers are either made in left-hand and right-hand pairs or fitted with double irons that mirror each other and enable the tool to be used in either direction.

Being able to approach the work from either end gives these tools a distinct advantage over an electric router, whose bit always revolves in the same direction and whose use can be difficult and dangerous if you attempt to feed the work in the 'wrong' direction. Furthermore, this form of hand router is designed to follow any curve and can be used on shaped workpieces difficult to rout or feed through a shaper.

CUTTING A DOUBLE-AXIS MOULDING

IMAGINE, FOR EXAMPLE, YOU WISH TO FORM a corner bead on a curved section of woodwork. A corner bead is a bead with a quirk, or small groove, on both sides, commonly used to round and protect otherwise vulnerable sharp edges. If you set up an electric router to cut the quirk on the flat face, you will have to readjust its fence and change the bit when you come to cut the quirk on the second, curved face. The difficulty is compounded should you want to cut the quirk on an inside curve instead of an outside curve (see FIG. 343). With a circular beading tool, however,

PRE-ELECTRIC ROUTERS

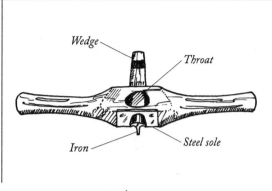

FIG. 344   COACHMAKER'S HAND BEADER

there is no setting up to be done at all; the tool will work any two adjacent faces regardless of the direction or axis of the curves. Furthermore, since the iron is two-sided, the tool can be worked in either direction, making it in effect both a left-handed and a right-handed tool (see FIG. 344). Hand beaders and other forms of moulding routers (FIG. 345) were often user-made,

and as such can be made in any size, to fit the work in hand.

Side or corner beads, incidentally, are but two of the more functional mouldings that can be incorporated into your work. They are not merely ornamental, creating extra lines of shadow to define the contours of a piece of work, but also very practical, since they constitute a good way to save otherwise square and vulnerable corners from unsightly wear. Practically all older door and window trim was treated this way for this very purpose. Wooden beading planes (see chapter 27) are all very well for straight edges, but when working beading in and on arches, curved door or window frames, round wooden lids, shaped chair backs, or indeed anything that is not straight, the hand beader is indispensable. Although it excels in creating corner beads, it can, of course, also be used to cut simple side beads.

THE QUIRK ROUTER

A CLOSELY RELATED HAND ROUTER, AND one that is just a little more sophisticated, is the quirk router (FIG. 346). A quirk, as mentioned before, is a narrow groove usually associated with a moulding, such as a quirked ogee (FIG. 347), but as far as this tool is concerned it simply means any narrow groove. The narrowness is also open to interpretation, for it may be varied from very narrow to quite wide. Once again, this router is for working quirks or grooves in surfaces curved in any direction (see FIG. 348). Although many quirk routers were hand-made, examples were also manufactured by famous companies such as Marples™, Mathieson™, and Preston™, and most manufacturers offered different models varying in sophistication as well as size.

Most quirk routers have adjustable fences, and the better ones have differently shaped fences to enable them to work concave and convex surfaces. The fences are, of course, adjustable, so that the groove may be worked at varying distances from the edge, and, moreover, they may be fixed on

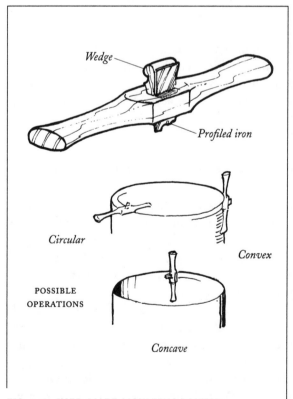

POSSIBLE OPERATIONS

Circular

Convex

Concave

FIG. 345   USER-MADE MOULDING ROUTER

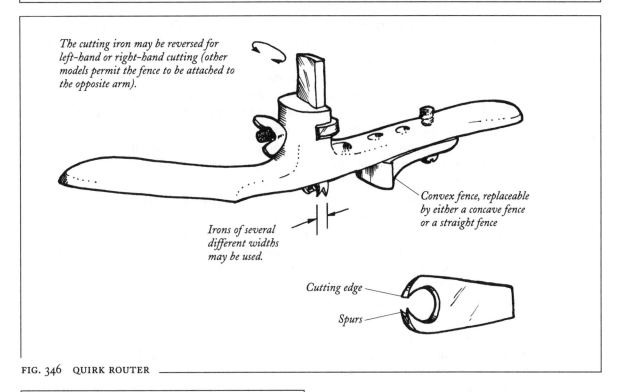

The cutting iron may be reversed for left-hand or right-hand cutting (other models permit the fence to be attached to the opposite arm).

Convex fence, replaceable by either a concave fence or a straight fence

Irons of several different widths may be used.

Cutting edge

Spurs

FIG. 346   QUIRK ROUTER

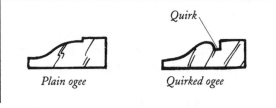

Quirk

Plain ogee   *Quirked ogee*

FIG. 347   OGEE MOULDINGS

either side of the iron, making this tool right- and left-handed too, like the hand beader.

Since the iron may be raised or lowered any amount, from less than flush to a depth of up to almost 1 in., and since, in addition, other irons of different widths may be substituted, the range of sizes and dimensions of grooves that may be

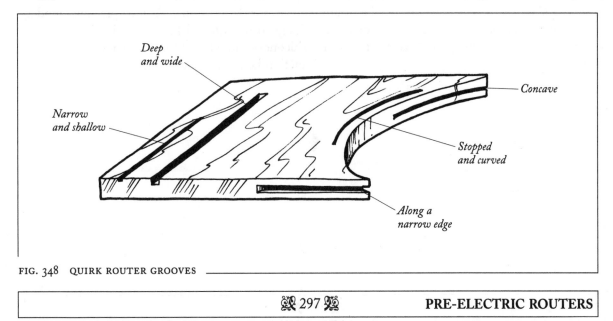

Deep and wide

Narrow and shallow

Concave

Stopped and curved

Along a narrow edge

FIG. 348   QUIRK ROUTER GROOVES

worked is very great. It will be readily understood that a groove of intermediate size may be worked by the simple expedient of cutting one groove and then resetting the fence to cut a partly overlapping or adjacent groove. It is worth noting that when doing this it is usually easiest to cut the groove farthest from the edge first, and then the groove, or part of the groove, nearest the edge.

The cutting irons of these tools are unusual and warrant some explanation. The business end is formed into a semi-circle, from which a section in the middle extending to the bottom edge has been removed. The forward tip thus left is filed in the center of its thickness so as to form two spurs, whose function is to sever the fibers of the wood being cut just ahead of the rear tip, which is sharpened straight across like a tiny chisel. This chisel-like edge then cuts and lifts out the wood that has been scored by the spur-like tip. The neatness of this design lies in the fact that since spurs and cutting edge are made from the same piece of metal, there is never any difficulty in aligning the spurs to the exact width of the cut as there sometimes is with tools having separate scoring devices. It follows, therefore, that great care should be exercised when sharpening these irons not to sharpen the spurs on the outside. Use a knife-edge slip stone only in the center of the spurs. From time to time it may be necessary to hone the sides of the cutting iron, but be aware that as when sharpening electric-router bits this will alter the width of the groove that the tool will then cut.

The practical uses of this tool are many, and range from routing small grooves needed for inlay to larger joinery operations such as routing grooves in curved framing members to receive curved paneling. The main advantage that this tool has over an electric router is that it makes no difference whether the work is straight or curved; you can go anywhere in any direction.

THE CIRCULAR PLOUGH

THERE IS AN ESPECIALLY INTERESTING TOOL that deserves notice at this point on account of its rarity and consequent high value. Most of the tools discussed in this book, while old, are not too hard to find and are certainly not expensive, even when compared to contemporary tools. The startling exception is the hand router referred to as a circular plough. It looks like a small wooden plough plane (see chapter 21) but its fence, which is usually metal, is flexible, and can be adjusted to match curves of different diameters, both convex and concave. Since it is much rarer than any of the other hand routers, owning it has become the privilege almost exclusively of museums and rich collectors. Beautiful French examples from the 18th century with finely made pistol-grips show up at auctions from time to time, to be knocked down for large sums. A less precious model, designed in 1846 and known for its designer as a Falconer's plough, sold at Christies, the London auction house, in 1981 for $2,035.

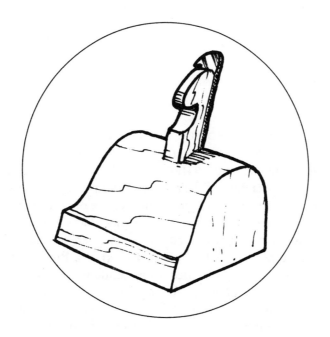

35

CHAMFERING DEVICES

'CANTUS FRANGERE'

WHEN A CHAMFER IS CALLED FOR THERE ARE TYPICALLY ONLY THREE TOOLS TO CHOOSE FROM IN MOST OF TODAY'S SHOPS: AN ELECTRIC ROUTER, A HAND PLANE, AND A DRAWKNIFE. THERE WAS A TIME, HOWEVER, WHEN CHAMFERS could be made with an ease and exactness difficult to achieve with the handtools mentioned above by using any one of numerous specially designed tools, each guaranteed to produce nicely executed chamfers for a variety of circumstances. Many of these tools are still to be found and might be used yet if their function were properly understood. But before describing the tools it will help to understand precisely what a chamfer is.

Although the word 'chamfer', which entered English via the Old French: *chan fraindre*, derives from the Latin expression: *cantus frangere*, which means literally 'to break an edge', its present meaning is much more precise than any random broken edge. 'To chamfer' means to bevel a corner

or edge equally on both sides of the original arris. In the case of an edge formed by the intersection of two surfaces at 90° to one another this results in a chamfered surface that is at exactly 45° to both surfaces. But — and it is important to bear this subtlety in mind — a chamfer formed at the arris of two surfaces meeting at any angle other than 90°, although extending equally into each surface, will no longer be at 45° to them, but rather will form an angle greater or smaller according to the angle of intersection of the two surfaces themselves (see FIG. 349).

This explanation should clear up two common misconceptions regarding chamfers: first, that they are merely any beveled arris which may or

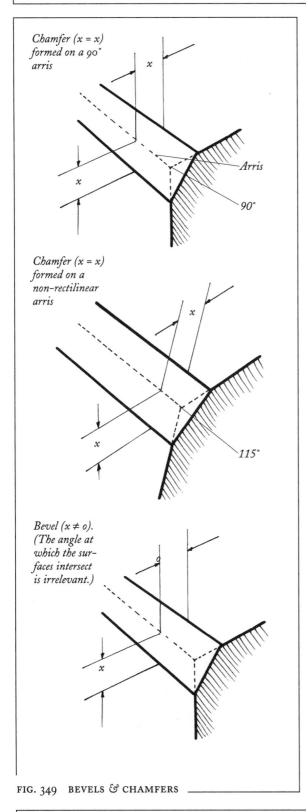

Chamfer (x = x) formed on a 90° arris

Arris

90°

Chamfer (x = x) formed on a non-rectilinear arris

115°

Bevel (x ≠ o). (The angle at which the surfaces intersect is irrelevant.)

FIG. 349 BEVELS & CHAMFERS

may not extend equally into each surface; and second, that they are simply and always a bevel of 45°. 'Bevel' is the term for any sloping edge. While a chamfer may also be described as a form of bevel, a beveled edge is not necessarily a chamfer unless it extends equally on both sides, whether in so doing it meets these faces at 45° or not.

The various tools and devices developed to form a chamfer on a given arris therefore have this in common: that they produce an equally disposed bevel. More than this is not always true. For inſtance, it cannot be taken for granted that any given chamfering tool is also convenient way of creating a bevel of 45°.

The underſtanding that chamfering is an ornamental and often practical design element used for many materials, such as ſtone and metal, should make it less than surprising that the use of chamfers is also common to very many branches of woodworking, all of which have developed their own means of creating them.

CHAMFER PLANES

THE LARGEST GROUP OF CHAMFERING TOOLS is that composed of the various chamfer planes used by joiners and cabinetmakers. Included in this group are some of the more sophiſticated devices ever devised for making chamfers, and indeed one particular model, the metal version once made by the Stanley Tool Company, has the diſtinction of being one of the moſt complicated and expensive planes in the entire woodworking world, commonly selling at auction for more than a thousand dollars, although when firſt put on sale a hundred years ago it coſt only three dollars, even when offered with extra beading and moulding attachments.

STOP CHAMFER PLANES

LONG BEFORE JUSTUS TRAUT PATENTED THE improvements which gave birth to the Stanley™

FIG. 350   STOP CHAMFERS

Plain ends

Moulded end

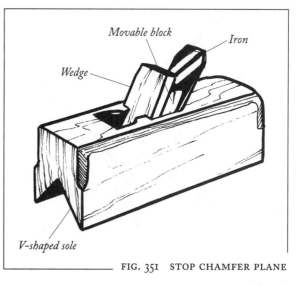

FIG. 351   STOP CHAMFER PLANE

Movable block

Iron

Wedge

V-shaped sole

metal chamfer plane, wooden chamfer planes were being made in several varieties. Of these, the commonest is known as the stop chamfer plane. To prevent confusion it should be noted that a stop chamfer (FIG. 350) is one which finishes before the end of the arris on which it is formed, rather than running off the end. The 'stop' is the end of the chamfer, and may be plain or moulded. Ironically, a stop chamfer plane cannot form one of these chamfers, since the front of the plane is always in the way. Even if the central part of the chamfer is made with the plane, the stopped ends must be finished with another tool, such as a drawknife. The use of the word 'stop' in conjunction with the plane refers to the depth stop which regulates the size of the chamfer to be formed, and has nothing to do with the kind of chamfer known as a stop chamfer.

Most stop chamfer planes are about 9 in. long, 3 in. wide, and about 2 in. deep (see FIG. 351). The sole of the stock is cut out in the form of an inverted right-angled 'V', one side of which is held tightly against the work as the plane is used. When the other side of the 'V' touches the work the chamfer is complete. Since their cutting irons are fixed at 45° to either side of the sole, stop chamfer planes can only cut chamfers on right-angled corners, but the width of the chamfer may vary considerably, as this is determined by how deeply the integral stop is set.

The simplest type is fitted with a movable block located between the cutting iron and the wedge. The bottom of this block is cut to conform with the plane's sole, and so acts as a simple and direct depth stop.

Somewhat more sophisticated is the boxed stop chamfer plane (FIG. 352). The throat of this plane is enlarged and fitted with an adjustable box called the sole box, the bottom of which forms a flat sole that rests on the produced chamfer. The amount by which the box protrudes into the V-shaped sole of the plane determines how wide the chamfer will be, for the iron is positioned closely behind the box, the plane's mouth being formed at this

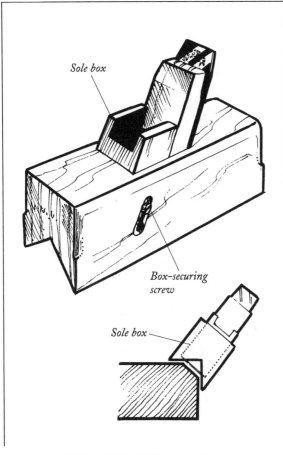

Sole box

Box-securing screw

Sole box

FIG. 352 BOXED STOP CHAMFER PLANE

conjunction of box and iron. It can be difficult to secure the wedge and simultaneously maintain the desired relationship between box and stock but the effort is worth while since the box provides an extra surface together with one side of the V-shaped sole with which to bear on the work. Better grades of boxed stop chamfer planes include a screw, located in the side of the sole box, which passes through and is tightened against a brass-covered slot in the side of the stock, thereby making the securing of the sole box much easier and more positive.

The metal chamfer plane made by Stanley™ is a development of the movable box idea. The difference is that the box does not move within the stock, but rather slides up and down in front of the stock, to which it is of course attached, the iron being secured directly to the box. Not only is adjustment made easier but in addition the front section may be lowered until it is level with the bottom of the rear V-shaped section, thereby enabling the tool to be used as a regular bench plane. The front section may even be exchanged for an alternative section designed to hold various beading and moulding attachments. This last feature is very useful when making beaded or moulded chamfers, since it guarantees that the moulding will be formed directly in the same plane as the chamfer. But care must be exercised in keeping the moulding centered because as the moulding is worked more deeply the side of the sole tends to push the iron over to one side.

Mention should also be made of the various metal combination planes that were developed towards the end of the 19th century, many of which, including some modern descendants, remain popular to a limited extent even today. Among their numerous capabilities is often included chamfering, which may be effected somewhat differently from model to model; it is easiest with the Stanley™ 45 or the Record™ 045, since these are equipped with two fences that can be tilted to the required angle, transforming the plane into a close replica of the wooden stop chamfer plane, but with the added advantage of being able to form a chamfer on the arris formed by two surfaces intersecting at virtually any angle, rather than only one of 90°.

FENCED CHAMFER PLANE

THE FENCED CHAMFER PLANE IS PROVIDED with a movable fence to regulate the width of the chamfer. This removes the irksome necessity of resetting the iron every time a new measurement is needed (see FIG. 353). The fence itself forms the second side of the V-shaped sole, and by being moved in or out reduces or expands the amount of iron that is exposed, so controlling the width of the chamfer. An additional advantage of this type of plane is that since it is so easy to adjust the

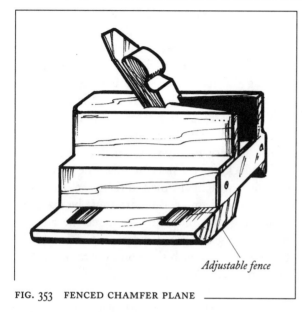

Adjustable fence

FIG. 353   FENCED CHAMFER PLANE

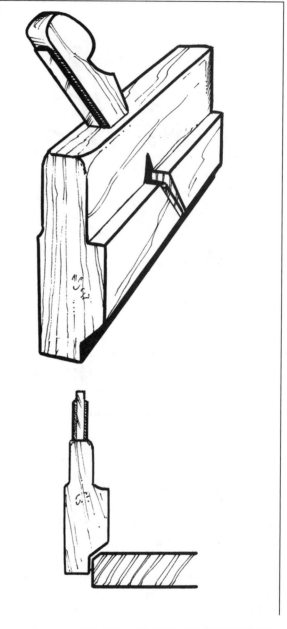

FIG. 354   CHAMFER MOULDING PLANE

fence, the chamfer can be started with guidance on both sides, making the job of keeping the chamfer at the correct angle relative to the sides of the work that much easier.

Incidentally, this is the system used by the Japanese chamfer plane, which is, however, an extremely uncomfortable tool for those workers accustomed to handled and larger Western tools. Since the recent introduction of many Japanese woodworking tools this readily available little tool has become quite popular, but although it is often supplied with a very good quality iron many woodworkers may find it is too small and too uncompromisingly awkward to hold because of the protuberant wingnuts.

CHAMFER MOULDING PLANES

THERE IS A THIRD GROUP OF PLANES, NOT all of which are strictly chamfer planes, but which by custom are referred to as such. To all intents and purposes these may be classified as moulding planes since they are made in the classic moulding plane shape. Of these the simplest has a straight-sided stock with a 45° sole. It is, in truth, a canted rabbet plane, and in fact one manufacturer, the Greenfield Tool Company, of Massachusetts, produced several of these planes with variously sloped soles and called them 'Special Rebate Planes'. With the addition of a fence either tacked to the work or fixed directly to the side of the plane, however, this qualifies as a chamfer plane since it will form a perfect chamfer (see FIG. 354).

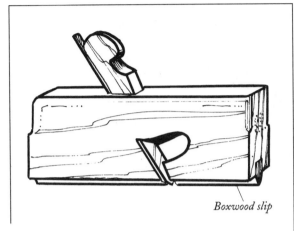

FIG. 355   DOUBLE CHAMFER MOULDING PLANE

Boxwood slip

Another variety of moulding plane also called a chamfer plane is the so-called double chamfer plane (FIG. 355), whose V-shaped iron projects from the middle of a stock fitted with a matching V-shaped slip of boxwood. While it is possible to use this as a reversible one-sided chamfer plane it is probably easier to use it as a V-grooving plane. One of the manufacturers of this kind of plane, Alexander Mathieson and Sons, of Glasgow, Scotland, also sold a metal-fronted wooden bull-nose plane which it called a 'Champhering Smooth Plane', illustrating thereby the high degree of adaptability possible in an age supplied with a super-abundance of handtools.

SHAVES & DRAWKNIVES

THE SECOND LARGEST GROUP OF TOOLS designed to make chamfered edges comprises a variety of ingenious shaves and drawknives. Doubtless the drawknife was the original method of producing chamfers, and is still used for this purpose where great exactness is not required, such as when roughly chamfering the edges of posts and beams in heavy construction and garden furniture. Despite this crude use it should be pointed out that in the past certain tradesmen whose work entailed much use of this tool were often possessed of a great deal of skill in using this

apparently guideless and free-form tool (see chapter 33). Bodgers (chairmakers) and coopers (barrelmakers) performed many operations to an astonishing degree of nicety with very simple tools, the simplicity of which often belies the centuries of development that gradually fitted such tools so well for their work.

In practice, if a chamfer is marked out exactly, a carefully wielded drawknife can produce a well executed chamfer. This is often, as mentioned earlier, the only way to make most stop chamfers. The various forms of elegant stop chamfers found on much furniture of the Middle Ages are evidence of the sophistication possible with this tool.

For the nervous or unsteady of hand there are, however, attachments which may be secured to the blade of a drawknife to form angled fences, which being adjusted as required will enable the tool to produce chamfers of a predetermined size. The one big advantage that a drawknife has over a chamfer plane is that it can produce chamfers on arrises formed by surfaces that meet at angles other than 90°.

The action of a spokeshave is similar to that of a drawknife except for the effect of the spokeshave's sole and mouth. These give rather more control to the tool and this also makes it more convenient for smaller work. Just as attachments may be used with a drawknife in order to provide fences for chamfering, so some spokeshaves were made with adjustable guides which made possible the working of perfect chamfers up to 1½ in. wide (see FIG. 356).

TOOLS FOR CURVED WORK

SPOKESHAVES MAY BE USED TO FORM chamfers on small sections of straight work, but if any length is involved it is more convenient to use a plane. Planes are all very well for general woodworking and most cabinetmaking, but certain trades such as coachbuilding and carriagemaking commonly dealt with complex, multi-directional curves and consequently required more versatile

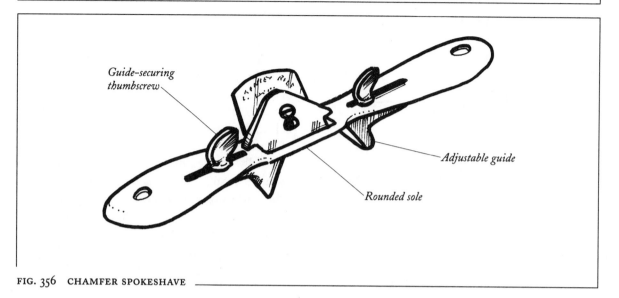

Guide-securing thumbscrew

Adjustable guide

Rounded sole

FIG. 356   CHAMFER SPOKESHAVE

tools. Where the spokeshave excels is in the area of curved work. A spokeshave fitted with adjustable chamfering guides, as well as a sole that is convex, can follow concave sections almost as easily as convex or straight sections. Such a tool is especially valuable when you are engaged in non-rectilinear contemporary furnituremaking.

CORNER ROUTER

THE CORNER ROUTER CONSISTS OF A TWO handled square wooden stock, in the bottom of which a V-shaped notch is cut (see FIG. 357). Into this notch protrudes a square iron for working chamfers or other shaped irons for working other profiles. The deeper the iron is set the wider is the chamfer that is formed, primarily by a scraping action. Although called a router, this tool is actually more closely related to a scratch stock (FIG. 358) — typically a user-made tool consisting of a blade filed to a desired profile and held in a wooden stock designed to be run along the edge of a workpiece, often curved, to form a moulding for which there is no specific moulding plane or other tool available. Since the corner router is hardly bigger than a spokeshave, it is ideal for curved work in any direction.

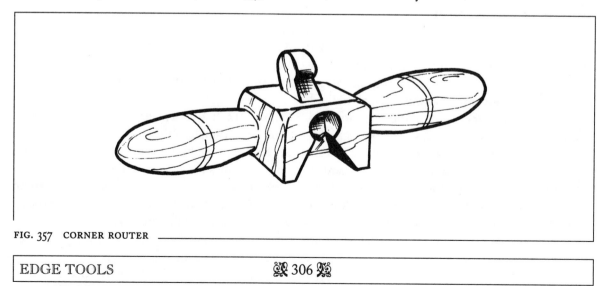

FIG. 357   CORNER ROUTER

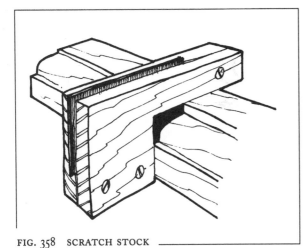

FIG. 358 SCRATCH STOCK

COOPER'S CHAMFERING TOOLS

TWO OTHER TOOLS ONCE COMMONLY used by coopers for chamfering various parts of barrels are the cooper's chamfering knife (FIG. 359), which operates on the principle of a beam compass, and the cooper's chamfering plane, which also has an adjustable pivot point, but instead of a canted drawknife-type edge is fitted with a small block containing a wedged iron. Both tools are ideal for creating chamfers on circular work. They operate on the same principle as a modern electric router that is mounted in a circle-cutting jig.

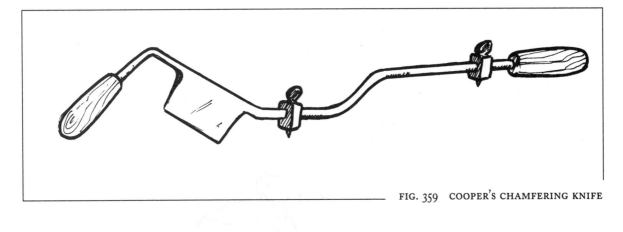

FIG. 359 COOPER'S CHAMFERING KNIFE

VI
BORING TOOLS

36

BORING TOOLS

BRADAWLS TO BEAM BORERS

WHEN WE THINK OF BORING, THE ELECTRIC DRILL COMES TO MIND. THIS TOOL HAS SEEN SOME INTERESTING IMPROVEMENTS IN RECENT YEARS, MOST NOTABLY THE INTRODUCTION OF CORDLESS VARIETIES. ALTHOUGH INFREQUENT OR irregular users may find the requisite recharging schedule inconvenient, it cannot be denied that liberation from the tool's previously essential umbilical cord is a very great advantage.

Contemporary technology has thus brought the form of the tool full circle; once again it is possible to bore or drill from high up on a ladder or in tightly cramped crawl-spaces without the constraining tangle of power cords. While it is true that the electric drill offers the benefits of increased power, it should not be forgotten that before its introduction holes were made wherever and however needed with a variety of handtools specially adapted for various tasks. Many of these tools can still be found, and familiarity with them

can prove very advantageous when a power drill, cordless or otherwise, is unavailable.

To avoid any confusion with terms that are sometimes synonymous and sometimes not, the following differences in usage — which are more conventional than strictly logical — should be noted: Both 'boring' and 'drilling' mean the same thing — to pierce or make a hole — but when metalworkers refer to a 'drill' it is the actual drill bit that is usually meant; when woodworkers say 'drill' they usually mean the tool that holds the drill bit. Woodworkers normally specify the bit more exactly than do metalworkers, referring, for example, to an auger bit or a drill bit, as the case may be. Thus, in this chapter, when the word

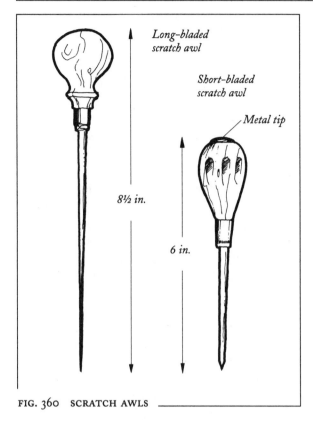

Long-bladed scratch awl

Short-bladed scratch awl

Metal tip

8½ in.

6 in.

FIG. 360   SCRATCH AWLS

'drill' is used it will usually be modified by a prefix to indicate a specific boring tool or modified by a suffix to indicate a specific form of bit. Used on its own it should be understood to refer to the entire tool rather than the bit held by the tool.

AWLS & GIMLETS

STARTING WITH THE SMALLEST MEMBERS OF the boring-tool family we immediately run into an area of common confusion concerning the difference between awls and gimlets. Both make small holes for starting screws or nails, or even for simply enabling other materials to be passed into or through the material being pierced. But the way in which they do so is different: an awl comes to a conical or chisel-shaped point; a gimlet is provided with a screw at its tip, like a miniature auger bit, described below. Gimlet, sometimes spelled 'gimblet', is actually the diminutive form

of the now obsolete word 'wimble', which meant practically the same as an auger; so think of a gimlet as an 'augerette' and you will not confuse gimlet with awl.

Almost every trade possessed its own variety of awls; there are belt awls, carpet awls, upholsterer's and cane-seater's awls, entering awls, garnish awls, stabbing awls, stiletto awls, straining awls, trimming awls, boatmaker's and sailmakers's awls, and shoemaker's pegging awls, amongst many others. However, so far as woodworkers are concerned, there are but two kinds of awls: bradawls (so common as to be spelled as one word) and scratch awls (FIG. 360).

Of these two, only the bradawl is a true boring or hole-making tool, since the scratch awl, as the name implies, is a marking tool used to scratch a mark in the wood. If its point is kept sharp it can be very useful for defining a very precise point or line, but if abused and allowed to become blunt it makes a mess, tearing the fibers of the wood across which it is dragged. For this reason a marking knife is commonly preferred, but the scratch awl has the advantage that when sharp it is less likely than is a knife blade to run into and follow the grain instead of the desired line. For fine delineation a long-bladed scratch awl is an elegant tool, whereas the commonly available shorter and stouter design is well suited for marking points and if necessary being struck with a hammer to make a deeper indentation, in the manner of a metalworker's center punch.

The bradawl (FIG. 361) is fitted with a steel blade from about 1 in. to 3 in. long finishing in a

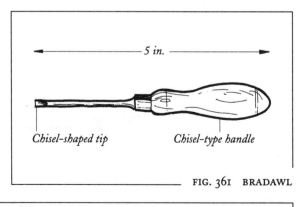

5 in.

Chisel-shaped tip   *Chisel-type handle*

FIG. 361   BRADAWL

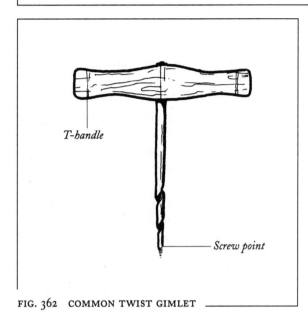

T-handle

Screw point

FIG. 362   COMMON TWIST GIMLET

small chisel-shaped point. Its handle is invariably straight and turned like a small chisel's handle, in distinction to a gimlet's handle, which is set at a right angle to the blade. Its use, which is not always properly understood, is as follows: The chisel-shaped point is pressed into the wood at a right-angle to the grain, and then the tool is twisted back and forth so that it works its way

into the wood by pushing the fibers apart. If started with the point parallel to the grain one has less control over the actual point of entry, and furthermore runs the risk of splitting the wood to an extent larger than the hole is desired to occupy. This tool must therefore, like the scratch awl, be kept sharp and not be allowed to bang about in the toolbox so that its little chisel point gets blunted.

The gimlet, which also exists in a surprising variety of types including those known as bell hanger's gimlet, boat gimlet, brewer's gimlet, farmer's gimlet, gutter gimlet, pod gimlet, shell gimlet, ship gimlet, skate gimlet, spike gimlet, spile gimlet, spout gimlet, sprig gimlet, twist gimlet, wheeler's gimlet, and wilk gimlet — some of which terms refer to designs and others to purposes and trades — is invariably furnished with a handle forming a 'T' with its metal shank. Its other salient characteristic is that whatever the further design of the shank, it always starts with a screw point (see FIG. 362). While this initially pulls the tool into the wood, pushing the fibers apart just as does the bradawl, once the tool is entered into the material it then cuts shavings and so enlarges the hole.

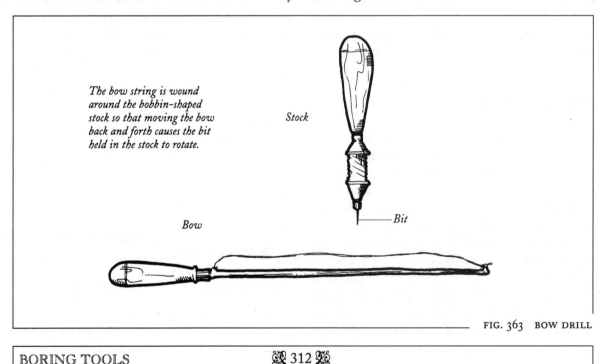

The bow string is wound around the bobbin-shaped stock so that moving the bow back and forth causes the bit held in the stock to rotate.

Stock

Bit

Bow

FIG. 363   BOW DRILL

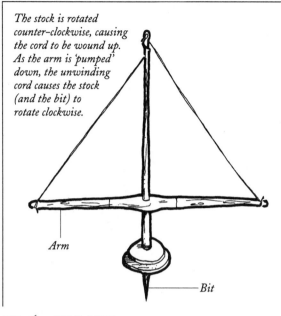

The stock is rotated counter-clockwise, causing the cord to be wound up. As the arm is 'pumped' down, the unwinding cord causes the stock (and the bit) to rotate clockwise.

Arm

Bit

FIG. 364   PUMP DRILL
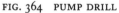

HAND DRILLS

TOGETHER WITH SIMPLE COPPER AWLS, drills have been known in various forms for a very long time, as shown by representations of clearly recognizable tools on ancient Egyptian buildings and artifacts starting around 2500 B.C. The variety common among the Egyptians, as well as among the Greeks and Romans, and which has remained essentially unchanged to this day in many parts of the world, is the bow drill.

The bow drill (FIG. 363) consists basically of a straight or bobbin-shaped stock that holds a drill

bit turned by means of a string or cord wound around it. It is supposed that the earliest version must have been developed from the string of a bow being wrapped around an arrow, hence the name. A more recent design known as a fiddle drill consists of a rod that is straighter rather than curved, similar to a violin bow, with a slacker cord attached to it.

Although primarily used for relatively small holes, larger bow or fiddle drills are used with pads or breast plates in the manner of a modern breast drill.

Despite its antiquity the bow or fiddle drill is the one type of drill that may now be considered truly obsolete so far as Western woodworking is concerned. Its close relative the pump drill, on the other hand, is alive and well in an albeit much modernized form known commonly by its new name of push drill. The original pump drill, like the bow drill, was worked by means of a cord wrapped around the stock (see FIG. 364). But unlike the bow, which was worked by being moved from side to side, the arm to which the pump drill's cord was attached was pushed up and down. Since the stock and its bit must be able to rotate in both directions, its use is confined to relatively hard materials such as very dense wood, china, or stone; used in softwoods the bit is liable to stick and be unable to rotate backwards.

The up-and-down motion of the pump drill's bow led directly to the invention of the Archimedean drill (FIG. 365). The name does not indicate an ancient Greek origin but simply a

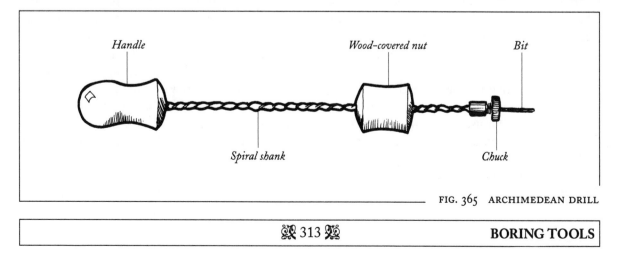

Handle

Wood-covered nut

Bit

Spiral shank

Chuck

FIG. 365   ARCHIMEDEAN DRILL

BORING TOOLS

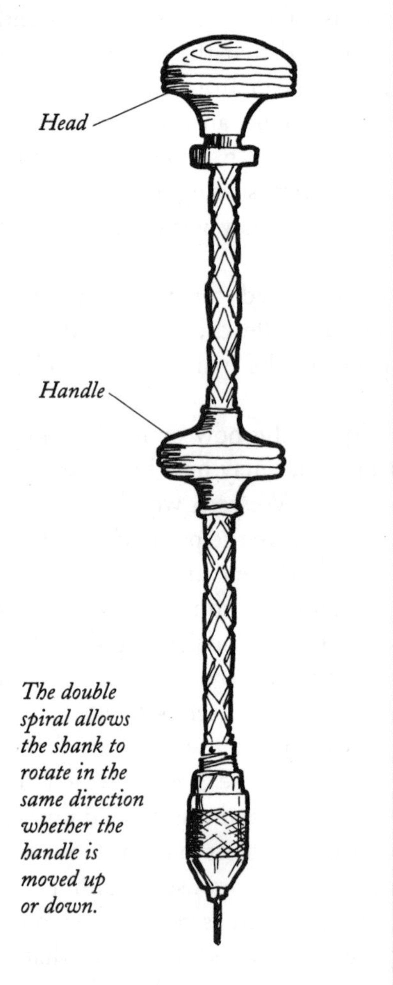

Head

Handle

The double
spiral allows
the shank to
rotate in the
same direction
whether the
handle is
moved up
or down.

FIG. 366   ARCHIMEDEAN DRILL

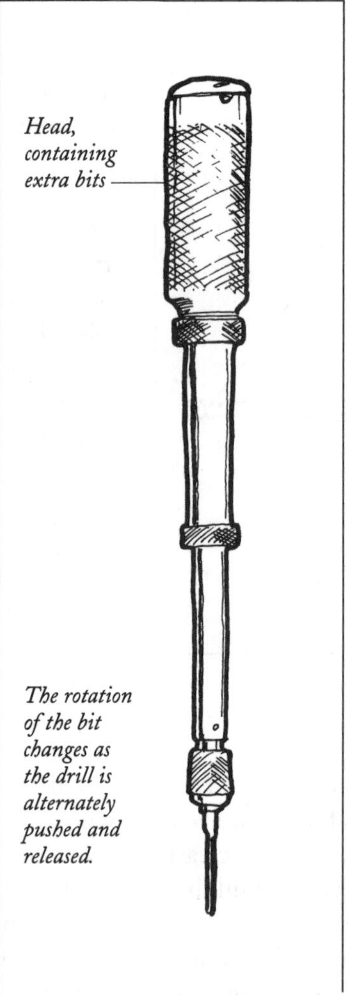

Head,
containing
extra bits

The rotation
of the bit
changes as
the drill is
alternately
pushed and
released.

FIG. 367   PUSH DRILL

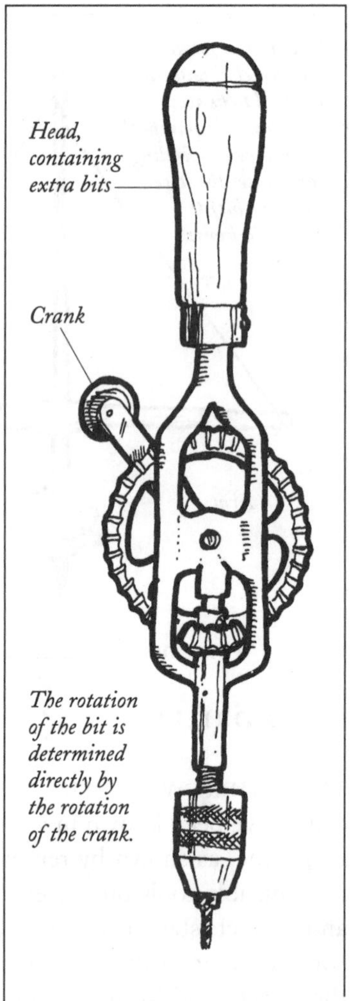

Head,
containing
extra bits

Crank

The rotation
of the bit is
determined
directly by
the rotation
of the crank.

FIG. 368   HAND DRILL

19th century awareness of the Archimedes screw water pump, which raises water by means of a rotating screw, commonly used in the Levant. The Archimedean drill consists of a spiral shank rotated by a usually wood-covered nut that is moved up and down the shank. Since the drill turns in both directions, the bits used are made also to cut in both directions. The chief advantage of this drill is that being small and slender it is admirably suited for use in confined spaces where the use of an auger, a brace, or even an electric drill would be difficult or impossible.

One improvement over the basic Archimedean drill was a type fitted with a ratchet in the handle allowing the drill bit to revolve in one direction only. From this type, with its obvious advantages over the bow drill, it was a small step to the double-spiral Archimedean drill (FIG. 366). The double spiral, together with a reversing device in the handle, enables a constant forward motion to be maintained regardless of the direction in which the handle is being moved. These tools, once quite common — the Stanley Tool Company marketed a 'reciprocating' double-spiral Archimedean drill for a considerable time — are now rare but the principle behind them lives on in today's spiral ratchet drill and screwdriver. In fact, the modern push drill (FIG. 367), most commonly exemplified by the Stanley™ model, is a direct descendant. This tool possesses the great added advantage of needing only one hand to operate it. Unlike its bigger cousins, however, which can revolve in one direction or the other as required, the push drill still requires bits formed to cut in both directions. This makes boring faster but can sometimes cause problems in extracting the bit. For this reason, the push drill is really only useful for boring relatively small holes.

Of all the various hand drills, the one that is usually meant when the term is used today, and which requires no other qualifying adjective, is the one thought to have been invented in France towards the end of the 18th century.

Brought to its present level of perfection as a result of American innovations developed in the technologically fertile period following the Civil War, the hand drill (FIG. 368) takes advantage of bevel gears used in various combinations and improved chuck designs. The hand drill is an ideal tool, compact and lightweight, capable of positive movement in either forward or reverse direction, and, moreover, very efficient as a result of the different gearing ratios made available by altering the relative sizes of the bevel gears. The hand drill continues to be made in numerous different designs, although older models are frequently far superior to those made today. Apart from extras such as hollow handles containing a selection of drill bits, and side handles attachable on either side, older castings are frequently stronger and prettier and often have extra gears to provide a more positive movement as well as adjustable cranks which can offer different speeds.

When contemplating the purchase of an older hand drill it is important to check the operation of the gears. Are they smooth and tight or are the bearings worn and the wheels and gears loose and sloppy? It is hard to bore with exactness if the tool is wobbly and shaky, although sometimes it is possible to readjust the gears by means of screws. Also important is the condition of the chuck. A description of chuck design is a study in itself, but what you should be most interested in is whether

the chuck will hold the appropriate bits securely, and if not, can a replacement chuck be fitted? Very often this is easily possible, and an excellent tool that requires only minimal adjustment and refurbishing can be had for a few dollars.

The same cautions are applicable to breast drills, which term today refers to larger hand drills of the sort just described additionally fitted with some form of pad enabling the tool to be held firmly and comfortably against the chest, thus leaving both hands free, one hand for turning the

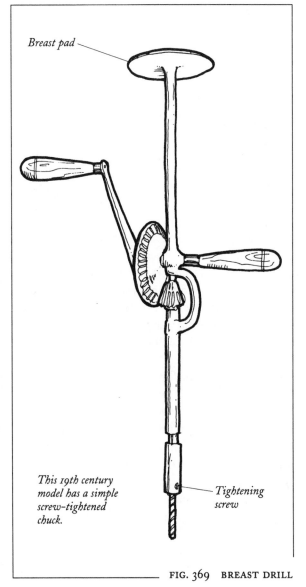

Breast pad

This 19th century model has a simple screw-tightened chuck.

Tightening screw

FIG. 369 BREAST DRILL

crank, and the other for holding the side handle. Older models dating from the middle of the 19th century usually have simple tapered-socket or screw-tightened chucks and large saucer-shaped breast pads (see FIG. 369). Although simple in design they are enormously effective and should not be passed over out of hand. Of course, more recent models may be expected to possess more modern chucks, but contemporary tools are rarely equipped with such niceties as built-in levels to facilitate accurate horizontal boring or gearing choices for different speeds and woods, things that are frequently found on earlier varieties.

THE VENERABLE AUGER

UNTIL VERY RECENTLY THE CURIOUSLY named and venerable auger was the only method available to the woodworker for boring large holes. The tool and its name have an interesting history. The word 'auger' has lost its initial 'n', and changed somewhat over the centuries, and as a result appears almost indecipherably foreign. But the Old English word: *nafu-gar,* from which it derives, gives a clue to its original purpose, especially when we learn that *gar* means 'piercer' or 'borer', and that *nafu* is the same word as nave: the central part of a wheel into which the axle-tree is inserted. Hence the [n]a[f]uger was the tool used to bore the nave for the axle (and the ends of the spokes).

Its distinctive wooden handle, fitted to the metal shank so as to form the shape of the letter 'T', is more vulnerable to wear and decay than the shank itself, so it is no wonder that only the metal parts survive from numerous Roman examples. However, many prints illustrate the use of this easily recognizable tool throughout the Middle Ages, up until which time the cutting part was invariably spoon-shaped. Thereafter, the nose auger made its appearance. This has the shape of a half cylinder with the very tip bent so as to form a cutting edge which cleans out the hole being made and at the same time helps keep the auger firmly in contact with the wood to be cut, which process is difficult if undertaken only by the pressure of one's hands, which must necessarily be removed every time a complete revolution is made. Eventually, towards the end of the 18th century, the now familiar twist auger (FIG. 370) was developed and became most popular.

Needless to say, a great many varieties of all three basic types have been developed over the years, many for specific trades — such as the blockmaker's auger, carpenter's auger, chairmaker's auger, clogger's auger, cooper's auger, shipwright's auger, coachwright's auger, and the wheelwright's augers — as well as many for purposes that were non-trade-specific — such as the brick auger, coak-boring auger, deck-doweling auger, counter-boring auger, raft auger, railway auger, and the slotting augers.

A third large classification might also be listed describing various types of designs for augers, but suffice it to say that an auger exists for almost every hole-boring operation ever conceived.

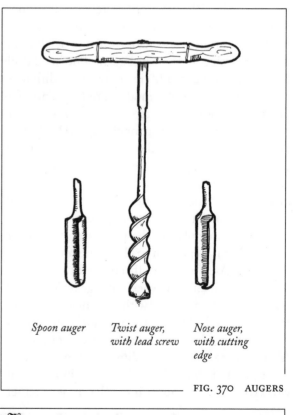

Spoon auger   *Twist auger, with lead screw*   *Nose auger, with cutting edge*

FIG. 370   AUGERS

It should be noted, however, that one so-called auger still readily available and commonly known as a hollow auger is, in fact, no auger at all, but rather a form of bit, since it does not make any sort of hole but merely shapes a round tenon that may be fitted into a hole. To call it a hollow bit is hardly more exact, but it has no other name.

Another point of interest concerns those tools known as 'nut augers' or, as they are sometimes

referred to, 'carpenter's nut augers'. This is not a variety of auger made for a specific purpose, but rather a description of a method for attaching auger handles.

Inasmuch as carpenters and house framers frequently found it necessary to provide themselves with augers of various sizes for boring holes in the timbers and beams of heavy timber-framed buildings, augers were sometimes made with detachable handles, so that a single handle might serve several tools (see FIG. 371). The earliest method of accomplishing this was to forge the handle end of the shank into a ring into which a removable handle might be fitted as needed. These augers are known as eyed augers.

A latter development that provided a more secure attachment was the cutting of a thread on the handle end of the shank. A hole was made in the center of the handle, which was placed over the threaded shank either to rest against a bolster or, more securely yet, to be tightened by the nut onto a tapered section of the shank, and secured by means of a washer and nut, hence the name.

The latest development of the auger is not strictly an auger, but since it employs the same form of auger twist-bit and is used for the same purpose as many augers this is as convenient a place as any to mention it. The boring machine (FIG. 372) largely replaced the carpenter's auger for the purpose of boring large beams when peg or trenail holes were required in mortise-and-tenon joints. The auger twist-bit is held in a metal frame that may in some models be variously positioned to bore holes at different angles, and while the operator sits astride the wooden platform to which this frame is attached, the bit is turned by gears operated by two hand-held cranks.

Depending on the pitch of the lead screw formed on the tip of the bit the rate of boring can be adapted to the density of the wood. Lacking a ½ in. electric drill — which, it should be noted, does not have the secure angle-alignment of the boring machine — there is no more efficient way of boring large holes in big beams than with a properly adjusted boring machine.

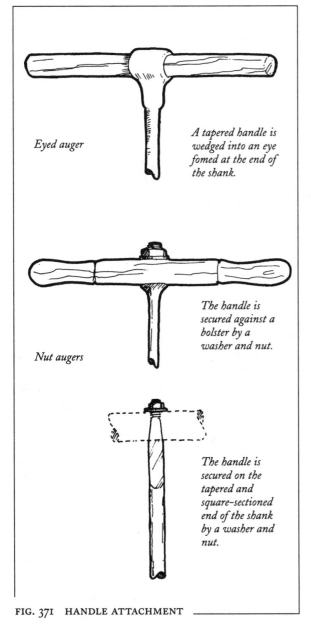

Eyed auger

A tapered handle is wedged into an eye fomed at the end of the shank.

Nut augers

The handle is secured against a bolster by a washer and nut.

The handle is secured on the tapered and square-sectioned end of the shank by a washer and nut.

FIG. 371   HANDLE ATTACHMENT

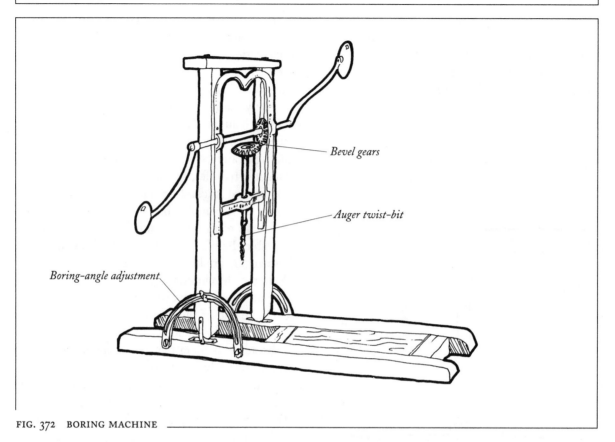

Bevel gears

Auger twist-bit

Boring-angle adjustment

FIG. 372 BORING MACHINE

THE BRACE & BIT

MUCH BEEN WRITTEN TRACING THE development of the brace and bit, which is all the more surprising when one considers that it is among the most recently arrived of boring tools, not being known before the 15th century. One surprising fact is that although metal versions were available by the 16th century there was a very long period when wooden forms predominated. Inevitably, improvements providing greater strength led to the acceptance of almost totally metal versions, but before this point was reached, the brace had become one of woodworking's most glorious tools, and it is probably true to say that along with the wooden plough plane no tool has been as much studied or as covetously collected as the wooden brace.

As previously mentioned, the first braces were made entirely of wood, but were by their very shape, at the narrow cross-grained parts forming the arms of the crank, subject to breakage. It is the crank — the very feature that makes a brace so superior to the auger — which enables the brace to be used in a continuously circular motion, thereby avoiding the stop-and-go action of the auger which occurs with every revolution as the position of the hands is changed. To strengthen these weak areas metal facings were added, hence the term 'plated' brace (see FIG. 373). Subsequent improvements included the development of frames stuffed with wood infill and advances in chuck design. From the earliest beech models of the 18th century to magnificent, brass-framed, ivory-ringed, ebony and rosewood examples such as the 'Ultimatum' or 'Ne Plus Ultra' of the late 19th century (see FIG. 377, chapter 37), no more handsome boring tool was ever made.

More important, however, are the variations that were made on the many metal versions that

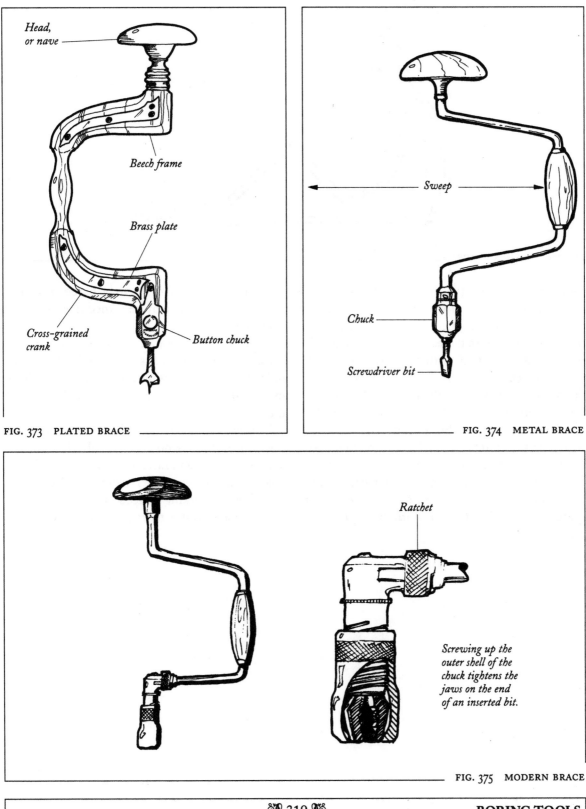

Head, or nave

Beech frame

Brass plate

Cross-grained crank

Button chuck

FIG. 373   PLATED BRACE

Sweep

Chuck

Screwdriver bit

FIG. 374   METAL BRACE

Ratchet

Screwing up the outer shell of the chuck tightens the jaws on the end of an inserted bit.

FIG. 375   MODERN BRACE

BORING TOOLS

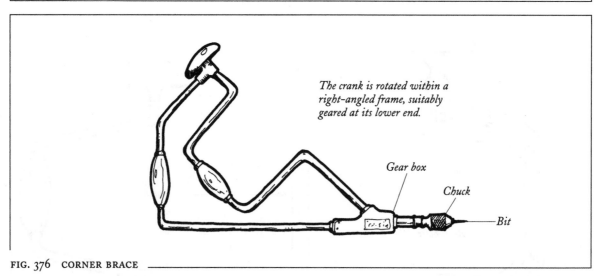

The crank is rotated within a right-angled frame, suitably geared at its lower end.

Gear box

Chuck

Bit

FIG. 376   CORNER BRACE

followed. Although it is the size of the sweep of the crank (see FIG. 374) which gives the brace its power — the larger the sweep, the greater the torque and therefore the easier it is to bore a hole — it is the crank itself, with sweep large or small, which sometimes operates to the tool's greatest disadvantage by being in the way when the tool is used in narrow quarters. In order to overcome this problem most modern braces (FIG. 375) are fitted with reversible ratchets, which allow the tool to be rotated throughout only a part of its full circle. Sometimes, however, even this arrangement can be inconveniently restrictive, and so the corner brace (FIG. 376) was devised. With this tool the bit

can be presented to the area to be bored at such an angle that the crank may be turned freely without interference.

A further refinement of this idea is the angular brace extension. This fits into the brace's chuck and, by means of a universal joint adjustable to any desired angle, the bit may then be used in almost any position.

A similar idea, but one which is not strictly a brace since there is no crank involved, is the so-called hand ratchet brace, which looks exactly like a large auto-mechanic's ratchet fitted with the typical woodworking brace's mushroom-shaped head, or nave, as it is more properly known.

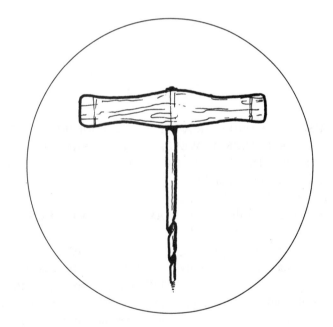

37

BITS & PIECES

MORE THAN BORING

A BIT IS A TOOL USED IN A DRILL OR A BIT BRACE TO BORE A HOLE. THERE ARE MANY BITS THAT DO OTHER THINGS AS WELL, SUCH AS REAMING, COUNTERSINKING, AND TURNING SCREWS, BUT IN GENERAL THE TERM 'BIT' IS UNDERSTOOD TO REFER TO a tool that makes a hole. The action of making a circular hole is generally referred to as 'boring', but some people also use the term 'drilling'. The former term implies a rotary action, whereas the latter term originally implied the simple piercing of material whether by circular boring or any other method.

Since the most usual tool used by the woodworker for making holes is known as a drill, to talk of drilling is quite understandable, if also sometimes a little confusing, especially when drill bits are confused with drills. And to make matters worse, the metalworker calls all his bits 'drills', whereas the woodworker understands 'drill' only to mean the tool that holds the bits.

AVOIDING CONFUSION

THE CONFUSION CAN PERHAPS BE AVOIDED if we restrict the usage of the various terms as follows: Let 'boring' be the verb used to describe making the hole — with whatever tool and in whatever fashion; let 'drill' be the noun referring to those tools — such as the electric drill, the cordless drill, or even the Archimedean drill — that hold and operate the bits; and reserve 'bit' or 'drill bit' for the accessories that actually cut the holes. The only exception to this system is that class of boring bits known as twist drills.

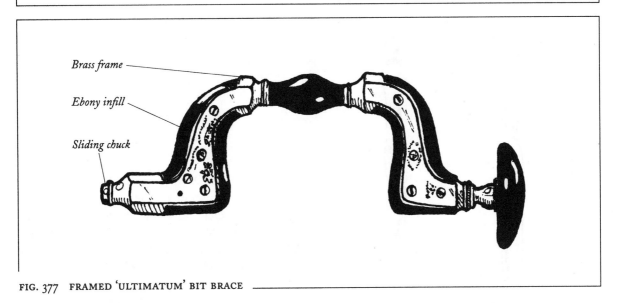

Brass frame

Ebony infill

Sliding chuck

FIG. 377   FRAMED 'ULTIMATUM' BIT BRACE

THE BIT BRACE

ONE OF THE QUINTESSENTIAL EMBLEMS OF woodworking along with the plane is the old-fashioned framed brace (FIG. 377). Since the advent of the electric drill, and especially since the development of the cordless electric drill, the bit brace, or brace as it is more usually referred to, has very nearly disappeared from the average toolbox. With it has gone the amazing selection of bits that were designed for a wide variety of jobs, to be largely replaced by the high-speed spade bit and twist drill. There is no denying the efficiency of a completely portable powertool, unfettered by extension cords, that can be carried anywhere and operated with one hand, and which is equally useful for boring holes or driving screws. But as with many modern powertools, a certain amount of sophistication has been lost along the way in the pursuit of speed and ease of use.

Despite the almost complete abandonment of the brace for the electric drill, many people are still familiar with the standard 'iron' brace, now usually made of steel (see FIG. 375, chapter 36). Fewer may be familiar with its predecessor, the wooden bit brace, even if images of traditional, hand-crafted woodwork are conjured up. But very few indeed would recognize any of the bits these

tools used and may still use to advantage. Speed and power are not everything, and more than one woodworker has been frustrated by a low charge or a dirty or worn variable-speed trigger on the electric drill causing the bit to plunge wildly out of control and damage the workpiece just at that moment when something of a certain nicety was being attempted. Furthermore, not all holes are intended to be created equal. The wide selection of special-purpose bits that can be used in a brace can make possible boring operations that are difficult to differentiate with an electric drill, or even its more powerful cousin, the drillpress.

Braces are still plentiful and cheap. They are designed with a wide variety of chucks to hold the bit, and many are also equipped with ratchets to allow the direction of rotation to be controlled. Nevertheless they are all easily understood if disassembled, and it is not hard to judge the quality or usefulness of any brace under consideration, even at a fleamarket or yard sale.

THE MYSTERY BITS

BIT-BRACE BITS ARE MORE OF A MYSTERY, however, especially as they tend to be dirty, rusty, mixed up with a lot of other unidentifiable tools

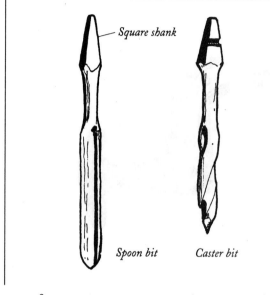

Square shank

Spoon bit   *Caster bit*

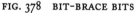

FIG. 378 BIT-BRACE BITS

to do with metalworking, and hard to reach at the bottom of bins or boxes of 'contents'.

The first clue to identifying a bit designed for a bit brace is its square shank (see FIG. 378). In a pinch many braces will hold bits with round shanks, but the jaws of most chucks are designed to grip most securely those bits with square, tapered shanks. Iron braces hold the bit by the chuck being tightened on the bit; wooden braces were made with a variety of chucks that became increasingly sophisticated with time. Early braces simply received the square shank of the bit and employed a screw to fasten it; later models were often fitted with various spring-loaded pins that engaged a slot or groove filed in the side of the square shank. Bits were specially filed to fit particular braces or left plain for the owner to file a notch to suit any given brace. Some bits may be found that have more than one groove filed on different sides of the square shank, indicating their use in various braces. But with or without these grooves almost any square-shanked bit can be accepted by almost any iron brace. That having been said, however, it should also be noted that as with almost every other successful class of woodworking tool, the brace has been made in a large

number of sizes, and it is quite possible to find an extra-small brace (perhaps once forming part of a set of variously sized tools) that will not accept a particular bit (perhaps an extra-large size bit designed for an extra-large brace).

AUGER BITS

AUGER BITS ARE SO CALLED SINCE THEIR design is reminiscent of the augers described in the previous chapter. They constitute one of the major classes of bits: those characterized by being formed into twisted spirals, usually with spurs to cut the fibers of the wood, one or two cutting edges to cut away the wood between the severed fibers, and a threaded point that pulls the bit into the wood.

There are single spiral bits with one cutting edge, double spiral bits with two cutting edges, and close and open spiral auger bits, as well as short auger bits also known as dowel bits, all of which are made in a range of sizes, usually increasing by eighth-inch increments, from as small as ⅜ in. in diameter to as large as 2½ in. in diameter. The size of these bits is commonly stamped on the square part of the shank: a number from 3 to 20 refers to how many eighths of an inch comprise the diameter. Especially long auger bits, usually made in a narrower range of diameters, are sometimes sized in sixteenths of an inch, and some high-quality bits were even made in one-thirty-second-inch increments.

The reason for so many types is due to the variety of material that might need to be bored. Finely threaded points on the end of an auger draw the bit more slowly into the wood and make cutting hardwood a little easier since less wood is removed with each rotation. Coarser threads pull the bit more quickly into the wood and result in a thicker shaving, ideal for softwood (see FIG. 379). A double-twist bit with two cutting edges has advantages over a single-twist bit with only one cutting edge when working with wood that is more seasoned. Double-twist also means two

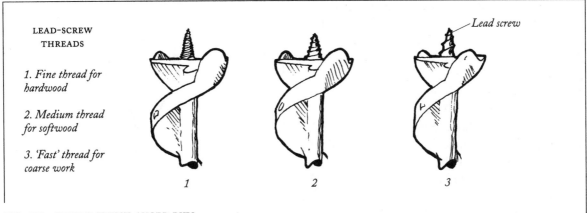

LEAD-SCREW
THREADS

1. Fine thread for hardwood

2. Medium thread for softwood

3. 'Fast' thread for coarse work

1   *2*   *3*

FIG. 379   SINGLE-TWIST AUGER BITS

spurs, which make accurate scribing of the hole to be bored an easier proposition — something that can be hard to accomplish with spade bit driven by an electric drill.

Being aware of these niceties will enable you to judge the condition of an auger bit beneath its dirt and rust. It must, of course, be straight. If it has been overly forced or otherwise abused the bit may be bent. It is hard but not impossible to straighten a bent bit, but its integrity will remain suspect, for the bending and straightening may have weakened it and it may unexpectedly bend again — with potentially dangerous results.

The all-important lead screw should not have been damaged by clumsy sharpening of the spurs or the cutting edges. An old trick for clearing clogged threads is to hold a clothes-pin over the lead screw tightly while turning the bit. Using a fine thread in softwood or wet wood will clog the threads, as will applying insufficient pressure when beginning to bore: the threads formed in the wood will strip out and fill up the screw so that it can no longer bite into the wood and will simply spin in place.

The spurs and the cutting edges are not hard to sharpen using a small double-ended file with alternate safe edges known as an auger-bit file (FIG. 380), but all too often the spurs will have been sharpened on the outside instead of only on the inside, with the result that the circle they

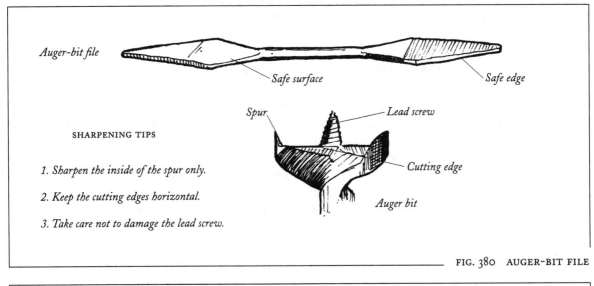

Auger-bit file

Safe surface   Safe edge

SHARPENING TIPS

1. Sharpen the inside of the spur only.

2. Keep the cutting edges horizontal.

3. Take care not to damage the lead screw.

Spur   Lead screw

Cutting edge

Auger bit

FIG. 380   AUGER-BIT FILE

scribe is narrower than the diameter of the bit. When sharpening the cutting edge or edges of the bit itself it is important to keep them truly perpendicular to the shank. If through inattentive sharpening they are made to slope, they will not hit the wood along their length or together at the same time, making boring considerably harder.

The majority of holes bored with an auger bit will ideally be perpendicular to the surface of the wood — this is what the tool was designed for; angled holes are more efficiently bored with the differently designed forstner bit (FIG. 383) — and every woodworker soon learns a number of tricks to guarantee accuracy. Almost every old book on woodwork recommends boring with a trysquare stood on end near the bit to provide a reference against which to compare your boring angle, but it is hard to get the trysquare close enough to the bit for this to be of much use. It is just as efficient to learn to use some other reference such as the surface of the bench or the wall glimpsed out of the corner of your eye. It also helps to position the workpiece so that the hole to be bored is either perpendicular to or in the same plane as the work-bench. The eye has difficulty consistently judging intermediate angles. How you hold the brace can affect the accuracy of the boring. It is almost always better to position the pad of the brace against some part of your body — a thigh, your abdomen, a shoulder — so that it may be held perfectly upright or horizontal.

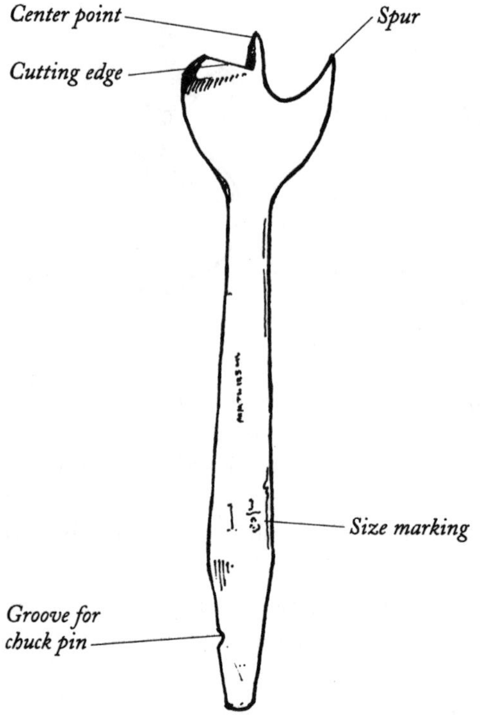

FIG. 381   CENTER BIT

center point for orienting the hole to be bored, a spur to cut the fibers at the outside of the hole, and a sharpened cutting edge for lifting out the waste. Simple to use and maintain, they exist in a large number of sizes from ³⁄₁₆ in. in diameter to 2½ in. in diameter. Their main disadvantage is their comparative shortness.

CENTER BITS & OLDER VARIETIES

BEFORE AUGER BITS EXISTED THE WORLD OF boring was filled with different designs such as gimlet bits, center bits, spoon bits, nose bits, caster bits, taper bits, and countersink wimbles. Some had screws at their tips but most did not. Many scraped rather than cut since they had been designed for boring tools that were reciprocating like the bow drill or today's push drill rather than fully rotational. One of the most successful bits was the center bit (FIG. 381), which possessed a

TWIST BITS

A LARGER GROUP, SECOND PERHAPS ONLY to auger bits, is the twist-bit family. These are very closely related to metalworking drills, and are made in a wide range of finely graduated sizes, all sizes being made both long and short. Especially long versions used to be known as bell hanger's twist bits, and until recently were used by tele-phone linemen for boring holes for thin wire through walls. Many of these have a small hole bored through the tip in which a wire to be passed

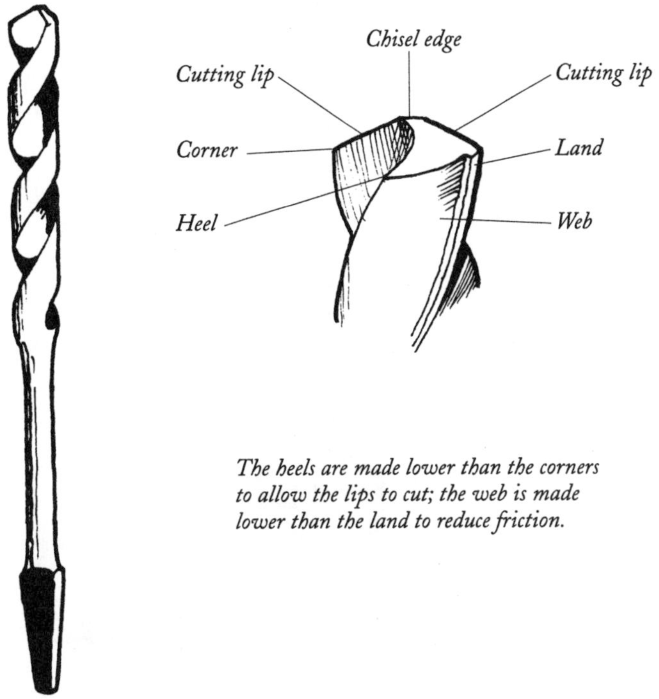

Cutting lip

Chisel edge

Cutting lip

Corner

Land

Heel

Web

The heels are made lower than the corners to allow the lips to cut; the web is made lower than the land to reduce friction.

FIG. 382   WOODWORKING TWIST BIT

through the bored hole may be fixed (and then wrapped around the flutes of the bit), making it easy to thread the wire through a hollow space.

Most people think that twist bits are properly intended only for use with hand drills. In truth, only those with round shanks are meant for hand drills; square-shanked twist bits are meant, like all other square-shanked bits, for use in a bit brace. Round-shanked twist bits are designed to be held by the three straight-faced jaws found in the chucks of most hand drills and drillpresses.

The geometry of the spiral flutes and especially the tips of twist bits intended for woodworking is different from that of metalworking bits, and for a twist bit to work efficiently it must be carefully sharpened at the proper angle (see FIG. 382). This is made easier if a shop-made or a commercially made jig is used to hold the bit in the proper relation to the grindstone. The difference between

a blunt or wrongly sharpened bit and one in good condition can be astonishing, and learning to sharpen properly is well worth the effort.

A nice variation on the woodworking twist bit consists of a brad-pointed bit, made with spurs and horizontal cutting edges in the manner of good auger bits. Both these features are of especial use when boring with a hand drill or an electric drill and when the more absolute control afforded by a drillpress is unavailable. Brad-pointed bits are used for making holes smaller than a regular auger bit can produce. Since they lack a lead screw, they require a little more pressure to cut, but since their diameters are small this is not excessive.

Of all the remaining bits that can be used in hand drills or braces, the forstner bit (FIG. 383) deserves mention. Its spur is nearly a complete circle, and this enables it to begin boring a hole at virtually any angle without the bit walking away

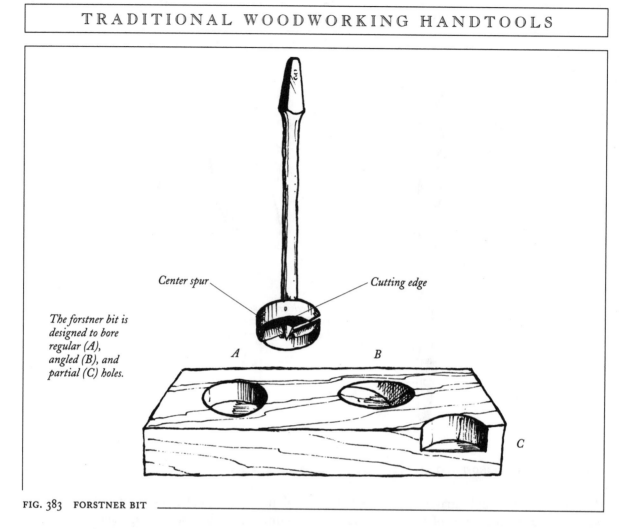

Center spur   *Cutting edge*

The forstner bit is designed to bore regular (A), angled (B), and partial (C) holes.

A   *B*

C

FIG. 383   FORSTNER BIT

from the desired location. An extra advantage is that it more nearly bores a flat-bottomed hole, its point producing only the smallest depression, unlike an auger bit, whose lead screw can burst through the floor of a hole bored too close to the other side of the workpiece.

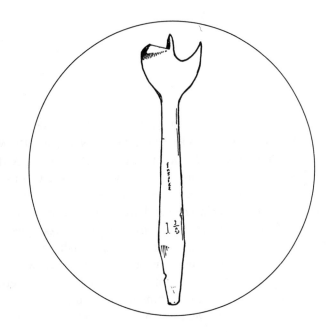

38

THREADING TOOLS

SCREW BOXES & WOOD TAPS

THREADED METAL ROD IS NOW SO UNIVERSAL AND EASILY OBTAINABLE THAT THE USE OF WOODEN THREADS IS RARELY SEEN. NOT SO LONG AGO, HOWEVER, AN ALMOST ENDLESS VARIETY OF THINGS WERE ASSEMBLED, ADJUSTED, AND USED WITH THE help of wooden threads. Many woodworkers are no doubt familiar with wooden-threaded handscrews, most of which have now been replaced commercially by the Jorgensen™-type handscrew (FIG. 13, chapter 2) which uses metal threads, and many others have probably seen old woodworking benches fitted out with vises operated by large wooden threads (see FIG. 4, chapter 1). But just as common when these items were new were wooden threads used in cider presses, printing presses, the adjustable arms of plough planes, broom handles, drawer knobs, lathe poppets, all types of furniture including early knock-down fittings such as bed parts, and a host of other everyday items.

The two tools used to make these threads, the screw box and its partner the wood tap, are simple and easily made, as proved by the fact that as many user-made examples survive as do models made commercially. They may still be used by the average woodworker with great effect and can often add that extra something to an otherwise run-of-the-mill project.

As with many other basically simple tools, the screw box is of great antiquity and its origins may be traced far back into the classical world. Archimedes, a Greek who lived around 250 B.C., is credited with the discovery of the principle of the screw, Pappus of Alexandria recorded a method of designing threads in the 4th century, and the

Romans too are known to have used screws, and therefore obviously to have had screwmaking tools.

By the early 18th century the screw box as we know it today was fully developed. Numerous descriptions and illustrations abound in books, treatises, and encyclopedias of the period. By the mid-19th century, screw boxes were being made commercially in great numbers by such British firms as Alexander Mathieson and Sons in Glasgow, Scotland, James Howarth in Sheffield, Holtzappfel in London, Marples and Sons, Moulson Brothers, and Ibbotson Brothers. For some reason, American makers are unknown, but the existence of large numbers of foreign-made tools all over America demonstrates their equally common use on both sides of the Atlantic.

Despite their relative abundance and popularity, however, there was little if any standardization with regard to thread sizes and pitch. Along with the increased availability of threaded rod, it was this very lack of standardization that led to their decreased manufacture and use. As of 1997 there remained only one major manufacturer of screw boxes, ironically an American firm: Connover Woodcraft, of Parkman, Ohio. The reason that a lack of standardization should have removed so popular and common a tool from the toolkit can be found in the fact that a screw box without a matching tap is about as effective as one hand trying to clap. Since the two items appear to have had a great propensity for separation the moment they left the possession of their original owner, matched pairs are seldom found. This tendency in itself would not be so disastrous were taps made for one screw box interchangeable with those made for another, in the way that plough-plane irons of any manufacturer invariably work with any other manufacturer's plane (the wooden plough plane and its original set of irons being another notorious example of a tool whose parts seem to become separated at birth).

With this in mind, you will save yourself a lot of time and trouble if you restrict your purchases of threading tools, new or second-hand, to complete, matching pairs. It is possible, as many old-timers did, to use either a single screw box or a single tap to make its mating tool, but it may not be worth the effort considering the work involved, and the chances of subsequently finding a mate to whichever part you obtained singly are remote. This will be apparent from the fact that a typical 19th century tool merchant's catalog often listed as many as twenty different thread diameters, and none of the pitches or threads per inch of those twenty sizes might match those from another manufacturer's selection.

Despite the wide variety in sizes and styles, most screw boxes and wood taps are, however, remarkably similar in their basic design. Taking the time to examine their constituent parts and features, and thereby gaining a more thorough understanding of this basic design, will ensure more rapid success when you attempt your first wooden thread.

THE BOTTOM BLOCK

SCREW BOXES MAY BE MADE FROM A large variety of even-grained and close-grained medium hardwoods such as apple, pear, hornbeam, beech, rosewood, boxwood, and even walnut. European beech is the most common commercially used variety. Some makers also made cast-iron boxes, but these are relatively rare. The box consists of two parts: the bottom block and the upper block (see FIG. 384).

The bottom block is the smaller part and contains a hole of the same diameter as the rod to be threaded: the basic thread diameter. In order for the threads to be cut properly it is important that the rod be fed in with perfect alignment. This is precisely what the hole in the bottom block is designed to do. Consequently, in order to avoid any wear which might compromise the required alignment, the bottom block is often made of a harder material than the rest of the screw box. Beech screw boxes with boxwood bottom blocks are common, and metal bushings are sometimes

THREADING TOOLS

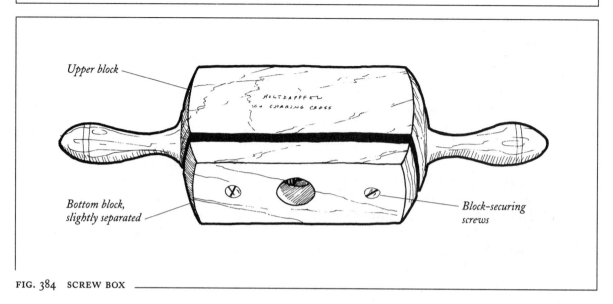

FIG. 384 SCREW BOX

found around the hole. The bottom block is fitted and held to the upper block with screws or with friction-fitted dowels (of which care should be taken when attempting to separate the parts), enabling it to be easily removed — for reasons explained below. It is also likely to have a shallow mortise or hole bored in its inside face to receive the end of the cutter-holding clamp, the which protrudes from the upper block.

THE UPPER BLOCK

THE UPPER BLOCK, WHICH IS CONSIDERABLY larger, is bored with a hole of the same diameter as the intended thread root (the diameter of the threaded rod as measured across the bottom of the threads), which is then tapped to the required size (see FIG. 385). Since wood is not as stable as metal, clearances between threaded rod and tapped hole

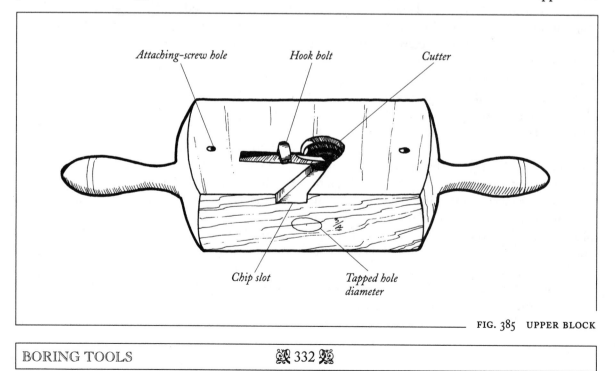

FIG. 385 UPPER BLOCK

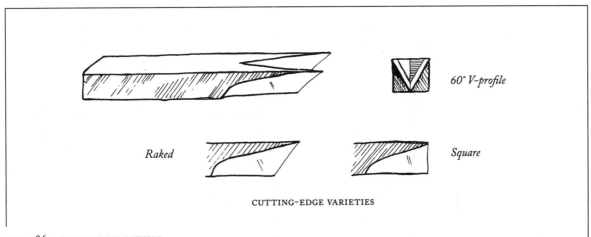

Raked *Square*

60° V-profile

CUTTING-EDGE VARIETIES

FIG. 386   SCREW-BOX CUTTER

need to be greater than is usual in metal. To guide the user as to the best size hole to be tapped for the thread made with any particular screw box, manufacturers frequently marked the upper block with an inscribed circle of the recommended diameter.

THE CUTTER

AT THE BEGINNING OF THE THREAD ON THE inside face of the upper block is fitted the cutter. The correct adjustment of this cutter contains the whole secret to the successful use of the screw box. Once you get this right everything else is plain sailing. But be the adjustment ever so slightly off and you will have no end of problems, and will probably (and mistakenly) be tempted to abandon screw boxes forever as old-fashioned, inefficient curiosities.

The cutter should be made from tool-steel, sharpened on the inside of a V-shaped edge. Although the end of this edge may be found either square or raked (see FIG. 386), the V-profile is invariably formed to a 60° angle. Interestingly, while modern analysis confirms 60° as being the best general-purpose angle, there is no knowing how the original makers arrived at the same conclusion. A process of trial and error would surely have left a trail of less successful angles behind.

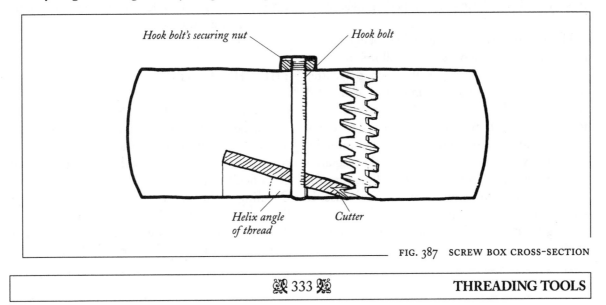

Hook bolt's securing nut *Hook bolt*

Helix angle of thread *Cutter*

FIG. 387   SCREW BOX CROSS-SECTION

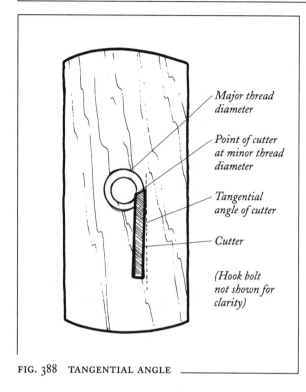

Major thread diameter

Point of cutter at minor thread diameter

Tangential angle of cutter

Cutter

(Hook bolt not shown for clarity)

FIG. 388   TANGENTIAL ANGLE

For this 60° raked or square cutter to work properly and easily it must be held in position to conform with two critical angles. The first demands that the cutter be properly aligned with the helix angle of the thread (the axial angle that matches the thread pitch) (see FIG. 387). Unless the mortise that the cutter sits in has been badly damaged and become enlarged by use or abuse, this angle should have been properly provided for in manufacture.

The second critical angle, while being largely governed by this mortise, also allows for user adjustment. It is the angle at which the cutter forms a tangent to the circumference of the rod being threaded (see FIG. 388). Assuming this angle to be correct, all that the user needs to do is correctly advance or retract the cutter until its point is exactly at the bottom of the required minor thread diameter (the bottom of the thread), since it is the cutter which defines this in use. If the cutter's tangential angle is too deep the cutter will dig in and jam; if it is too high it may not cut at all.

Recognizing which adjustments need to be made, and to what degree, becomes easier with a little practice at thread-cutting. It is ignorance of these various possibilities which can make trying to use a poorly adjusted tool an exercise in frustration.

The critical relationships which must exist between the cutter and the bored and threaded hole in the upper block having been described, it should also be pointed out that there is an amazing variety of techniques by which the correct adjustment is maintained. Quite a few commercially made boxes have hook bolts that are tightened by a slotted nut on the bolt where it passes through the outside of the upper block. Home-made methods include screws, nails, wedges, and sometimes just a friction fit in the cutter's mortise.

A useful tip that can help secure a loose cutter is to take a shaving or two off the inside face of the upper block so that the cutter is just a little proud of this surface. Then when the bottom block is fixed to the upper block it will press against the cutter and help hold it in position. Care should be taken that any pressure exerted in this manner does not also inadvertently alter the cutter's helix angle by tipping it in its mortise. But note that this method will only work when the bottom block is in place, which it will not always be, since when a thread is required to be cut right up to a shoulder the bottom block must necessarily be removed.

THE CHIP SLOT

ONE OTHER FEATURE OF THE UPPER BLOCK not to be overlooked is the chip slot, or mouth of the box, through which the chips taken by the cutter must exit the box. If this is clogged it will be difficult if not impossible to cut clean threads. Cleaning of this slot, together with adjustment of the cutter and the need to make shoulder cuts, are the three main reasons why the bottom block, as mentioned earlier, needs to be removable.

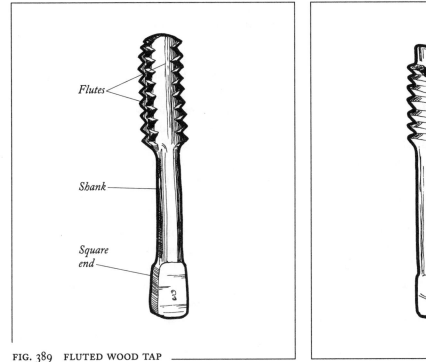

Flutes

Shank

Square end

FIG. 389   FLUTED WOOD TAP

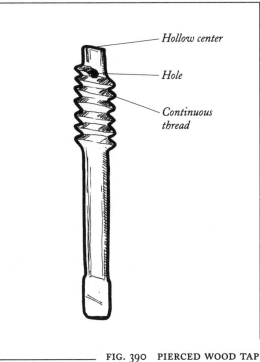

Hollow center

Hole

Continuous thread

FIG. 390   PIERCED WOOD TAP

HANDLES

THE LAST AND PROBABLY MOST SALIENT feature of screw boxes, at least of those designed to produce threads in stock over ¾ in. in diameter, is the furnishing of two integrally turned handles. Smaller boxes are in fact virtual boxes, and are designed to be held in the hand or a vise while the rod to be threaded is twisted through them, whereas when working on larger stock it is the stock which is secured in a vise while the screw box is revolved about it by the handles provided.

WOOD TAPS

SCREW TAPS ARE MADE OF STEEL OR forged iron in two main types: channeled and pierced. Both types may be found either straight or tapered to a greater or lesser extent. The tapering enables the thread being tapped to be cut gradually at first, thus reducing the initial force required. Straight taps would appear to be most

useful for bottomed threads, but a blind hole threaded all the way to the bottom is not a commonly required item in woodworking, and probably explains why this type is less common. Since it can require considerable effort to turn a tap in wood, especially for the larger sizes, tapering is a great help.

The tap may be supplied with its own handle secured by a tang or a nut or, as is more usual, with a square or rectangular shank or head designed to allow the tap to be turned by a key, a wrench, or an interchangeable tap handle of the kind commonly used with carpenter's nut augers (see FIG. 371, chapter 36).

The channeled or fluted type of tap (FIG. 389) is the commoner form, and usually consists of a slightly tapered tap with three, or most commonly four, flutes cut through the threads so as to form a series of cutting edges, which at the same time as cutting provide an escape route for the wood removed by the tap.

The second type (FIG. 390) is furnished with a continuous thread, the very first spiral of which is

THREADING TOOLS

pierced by a hole at its start so as to produce a sharpened profile of the thread which then cuts like a little chisel, the waste wood exiting through the hollowed center of the tap.

THREADING IN PRACTICE

ASSUMING YOU ARE PROVIDED WITH A properly matched tap and screw box it does not matter whether you cut the male or female thread first. When using the tap the important point is to be sure that you work with a hole bored to the proper diameter. As mentioned above this is often indicated on the side of the upper block. If not, measure the minor diameter of the screw and add a little for clearance. If the screw is not yet made, measure the inside diameter of the screw box and add a little. A 'little' is necessarily vague since in practice this depends on a number of factors such as how large is the thread and how green or dry is the material; but a little practical experience will soon make you a good judge of this.

If you use a tapered tap take care to re-engage the same previously cut threads each time you reinsert the tap after having removed it for chip ejection. A certain amount of downwards pressure is necessary to commence cutting the threads; if insufficient force is applied the tap will simply score around and around without biting into the wood. Once begun, however, the tap should feed itself in; the only force necessary — which can be considerable depending on the diameter of the hole being tapped — will be in rotating the tap.

Similarly, when using the screw box it is most important to start with a rod or dowel of the correct diameter. It must fit snugly in the unthreaded hole of the bottom block but at the same time turn freely. If you are using stock you have turned yourself or have just made with a dowel-making machine this is generally no problem. But beware

of commercially made dowel rod; it will have often dried out-of-round and not only be smaller than its nominal size but may be oval to boot. It helps to chamfer the end of the rod slightly and feed it forcefully at first into the box until the cutter has taken a bite; thereafter the threaded portion of the upper block will ensure that the rod is fed through at the proper rate. To make cutting easier you may back off the cutter slightly for the first pass and then reset it to cut to the full depth of the thread for the finish cut.

Practically all your difficulties will be found to be traceable to an incorrectly set cutter. If it is set too high you will not be able to make a deep enough cut and the rod will bind on the threaded portion of the box. If the cut appears deep enough but the rod is still hard to turn in the box then the cutter may be misaligned with regard to the helix angle. If one side of the cut thread appears polished this may indicate misalignment and you should reset the cutter in the opposite direction.

Even if the box turns well another problem may be created by the threaded rod itself. Not all species of wood are suited to being threaded. If the wood is too soft, the cut threads will chip off, or even worse, the rod will emerge from the box undersized and furry with few or no recognizable threads. Make sure the cutter is sharp and the wood is well seasoned. Experiment with different species; maple, birch, hornbeam, alder, boxwood, and lignum vitae are generally excellent, as are many fruitwoods. Hardwoods with porous grain like the various oaks are sometimes fine, but they can be prone to a lot of chipping at the threads. Walnut and beech, from which many commercial dowels are made, are not good choices. Green wood may produce long shavings and good threads but will then shrink to the point where the fit is too loose. One thing is certain, however: the first threads you produce will amaze your friends and delight you.

VII
MISCELLANEOUS TOOLS

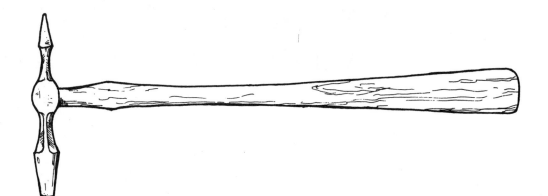

39

STRIKING TOOLS

'HAMMAR' & 'MALLEUS'

JUST AS THERE ARE MANY SYNONYMS FOR STRIKING DEPENDING ON THE SEVERITY OF THE BLOW, FROM GENTLE 'TAPPING' TO VIGOROUS 'POUNDING', SO THERE ARE ALMOST AS MANY NAMES FOR THE TOOLS DESIGNED TO INFLICT THESE BLOWS. FURTHERMORE not only the intensity of the blow but also the precise arena in which it is wielded gives rise to another set of classifications, with the result that this single class of woodworking tools probably contains more members than any other. The list may be nearly endless, but among those that come immediately to mind are the ball-pane hammer, blacksmith's hammer, brickie's hammer, claw hammer, carpenter's hammer, coal hammer, cobbler's hammer, cross-pane hammer, engineer's hammer, fiber hammer, lath hammer, lump hammer, panel-beater's hammer, pin hammer, planishing hammer, plasterer's hammer, plumber's hammer, rubber hammer, slate hammer, sledge hammer, tack hammer, toffee hammer, wooden hammer, square mallet, round mallet, bossing mallet, dresser, bending dresser, commander, bobber, and snatch. The list could go on and on. One current dictionary* lists over a hundred types; the number of more obscure, obsolete, and forgotten types is far greater.

If we restrict our discussion of this huge group of tools to those used in woodworking, however, we can divide the majority into two main groups: those with wooden heads and those with metal heads. Most members of the former group are now known as mallets, and those of the latter are

* R. A. Salaman. *Dictionary of Tools used in the woodworking and allied trades, c. 1700–1970.* London 1975

mostly called hammers. A separate name for two easily distinguishable classes of striking tools may seem reasonable enough at first glance but when you realize that the word 'mallet' comes directly from the Latin word for hammer: *malleus,* logic disappears.

Tracing the etymology of 'hammer' further confuses the situation. Supposedly related to the common Russian word: *kamen,* meaning 'stone' (whence Kaminski, meaning stonemason, one of the commonest Slavic names), the word 'hammer' came into English via the old German Teutons and the Scandinavian Norsemen, who both had a word like hammer: *hammar,* that had much to do with crags, tors, and other rocky, stony places. It is easy to see that a hammer might originally either have been an instrument for breaking rock, or an actual piece of rock itself, used for hitting other objects or enemies.

Why the Latin word for hammer should have become the word for a wooden-headed striking tool, and the Norse word the one used for a metal-headed version, could lead to a great deal of interesting speculation concerning the development of society, cultural biases, slavery, and the history of war, not to mention early carpentry practices. But whatever the reasons we are now stuck with them, and it remains the bane of every shop-teacher's life that he or she spends endless hours trying to drill into dull students' heads the fact that a mallet should be used for striking wood and a hammer for striking metal.

THE HANDLE

NEXT TO THE HEAD, THE HAFT OR HANDLE is the most important element of most striking tools. It is curious that beginners very often emulate what must have been the method employed by the original users of these tools — the original tools having had no handle — and hold the tool very near the head. It is a learned process to grasp the tool near the end of the handle, just as it was a slow development from hafting a crude lump of

rock to fitting an elegant and far more efficient handle to the tool. In fact, the impulse to use the tool by holding it close to the head is so strong that one 19th century manual on elementary woodworking* devoted an entire chapter to describing the different methods of wielding striking tools, emphasizing different grips near the end of the handle, and different wrist, forearm, and whole-arm motions to effect the swing.

The correct use as well as the correct fitting of a handle is actually more complicated and sophisticated than might be imagined. It is not just a question of extra leverage effecting a more powerful swing, there is also the delicate matter of balance and resiliency to be considered if the tool is to be used efficiently, especially for long periods of time. In this respect many older tools are far superior to contemporary ones. A closer look at some of the important features of these tools will make comparisons between older and newer tools easier.

THE COMMON CLAW

MENTION A HAMMER TO MOST PEOPLE AND the tool that comes most readily to mind is the carpenter's claw hammer (FIG. 391). It should be

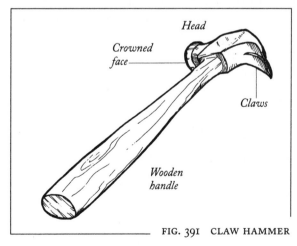

FIG. 391   CLAW HAMMER

* The Industrial School Association. *Wood-Working Tools; How to use Them. A Manual.* Boston 1884

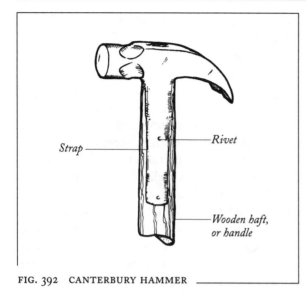

Strap

Rivet

Wooden haft, or handle

FIG. 392   CANTERBURY HAMMER

pointed out that of all striking tools the claw hammer is the most flawed, since its two avowed purposes, striking and clawing, are basically at odds with one another so far as structural design requirements are concerned.

It is not just that the older, wooden-handled tools do not have enough strength in the handle to stand up to much serious clawing or levering out of nails, but also that the two operations require mutually incompatible qualities of rigidity and flexibility. If the weakness of the wood were the only consideration then a metal-handled tool would solve the problem. But levering requires an unflexing, rigidly strong tool like a crowbar or prybar, whereas a tool used for striking blows requires a certain amount of spring or give in the handle if the shock of the blow is not to be painfully transmitted up the user's arm.

Even fiber-handled versions do not have the same balanced resiliency possessed by wooden-handled hammers. The proof of the matter is seen in the continued supremacy of wooden-handled framing hammers. These tools are essentially claw hammers that weigh considerably more than the standard 16 oz., used by carpenters pounding 16d nails into studs, joists, and rafters all day long. This is a group of woodworkers that has no time to spare for anything less than the most efficient

and practical tools; a group not likely to cling to old-fashioned ways for sentimental reasons. Even where power hammers and cordless drills have largely replaced hammer and nail, the 20 oz. framing hammer is typically fitted with a wooden handle. The metal-handled hammer even when sheathed with a rubber or plastic grip remains an inefficient abomination and neither extracts nails nor drives nails very well.

It is interesting to note that in the past before the introduction of metal-handled or fiberglass versions all sorts of dodges were tried to give a wooden handle sufficient strength to withstand the clawing forces, from deepening the eye in the head in which the handle is fixed to fixing straps to the head which ran down the side of the handle for varying distances. Some of these old designs bear quaint names such as the Canterbury hammer (FIG. 392), the carrick hammer, and the gentleman's hammer, but all were only partially successful. Even the best-made wooden-handled hammer will suffer damage if used too often to remove nails. The advantage of wood over metal is one of comfort, resiliency, and balance; it is a waste of these attributes to destroy the handle by inappropriate use.

THE WARRINGTON HAMMER

DESPITE THE PRE-EMINENCE OF THE CLAW hammer as the generic model for all hammers, the most usual form employed by woodworkers other than house carpenters — meaning woodworkers who work at a bench rather than on a building site — is the so-called Warrington-pattern hammer (FIG. 393). Instead of a claw this type has a straight pane (described below) used for starting pins and small nails.

There are other hammers that closely fit this description, including the Exeter pattern and London-pattern hammers, but it is the type first noticed as having been made in the Lancashire manufacturing town of Warrington since at least the middle of the 19th century that has come to

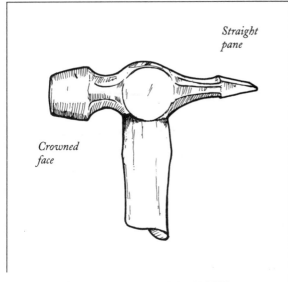

Straight pane

Crowned face

FIG. 393   WARRINGTON-PATTERN HAMMER

PANES & PEENS

IF THE OPPOSITE END FROM THE HAMMER'S face ends in a relatively thin wedge-like shape it is called in Britain a paned hammer; in America it is called a peened hammer. In both places it may also be referred to as a peined hammer, pronounced either as 'pane' or 'peen' depending on the user's preference. The origin of this curious word is obscure, but while there may be sound etymological reasons for both 'pane' and 'peen', 'pein', which gives first-time users pronunciation pains, is a 19th century manufacturer's invention and might be usefully ignored.

Both cross and straight panes are useful for starting small nails, although in fact their real purpose is for hammering out metal in ways not possible with a round face. An extension of this function has led to the provision of some tools with an almost spherical face (at the opposite end from the regular face), known perversely as a ball 'pane' — although round 'face' would be more accurate, since a pane is by definition wedge-shaped (see FIG. 394).

predominance. Originally made in a wide range of sizes and weighing from 5 oz. to 33 oz., but now generally available only in a couple of middling sizes, the Warrington-pattern joiner's hammer with its well-designed head and wooden handle is a joy to use.

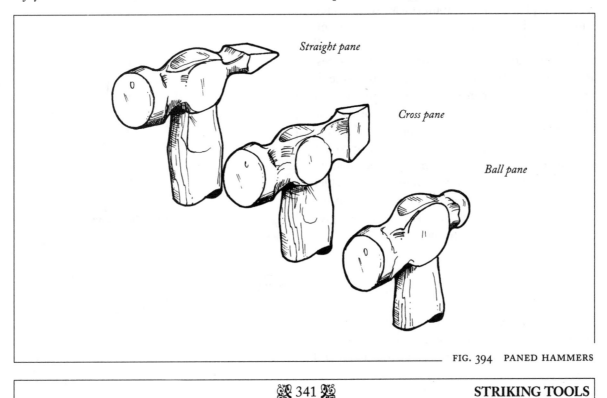

Straight pane

Cross pane

Ball pane

FIG. 394   PANED HAMMERS

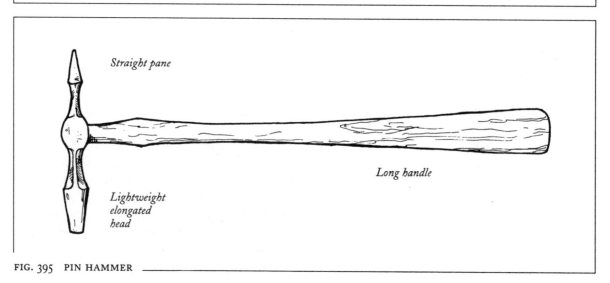

Straight pane

Long handle

*Lightweight
elongated
head*

FIG. 395   PIN HAMMER

SMALLER HAMMERS

BENCH WOODWORKERS POSSESSED OF A Warrington-pattern hammer can dispense with a carpenter's claw hammer but will find the use of one or more smaller hammers a great advantage. Of these there are many designs, old and new, including the magnetic-headed upholsterer's hammer, pin hammer, round-headed hammer, square-headed hammer, and tack hammer. Square-headed models are good for driving small nails close to adjacent perpendicular surfaces. Round-headed models, especially if the face is crowned (slightly convex), are good for driving brads, tacks, and small nails slightly below the surface without creating dings or 'moons' in the wood. And magnetic-headed models are of course a great convenience when using nails too small to be comfortably held between your fingers. Older hammers of this variety tend to have longer, more finely balanced handles (see FIG. 395) that give them an especially elegant look.

STRIKING GIANTS

AT THE OTHER END OF THE SCALE ARE THE heavyweight sledge hammers and commanders. Sledge hammers can weigh as much as 14 lb. and are commonly used by shipwrights, blacksmiths, loggers (for driving wedges), and even the home handyman (for pounding in fence posts and mailbox posts). Interestingly, there is no recorded use of one ever having been used in sledge-making, but this is due to the fact that the word 'sledge' in

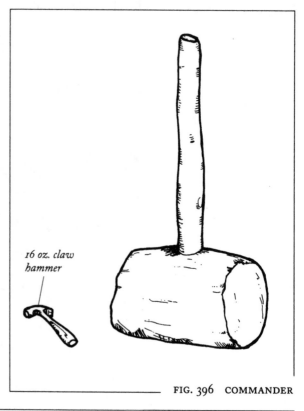

*16 oz. claw
hammer*

FIG. 396   COMMANDER

this case comes from the old English word: *slecg*, meaning 'slay', and points to its original use as a war hammer (probably by the bellicose Vikings and Saxons mentioned earlier).

The wooden commander (FIG. 396) is by far the largest striking tool of them all. Its massive head is usually nothing more than a particularly dense chunk of log with a long handle firmly fixed into it. If a commander is to be used for an extended period, rather than being made up for temporary use when settling heavy beams and posts into place in timber framing, and then discarded, its head may be banded with iron rings. Used like a giant croquet mallet, the commander is a far cry from lightweight carving mallets, which may weigh as little as 1 lb.

MALLETS

ALTHOUGH AS PREVIOUSLY MENTIONED THE word 'mallet' means hammer, in practice it refers to a wooden-headed hammer. The woodworker's mallet used primarily to hit wooden-handled tools like chisels and gouges is made in various sizes and various shapes. Round or oval heads turned from some dense wood like beech or lignum vitae, with the handle inserted into the center of the barrel (unlike carving mallets, whose handles are inserted into the end) are common, especially as user-made varieties, but so-called square-headed mallets have a distinct advantage. These mallets are not actually square, but merely flat-sided, the ends being cut at such an angle that they contact the object being hit squarely, even when the moment of striking occurs at the end of the arc of swing. The ability to make square contact, together with the fact that the squareness of the handles makes it easier to maintain the tool's proper alignment with the struck object (you can easily feel if you are holding the tool askew), is why this type is often preferred over the round type.

There is, however, another reason for their popularity, not so common now as formerly,

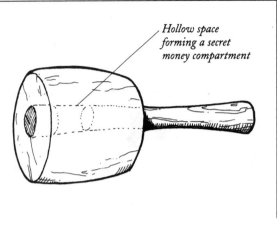

Hollow space forming a secret money compartment

FIG. 397   CARVING MALLET

which has to do with security. Harry Hems, the great Victorian woodcarver, once told a story bearing on this. During his youthful journeys through mid-19th century Italy, a country made dangerous not only by brigands and robbers but also by revolutionaries and Garibaldi's men, he sawed off the end of his mallet's handle, glued the very tip in place, and then replaced the bottom part so as to leave a secret gap in the head — and was consequently able to keep his money safe (see FIG. 397). He was able to do this only because the mallet's handle is inserted from the top — unlike a hammer's handle, which is inserted from below — and is kept in place by wedges, except, of course, for hammers of the adze-eye pattern; repeated use of the mallet consequently tends to drive the head ever more firmly down the handle.

A further testimony to this unique and secure method of hafting old mallets is the custom practised in England until recently of sawing recently demised carver's mallets in half lengthwise and then hanging them on the walls or beams of the carving shop. Even sawed in half the handles remain firmly fixed.

GOOD PRACTICE

IF YOU ARE LUCKY ENOUGH TO OBTAIN AN older mallet or hammer do not despair if the head

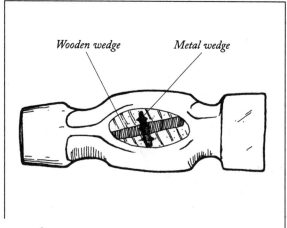

Wooden wedge   Metal wedge

FIG. 398   HAMMER-HEAD WEDGES

is loose. Apart from a damaged handle, a loose head is the most serious defect you may encounter, although potentially also the most dangerous. Chipped metal faces should also be avoided, and, of course, single-clawed claw hammers will never claw again — although this is not perhaps too much of a disadvantage apart from upsetting the balance of an otherwise whole head — but loose heads can and should be tightened. However, do not attempt this by the oft-repeated method of soaking the head and handle in a bucket of water overnight. This may be a good trick for providing the tool with an apparently secure handle if you intend to sell it immediately, but as soon as the handle dries out the head will loosen up again. Instead, replace the wedges, using wooden ones across the longest axis

of the end of the handle and ridged metal ones at right angles to these, as shown in FIG. 398.

Keep the face clean and polished; accumulated dried glue or rust and other debris can result in dangerously glancing blows and may even lead to potentially eye-blinding chipping.

Should the tool need to be rehandled, select the wood with care. It is important to choose material as straight-grained as possible, as well as a species that is both long-grained and pliable. Ash is considered by many woodworkers to be ideal, but hickory, the species most commonly used by commercial manufacturers, comes close in strength and comfort. A handle that is too stiff is not only liable to break but will impart no resiliency to the head. This resiliency not only makes it more comfortable to use but also makes possible the almost magical ability of being able to 'bounce' the driven nail below the surface of the wood without the hammer's face touching and marring the surface.

A little linseed oil on the handle from time to time will help prevent the wood from drying out and shrinking, but if the tool is used with care a natural patina produced by the oil and sweat of your own hand will result.

Remaining mindful of the huge variety of styles, shapes, and sizes will make discovery of older worthwhile tools at fleamarkets and antique stores far easier. And bear in mind that a broken or missing handle need be no deterrent to acquiring a better-quality 'tried and true' tool.

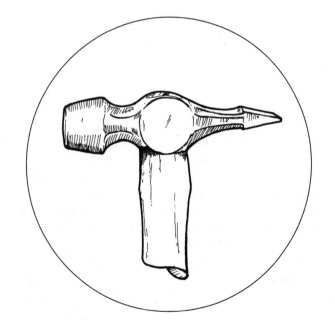

40

BENCH-TOP ACCESSORIES

THE SECRET WEAPONS

I F YOU WERE INTRODUCED TO WOODWORKING THROUGH THE MEDIUM OF THE TABLE SAW AND THE ROUTER, YOU ARE PROBABLY ACCUSTOMED TO USING THESE TOOLS TO PRODUCE FAIRLY EXACT WORK. APART FROM REQUIRING LESS EFFORT TO USE THAN many traditional handtools, modern powertools are also capable of nice adjustment and accurate use. Calibrated fences, graduated depth-stops, and other built-in guides all help in producing consistently straight and square work. The very thought of attempting to saw or to cut something by hand and producing a cut as nicely accurate as something passed across the tablesaw supported by accurately aligned fences and miter gauges can seem impossibly difficult unless you have spent years practising such a skill.

The imagined difficulty of readily obtaining the accuracy comparable to that possible with power-tools often discourages many people from using handtools. Whatever the attractions might be of

working with a beautifully made wooden hand-tool, whatever the romantic associations that may be conjured up by handling something that one of yesterday's craftsmen may have used, whatever the very real advantages regarding an operation not possible with more modern tools, if you have the idea that you will simply not be able to do the job to a sufficiently high standard you are likely to abandon the attempt.

Even a cursory look at the fine furniture made before electric tools became common is enough to convince most people that accuracy was far from unattainable. But the general assumption is that it was achieved only after long years of grinding apprenticeship and a painstaking development of

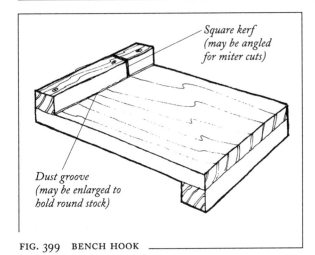

Square kerf (may be angled for miter cuts)

Dust groove (may be enlarged to hold round stock)

FIG. 399   BENCH HOOK

hand skills for which few people today have the time. It is, however, only partly true that many of the exquisite antiques we classify as Chippendale, Hepplewhite, Sheraton, Empire, and so on, were the result of years of accumulated hand skills. What is not generally understood is that the woodworkers who created these pieces did not simply rely on 'crude' handtools and years of skill, but also commonly employed a whole range of jigs and accessories to make their use of these tools easier, and to guarantee a level of accuracy every bit as fine as we expect and strive for today.

Many of these jigs are extremely simple to make and to use. Having a few of them around will often provide an alternative to the sometimes hard choice of whether to launch into a fully fledged operation on a stationary powertool such as a tablesaw, with all the necessary setup that may be worth while for a large job but which can be annoyingly time-consuming when there is only one small piece to cut, or to attempt the risky proposition of undertaking the job by hand in a fraction of the time but with less than guaranteed results.

SAWING JIGS

PERHAPS THE COMMONEST GROUP OF EASILY made jigs that will guarantee success when using

handtools are those employed in various sawing operations. Chief among these is the bench hook (FIG. 399). In its simplest form it consists of a small table with a lip at each end. The lips are arranged on opposite sides so that one lip 'hooks' onto the bench top and the other forms a stop against which the work may be held securely.

Its primary use is to hold a small workpiece securely when being sawed, without having to clamp or otherwise secure the piece. A flat board, about 9 in. wide by 1 ft. long, with 2 in.-square lips is easily made. Somewhat different proportions may also work well and merely be the result of using whatever scrap is handy to make the jig. Experience will soon demonstrate certain advantages that minor changes can offer, such as making the back hook — the piece against which the work is held — somewhat larger and perfectly true in relation to the bed of the bench hook. If a saw cut is made, through this hook down to the level of the bed, that is perfectly perpendicular, both to the plane of the bed and the back of the hook, the bench hook will serve as a reliable and square cut-off guide for the saw when trimming short pieces. This can be easier and safer than running very short pieces through the tablesaw.

Similarly, if the end of the back hook is made perfectly square, the side of the bed can be used as a small shooting-board to trim short sections; the square end of the hook will function as an exact stop.

Logical extensions of this idea include extra kerfs made in the back hook to guide differently angled cuts, including regular and irregular miters. This is a very common use for the bench hook. Consequently, position any nails or screws that you might use to attach the back hook only in places where such guide kerfs are not likely to be made. Remember that if the hook is attached only with such fasteners, rather than being glued in place along its entire length, a kerf made outboard of the end fastener will necessarily allow the last piece of hook to fall off! In any event, a clearly marked line indicating the position of the fasteners may save you the embarrassment of

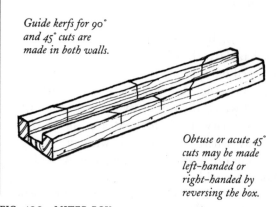

*Guide kerfs for 90°
and 45° cuts are
made in both walls.*

*Obtuse or acute 45°
cuts may be made
left-handed or
right-handed by
reversing the box.*

FIG. 400   MITER BOX

trying to cut a guide kerf through a hidden fastener.

Some people prefer bench hooks with relatively thin hooks. These allow easy clamping of stop blocks with small C-clamps, such stop blocks being very useful for repetitive cutting of similar lengths when the same guide kerf is used.

For a particular operation that you repeat often, a bench hook with a marked, or even completely graduated, hook can save considerable time. For example, I keep my bench hook marked so that I can saw the short dowels needed for dowel joinery to the same length without having to measure or mark the dowels every time.

The bench hook can, of course, be constructed so that either end may be hooked over the bench, thus providing you with two beds and a different selection of guiding kerfs. Undercutting the back hook (before attaching it to the bed) will prevent the workpiece being forced away from the hook by a buildup of sawdust and if it is undercut sufficiently may also prove helpful for holding round stock securely against the hook.

Small purpose-made miter boxes are an often overlooked aid to handsawing. While large metal versions complete with clamps and scales are expensive collector's items largely superseded by chopsaws, a simple miter box (FIG. 400) nailed together from scraps of one-by-two and provided with a carefully laid-out kerf or two can be a very effective way of making exactly angled cuts in small stock, especially in pieces too short to run safely through the tablesaw.

To make angled cuts in stock that is too large or unwieldy to be held in a miter box or run through the tablesaw, use the simple side guide. Every

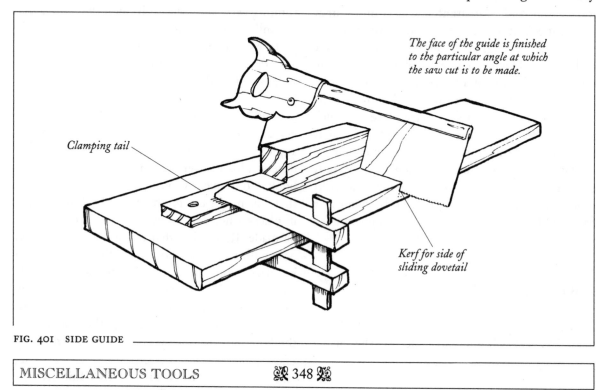

*The face of the guide is finished
to the particular angle at which
the saw cut is to be made.*

Clamping tail

*Kerf for side of
sliding dovetail*

FIG. 401   SIDE GUIDE

shop used to have one of these hung up for use when cutting the sloping sides of sliding dovetails in wide stock, as shown in FIG. 401, but its use is not limited to the angles required by dovetails.

The side guide is simply a block of wood against the angled end of which the backsaw may be held to guarantee the required angle. The other, non-angled, end of the guide is made thinner so that it may be conveniently clamped to the workpiece.

PLANING AIDS

IN THE SAME WAY THAT A PUSH STICK CAN be indispensable to a power jointer, there are certain devices that are equally useful when using handplanes. Although a well-sharpened plane can be considerably handier to use when working on small stock or short, odd-shaped workpieces than an 8 in. jointer, attempting to work completely freehand with the plane alone is something even the most skilled old-time craftsmen rarely risked.

The most useful adjunct to a handplane is a shooting-board. This easily made jig ensures the accuracy of the surface being planed. The most common form is designed to make edge-planing easy and accurate. The work is clamped (or simply held) on the board against a stop, and the plane is used on its side, the squareness of the plane's stock or body guaranteeing the squareness of the edge, as shown in FIG. 402.

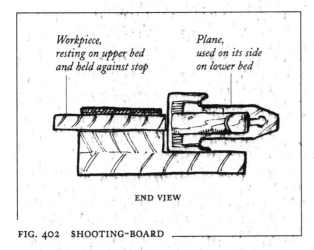

Workpiece, resting on upper bed and held against stop

Plane, used on its side on lower bed

END VIEW

FIG. 402 SHOOTING-BOARD

Shooting-boards can be made to any length practical for the work in hand. By altering the position or angle of the stock, different tapers or angles can be achieved. Their use is not limited to side grain; using a suitably constructed shooting-board to trim end grain will not only ensure a finished flat surface, which is difficult to achieve freehand when planing small pieces, but also remove the need to provide waste pieces behind the workpiece to avoid splintering off the rear of the cut.

Trimming the ends of splayed work can be particularly frustrating when you try to match the compound angles using fences and miter guides on the tablesaw, but by providing a shooting-board with appropriately cut wedges (see FIG. 29, chapter 3) or by using a shooting-board with adjustable stops, this type of work can be made considerably easier.

Planing miters by hand can often result in losing the perfect fit of the miter should the end become slightly rounded or otherwise trimmed out of the correct plane. The miter jack (see FIG. 31, chapter 3) solves this problem. The jack is held in the bench vise, and the work is held in the jack so that the surface to be planed protrudes slightly above the surface of the jack's jaws. It is common to protect the jaws by gluing a thin piece of card to their top surface, over which the plane is then run, automatically planing the surface of the miter to an exact 45° angle.

Somewhat more problematical is how to trim the ends of tall miters. There is, however, a special shooting-board designed specifically for this job known by the quaint name of a donkey's ear shooting-board (FIG. 30, chapter 3). It too is held in the bench vise, and the workpiece being held or clamped to it, accuracy is guaranteed — no skill being needed other than the ability to push the plane.

In the same way that the shooting-board takes advantage of the squareness of the plane's body to guarantee a square cut when planing long edges, an adjustable guide clamped to the side of the plane can be made that will produce a consistent angle other than one of 90°. The guide is no more than an angled strip fixed to the side of the plane so that when it is held against the side of the workpiece the plane's iron contacts the surface to be planed at the required angle. Although such guides can be quickly made from scrap as the need arises, various manufacturers have produced adjustable metal guides that may be quickly and securely clamped to the side of Stanley™-type metal planes.

One last planing jig that deserves mention is the sticking box. Few people are interested in making their own window sash anymore (although rabbeted sash bars may be needed for pieces that include glazed doors), but the sticking box, once commonly used in the production of such items, is very useful for planing other workpieces too narrow or small to be conveniently run through the tablesaw, run across the jointer, or even held in the vise for handplaning. The simplest form consists of a grooved bed to hold the narrow workpiece and a brad or small nail to function as a stop to hold the end of the workpiece. Secured this way, surprisingly small sections can be planed or even moulded.

CHISELING GUIDES

A CHISEL MAY BE THOUGHT OF AS A PLANE iron without a body. As such it is a totally free-hand tool, lacking even the sole of the plane's stock to guide it. While it is this very freedom for which the chisel is designed, there are occasions when what has to be chiseled requires a perfect accuracy difficult to achieve unaided. One very simple device is the chisel miter guide (see FIG. 33, chapter 3). A short length of scrap is provided with an accurate miter at each end and is then

attached on one side to another short length of scrap. When this second piece is clamped to a workpiece the back of the chisel may be slid down the face of the mitered piece to trim a small 45° miter, such as is commonly used at the corners of moulded frame-and-panel work, sash work and mitered rabbets, with the assurance of perfect accuracy.

BORING GUIDES

A HAND DRILL OR A BRACE AND BIT CAN BE particularly difficult to use with accuracy. Power boring in the shop is usually done on the drill-press, the usually adjustable table of which goes a long way to providing accuracy. Handtools can be especially useful when it is not convenient or even possible to bring the work to the drillpress, but used in awkward situations such as below a table top or on the interior of some cramped case-work accuracy can be annoyingly elusive. An extremely simple guide, however, can be made in a matter of moments — especially if you do have a drillpress. All that is needed is a short length of scrap pre-bored to accept the size bit you intend to use. The end of the bored scrap piece should be made perfectly square (or to the angle required), and is slipped over the bit and held against the work surface. You must, of course, make sure that the bit used is long enough to penetrate both the guide and the work to the depth required, and a mark or two may be necessary to align the guide properly, but by simply holding the guide to the work the hole will be bored accurately.

This type of guide can even be used with an electric drill, even when using spade bits. Simply bore the hole in the guide large enough just for the shank of the bit.

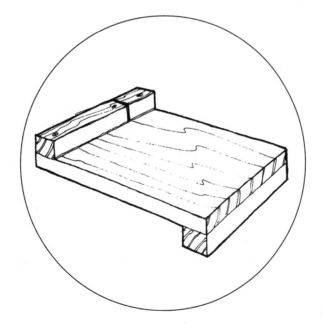

*

SELECT BIBLIOGRAPHY

THERE ARE SO MANY BOOKS ON THE SUBJECT OF WOODWORKING HANDTOOLS THAT TO ATTTEMPT A COMPREHENSIVE LISTING WOULD SERVE LITTLE PURPOSE HERE. MOREOVER, IN THIS COMPUTERIZED INFORMATION AGE THERE ARE SO many avenues open to anyone who would look that specialized searches are easier than ever and can produce more up-to-date and complete results than any single book's necessarily fixed bibliography. What follows, therefore, is a list of books that I have particularly enjoyed. Some of these titles are relatively obscure while others are common to many bibliographies, but all are especially pertinent to the further study of traditional woodworking handtools — if sometimes somewhat contradictory — and will provide further insights into the subject, from both an instructional standpoint as well as one of pure entertainment.

Eaton, Reg. *The Ultimate Brace: A Unique Product of Victorian Sheffield.* Heacham, England: Erica Jane Publishing, 1989.
    — The definitive illustrated study of one of the true handtool aristocrats.

Gaynor, James M., and Nancy L. Hagedorn. *Tools: Working Wood in Eighteenth-Century America.*

Williamsburg, Virginia: The Colonial Williamsburg Foundation, 1993.
— *A richly photographed introduction to the forms and varieties of British and American woodworking handtools in the 18th century.*

Goodman, W. L. *The History of Woodworking Tools*. London: G. Bell and Sons, 1964.
— *For many years the introductory authority and basic reference for students and enthusiasts of woodworking handtools.*

Grimshaw, Robert. *Saws: The History, Development, Action, Classification and Comparison of Saws of all Kinds*. Philadelphia: 1880. Reprint. Morristown, New Jersey: The Astragal Press.
— *The definitive work on 19th century saw technology, this is also an extremely useful text on many aspects of saw maintenance, from swaging to tensioning, flattening, and dent removal.*

Hack, Garrett. *The Handplane Book*. Newtown, Connecticut: The Taunton Press, 1997.
— *A beautiful, full-color book on the purchase, care, classification, and use of a great variety of handplanes.*

Halfpenny, William. *Magnum in Parvo: or, The Marrow of Architecture*. London: 1728. Reprint. Bronx, New York: Benjamin Blom, 1968.
— *An 18th century description and analysis of the proportional system commonly known as 'The Five Orders of Architecture', on which much 18th century design was based.*

Hampton, C. W., and E. Clifford. *Planecraft: Hand Planing by Modern Methods*. 1934. 7th imp. Sheffield, England: C. and J. Hampton, 1959.
— *The last and most complete word on planing in the period immediately before powertools became common in the average small shop.*

Hasluck, Paul N. *The Handyman's Book of Tools, Materials and Processes Employed in Woodworking*. 1903. Reprint. Berkeley: Ten Speed Press, 1987.
— *An encyclopedic, turn-of-the-century look at the tools and techniques practised by amateur woodworkers.*

Hayward, Charles H. *The Complete Book of Woodwork*. 1959. Reprint. New York: Drake Publishers, 1972.
— *While including the beginnings of machine-equipped home workshops, this still represents a thorough grounding in the use of traditional handtools. It assumes the use of powertools as labor-saving adjuncts to basic hand techniques rather than the other way round — which is the more contemporary and often limiting approach that has become common in shops deprived of the earlier handtool technology.*

Hayward, Charles H. *Practical Woodwork*. London: Evans Brothers, 1968.
— *One of Charles Hayward's many standard works on woodworking, this volume describes the fundamentals of woodworking by hand as practised in the first half of the 20th century. (Any other title by Hayward is also well worth examination.)*

Hibben, Thomas. *The Carpenter's Tool Chest*. Philadelphia and London: J. B. Lippincott Company, 1933.
— *An entertaining look at the development of a wide range of woodworking handtools from the dawn of history to modern times.*

Hodgson, Fred T. *ABC of the Steel Square and its Uses*. Chicago: 1902.
— *An extremely useful contemporary abridgement from one of this well-known architect's woodworking texts.*

Hummel, Charles F. *With Hammer in Hand: The Dominy Craftsmen of East Hampton, New York*. Charlottesville: The University Press of Virginia, 1968.
— *A handsome, large-format study of the tools, products, and business methods of a clock- and furnituremaking enterprise spanning the 18th and 19th centuries.*

Jones, Bernard E., ed. *The Complete Woodworker*. ca. 1900. Reprint. Berkeley: Ten Speed Press, 1980.
— *A comprehensive reference and instructional book on a wide range of processes and techniques common to hand woodworking in the 19th century.*

Jones, Bernard E., ed. *The Practical Woodworker*. ca. 1900. Reprint. Berkeley: Ten Speed Press, 1983.
— *A companion volume to the previous title, this contains further techniques and a wealth of practical applications.*

Kebabian, Paul B., and William C. Lipke, eds. *Tools and Technologies: America's Wooden Age*. Burlington, Vermont: Robert Hull Fleming Museum, University of Vermont, 1979.
— *A scholarly perspective on the interaction of handtool and powertool technologies in various woodworking trades with some interesting observations on current approaches.*

Landis, Scott. *The Workbench Book*. Newtown, Connecticut: The Taunton Press, 1987.
— *A handsome and enormously informative book on the history, use, and construction of a great variety of woodworking benches ranging from classical and medieval benches to benches for bodgers, boatbuilders, luthiers, carpenters, joiners, and cabinetmakers.*

Mercer, Henry C. *Ancient Carpenters' Tools: Together with Lumbermen's, Joiner's, and Cabinet*

Makers' Tools in use in the Eighteenth Century. 1928. 5th ed. New York: The Horizon Press, 1975.
— *The early 20th century successor to Moxon and Nicholson (see below), this book contains much information on woodworking tools from many cultures and periods of history still not duplicated in more recent works.*

Moxon, Joseph. *Mechanick Exercises: or the Doctrine of Handy-Works.* London: 1678.
— *Generally regarded as the first record of British woodworking tools and techniques, its plates have been used in so many subsequent publications on the subject as to have become as well known as those from Denis Diderot's 1751 'Encyclopédie, ou Dictionnaire Raisonné des Sciences, des Arts, et des Métiers'. A useful reprint of the 1703 edition was published in 1975 by The Astragal Press, Morristown, New Jersey.*

Nicholson, Peter. *Mechanical Exercises; or, the Elements and Practice of Carpentry, Joinery, Bricklaying, Masonry, Slating, Plastering, Painting, Smithing, and Turning.* London: J. Taylor, 1812.
— *Moxon's (see above) 19th century successor; my personal favorite and original inspiration.*

Proudfoot, Christopher, and Philip Walker. *Woodworking Tools.* Rutland, Vermont: Charles E. Tuttle Company, 1984.
— *A handsomely illustrated and well-documented guide primarily for collectors.*

Roberts, Kenneth D. *Some 19th Century English Woodworking Tools: Edge and Joiner Tools and Bit Braces.* Fitzwilliam, New Hampshire: Ken Roberts Publishing Company, 1980.
— *The ultimate resource on the development of the Sheffield steel and tool industry as related to woodworking tools.*

Roberts, Kenneth D. *Wooden Planes in 19th Century America.* 2 vols. Fitzwilliam, New Hampshire: Ken Roberts Publishing Company, 1978.
— *A detailed, illustrated compilation of American planemaking from the 18th century to the 20th century.*

Roubo, M. *L'Art du Menuisier Ébéniste.* 1774.
— *For French woodworking what Moxon (see above) did for Britain, but focusing on more sophisticated branches of the trade.*

Salaman, R. A. *Dictionary of Tools used in the woodworking and allied trades, c. 1700–1970.* London: George Allen and Unwin, 1975.
— *The one indispensable work on the subject.*

Sloane, Eric. *A Museum of Early American Tools.* New York: Funk and Wagnalls, 1964.
— *One of the most delightful of Sloane's uniquely illustrated books on the American past.*

Sutcliffe, G. Lister, ed. *The Modern Carpenter Joiner and Cabinet-Maker: A Complete Guide to Current Practice*. 8 vols. London: The Gresham Publishing Company, 1902.
    — *A complete reference to the 19th century woodworking trades: timbers, tools, machines, designs, and practices.*

The Industrial School Association. *Wood-Working Tools; How to use Them. A Manual*. Boston: Ginn, Heath, and Company, 1884.
    — *A beginner's book, valuable for understanding the attitude towards handtools and techniques before the advent of powertools.*

Walker, Philip. *Woodworking Tools*. Princes Risborough, England: Shire Publications, 1980.
    — *One of a fascinating illustrated series of small but packed booklets on trades and handicrafts of the past.*

Wheeler, William, and Charles H. Hayward. *Practical Wood Carving and Gilding*. London: Evans Brothers, 1963.
    — *Still possibly the best introduction to two areas of woodworking that continue to rely largely on handtools and hand methods.*

Wildung, Frank H. *Woodworking Tools at Shelburne Museum*. Shelburne, Vermont: The Shelburne Museum, 1957.
    — *A useful pamphlet and guide to a fine collection.*

*

TOOL ASSOCIATIONS

Early American Industries Association: 167 Bakerville Road, S. Dartmouth, MA 02748
Mid-West Tool Collectors Association: 7201 Danny Drive, Saginaw, MI 48603
Preserving Arts & Skills of the Trades: 5200 Lawton Avenue, Oakland, CA 94618
Tools and Trades History Society: 60 Swanley Lane, Swanley, Kent, BR8 7JG, England

*

TOOL DEALERS

Arnold and Walker: 77 High Street, Needham Market, Suffolk, IP6 8AW, England
Bristol Design (Tools): 14 Perry Road, Bristol, BS1 5BG, England
William A. Gustafson Antiques: Box 104, Austerlitz, NY 12017
The Tool Shop: 78 High Street, Needham Market, Suffolk, IP6 8AW, England
Old Tool Store: Ashley Iles, Lincolnshire, England
Tom Witte's Antiques: P. O. Box 399, Mattawan, NJ 49071

*

TOOL AUCTIONS

Brown Auction Services: Pownal, Maine
Richard Crane: Hillsboro, New Hampshire
Fine Tool Journal: Pownal, Maine
Tool Shop Auctions: Needham Market, Suffolk, England
David Stanley Auctions: Osgathorpe, Leicestershire, England

INDEX

Numbers in bold face (e.g., **246**) indicate pages with illustrations.
References to ranges greater than two pages (e.g., 102–104) may
also include illustrations.